I Remember Too Much

~

I Remember Too Much

~

89 Opera Stars Speak Candidly of Their Work, Their Lives, and Their Colleagues

Dennis McGovern
and
Deborah Grace Winer

WILLIAM MORROW
and Company, Inc.
New York

The authors wish to thank David M. Reuben and the Metropolitan Opera Press Department for production photos and head shots used in the book. We also thank *Opera News* magazine and are grateful to the artists who made their photo collections available to us.

Thanks also to Bill Ray for the photograph of Garson Kanin, Larry Lapidus for Rosalind Elias and Carol Neblett, and Ed Jablonsky for *Porgy and Bess*.

Library of Congress Cataloging-in-Publication Data

McGovern, Dennis.
  I remember too much : 89 opera stars speak candidly of their work, their lives,
  and their colleagues/Dennis McGovern and Deborah Grace Winer.
    p.   cm.
  ISBN 0-688-08447-8
  1. Singers—Interviews. 2. Opera—New York (N.Y.) I. Winer,
Deborah Grace. II. Title.
ML400.M4   1990
782.1′092′2—dc20   89-13876
                                                                    CIP

Printed in the United States of America

First Edition

1 2 3 4 5 6 7 8 9 10

BOOK DESIGN BY RICHARD ORIOLO

We dedicate this work to our parents,
Mr. and Mrs. Joseph McGovern and
Dr. and Mrs. N. J. Winer,
and to our families
and friends

PREFACE

~

When we first told friends, and anyone else who would listen, that we were planning to spend the next year with almost ninety opera singers, we were greeted with a lot of knowing snorts of "Good luck." Prima donnas, after all, have the reputation of being, well, prima donnas.

While we were touched by public concern for our egos, it turned out no one need have worried. The singers were warm, imaginative, sensitive, blissfully idiosyncratic people. They spoke with earnestness, candor, and, above all, tremendous respect for their art form. Often they welcomed us into their homes to extend their hospitality and cooperation. They gave freely of their time and photo collections. We were accommodated, coddled, kissed, fed, instructed, and adopted.

Naturally, we would have loved to talk with artists like Ezio Pinza, Mary Garden, Mario del Monaco, and the ultimate comprimarios, Mathilde Bauermeister and Thelma Votipka, but fate had already intervened. Fortunately, only a few living artists were inaccessible or uncooperative. But that's another—and much shorter—book.

Our odyssey started during a torrential downpour when we arrived at the doorstep of Bidú Sayão, who lavished concern on her nearly drowned visitors. Eighty-eight artists later, it ended backstage at the Met during *Götterdämmerung,* with Franz Mazura chainsmoking in his dwarf's costume, and Fafner and Fasolt playing poker in the background. In between was a parade of priceless moments and unforgettable impressions: Christmas cookies at Fiorenza Cossotto's; Patrice Munsel's dog, Heathcliff, which tromped back and forth over us, licking the tape recorders; Martina Arroyo's sing-along canine; the humor and friendship of Anna Moffo, who greets workmen in her apartment with a cheery "Hi, boys!"; Sandra Warfield admitting she was "scared to death," but loosening up to downright chattiness before the interview's end; Neil Shicoff excusing himself during a telephone conversation to Windex the TV screen; Licia Albanese's maternal restaurant advice: "You don't want the gnocchi—is too heavy for today"; watching Brenda Lewis fix the screen door of her Connecticut home; a late-night dessert-fest with Evelyn Lear and Thomas Stewart, who gently escorted his mother-in-law upstairs with a buoyant "Come on, Mom!"; Renata Scotto's discourse on being the mother of teenagers; Ramón Vinay singing "Happy Birthday" over the phone; in her last interview, Zinka Milanov, resplendent in leopard—a true original; Joan Sutherland's reaction when we asked about her future plans: "I've worked hard enough—I'm just going to put my feet up and relax!"

The impetus for this book came from the family reunion we hosted for participants in Garson Kanin's 1950 Met *Fledermaus,* which reunited Mr. Kanin with Brenda Lewis, Patrice Munsel, Regina Resnik, and Risë Stevens.

We would like to thank Regina Resnik for the book's title, and for their invaluable help: the Metropolitan Opera Press Office, the Metropolitan Opera Archives and Archivist Robert Tuggle (author of *The Golden Age of Opera*), the staff of *Opera News,* Philip Caggiano, Elizabeth Diggans, Gregory Downer, F. Paul Driscoll, Regina Fiorito, Gerald Fitzgerald, John Freeman, Marylis Sevilla-Gonzaga, Edward Jablonski, Timothy Jenkins, Ahna McCracken, Karen Nelson, John Pennino, Martin Sokol, Barry Tucker, Victor Vail, Martin Waldron, Jessica Daryl Winer, all the managers and press representatives of the singers involved, and our editor, Maria Guarnaschelli. Portions of the *Fledermaus* and *Carmen* chapters, as well as brief portions of individual interviews, have appeared in *Opera News* and *Dial*.

Most of all, our heartfelt gratitude goes to the gifted artists who have given so generously of their time and confidence in order to make this project possible.

DENNIS MCGOVERN
DEBORAH GRACE WINER

CONTENTS

~

Opera singers are not like other people.
We're all meshugge. *We live life like it's an opera.*
If someone dies, they die a Horrible Death. If they're
sick, it's a Terrible Sickness. Our tragedies
are bigger—but therefore our
joys are bigger. We belong
in a different cage.
—BRENDA LEWIS

I Remember
Too Much

~

DIE FLEDERMAUS

~

I can't remember a thing!
–PATRICE MUNSEL

I remember too much!
–REGINA RESNIK

Music by Johann Strauss II
Original libretto by Carl Haffner and Richard Genée
from the play *Le Réveillon* by Henri Meilhac and Ludovic Halévy
English libretto by Howard Dietz
Directed by Garson Kanin

ROSALINDA .... *Brenda Lewis, Regina Resnik*

ADELE.. *Patrice Munsel*

ORLOFSKY.................................... *Regina Resnik, Risë Stevens*

There is a talent in the American theater to rouse the Metropolitan out of its Rip Van Winkle sleep of twenty years since 1930. Whether the eventual judgment is that it's delightful but we can't afford it, or it's delightful and we must afford it, the fact remains—it's delightful.
—*SATURDAY REVIEW*, JANUARY 6, 1951

*T*he delight, of course, was *Fledermaus*. Rudolf Bing's sparkling resurrection of the classic Viennese confection opened on December 20, 1950, in one of Bing's first presentations as the Metropolitan's new general manager.

Operettas come and go with the whims of public fancy. Offenbach's

Grand Duchess of Gérolstein opened to glorious reviews and delighted audiences of its day, but has almost totally disappeared from the scene today. So have most of the 150 once-popular works of Franz von Suppé. Even Strauss's *Gypsy Baron,* his only other surviving operetta, palls next to *Die Fledermaus.* This story of the Eisensteins and the good life in mid-nineteenth-century Vienna, before its decline, is the quintessential Viennese operetta. It has been done every way but in the nude and still packs in audiences. The Met, Covent Garden, Paris, and of course Vienna still carry the work in their repertories, as do smaller houses and universities all over the world.

The operetta has turned up on Broadway in at least three different versions: a not very successful 1929 production entitled *A Wonderful Night,* featuring a young actor named Archie Leach, soon to become Cary Grant; the 1933 *Champagne Sec,* starring Peggy Wood, who had already earned her operetta laurels in Noel Coward's *Bitter Sweet;* and *Rosalinda,* in 1942, which had the dubious honor of introducing Shelley Winters to the musical theater and vice versa. The London stage, not to be outdone, produced *Gay Rosalinda!* employing the talents of Cyril Ritchard. Filmed numerous times, *Die Fledermaus* also inspired several ballets.

It is strange that so animated a masterpiece could have come from such reticent beginnings. Basically, the theater made Johann Strauss nervous—a real aberration in culture-crazed Vienna. He much preferred, with his orchestra, to be the arbiter of the Austro-Hungarian Empire's taste in dance music, carrying on his "Waltz King" birthright from his father. He was also sobered by his music's first brush with words—a disastrous presentation of "The Blue Danube," set for the Men's Choral Society. As the legend goes, it took a passing word of encouragement from his friend Jacques Offenbach, whose popular Parisian parodies had left the Viennese public hungry for homegrown operettas, to interest him in theater music. In addition, there was a conspiracy by Strauss's aging wife, Jetty, and impresario Maximilian Steiner of the Theater an der Wien, who trooped an assortment of singers into Johann's workroom one day to present him with a *fait accompli:* his own music, stolen by Jetty, to which Steiner had had words added. Jetty, growing weary of Johann's inattention and extracurricular dalliances, hoped her husband's liaison with the theater would bring some much-needed glamour to both their lives. She was determined, and he gave in.

After one false start by Strauss, *The Merry Wives of Vienna* (which he withdrew after a dispute over the leading lady), and two modest successes, *Indigo and the Forty Thieves* and *Carnival in Rome,* Steiner acquired the rights to a wildly successful French farce, *Le Réveillon* (The Morning After), by *Carmen* librettists and Offenbach collaborators Henri Meilhac and Ludovic Halévy (nephew of Fromental Halévy, *La Juive*'s composer). They, in turn, had adapted their comedy from a German farce, Roderich Benedix's *Das Gefängnis* (The Jail Sentence). To Viennize it and tone down its blasphemous and subversive qualities (especially a Christmas Eve ball), Steiner engaged librettists Carl Haffner and Richard Genée. For the first time, Strauss was completely carried away by a libretto. Holed up in the country, he toiled in a frenzy for forty-three days and nights, ignoring sleep and food and Jetty, and emerged with *Die Fledermaus,* his masterpiece.

Unfortunately, the crippling stock-market crash of almost a year before made *Die Fledermaus* a nostalgia piece even before it reached the stage on April 5, 1874. In the shadow of bankruptcies, suicides, and the doomed empire, no one was in the mood for conjuring up the champagne and fancy-dress balls of vanished golden days. But the lukewarm reception didn't stick. By November, the operetta had reached New York, bowing first in German at the Stadt Theater, then in English at the Thalia. It was embraced by cities across Europe and the United States, returning in triumph to Vienna in 1894 under Gustav Mahler's baton.

The Metropolitan Opera first mounted *Die Fledermaus* with a cast that included Marcella Sembrich, Bella Alten, and Andreas Dippel. It was the annual Director's Benefit, and ticket prices were doubled. While the critics didn't rave, the audience was treated to a galaxy of second-act additions to the evening. Prince Orlofsky's party guests included Lillian Nordica, Louise Homer, Eugenio Giraldoni, and Enrico Caruso singing the quartet from *Rigoletto;* the trio from *Faust* was performed by Emma Eames, Pol Plançon, and Francisco Nuibo. The operetta was virtually swamped by the guest artists, who also included Alois Burgstaller, Olive Fremstad, Antonio Scotti, and a host of others. W. J. Henderson of the *New York Sun* complained: "Last night's presentation was inflated beyond the market value of operetta. . . . Certainly, those who attended it were not invited to consider it purely in the light of its adequacy as an interpretation of a delightful musical comedy, for in the yawning gulfs of the Metropolitan Opera House the plentiful dialogue was bound to be lost. . . . The truth seems to be that people were asked to be astonished at the general lavishness of expenditure and to gape at the appearance of Caruso, Nordica, Fremstad and the rest."

The first half of the twentieth century saw *Die Fledermaus* decline as a classic opera-house staple, leaving the more popular media to have their way with it. It was Rudolf Bing who restored it to its well-deserved operatic stature. In 1950, during his inaugural season at the Met, he realized some major changes had to take place. Chief among them was bringing some sort of unity and sense of concept to the company's productions. Perhaps there was little he could do with the old bread-and-butter productions of warhorses like *Carmen* and *Aida,* but with new productions he could start to make his presence felt—and he did.

The noted stage director Margaret Webster was hired to stage the opening-night *Don Carlos* in 1950. Later that season, Bing lured to the Met Garson Kanin, Broadway director and author of *Born Yesterday;* with his wife, Ruth Gordon, he'd written the best of the Katharine Hepburn–Spencer Tracy films. Kanin was to stage Bing's "special project"—a *Fledermaus* with a new English libretto, which Kanin was to write. He was joined in the endeavor by lyricist Howard Dietz, whose Broadway and Hollywood successes included *The Band Wagon* and *Inside U.S.A.* They formed a creative team that would be followed in subsequent Bing productions by such theatrical luminaries as Alfred Lunt, Tyrone Guthrie, José Quintero, Joe Mankiewicz, Cyril Ritchard, and Cecil Beaton.

Fledermaus, as it was known (minus the *Die*), immediately became a standing-room-only theatrical event in New York and everywhere else it played. It remained just that for years to come, and some of the divas to grace the work in its revivals were Mary Costa, Phyllis Curtin, Hilde Gueden, Dorothy Kirsten, Anna Moffo, Eleanor Steber, Laurel Hurley, Roberta Peters, Kitty Carlisle Hart, Jean Madeira, Jarmila Novotná, and Blanche Thebom.

Recently, five veterans of the Bing production were reunited to reflect on their common experience. Director Kanin was joined by Patrice Munsel and Risë Stevens, the original Adele and Prince Orlofsky; Brenda Lewis, Rosalinda both in the house and on tour; and Regina Resnik, the only singer to perform both Rosalinda and the Prince on the Met stage.

PATRICE MUNSEL: I can't remember a thing!

RISË STEVENS: I can't either. How long has it been?

REGINA RESNIK: I remember too much!

GARSON KANIN: It was Rudolf Bing's first season at the house, and he had very specific ideas about what he wanted. He wanted *Fledermaus* in English, and he spoke to several directors and librettists and tried to talk them into doing it. I think to a man, we all turned him down. Well, Mr. Bing is a terribly persuasive man, and he just wouldn't take no for an answer. All at once I found myself doing it. I suggested Howard Dietz, who was much more receptive about the whole idea. He undertook the job, and we were in rehearsal.

STEVENS: And you were stuck with us.

KANIN: And happily so.

To sing Rosalinda opposite Richard Tucker's Alfred, Bing chose Ljuba Welitsch. Famed for her Salome, rather a different brand of heroine from the more restrained Mrs. Eisenstein, Welitsch gamely tackled the English libretto and Dietz's Broadway-tinted lyrics. In a recent letter from Vienna, the soprano recalled her *Fledermaus* experience. "Yes," she wrote, "I remember the *Fledermaus* with Mr. Kanin very well. One thing I remember is when he ordered me where to go on the stage, he always called me 'Beauty.' Of course I was not a beauty, I was only young and also a bit fat. But it was nice to hear it. Which woman wouldn't like to be called like that? He was a real gentleman."

RESNIK: All of us who were going into second casts were sitting out there watching, and Ljuba was struggling with her English. She had to say to Alfred, "I love your high notes." So we all hear her tell Tucker, "I luff your high notts."

MUNSEL: Oh, of course, I remember that!

RESNIK: So everybody panicked and they decided that they had to change the words, and Howard said there was no other word for *notes*. And Garson would go, "Say *notes*!" and Ljuba says, "That's what I say—*notts*!"

Kanin recalled how the unknown Roberta Peters had come to rehearsals to observe Munsel's Adele.

S T E V E N S : I think she'd just made her debut.

K A N I N : [to Munsel] You weren't much older than that then.

B R E N D A   L E W I S : Oh, Patrice was a prodigy!

K A N I N : So little Roberta would come around to these rehearsals as long as they went on.

M U N S E L : If I'd seen her, I'd have killed her.

S T E V E N S : In those days, Patrice, she didn't mean anything.

L E W I S : You were already well established.

M U N S E L : Oh, I'd been there for years.

R E S N I K : You had roots!

M U N S E L : [to Stevens] I'd been there since you were pregnant with Nicky, and Jimmy Melton used to pick you up and swing you around. And as you got more and more pregnant, you got heavier and heavier.

R E S N I K : Jimmy Melton! He was on the record.

Part of Bing's plan for the Met's financial turnaround was to produce an "original cast album" for his *succès d'estime,* a recording that, in the minds of the public, would be totally connected with the production. An agreement to record the work was made with Columbia Records before the production opened, but the project ran into trouble. First came a change in conductor, from Fritz Reiner to Eugene Ormandy; then came Bing's underestimation of the cost of extracting his singers from their contract agreements with other record companies.

The original-cast-album idea was never to see the light of day, but two different *Fledermaus* recordings were released that year, with the Met cast divided between them: one from RCA, with Munsel and Stevens, led by Reiner with a translation by Ruth and Thomas Martin; and the Met-sanctioned Columbia recording, in the Kanin-Dietz translation, with Welitsch, Tucker, and Ormandy, rounded out by Set Svanholm and Martha Lipton.

M U N S E L : We couldn't appear in the original recording together because we were all with different record companies and they wouldn't release us, which was ridiculous. I didn't do it because I was with RCA.

S T E V E N S : The same thing with me, too.

R E S N I K : The version we did was Risë, Patrice, myself, Jimmy

Melton, Jan Peerce, and Robert Merrill. They got Reiner to do a highlights recording, but in the Martin version—as Columbia had the rights to the lyrics.

K A N I N : We wound up with Lily Pons, who made a hash of Howard's lyrics.

S T E V E N S : I didn't know that.

L E W I S : You've never heard it?

S T E V E N S : No. I wish I had.

K A N I N : She hit some beautiful notes, but you couldn't understand a word.

R E S N I K : And you understood Ljuba?

L E W I S : I've got to tell you something. She's still the great lady. The last time I sang in Vienna, she came backstage to see me and she said, "They are still doing *Fledermaus* in New York?" I said, "Yes," and she said, "Tell them Ljuba is still alife! Still alife!" She was so sweet.

Opera audiences today are accustomed to seeing *Candide, Sweeney Todd, Show Boat,* and other not strictly operatic works occupying the opera house. But by using *Fledermaus* to launch his crusade to utilize Broadway talent and bring theatrical know-how to the opera stage, Bing took an important step toward raising the theatrical standards of opera—an art form, after all, that is ideally the perfect blend of music and dramatic content. The growing sophistication of audiences conditioned by the three-dimensional Rodgers and Hammerstein characterizations in musicals like *Oklahoma!* and *South Pacific,* and increasingly expert Hollywood productions, called for the infusion of theatrical enrichment into the opera house. Think how funny a turn-of-the-century diva acting up a storm would seem by today's standards.

Bing followed the *Fledermaus* by transforming the Met's repertory with Tyrone Guthrie's striking *Carmen,* Alfred Lunt and Cecil Beaton's elegant *La Traviata,* Lunt's *Così Fan Tutte,* Joe Mankiewicz's ambitious *La Bohème,* and Cyril Ritchard's delightful stagings of Offenbach's *Tales of Hoffmann* and *La Périchole,* whose introduction into the Met lineup was a direct result of *Fledermaus*'s runaway appeal.

K A N I N : The first night, I remember, Howard Dietz took his little six-year-old daughter to the grand opening of *Fledermaus.* It was white tie, and Howard got her an evening gown and a little mink coat. They stepped out of the limousine and he was so thrilled—he was so touched and moved, with tears in his eyes. He took her hand and said, "Oh, darling, I hope you're going to like this." She said, "I will, Daddy, if there's no singing."

STEVENS: Well, one thing I'd like to make clear: When *Fledermaus* came into being, we had an entirely different kind of audience come. You know, we had not only an opera audience showing up, we had Broadway. It was a sweep of people who had never entered the opera house before. And the reviews were so fantastic.

LEWIS: It opened it up to the theater community of New York.

RESNIK: Risë's very right, because this innovation put *Périchole* and those things in the picture—

MUNSEL: Thank God!

RESNIK: —to bring something light into the opera house.

KANIN: Well, I remember that Bing used to come to almost every rehearsal. One day I came and sat beside him, and he was just simply *kvelling* over it—and he was sort of conducting.

MUNSEL: Oh, he would conduct in every performance. With a banana, always with a banana.

STEVENS: And in the wings, he would try to conduct.

Kanin asked Bing why he came so often, and he said, "Because this is the most impressive work in the repertory." When asked why, he answered, "Because the most difficult and rare thing in our world is to be light and great."

KANIN: The problem was he wanted to do another on top of that, but we never really could find one.

STEVENS: How many *Fledermaus*es are there?

Laymen, and even theater professionals, often don't realize that it is not unusual for the leading players in an operatic performance to meet each other for the first time minutes before going onstage. Countless artists sing without ever having been on the sets, worn the costumes, or worked with the conductor before. It's just a fact of operatic life. Rehearsals, especially in a company the size of the Met, are kept at a minimum. But because of the importance Bing attached to the theatricality of this work, he allowed fifteen rehearsals for *Fledermaus*—an unheard-of number in those days, when three or four were considered more than generous.

KANIN: This was given to me as a tremendous boon.

SINGERS: Well, it was, it was! Nobody got that!

KANIN: I know, but I came from the theater, where we were accustomed to getting at least five or six weeks.

MUNSEL: Ugh, we should be so lucky!

KANIN: Well, on the other hand, in the theater we're not accustomed to a cast turning up letter perfect and note perfect—that doesn't happen.

STEVENS: Well, you'd better at the opera—

KANIN: But when these guys came in, all of us from the theater were astonished. The very first day, they knew every note, every word, so it made it a hell of a lot easier.

MUNSEL: And we could have a lot of fun.

LEWIS: Then you're free. You're free to do whatever's needed.

The meeting of two cultures—the theatrical and operatic establishments—didn't always go smoothly, especially in the beginning. Conductors, who had long been supreme commanders over opera productions, suddenly had to bow to the authority of star directors. Singers, who were often used to "just going out there and singing," had to cope with the frustrations of fitting into a director's concept of character and stage business. Theater people, on the other hand, weren't used to the lack of adequate rehearsal time and often had to juggle the singers' musical priorities with the flow of the drama. Not the least of the directors' nightmares was controlling the choral masses, which inundate almost every Met production.

MUNSEL: I remember in *Bohème,* Joe Mankiewicz had trouble getting people to move. He gave the chorus individual characterizations to work with, and they were all going crazy. They would move for just the moment they weren't singing, and the minute they would start to sing, they'd stop dead in their tracks and focus on the conductor. And he was going crazy.

RESNIK: Well, at least those weren't the directors who came to the theater who then said, when the procession was over in *Cavalleria,* "I don't have enough music—I still have people on the stage."

K A N I N : There was one sticky little thing. Well, how many people are there in the chorus? In any case, my assistant and I were struggling with rehearsal methodology—how was I going to communicate with that many people on the stage? What do you say? "The girl next to the fellow with the red hair, would you go . . . ?" It was almost impossible. So we got the idea of making up—

R E S N I K : H, double H, A—

K A N I N : —placards that we hung around their necks, and this went all right for a few minutes. And there's always got to be one SOB in the party, and one guy in the chorus protested. He thought that somehow it was demeaning to him. I tried to reason with him and say how much easier it would be for them and more convenient for me—and it went as far as calling their Equity, and the union stood by me. And that's how we were able to rehearse with great efficiency, because all I had to say was "Would A, C, F, G come forward," and it was very easy to handle.

S T E V E N S : Except they kept forgetting what they had on.

M U N S E L : Well, thank God it was such a hit, because then it inspired *Così Fan Tutte* and *Périchole.*

To complete Bing's dream cast—which also included Wagnerian tenor Set Svanholm, displaying a heretofore unseen gift for comedy as Eisenstein—the role of Frosch, the drunken jailer, had to be filled. Though the character appears only in the last act and doesn't sing, a comedian who could command the stage, as well as holding his own with the stellar operatic cast, was needed. Danny Kaye seemed to be everyone's first choice, and when he proved unavailable, Milton Berle, Zero Mostel, and Groucho Marx, among others, were considered or contacted. In the end, it was actor-comedian Jack Gilford who opened to rave reviews. His casting sustained a career derailed by the blacklist of the early fifties. He appeared at the Met while working on Broadway both in *A Funny Thing Happened on the Way to the Forum* and later in Peter Ustinov's hit comedy *Romanoff and Juliet.* Gilford became thoroughly identified with Frosch and remained with *Fledermaus* for years to come, relinquishing performances now and then to Jack Mann.

RESNIK: I have a sweet recollection of Jack Gilford on opening night. We were friends, and Jack said to me, "Regina, what happens about the projection?" I said, "Jack, don't worry about it." It was the old house, you know. "But aren't there any hidden microphones around?"

STEVENS: Wasn't he the one who asked for one of those little microphones around the neck?

RESNIK: Right, right! He said, "Can't I get one of those little things around the neck so my voice can project? I'll get hoarse. I feel like I'm screaming my head off! I'm making my debut at the Met! My heart's pounding. I don't know what to do—I don't think they can hear me in the twentieth row!"

MUNSEL: You look exactly like him, too. You're doing him perfectly! I remember he was nervous.

STEVENS: He was terrified that night.

RESNIK: I went backstage before his act and I kicked him in the pants and all that, and he went out and did his walled-in thing.

LEWIS: And he was marvelous.

RESNIK: He was so miserable that night.

LEWIS: He was perfect in it, though, in every way. He wasn't at all vulgar.

KANIN: And he was probably in it longer than anyone. Whenever he signed a contract for a Broadway show, there was a stipulation that if they ever needed him for one or two nights, he could get out.

RESNIK: He's sweet. A sweet comic.

MUNSEL: A very funny man.

In 1921, the Moravian soprano Maria Jeritza made her Metropolitan Opera debut as Marietta in Korngold's *Die Tote Stadt.* She went on to become a great favorite with American audiences, becoming the Met's first Turandot and a crowd-pleasing Tosca who was famous for singing "Vissi d'arte" while lying prone on the floor. Her final appearance as Rosalinda came on February 22, 1951, when for the first time since 1932 and at the age of sixty-three, she asked to sing it once again.

RESNIK: That night Jeritza came to sing—

MUNSEL: Oh, that was awful.

R E S N I K : They said, "Madame Jeritza is coming. It's her sixty-third birthday, and she would like very much to sing Rosalinda."

M U N S E L : Oh, that was a killing evening!

R E S N I K : I couldn't not defer a performance—I was a weekly artist then. So she and Ormandy had a big confab, and they transposed the "Czardas" down a third. Should anything have gone wrong, I was in the house to step in. She was petrified, but in the end, she was like a baby. She was so thrilled to have gone through it. She sent me roses afterward. We remained friends to the end of her days.

The *New York Daily News*'s John Chapman wrote kindly in the next morning's paper: "It was a happy evening, and after it was all over, it still was Maria Jeritza's. She was gallant, she was handsome, and she was loved. No lady of her years could ask for much more than that, and this is why I hope that Miss Munsel, who is now scrambling to the top of the operatic ladder, may have at some distant time a night such as Jeritza had last evening in *Fledermaus* at the Metropolitan Opera House."

M U N S E L : That was a devastating evening—

S T E V E N S : I wasn't in that.

K A N I N : Were you in that, Patrice?

S T E V E N S : Patrice was in that for the whole run.

M U N S E L : I guess so, until, until—

S T E V E N S : I don't know when Roberta came in. Roberta came later. But I only did four Orlofskys. Later there was Novotná and Blanche Thebom.

M U N S E L : But that night was so terrible—Jeritza just couldn't do it. And some people like Mr. Bing thought it was very funny. It was devastating. I came onstage stage left, and came around stage right to make another entrance, and Bing was standing there laughing hysterically, eating his usual banana, and he thought it was very funny. And it was a cruel, cruel evening. She just couldn't do it. I ended up in tears; I could barely get through it. The critics were very kind, but it was kind—not good. It was almost painful to be onstage with her, and of course, she had to learn it in English. She had always done it in German, and didn't have enough time to really learn it, so that she was a nervous wreck and she forgot tons of things.

L E W I S : And she did it only once?

MUNSEL: Just once.

STEVENS: Wasn't that a special kind of gala thing?

RESNIK: Yes, it was a gala.

MUNSEL: And her husband had given a big donation, but the day
that those seats went on sale, there was a bigger queue in front of the
box office than they had seen in a long, long time.

STEVENS: Oh, come on, we didn't do so badly there. We had quite
a crowd out there.

To capitalize on the success of his brainchild, and to bring some
always welcome revenues to the Met's coffers, Bing decided to send out
a special touring company—separate from the regular annual spring
tour—during the 1951–52 season. A young cast was hired, including
Jack Gilford from the original production, and with Brenda Lewis as
Rosalinda, and the original was reproduced. Soprano Virginia Mac-
Watters, the tour's Adele, managed the incredible feat of singing all 144
performances, earning her a special letter of commendation from the
general manager. Every now and then Met stars such as Regina Resnik
and Marguerite Piazza were brought in to spell Miss Lewis. The tour
opened in Philadelphia on September 22, 1951.

Unfortunately, despite a critical success and the pleasure of all who
saw it, the tour was abandoned in February 1952 at its scheduled halfway
mark, and ultimately had to be branded a financial loss, a victim of
circumstances. Not to be outdone, impresario Sol Hurok had sent out
another *Fledermaus* tour with former Met star Irra Petina and Adelaide
Bishop. The cities he booked coincided with the Met tour and often beat
it to the stage, causing an overabundance of a good thing and a lot of
confusion about which was the "real" *Fledermaus.* The Met tour's
problems were not caused by a lack of polish, however: According to
the bible of show business, *Variety,* of September 24, 1951, "Everything
about the production spells class and good taste, and the cross country
tour should bring a lot of enjoyment to a lot of playgoers."

The tour was eventful beyond the tireless performances of its company members. An arbitrated dispute between the American Guild of
Musical Artists and Actors Equity resulted in a change in booking in
Washington, D.C., because the Daughters of the American Revolution
owned Constitution Hall and blacks weren't admitted, while Equity
forbade its members to perform in segregated theaters. The DAR, of

course, had just a few years earlier banned Marian Anderson from the hall, prompting Eleanor Roosevelt to extend to her an invitation to sing at the Lincoln Memorial. The *Fledermaus* tour made its home instead at the Gayety, an old burlesque house in the seediest part of town. The house was refurbished for the occasion.

In another incident, the company was met by pickets in Syracuse, prompted by the blacklisting of two of its members, Gilford and Miss Lewis, by Red Channels, a national organization operating out of that upstate New York town. To show the Metropolitan's support for its artists, Bing flew up to Syracuse himself, personally escorting the cast through the picket line.

L E W I S : I think the tour gave a great service to all the people who saw it. There was one evening which stands out in my memory. That was the night that Donald Dame died in Lincoln, Nebraska. He died in the afternoon before the performance. It was in February, and the traveling conditions were terrible, and many of the people came during blizzard conditions. A lot of the people knew the weather conditions would be prohibitive, so they left the night before, because they'd had their tickets for months and they weren't going to miss it, regardless. The scenery came in late and the show didn't finish until one or one-thirty in the morning. After it was over we went to a diner near the train station—we had to make our way through the drifts. As we walked into this little smoky diner, here were all these middle-western country people, and they started to applaud and carry on like crazy. We graciously acknowledged it and sat at a table, and one woman came over to us, her eyes absolutely brimming with tears, and said, "How wonderful that you came and gave this to us." It was, I think, the first time I realized what being a performer really meant.

K A N I N : A touring performer.

L E W I S : For them it was a gift. We brought an image of something they'd imagined, where they could laugh and enjoy it, with costumes and bustles and color and sparkle.

When he was planning *Fledermaus,* Bing originally chose the Hungarian perfectionist Fritz Reiner as his conductor. A man with definite ideas, Reiner led over 140 performances at the Met through the years, before leaving it to conduct the Chicago Symphony. A complex character, he dropped the oft-quoted remark "When I am conducting opera, I'd rather be conducting a concert; and when I conduct a concert, I'd rather be in the opera pit. It's been like that all my life. . . ." His life was cut short in 1963 when he died of pneumonia while preparing a production of *Götterdämmerung,* which would have marked his return to the Met.

K A N I N : Now that dear old Fritz Reiner is no longer with us—

L E W I S : Now you can tell.

K A N I N : Well, we can speak frankly. As you all remember, it was Fritz Reiner who was the original conductor announced to do *Fledermaus.*

L E W I S : In fact, he started with the rehearsals.

K A N I N : He did. Well, there came a moment—somewhere in the second act, I think—I wanted it to seem kind of sexy, so I asked the chorus people to sit down and maybe embrace in couples onstage, and I thought it looked fine. Reiner said, "No, no, that's impossible. They can't sing sitting down. I want them standing, I want them facing me, and I want them watching me."

S T E V E N S : That's extraordinary for him, because he was not like that at all in *Carmen.* You didn't have to look at him—

K A N I N : Well, he was like that with me. And not only like that, but absolutely nasty about it.

L E W I S : That he was good at.

M U N S E L : I remember all of this now.

K A N I N : So I went to Mr. Bing and told him good-bye—I didn't want the job.

R E S N I K : "Him or me"?

K A N I N : I didn't put it that way. I just didn't want to be involved if I was just going to be vetoed on every major idea.

S T E V E N S : Boy, he wasn't like that in *Carmen.* You never had to look at him for one minute. He was so fabulous.

M U N S E L : I had to look at him. He was the only conductor I ever paid any attention to.

L E W I S : You had to, because his beat was so tiny.

M U N S E L : It was only for the first-violin section.

L E W I S : Tinier than that.

R E S N I K : I used to call it his little chocolate square.

K A N I N : Well, Bing called us together for a meeting in his office. Reiner said to Bing that either he was the boss or he wouldn't do it.

S T E V E N S : That's incredible—I never had any problems with him.

M U N S E L : Maybe he learned from that experience.

K A N I N : That could be.

R E S N I K : One of the greatest things that ever happened to us in our lives is that people like Reiner would sit with us and rehearse for hours. I wish that young singers had that today.

L E W I S : Well, there are no conductors around now who know the score, have that authority, and they don't want to work that hard.

The ladies recalled the softer side of Fritz Reiner:

R E S N I K : Patrice was wearing her first contact lenses—

M U N S E L : My first, and they were the big ones.

R E S N I K : —Jan Peerce was wearing the Cyclops, and I wasn't wearing contacts yet at all. After Act One, one night, to show you the other side of Reiner, he said to the stage manager, "Send me in the three blind mice." We all came to his dressing room. He said to me, "You I forgive; you're not wearing the lenses. [Indicating Munsel] You I don't forgive; look at me." To Jan Peerce he said, "You just sing. Sing good." All three of us couldn't see a thing. I couldn't see a thing for years. I saw the audience for the first time ten years ago.

K A N I N : How do you like it?

R E S N I K : I hated it.

M U N S E L : It's terrible.

L E W I S : I wore them once and that was it.

S T E V E N S : [shrugs] I liked it.

M U N S E L : I got my first lenses for that *Don Giovanni,* and they were the big ones. And first I had all the things that I'd have to act on moved way down front because I couldn't see anything, and then I got these huge lenses, and they put them in that day. The only day I ever put them in was the day of that performance. And I got bubbles in them. The man who made them for me came and put them in for me. I went out onstage and they filled up with bubbles, and all I could see were thousands of lights from the foot, from the top—I was totally blind. And I staggered to the wings when I finished singing the first bit, and I called for my maid to come quickly with my suction cups—because you took them out with suction cups—and I would go out and sing a little bit, then I'd run to the wings and pop one out, go and sing a little and run back to the wings to pop the other one out.

R E S N I K : The only one who wore them well was Jan.

L E W I S : But he only wore one—he only wore one lens.

M U N S E L : I couldn't see anything.

K A N I N : Well, we didn't really finish the contretemps involving Reiner and myself. Because all of these women are his supporters, but—

M U N S E L : No, I'm not.

K A N I N : That's the curious thing about the bubble reputation, because he could have been very sweet and adorable to them, but to me, he was an out-and-out SOB.

L E W I S : Well, that's what he was to most people.

S T E V E N S : No, that's not true.

K A N I N : He was mean—

L E W I S : To his orchestra musicians?

S T E V E N S : He was marvelous to me.

L E W I S : I could tell you stories about some of his orchestra musicians—

S T E V E N S : I loved him.

K A N I N : —he was uncooperative—

R E S N I K : He was a very difficult man; we all adored him.

M U N S E L : He didn't help me.

K A N I N : —he just happened to pick the wrong adversary in me, because I didn't need the goddam job. I didn't want it; I was doing it as a sort of a favor to the Met and to Bing. I had other work to do, which was more important and far more lucrative and more interesting to me. I didn't care about losing the job, and I simply went in and said I didn't want to do it. So he called us both together for a meeting in his office, and the three of us sat there, and it was at that moment that our friend Reiner really displayed himself, because he thought he could really prevail, and so he took the position that was absolutely uncompromising. I said absolutely nothing. I didn't open my kisser, which is a trick I've learned through the years—the less you say, the better. Bing said to him, "If that's your position, I don't want you to do it." He was stunned, and said, "I want to do it," and Bing said, "It's not only Kanin, but I'm going to bring in many, many stage directors, as important as I can get, because I think that's what this company needs, and the conductor will have to learn how to cooperate with them. Conductors will no longer be in complete charge of the staging and the scenery and the lighting and so on."

STEVENS: He sure changed his tune later, because later when Sir Tyrone Guthrie came in and worked with me on the *Carmen,* I want you to know, he did not have that kind of attitude.

RESNIK: No, he didn't—he changed after that.

MUNSEL: Well, maybe he learned something.

KANIN: Wait, wait, wait—Tony Guthrie was living with me at the time—

STEVENS: We didn't have any of those problems.

KANIN: I know, because Tony Guthrie was a man of tremendous power and importance.

MUNSEL: He probably learned.

KANIN: And I don't think he would have taken one bit of horseshit from Reiner.

RESNIK: And he didn't.

KANIN: But I was not in that position with him.

LEWIS: You didn't have a title.

RESNIK: Also, I think it was because it was the *Fledermaus.* It was a lighter piece—

KANIN: Regina, no one, no one would tell Tony Guthrie what to do or how to do it or change a concept that he had—not at all.

RESNIK: I think it was easier for Reiner to take a backseat on *Carmen* than on *Fledermaus*—I don't know why.

KANIN: Yeah, that could have been, too.

RESNIK: By that time he'd been at the Met for some years.

MUNSEL: And he saw how successful those things were.

LEWIS: But it was a whole new field—

STEVENS: Because he was *very* cooperative, very cooperative.

KANIN: Well, as the girls suggest, he may have learned. Oh, I know every detail of that *Carmen,* because he used to come home every night and tell about the rehearsal.

S T E V E N S : Reiner was really relentless. I mean, he worked from ten in the morning until midnight; all he did was break for lunch and dinner.

R E S N I K : But Risë, is that the greatest thing that ever happened to us in our lives? That people like Reiner sat at the piano with us and rehearsed?

S T E V E N S : Right, right. Endlessly.

R E S N I K : When we got onstage there was no way for it not to go well, except if we were sick. We were hoarse when we got home, we got up the next day and we sang again, and he was at the piano playing all the time. I wish the young singers had that today—the benefits we had.

L E W I S : He was a master.

R E S N I K : Despite his tremendous temper.

Reiner's replacement in *Fledermaus* was Eugene Ormandy, as famous for his memory as he was for leading the Philadelphia Orchestra, which he did for forty-two years. He frequently conducted without a score. Though Ormandy was a Hungarian by birth like Reiner, their temperaments were completely different. When once asked if he missed having a family, Ormandy replied, "I really have 104 children. My orchestra. A very nice and friendly menage."

M U N S E L : Ormandy just went with you all the time.

L E W I S : He had never conducted opera, so in a sense, he felt he'd better do what was being done, not throw his weight around—so it was easy to work with him.

M U N S E L : He would do anything.

K A N I N : I remember him saying to all of you at one of the early rehearsals, "You just do whatever you like and I will accompany you." Well, that was reassuring, you can imagine.

Die Fledermaus has always been a favorite choice for gala performances, ever since somebody had the notion that Prince Orlofsky's second-act ball could provide even more entertainment than was actually in the libretto, and the concert-within-the-opera was born. Traditionally done on New Year's Eve or other special occasions, this serendipity has offered some of the most priceless moments operagoers have ever witnessed, with impromptu appearances by surprise guests from all corners of the performing arts.

Sometimes the novelty was an altered text, as on New Year's Eve of 1952 when in Orlofsky's aria Risë Stevens interpolated:

> *The op-er-as that must be your choice,*
> *If you like plays that sing,*
> *Are solely dependent on one voice,*
> *The voice of Rudolf Bing.*

In 1953, *Fledermaus* featured Alicia Markova in a special divertissement that was her last appearance at the Met. In 1954, a miniature piano was rolled out onstage to accompany the suddenly visible Vienna Boys' Choir in two selections. On New Year's Eve 1955, Renata Tebaldi sang three selections, and Jarmila Novotná as Orlofsky interpolated:

> *But if you think that life will be tough*
> *For dear old Foster Dulles,*
> *Just think that Bing had Milanov,*
> *Tebaldi and La Callas.*

In a recording led by Herbert von Karajan with Hilde Gueden, Erika Köth, and Regina Resnik, featured among the party guests are Renata Tebaldi singing the "Vilia-lied" from *The Merry Widow*, Birgit Nilsson tripping the light fantastic in "I Could Have Danced All Night," Leontyne Price singing her incomparable "Summertime," and, in an unparalleled interpretation, Giulietta Simionato and Ettore Bastianini at their Wild West best in "Anything You Can Do," from *Annie Get Your Gun.*

R E S N I K : I enjoyed New Year's Eve the most. When Garson wasn't there—

L E W I S : You could do what you wanted.

R E S N I K : I did what the hell I wanted.

L E W I S : And there was always champagne.

M U N S E L : New Year's Eves were fun for all of us because we never really knew what ballets there were and who was going to come on to sing. Guest appearances were always a surprise.

KANIN: At the end of the second act, on the second curtain call, members of the chorus dressed like janitors, sweeping up after the party. On New Year's Eve, as an extra added attraction, it was Bing and his whole staff who would come out with mops and brooms.

On April 22, 1972, the end of an era in American operatic history was marked by a gala at the Met honoring Sir Rudolf Bing. The festive evening featured appearances by over forty stars from the Bing era. After singing Salome's "Ah, du wolltest mich nicht," Birgit Nilsson presented Bing with a bronze bust of himself, designed by Virginia Page, on a silver tray. It was even rumored that Sir Rudolf had been seen shaking hands with a music critic after the performance—surely a once-in-a-lifetime happening.

RESNIK: When [Met administrator] John Gutman came to me and said, "We want you to participate in the Bing gala," I said, "Lovely. I'd like to sing ———" and he said, "No, I'm sorry, it's already taken." I said, "Who's taking a potshot at Mr. Bing? Is anybody going to sing about him?" I came up the next day with writing Orlofsky lyrics to Mr. Bing, and he said, "I have a ticklish problem. Nobody's in costume tonight." He wanted it to be a surprise, so he went to Bing and told him, "I want Regina to sing something, and I want it to be a surprise, but it has to be in Orlofsky's costume." And Bing said, "If Regina will make it funny, do it." I looked at the program—dead serious; and so we concocted it, John and I wrote the lyrics together. Mine were racier, and he took some out.

Some less racy lyrics that stayed in were:

All his productions were cheaply done:
he saved the nickels and dimes!
He loved the critics—every one,
he even loved the Times!

When *Die Fledermaus* was written, the authors decided that writing the part of the postpubescent Prince Orlofsky for a woman to sing would lend just the right touch of outrageous eccentricity to the already decadent scenes of Viennese party life. Not that it hadn't been done before. From the Handel operas to Cherubino in *The Marriage of Figaro,* to Hansel, to Octavian in *Der Rosenkavalier,* mezzo-sopranos have long enjoyed striding across opera stages in trousers, displaying newly acquired manly charms. But Orlofsky is different—no mere page boy in a white wig. Autocratic and bored, he demands to be entertained.

The tradition was kept until Max Reinhardt's Berlin production in 1929, when in the course of rejuvenating and updating the work, he broke the sex barrier by casting Oscar Karlweis as the first man in history to play Orlofsky. Since that time, the pants have been worn by both sexes, depending on the production and the director's mood.

RESNIK: The Viennese were getting away from using women. To this day they're using men. The Met kept the tradition all the time.

KANIN: What is Orlofsky's vocal range?

MUNSEL: Anywhere.

LEWIS: You can do anything.

STEVENS: That aria's a nothing aria, let's face it.

RESNIK: It's not such a nothing. What it is, it's really too high for all of us—way too high.

STEVENS: Well, first of all, it's written so badly—come on—it always sounds like you have the hiccups.

LEWIS: Maybe that was intended.

RESNIK: When I recorded it with Karajan, he suggested a transposition down a third, to sound more like a man.

[Stevens hiccups a few bars.]

RESNIK: Well, he wanted him to sound eccentric, I guess.

MUNSEL: It was eccentric, it was eccentric.

When Bing first approached Risë Stevens to do the role of Orlofsky, she didn't want to take it. Although celebrated for her Octavian, she needed a good deal of convincing to take on the Prince. Though identified with the role, Miss Stevens sang it only six times, but recorded it twice.

STEVENS: I remember my husband and I sat down with the whole group to decide how I was going to do Orlofsky. Everybody was throwing in advice. I wore a monocle, I had the moustache, and I found a huge cigarette holder—

MUNSEL: A very long cigarette holder—nobody could get near her.

STEVENS: —and these long cigarettes. It was so outrageous for a woman to walk out on the stage like this. They said, "You're not really going to do this," and I said, "Darned right I am." And I even went out and bought shoes—what did they call them—

RESNIK: Adler elevator shoes.

STEVENS: Adler elevator shoes!

RESNIK: I still have mine.

STEVENS: They were black patent-leather men's shoes, my size. I only did five or six performances.

KANIN: But you came back in later years.

STEVENS: No, that was it. I never did it again. I don't know why—I just had other things to do.

KANIN: We just think you did it more often because you were inimitable.

RESNIK: I certainly didn't even try to imitate you. Impossible.

STEVENS: [to Munsel] You were in it for a long time.

MUNSEL: I guess so. The first year I had to stop singing, though, because I was very pregnant with our first baby. Bing finally came to me and said, "Pat, I think it's time to quit for the season because I can't tell whether the bustle's on the front or the back." So I quit for the season.

For a new wrinkle on the perennial controversy about opera in English, consider that, with due respect to tradition, *Fledermaus* in a comprehensible language is appreciated by all, cast and audience alike. A new wrinkle on *Fledermaus,* in turn, appeared in 1986, when in its new production (the first since the Kanin-Dietz), the Met presented a bilingual version, with dialogue in English but sung in German—a mix disorienting to anyone but a schizophrenic UN translator. When it was first announced, the choice took everyone by surprise.

KANIN, LEWIS, MUNSEL, RESNIK: In German! *Why?*

STEVENS: I know nothing about it.

RESNIK: Zey are goink back to Vienna.

LEWIS: Ja!

MUNSEL: Oh, my God!

RESNIK: That spells trouble.

STEVENS: I have nothing to say.

MUNSEL: Oh, that's tragic.

KANIN: Does anybody know why?

LEWIS: You don't please either camp.

MUNSEL: Obviously someone said, "Let's go back to the classics." It's like opening all the cuts in an opera.

RESNIK: I think the reason we had so much fun in that version was because we understood the colloquialisms and we liked what we were singing.

LEWIS: It was part of our culture.

MUNSEL: It was the first time an audience had gotten all the jokes—all the laughter was there.

LEWIS: You didn't have to drop your pants to make them laugh.

MUNSEL: And it was such a joy to do.

Few visits to the theater can be as exhilarating as a visit with *Fledermaus*. Unlike the pleasant but flimsier examples of Viennese operetta, and more than stalwart survivors like *The Merry Widow, The Student Prince, Maytime,* or even Strauss's own *Gypsy Baron, Fledermaus* has an enduring magic that delights its audiences—sweeps them up into an intoxicating, bygone world and sets them gently down again, leaving them to waltz to their taxis as they exit the theater.

KANIN: If you're asking why it's so successful, it's because there's something beneath it that—

LEWIS: It had everything in it.

RESNIK: It was a thing of its time.

MUNSEL: And the music is shmaltzy.

LEWIS: And it's not repetitive and not derivative—it's the essence of what Strauss had to offer.

STEVENS: It's very Viennese, let's face it.

LA TRAVIATA

~

I like on the stage fairyland stories—beautiful, elegant.
—LICIA ALBANESE

Music by Giuseppe Verdi
Libretto by Francesco Maria Piave
from the play *La Dame aux Camélias*
by Alexandre Dumas *fils,* from his novel

VIOLETTA................. *Licia Albanese, Patricia Brooks, Anna Moffo,*
Jarmila Novotná, Bidú Sayão, Renata Scotto,
Joan Sutherland

ALFREDO................. *Alfredo Kraus, Neil Rosenshein*

GERMONT............... *Robert Merrill, Sherrill Milnes*

*I*n the glittering Paris of the 1840s, a young rake known as Alexandre Dumas *fils,* while not writing, dallied with one of the city's most desirable courtesans. Alphonsine Plessis, a country girl, had come to Paris in her teens, and in the interests of fashion promptly changed her name to Marie Duplessis. She speedily became queen of the demimonde before dying of tuberculosis on February 2, 1846, shortly before her twenty-second birthday.

Holed up in a country inn, Dumas exorcised his grief by writing, *La Dame aux Camélias,* a fictionalized account of their affair, naming the characters Marguerite Gauthier and Armand. The novel's scandalous popularity was exceeded only by that of the stage version, the "immorality" of which appalled and/or fascinated everyone who saw it. Among the latter group was Verdi, who saw the play on a trip to Paris. He decided this would be the subject to fill the commission he had just received from the Teatro la Fenice.

Though many found "Can a tubercular demimondaine find happiness with an innocent young man from Provence?" a lurid question, the intimate, domestic story set against a bourgeois background appealed to Verdi. "Everyone complained when I proposed putting a hunchback on the stage," he wrote. "Well, I wrote *Rigoletto* with great pleasure."

Mlle. Duplessis was apparently not only a magnificent specimen, but quite a busy one; her list of lovers reads like a veritable who's who of Parisian society and includes Franz Liszt. She is buried below Sacré-Coeur, where to this day, La Traviata (or "the misguided girl") receives a steady stream of callers.

"Some persons say I am too big for the role. Others say I am too ugly. But that shows they do not know their history," said Rosa Ponselle as she was about to sing her first Violetta. "I have a picture of the famous courtesan who was the living counterpart on whom Dumas based Camille. Anyone may see the picture and judge for himself if she is not larger than I am. And as for ugliness, Clara Morris, America's most famous portrayer of Camille, was known as one of the homeliest women on the stage. . . . I am at least no bigger than the original, and no uglier than the most famous actress who ever played the part."

ANNA MOFFO: I'm a firm believer you should always look in the mirror and say, "Do I have the fifty percent to start with? Can I look like Violetta, can I look like Tosca, can I look like Manon?" Then, "Well, not exactly, so I have to do this, or that, or costume myself, or lose fifty pounds. . . ." But you always have to start with that. I think the mirror tells us what we should do—not always, but it's an indication.

JOAN SUTHERLAND: My main problem was that I never looked like Violetta. I never looked like many of the characters that I played. On a big stage, I suppose I pass.

LICIA ALBANESE: For *Traviata,* you must make yourself very tall onstage, very aristocratic.

SUTHERLAND: I was always tall, so it was always great for me if the rest of the cast was larger than I was. But I very often found myself with a very short tenor, and that always puts one at a disadvantage—or one feels it does. But then later on, I usually had larger people. I don't know if the tenors are growing larger or what!

RENATA SCOTTO: We have this beautiful being in Violetta. She is a woman who never knew how to live a normal life, a good life. She sold herself, her body, and she thinks it's enough for her to have a good living, a beautiful house, and lots of friends. But inside her it's very cold and nothing else, because everybody likes her only because of her body.

Having performed *La Traviata* over four hundred times, Anna Moffo has made Violetta her signature role. "Her voice is a warm, vibrant, agile instrument," according to *The New Yorker.* "Her acting is skilled and heartfelt. One would have to look far to find a contemporary singer better suited to the role."

MOFFO: In many ways, I think Violetta suits me. I have to work much harder in something like *Butterfly,* where I feel I have to make myself minuscule.

In 1953, Renata Scotto made her formal operatic debut in *La Traviata* in Milan. Actually, she had debuted a few years earlier as a teenaged Violetta in her hometown of Savona, Italy.

SCOTTO: It's a very romantic period, Verdi's period. But the character of Violetta, even though it is a romantic character, can also be a modern character. As a human being, she can be anywhere at any time.

Of Bidú Sayão's Metropolitan Violetta in 1940, one critic wrote that she "graced the part with beauty, charm and great poignancy."

BIDÚ SAYÃO: She was the kind of woman who used men. She knew they wanted her and she used them. But when Alfredo came along, finally, here was one who was different.

Jarmila Novotná brought all of her consummate acting skill to the role of the dying courtesan. She debuted in the part in 1926, in her native Prague.

JARMILA NOVOTNÁ: She is a rather frivolous, pleasure-loving creature, used to luxury, not believing in loyalty and love, easily changing lovers—so one can play her that way.

In 1960, the New York City Opera presented a controversial new production of *La Traviata* with Patricia Brooks and Plácido Domingo. According to the director, Frank Corsaro, "Pat Brooks was the most human Violetta I've ever seen. She was able to approach and scale the character in all its ramifications, and caught things that are only hinted at in the score."

PATRICIA BROOKS: I had done the role only once before this production, out on Long Island. I was very influenced by Greta Garbo in the movie, and having worked with Uta Hagen as an actress years ago really gave me a lot of ideas on the part. Frank took some, and some he didn't want. Violetta has never been alone. She is being kept by the Baron in the first act, so you have to deal with the falseness of that life, because there was a limit to the kind of relationship they had. He was just someone who liked to put her on view for people. I would never see him during the day; he'd be busy, so I would spend a lot of time alone. Then he would present me with jewels and beautiful dresses, and want me to present myself to other people. That would make him more important. At the beginning of the opera, this is my life, and I've just had it. It's been wonderful and secure, but I can't bear it anymore. I'm ready to say good-bye.

Licia Albanese did not sing Violetta until she came to the United States, where, beginning in 1942, she sang the role seventy-two times at the Met alone, a record for that house.

ALBANESE: When I was singing Traviata here, I saw the Greta Garbo Traviata, which I adored. I also saw many French and Italian Traviatas in the movies, but they weren't like Garbo. But when Alfredo says, "In this park, where I first saw you—" Traviata looks at the public and becomes more like she feels—really fantastic and healthy. You look far away. Garbo did that, too. Then she starts, "Oh, come on, don't say all these things," making a joke. "If this is true, just go away—you can love me like other men."

BROOKS: I read everything I could about Dumas's Camille and gave it the preparation a straight actress goes through, where you make up a history of what she was like as a child, then growing up, and her family—or lack of one. There were things I had decided about her house, what her favorite colors were, and how I dealt with men, even to the point of how we would make love and how I'd play that. The first lovemaking experience I had, who I was with, and all the details—things like that. This all helped me enormously. Then suddenly, it became "what I like" and it wasn't "she" any longer. I became posessed with the part.

SAYÃO: She didn't want anything except the big apartment, jewelry, belongings. She lived for excitement. But after she finds this boy who gives her all this devotion, she falls in love with him, instead of just using him. She changes.

ALBANESE: Sometimes, when they had dances with friends, they told dirty stories, like we do—well, not very dirty—risqué. They used to, because they were all kept women. And she was dancing the waltz and the mazurka. But not vulgar. I don't like things vulgar onstage.

MOFFO: It's very easy to make Violetta not a modern character, and she's a very modern character. My thought is always that her coping, when she's so sick, is the key to her strength. She has great moral strength.

If Verdi wrote *La Traviata* with great pleasure, the same emotion did not extend to the pleasure of March 6, 1853, which by all accounts was pretty ghastly. The voluminous Mme. Fanny Salvini-Donatelli drew howls from the audience as she gamely attempted to waste away as Violetta. The tenor, Lodovico Graziani, was hoarse, and baritone Felice Varesi hated everything about Germont *père*. Verdi had even received an anonymous letter begging him to recast it. After the premiere, he wrote the oft-quoted note *"La Traviata* last night—fiasco. Was the fault mine, or that of the singers? Time will be the judge."

Fourteen months later, on May 6, 1854, the work was presented again in Venice—this time at Teatro San Benedetto, with Francesco Maria Piave directing and the more suitable Maria Spezia as Violetta. After its unqualified success, Violettas immediately began coughing across opera stages all over Europe and America, where it premiered at the New York Academy of Music on December 3, 1856, with Anna de la Grange. The *Traviata* story has had many incarnations, including *Camille,* a 1930 opera by Hamilton Forrest, and most notably, Greta Garbo's film *Camille.*

N O V O T N Á : Violetta is a role that allows you a wonderful chance to display all the areas of talent—vocal, dramatic, and physical.

S U T H E R L A N D : Violetta is a wonderful, absolutely fantastic role. She's so complete as a woman. Of all the roles I do, she is so much more real.

M O F F O : Violetta is a pure character. Through the opera, she cannot have any gimmicks. Even at her most courtesan self, she's a lady of great class. Her whole manner of acting, to anybody—that to me is very important in the first act.

Director Max Reinhardt staged a production of *Traviata* in 1929 Berlin. Reinhardt dominated German theater until he was forced to leave his homeland in the early 1930s. Director of the pageant play *The Miracle,* which toured worldwide, he staged *A Midsummer Night's Dream* at the Hollywood Bowl in 1936, committing the production to film the same year, with a cast including Mickey Rooney, James Cagney, Anita Louise, Dick Powell, and Olivia de Havilland. Among his forays into opera was the staging of the first *Der Rosenkavalier,* premiering on January 26, 1911, in Dresden.

N O V O T N Á : I had not only the joy but the great privilege to work in Berlin with Reinhardt, and I sang *Traviata* there in 1929—can you imagine? He was very influential in making us see that every character in opera must be different. You must penetrate the character, go through the whole life of such a person. For artistic performance, it is not enough to simply master the technical demands. You must penetrate the music and express your own, individual conception. In *Traviata* you have so many things: She must look well, sing well, act well. All these things together make a great Violetta. I don't know, maybe I was able to express it like an actress, almost. Manon and Violetta are almost the same character, don't you think? They are similar because of the pleasure which they love; more, probably, than what life can give them. But when the love really comes—my God, then they give it up. So you see, it is probably in every woman's heart that love can do miracles. It is the strongest thing we can have.

S A Y Ã O : But Violetta had become a lady and she had manners. She was not vulgar at all—a very distinguished lady.

S C O T T O : We must understand the meaning of this character of a woman who didn't find her life worth living in the right way. Of course she's sick, and she wants to get out of her life the most she can, because she knows she's going to die. And she's very beautiful and likes to get men only to pay for her lifestyle. She's a prostitute with feelings that she has never dared to take out of her, but she has them inside of her.

M O F F O : Each production was different; each director was different. Somebody would always ask me for something that surprised me. Like I did it in Florence, and a man told me Violetta was really not only an alcoholic and a dope addict, but she was also into cigars, and he wanted me to smoke these little cigarillos. I mean, I was the one who said, "No blowing out of candles in the first act!" I was never a hysterical diva, but there was one thing about the smoke—I couldn't risk breathing in any sulfur from the candles or anything.

A L B A N E S E : The opera is something educational; you have to educate people. Not like you see now in the movies. In my time, or my mother's time, they never kiss. If they kiss, or if they try to—I don't want to see that man anymore. This is no good for young people. For young people, it's nice to learn how to approach love, because if they love too much they kill themselves. If you approach it in a very bad way, it's not pleasant. So with Violetta, from the first act until you die, you are an aristocratic person.

M O F F O : I mean, Flora is a real—well, she's really off the street. Violetta, no matter what she does, is really a grande dame.

A L B A N E S E : And they make Flora too young! Flora is an old woman. Flora makes appointments for Traviata. She had been a beautiful woman of the world—but then she was not rich, so she began to make appointments.

M O F F O : The way you realize how wonderful Violetta is is when you go to Flora's house and realize how tacky, tacky—great in bed, maybe, but tacky. Violetta is a deluxe courtesan. She is very bright, very aristocratic in her conversation, the way she moves. She's really a desirable woman because she's not just gorgeous, she's fun, she's articulate, she's a lady.

N O V O T N Á : I wouldn't say Violetta is a grande dame, but she's a dame.

Though the kept woman is by no means a uniquely French invention, the demimondaine was hands-down the deluxe model, a product of careful grooming, exemplified by the rigorous training that Gigi received at the hands of her aunt—everything from how to dress to choosing the right cigar.

A L B A N E S E : Traviata finds herself in this condition because she was a young girl in the big city, Paris, and was sent flowers and all that.

M O F F O : The wonderful thing about Violetta, or Marguerite Gauthier, is that she experienced in such a hurry—in twenty some-odd years—what most people experience into their forties. And she concentrated her experiences so much—everything that happened to her. Her love for Alfredo—every time I do it I realize how much more consuming it is, like her illness, because she knows she doesn't have any time. Every *Traviata* for me changes, still. Because I know a lot more about a lot of things that I didn't know about then. It's the old thing when you're first starting and they say, "You can't be a virgin and sing *Traviata*"—and I would say, "Ha ha ha." But yes—and be careful how you word this—it's experience.

A L B A N E S E : You find the books a great help. Then you really see the life of this woman. She starts the life young. She learns how to dance, how to speak languages, to play the piano. This is the book. And the old Count had lost a daughter, so he took this girl and made her like a daughter—not a sweetheart. Afterwards, she was so beautiful to all the counts, the barons, and all the great society, so she became *la dame du monde*. And everybody walked by not to look because she was a bad girl—but everybody was looking at her, what dress she wore, in the opera house or the park.

S A Y Ã O : Violetta is a completely different role than Mimì—Violetta changes.

BROOKS: There's a definite progression, a definite change in the woman.

SAYÃO: The first act is completely different from the second act, or the third or fourth.

MOFFO: I don't think Violetta changes at all. People don't change. I think she's the same person when the curtain opens; I just don't think she's been able to deal with that. First of all, when she looks at Alfredo, she knows—he's the one. "He may not want me; too bad I'm a courtesan." But it's the first time. The only thing that changes is she's able to relax with the situation. She's no longer interested in making a living. She cancels out everything else. She suddenly realizes this is what has been foremost in her mind—she just never thought it was going to be in the cards for her.

NOVOTNÁ: Mimì is a completely different personality. Mimì is just a delightful creature, and that should come to be seen on the stage.

SAYÃO: Mimì is always the same. She's sick in the beginning and she dies of the same sickness. She loves him at the beginning and the end of the opera. The only big change in her life is when she learns he is annoyed with her, when she hears him tell Marcello, "I can't live with her anymore." Violetta was also a very poor girl, but she was very ambitious and moved to Paris.

In the centuries before streptomycin and good hygiene, pulmonary tuberculosis almost always proved fatal. Usually contagious, it claimed victims not only from the general population, but among opera heroines like Violetta, Mimì, and Antonia and her mother. Had the composers followed through, the end result of all that conspicuous coughing would have been a tubercular ward occupied by Musetta, Rodolfo, and his three roommates, Alfredo, Flora, and Dr. Miracle. Occasionally, with rest and good care, a patient did recover, but not often—and never in opera.

ALBANESE: They all died with TB, because they used to wear light things. And to die with TB was *romanticismo*.

SAYÃO: Violetta was very sick, but it really didn't bother her. She wouldn't let it.

ALBANESE: I went to see TB people in the hospital in Italy, although I did my first *Traviata* in this country. But I went just to look—what kind of cough, and this and that. When you cough, you have to cough dry, not like you have a cold. And then they come out without a handkerchief! A handkerchief is always elegant. [Coughs gently into her hand.] Even to make the face, you want to avoid to cough. Also, I remember when I was young, we went to the little town where my mother was born, to see her cousin. A beautiful home. And my mother said, "How's Maria?"—one of the daughters. And my cousin said, "Oh, she's not well; she has TB." And she came in like Traviata in the first act. And you know, I will never forget that. Tall and beautiful and oh, so happy to see my brothers and me. She was eighteen or twenty years old. The skin was alabaster, and big eyes—you know, when you have a fever, your eyes are shiny. And I was a kid then; I never thought to sing *Traviata*. But when I did, I always thought of her. She said, "See, I am so happy today, I don't need any medicine. Look at this table, it's full of medicine! When you go, throw it all out." And she was so gay, dancing, playing the piano. I will always remember.

S C O T T O : Alfredo was looking at her for one year without talking to her. One year, just looking at her—I mean, this is romantic! But when they finally talk to each other, he says, "I love you," and she says, "Oh, come on—nobody loves me." And this is very Violetta, very much the way she lives in the first act. Nobody really loves her for what she is; they love her because she's beautiful.

A L B A N E S E : Alfredo comes, and she makes a joke of his love. It cannot be true. And he says, "Well, if you were mine, I would take care of you." Then she wakes up: "Nobody took care of me; nobody would love me like you do." But you say it always with elegance: "Dite davvero." One time I was up, one time I sat down, one time I was at the table, then slowly you can sit in the chair near the table. And when you sit, it's not just any way, but *posizione*—you must sit elegantly, with your fan.

M O F F O : In the words of Licia Albanese, as she said to me, "Anna *mia,* after me, you're the best Violetta."

Born aptly in the Canary Islands, of Austrian descent, Alfredo Kraus made his operatic debut in Cairo as the Duke in *Rigoletto*. His vocal longevity owes a debt to the fact that he restricted his repertory to virtually a handful of roles, all suitable for his high yet light and elegant tenor.

ALFREDO KRAUS: I am Alfredo twice—Alfredo Kraus and Alfredo Germont. I have sung the role with almost all the most famous sopranos in the world: Renata Scotto, Anna Moffo, Rosanna Carteri, Marianna Nicolesco, even with Magda Olivero, which was a fantastic experience; and of course, I can't leave out Maria Callas. But with so many others, also.

MOFFO: Kraus, of course, was my first Alfredo. He was my first everything—my first Duke, my first *Puritani,* my first *Pearl Fishers.* He's just the greatest tenor I maybe ever worked with consecutively. He's so reliable and so secure—and just marvelous. He was very elegant, always. And what I like about him so much—he's always stuck with his repertoire. That's why, while he's here with us on earth, he'll still be singing those high Cs.

KRAUS: Alfredo has to change a little with each different Violetta. The psychological part is almost always the same, but the reactions with one or another soprano could be different. You also have to adjust the way of singing, because every soprano has a different pitch. And rehearsals at the piano, and on the stage, are very important beforehand, because I imagine that most sopranos have a different idea of what Violetta is like. Different personalities always make for different performances.

NOVOTNÁ: Alfredo's sincere love opens a new world for Violetta. And she learns to love as never before, and she gives up all her frivolity.

BROOKS: Also, his sending me gardenias when I have been sick—it was very touching, but I am not about to show that I was touched by this young man and the flowers.

MOFFO: He must have been considerably younger, not only in years but in experience. And she was a very mature twenty-five or so.

SAYÃO: She had always wanted to have fun, to have a good time. She had wanted happiness—but love? She wanted to be queen of the parties and have the jewelry and fun and champagne; she didn't want love. But he persists so much, she gives everything to him.

NOVOTNÁ: She loves Alfredo so, so strongly that nothing else matters. His love gave her more than all those loves that didn't mean anything. When all that is gone, she is absolutely dedicated to Alfredo.

MOFFO: When she meets Alfredo, she has so little time, and she's the only one who knows. And she has all she wants to do—above all, for him.

S C O T T O : That's why she's afraid to look into herself. And she lives in a lifestyle where she doesn't even have a moment to look into people. The people she's with are not worth a penny. They live— well, you know what kind of life. Her house is a bordello.

A L B A N E S E : I sang with beautiful Alfredos. Richard Tucker, Charles Kullman. *Elegante.* They came in with such elegance. And when Alfredo first comes in, he shouldn't show he's the man of Germont. No. He's young—he was never in a fancy house before. Gastone took him. He should look at Violetta all the time, and she feels this look. I used to tell the *tenore,* "You look at me when I come and go, because you fell in love with me when you saw me. And you're young. You have to follow me with your eyes." And I feel this on my back. And when I turn around, he turns—you know, like a young kid; when you look at them, they turn around.

N O V O T N Á : Jan Peerce was a wonderful Alfredo, I remember. Although he was not somehow very handsome, it did not matter at all. He sang it beautifully. I liked him quite well.

M O F F O : Jan Peerce was an extraordinary Alfredo. He was possibly the finest musician. You know, he was a violinist. He was so wonderful in his phrasing; he was simply the consummate artist. And you know, because of this wonderful musicality, he became ten feet tall. And he was also memorable the time he lost a contact lens during the first act. So it was a little bit like *Bohème,* under my hoopskirt looking for this contact lens. But he was fabulous. And Tucker was extraordinary. The recording I did with Tucker and Bob Merrill for RCA came out very well—it was so great to have them as colleagues.

In 1941, Richard Tucker sang his first Alfredo at the Al Jolson Theater in Manhattan. He later said, "My Boro Park friends were there, and of course, half Temple Adath Israel was there, too. My costume didn't fit worth a damn—it was an old swallowtail outfit which made me look like a mortician." But morticians seldom get to speak words like "Oh, quanto' quanto v'amo, quanto v'amo . . ." No matter how he looked, Tucker's sound will never be matched.

M O F F O : Richard was a wonderful Alfredo.

S C O T T O : From the moment Alfredo says, "No, I really love you," this is what gets Violetta in trouble—big trouble. Because from that moment she realizes that there is maybe someone who really loves her. And maybe he's the one that, inside, she was always looking for.

M O F F O : Flora is the only one to say, "But you know what you really are?" She has put it in black and white. Because that kind of life is like being on a merry-go-round. You don't like yourself, maybe, but I don't think you stop and think about it.

A L B A N E S E : She fell in love and starts to suffer.

M O F F O : Di Stefano was a wonderful, wonderful Alfredo—and he hated every minute of it. I did it with him in Mexico City, where I was panting so loudly because of the altitude. Pavarotti was wonderful and so was Plácido Domingo.

B R O O K S : Domingo was so tender—he likes women. He was the ideal.

A L B A N E S E : Then she takes the camellia. You must have a camellia: one white, with a little red in it, and one red. And you say, "Quando sarà appassito." The book says, "When it changes color." And the meaning is that she had her period. Eight days a month, nobody could approach her, when she wore a red camellia. When she wore white, everybody could knock at her door, *sì*. But today they don't do it!

M O F F O : I wouldn't cross Licia. She was a very fine Violetta. I've heard this about the camellia all my life—but in my case, I think no camellia is quite sufficient to make the point. Closed. Well, I never gave out any reds—I'll let it go at that.

B R O O K S : He protests his love, and to protect myself I say, "Oh, you can have me. Just pay the money and that's it for a night, or for a week if you can afford it." But when he goes away and I sing the aria, I realize this is the first person I've met who loves me for myself. He is doing something just for me.

S C O T T O : In "Ah, fors' è lui," she says—and it's an effective thing—"Maybe he's the one I was looking for," and she sings this wonderful aria. "I feel something I always wanted, but was almost afraid to look into." So this is an aria that talks about how he may be the one. And after that, she says, "Oh, I'm crazy—it's impossible." I believe the "Sempre libera" is the most exciting moment in the first act, because she really gives up and says, "No, this is really the life I'm born to live, and this is the way I want to live." And the words are beautiful. They say, "I'll here, all alone, by myself, and abandoned in this desert. So many people!" And you know, it's true, because you can really be alone in a place like New York City. And she says, "No, I'm alone, and I have to go on." But this is only the first act. Finally, she wants to try, and she changes her life completely.

B R O O K S : Frank Corsaro suggested that the first part of the "Sempre libera" is sort of seductive—always full of life and full of fun. Then the second part, I'm dealing with my sickness; that it's almost ironic this new person has come into it and I have this terrible sickness. The aria itself isn't as difficult musically—or it wasn't for me—as the end of the second act, since my voice wasn't that heavy. It was always lighter.

M O F F O : The artist only has to do what Verdi wrote—and he wrote it very well. The coloratura, to me, represents the frivolity of Violetta, which is fake. She already knows, when she says "Ah, fors' è lui," that she's been hit very hard by Alfredo. But then she says, "No, it can't be. I won't let myself go into this." And that's fake. She will not admit it and fights the fact that she's really fallen for this guy.

N O V O T N Á : It is really lyric, not a coloratura role. And it's not four voices, as they say. You see, almost every soprano tries to sing Traviata—some better, some less so. But it should not be any dramatic soprano.

M O F F O : I don't believe you need four voices to sing the role. Any really good lyric soprano can. The first act, it's not Zerbinetta—it's a lyric agility, a heavy agility, not to be confused with any kind of real coloratura piece.

The prima donna who made *La Traviata* famous was Marietta Piccolomini, a popular soprano of the 1850s, who apparently had everything a girl should have except vocal ability—a detail not overlooked by critics of the day. A practical soul, she explained, "They call me little impostor, and they give me bouquets, applauses, moneys—why not be a little impostor?" Later years saw the role in more capable hands.

In 1961, Joan Sutherland's Met debut as Lucia was considered important enough to make the front page of *The New York Times*. Apart from her glorious voice, her engaging personality and infectious sense of humor have made her one of the most beloved singers of her generation.

S U T H E R L A N D : You sing with the voice that you've got. You just tackle something, and you do it. I understand what they mean about different voices for the role; you have to have the agility and the heights for the first aria, but you also have to have a good solid sound for the last half of the first act and the second act.

S C O T T O : I believe that sometimes Violettas look only at the first act, so they think when Violetta has a good coloratura and a high tessitura, that's enough to sing Violetta. And it's not. No. The rest is much more difficult. A successful Violetta should look much further into the opera.

S U T H E R L A N D : You have to have control over the voice and not let it get too high at first, and also not push on the middle or the bottom of the voice. Otherwise, you won't get it back up again. You can't let it get too high too soon, or you'll be in trouble before you get to the end of the second act.

S A Y Ã O : Everything comes down to the words—that's where we get the true interpretation.

N O V O T N Á : In the beginning, it is necessary for the color of her voice to be that of a young girl. If one is lyric, or lyric-spinto, then anybody can sing it; and everybody did.

M O F F O : I remember discussing it at length with Joan, and we both agreed we'd go out and do Lucia's mad scene three or four times consecutively, but not that first act of *Traviata,* because it's so hard. The "Sempre libera" is really very hard after this long and very frivolous act of hard singing—and you still have the whole opera to go.

A L B A N E S E : And in the "Sempre libera," you have to build up the phrases a little hysteric, because TB people are hysteric.

N O V O T N Á : If one has agility of the voice for the beginning, then there won't be any more difficulty. It is the first act. To do it really beautifully and believably, it is a lighter coloratura.

A L B A N E S E : I used to take a note, with my back to the public, then turn around. Those are tricks. To do pianissimo, when you open the fan. That's the way to do it. But no—they do it fortissimo—*finito!*

N O V O T N Á : Later on, for the voice it becomes more normal, like *Bohème* or any other opera.

S A Y Ã O : Learning *Traviata* was the most difficult for me. Not the first act with the aria that everyone thinks is so difficult—that was easy for me as a coloratura. No, what was difficult for me was the second act.

B R O O K S : The end of the second act was always more difficult for
me because my voice just wasn't really comfortable with that music.
It was very, very hard.

S A Y Ã O : Because Verdi was very cruel—he wrote that opera for a
dramatic coloratura.

Act Two has Violetta and Alfredo living in unwedded bliss in the
country, an arrangement that didn't endear either play or opera to the
wags and moralists of the day, who saw the work as championing free
love. Verdi and Piave thought historical trappings would make the
opera more palatable, so they set it back in the early 1700s, a practice
that continued for many years. Of course, Verdi was raising eyebrows
himself in Busseto due to his scandalous living arrangements with
Giuseppina Strepponi, whom he eventually married in 1859.

"I loved placing Violetta in the cottage where she belonged," says
Corsaro. "Here was this lady trying to live a regular bourgeois existence,
after what she had been used to. She's basically a good, religious girl,
and superstitious; so we tried to concentrate on the simplicity, so it
would jolt with the garish third act."

A L B A N E S E : In the second act, she's a little more mature, because
this man loves her, takes care of her, which nobody ever did . . . and
you become a little older.

M O F F O : When we see her again, it's this big heavy relationship. She
gives up everything, being in the country. They're not in Paris with
all the fake people. There is no more courtesan atmosphere. Everything has a certain purity, because it's in the country. One has the
feeling she goes out with a basket in the morning and gathers eggs
or whatever. Sure, that's the real Violetta.

S C O T T O : Here we have the drama, when we go into the second
act, and this woman finally finds her life as a woman, as a human
being. Happiness, everything she's ever wanted, she finds in Alfredo.
And at this moment, society comes with the figure of the father.

R O B E R T M E R R I L L : I was a bad boy. I was telling all my
Violettas to leave my son alone.

S A Y Ã O : His father starts to tell her that this is very wrong, and she
is doing a big damage to the family and its reputation.

S C O T T O : The meaning is "You are a prostitute, and so why do you bother with a good guy like Alfredo and a good family like mine? You come and spoil everything." And he's so rude with her.

SAYÃO: She is very dignified. She says, "I never took one penny from your son."

For many operagoers, the name Robert Merrill is synonymous with Germont *père*. "For purity of vocalism and the achievement of the greatest degree of vocal nuance, the honors of the evening must go to Mr. Merrill," remarked a critic about one of Merrill's performances in the role. "As a vocalist he is superb. His voice is one of wide range, richly resonant and of beautiful quality, and his use of it is always admirably intelligent."

MERRILL: I sang the role with Toscanini in 1945–46. And he didn't know what I looked like when he engaged me. I had a radio show then on NBC and he was the conductor of the NBC Symphony, and he heard me sing the aria and engaged me sight unseen to sing the part of Germont—and Germont's forty-eight years old. I was twenty-six and looked nineteen. When he finally saw me, we were at a rehearsal, and he just kept staring at me and didn't say anything. He suddenly realized, "I made a big mistake—I engaged a boy, a kid, to sing this role." He finally brought me to the piano and said, "Well, are you a father?" And I stuttered and said, "No, I'm not even married, Maestro!" And after another minute or two of silence, he sat down and went through my entire part. After he finished, he looked at me again and patted me on the shoulder and said, "All right, I will make you a father." So I was only twenty-six years old and Toscanini helped make me a father. But after all, my son was only supposed to be sixteen or seventeen, so I almost could be his father. Can you imagine being the father of Richard Tucker?

ALBANESE: The father tells her to leave Alfredo because "the fiancé left my daughter." And she says, "I promise." It breaks her heart.

SHERRILL MILNES: Germont is traditionally the "bad guy" in the opera, but he's not a bad guy. He's doing what he considers best for his family. I think he considers that Violetta and Alfredo really love each other, but it's still the right thing in his mind. He knows she's going to die, and I think he's truly sympathetic to that.

M O F F O : One thing that's always puzzled me about *Traviata* is with such a consuming love, why does she make this almost futile sacrifice? I always said, "She knows she's going to die; why doesn't she live this thing out and let the sister worry about it afterward?" But she doesn't. She's kind of a martyr from the word *go*.

N O V O T N Á : You see, she knows that she is sick. She's coughing all the time; she's got the tuberculosis. So she thinks, "Sacrifica, e che morrà"—"Tell the daughter Violetta is sacrificing herself, but she will die." So it is already with this in mind that she thinks, "My life won't be very long." Nice person, I must say—beautiful.

S C O T T O : Inside of her, Violetta knows that society rejects people, and she takes their side. She understands exactly what she is, and she sacrifices her life, because she made a mistake and she's going to pay for the mistake, and she wants to pay. She realizes how much more important it is to have a good life. But it was "Nobody loves me—they only want my body." What kind of life is this?

N O V O T N Á : She was somehow big-hearted. She almost wanted to make the other girl happy. As a woman, she is very, very sensitive and very nice. Because I would have fought for him. "Hell," I would say, "thank you very much, but go out." But not she.

S C O T T O : Then she realizes how beautiful to be like the sister of Alfredo, because she is so pure, and she has everything ahead of her. Why should she spoil the life of such a young, beautiful, and pure girl?

A L B A N E S E : Even the words *"sì bella e pura . . . bella,"* she says, "I am beautiful, too. *E pura*—I was never pure." She doesn't remember. See, and at that time, to be pure was something.

S C O T T O : The father sees her only as a prostitute who takes Alfredo away from his family, his good society, and provincial town.

N O V O T N Á : You know, the most wonderful moment in the opera is when she sings "Dite alla giovine." It must be acted very simply, no big gestures, almost solely through the voice.

S A Y Ã O : She had become a lady by this point. No one could tell she was a prostitute.

M O F F O : I'm madly in love with my husband, and if somebody came to me and said, "Well, his sister . . . and there's this big problem . . ." I don't mean I don't care about his sister, but my priority would be my man. If his sister never gets married—and I think I'm a rather nice, sensitive person—well, she can get married when I'm gone. You know what I mean?

S C O T T O : There is one moment in the duet when she answers to him. She makes up her mind and says, "OK, this man comes here, to *my* house, and treats me very badly. Now I know I have to do something—not for him, not for Alfredo, but for myself—which is to redeem myself to a good life. What I will do is I will make him a very small person, and I will show him." Not that she's doing this to be proud, but she is far above him. He's talking father talk and she is talking human being talk.

Sherrill Milnes, one of the world's leading Verdi baritones, has sung Germont far and wide. The first time he harassed a Violetta at the Met was on June 2, 1967.

M I L N E S : It's an opera that does not need a lot of staging for the Germont, if you know the part. There are some productions where you can go in, and once over lightly, and you're ready to perform. For the Germont only, not the Violetta. It never matters, because Germont is never in an environment that he knows. So if Sherrill Milnes finds himself in a strange place doing Father Germont, who's in a strange place, it's OK that he checks the chairs—"Where am I going to sit?" With Scarpia, he should never have to look where he's going: He just reaches out and the chair is there.

S C O T T O : He is very rude with her and they have a confrontation. She stands in front of him and says, "How dare you talk to me like that?" And they have like a duel. He says terrible things to her, like "Don't you think that in a few years, you are going to be old and ugly, and he will not see you anymore? He's young and beautiful, and you're going to be old and ugly." I mean, this is what he is saying to her. And they have this terrible duet—I mean, it's beautiful, but it's terrible.

M I L N E S : There have been productions where he has a checkbook, and he comes in really cold and wants to pay her off: "How much?" I refused to do it quite as coldly, because I thought in the music, that Verdi had him being very conciliatory. There are those beautiful Verdi lines. The music is too sincere to be fake sincere. So I did the check business, but changed the timing of it and took out some of his rudeness. And the fact that he comes in hat in hand—although he could come in with his hat on his head, but it messes up your hair. It sounds like a dumb thing, but you don't want to do the rest of the scene with a dent in your hair.

A L B A N E S E : It's a big sacrifice for her, and how! It breaks your heart. And Traviata, in the second act, we see her *annientata*—to be like this, you're really crushed.

M O F F O : That Violetta is willing to do this—the whole duet with the father makes more and more sense to me as time goes on, much more meaning for me than when I first started.

S C O T T O : Of course, this will be the reason for her to die sooner, I think. She understands that for her, there's no hope. She has to give up Alfredo and happiness, and sacrifice her own life for a good family: society. Society rejected her and she cannot rehabilitate her life. She tries. It's like a prostitute today who wants to get married, have children and a good husband. I mean, I don't know if this is possible, because of society.

M O F F O : Before, with her situation, being sick, it's been very hard for her to be real. She has to pay for her medicine, pay the doctor. She drinks champagne to forget all these guys she's going with. But the real Violetta is a very down-to-earth, nice lady.

S C O T T O : As a human being, she is ten times more of a good person than the father is. He's a very average person, but she gives up her whole life for the good of the society.

M O F F O : It takes the right guy to bring that out in everybody, doesn't it? She really is crazy about Alfredo, and as we all know, love is everything. People do incredible things for love: They kill for love; they steal for love. And Violetta gives up a lot.

M I L N E S : I did a few *Traviata*s once in Hamburg with an iron curtain singer—I'll leave it at that—and she had obviously been coached that "Western singers will upstage you or do something; don't pay any attention, just sing out." So she would do that, and everything was just general. I think I gave it the best reading possible, but it was much harder. In every place where he interrupts, "You may be pretty now, but this is what's going to happen," you can do it soft or hard. I used the cane to strengthen the points, which is stronger than a gesture or a look. And if I had really tried to eyeball her and make a connection, it would have looked like I was the child and she was the dominant personality. And I still had to be faithful to Verdi and the places where Germont is sympathetic—because he is, when he finds out this is a finer human being than he had thought—and there is a line and a change of feeling toward her through the duet. It's very clear. So to be equally or more dominant, I looked at her more than she did at me, but not as much as I would look at a softer Violetta, like Anna Tomowa-Sintow or someone who is more sympathetic.

M E R R I L L : My twenty-fifth anniversary at the Met was with *Traviata,* and they opened the curtain on the gambling scene, with these luscious Cecil Beaton sets, and Mr. Bing came out and introduced seventeen Traviatas I had sung with. That night I was singing with Joan Sutherland, but I hadn't realized I had sung with that many Violettas. I debuted in '45 with Licia Albanese, who was always the sweetest, kindest woman. As fate would have it, when I auditioned on the radio, she was the hostess. This was before I knew I was going to sing at the Met, and she said, "Someday I'm going to sing with you." So my first was Licia, then Tebaldi and Moffo and Scotto and Dorothy Kirsten. They were all great, all with different personalities and different emotions. They all sang beautifully. Licia, of course, is very emotional. She threw herself at me, and that's what Licia was. Anna Moffo sang it beautifully and interpreted it well, and she looked absolutely beautiful. And you know, the last scene was really very touching.

M O F F O : Bob Merrill had a terrific debut in Italy. It was '69 or something, and I can't believe he hadn't made his Italian debut till then. But we were singing in Venice, and it was one of those hot, hot, hot days, and the Fenice was inaugurating its air conditioning. It was on in the audience, but the dressing rooms were hot. And when the curtain opened, you got this blast of cold air, so it was just like being hit with a Sherman tank, and I just felt awful. And in the second act, he comes in: "Madamigella"—and I went out like a light, fainted. And Bob, who always said, "Well, you know, you're such a great actress, I'm not surprised at anything you do," thought this was part of the scene and kept singing. So pretty soon, he goes over and says—in English—"Maestro, I think the *signora* is sick." It was so funny—and all of this was told to me. Out cold. My blood pressure, they told me, was like—what—a newly born chick? They gave me some adrenaline, and I finished the performance. Mario del Monaco was there. Dorothy Kirsten was there. Dorothy offered to continue the performance, and del Monaco was up there unlacing my dress— "She's gotta breathe, she's gotta breathe." I was so sick. And for the rest of my life I felt I had to make this up to Bob. I was so embarrassed.

M E R R I L L : All my Violettas were different emotionally. Tebaldi, of course, sang it beautifully and interpreted it well, but she didn't move much; I had to move toward her and react. But she interpreted the music beautifully. Her passion was in her singing. Eleanor Steber was wonderful in the role. Dorothy Kirsten was very musical, and she acted very well and she reacted. This is an important thing for a colleague, because if they're cold and don't react, then it's difficult for you to react. It works both ways.

S C O T T O : So Violetta gives up Alfredo to redeem herself. A plea for forgiveness to God. She becomes a martyr, I believe—and that's the greatness of Violetta.

Some directors have departed from tradition in creating the scenery for the opera. Perhaps because he was uninitiated as an opera fanatic, Alfred Lunt dispensed with the usual second-act interior that the libretto calls for, and instead persuaded Cecil Beaton to design an idyllic porch and garden setting for their 1966 Met production.

M O F F O : *Traviata* is an opera that can be done of a very big stage— Verona or Central Park—or you can do it in your living room. But wherever you do it, it cannot lose its focus. There are parts that have to stay very intimate. When I came to the Met in '59, there was a production that had a little gazebo in the second act, in the middle of the stage, to make this intimacy between Germont and Violetta. You have to know when to make things big and when to make them small. I don't know that a lot of directors know they have to do that.

In the Dumas play, Germont may have a respectable family, but he also has a respectable appreciation for beautiful women, including Violetta.

A L B A N E S E : She was the sweetheart of the father. She went with him, too. But the father didn't tell the son.

BROOKS: At times with the father, I would play "seduce," and I wouldn't really be trying to seduce him, but only to give that color to the music and the voice. It's tricky to explain.

SCOTTO: In the opera, no. We always say in rehearsal that Germont wants to go with Violetta himself—this is a joke.

MOFFO: All those things don't make a difference in the end result, but it makes Violetta more defined, his character more so. But you have to have a Germont who can do that successfully.

SAYÃO: In the original play, I believe Violetta was actually Germont's mistress. The fact that he wanted his son, this innocent young thing, to leave this—what shall we call her—not a call girl, but a painted woman. Well, maybe there is jealousy there. But no, I never consciously played it for that.

BROOKS: You pick certain colors and explore them. I found myself looking at Dominic Cossa and thinking, "His ears are just like Plácido's—the similarities between father and son! And now he's trying to hurt me, and treat me this way. Plácido—I mean, Alfredo—has never talked to me about his sister!" The real Camille was shared by both father and son—but it didn't really work for us.

MOFFO: There are two kinds of attitudes toward the baritone. I've done it where the baritone is all square Papa. And I've done it where the director's said, "Well, he comes in, and he ain't so old, and he says, 'Boy, my son's got good taste.' And he doesn't mind paying for it, either, if he thinks he can get it." It's a whole other approach, and a very interesting one for Violetta. Because that to me is much more shameful than having money thrown at me—is Papa trying to make out with me? It shows how young Alfredo is, and how she appeals to men with great experience, because she's so unusually fine. I mean, Germont would never ask Flora for a date, but he'd ask Violetta any time. She's very rare.

MERRILL: I've done the role over two hundred times. Germont was my debut role, November 15, 1945. I was a pretty young man to be singing that role. I guess it's better, vocally, when you're young. It's not an easy part. And it's not the longest role. But that second act, which is almost twenty minutes long, is all singing—pure singing. So when you're younger, the voice is probably fresher. But I sang it until my last year at the Met, thirty years later.

MILNES: My Germont, of course, changes with each Violetta,

depending how soft she is, how vulnerable. And the sound, the timbre, and the way the body looks and moves. Or how hard they are—how they look at you.

MERRILL: Let's face it, the older I got, the less makeup I needed. But as I matured, I wasn't so vocally conscious from a technical point of view. You learn that with any performance, you can't go worrying about the high notes, thinking about the arias only, if you're responsible. That's fine, but you have to think about the whole thing.

MOFFO: Vocally, the second act is only an extension of her predicament. It's still the same voice and it shouldn't be a big, heavy, gutsy soprano—because then where's the frailty? Where is her illness? I mean, you have to hear her, but she's the same Violetta as in the first act. She can't suddenly become Isolde.

SAYÃO: You have to have big voice in the second act, almost like a dramatic soprano. He wants a big voice, with tremendous agility. All the singers of the past were this way. And it's the same for the tenor and the baritone. Everybody was like Patti: They started with a big voice in the center. You have to have a terrific technique.

SUTHERLAND: I used to find, when I first started singing it, that the second act was very difficult. I always loved the first act, and of course the last, which is a dream for a singer. The second act was very hard for me because very early on, before I'd even done the role, I saw Callas do some performances; and like with her Norma, and other things I would see her do, it was very difficult for me not to copy what she had done. Of course I didn't have the physical attributes that she had. But I did find that the second act was hard for me, and the more I did it, the easier it got.

SAYÃO: I think he wrote the role for a dramatic coloratura—someone who can sing Norma—just like they used to call Sutherland a dramatic coloratura. Today it's difficult to find that. But even in my time, it was very difficult for singers to sing that aria in the original key. Now, of course, they transpose, but those high Cs and Ds . . . And then on the stage, you must act and you must feel, and it's very hard—it's not just the high notes. It's having the body and the expression and the drama. I was scared to death to sing the second act. I didn't think I had the voice enough to sing those arias and go on to the duets.

SUTHERLAND: But *Traviata* is a piece of cake compared to *Anna Bolena* or *Norma*—come on!

S C O T T O : One of the best moments, where the soprano really has to give herself, is "Amami, Alfredo." This is the apex—where she really is desperate, because with "Amami, Alfredo," her life ends, really. For sure, she's going to die, because she's sick—but also because this is it. And I think it has to be desperate. It's so beautiful—so much in the character of *La Dame aux Camélias*.

Pursuant to his belief that theatrical talent belonged onstage in an opera house, Rudolf Bing had brought Alfred Lunt to the Met in 1951. The actor-director had staged a successful *Così Fan Tutte,* also making a costumed guest appearance onstage on opening night. Now he teamed up with Cecil Beaton, who designed the sets and costumes, to create the 1966 *La Traviata* starring Anna Moffo, Robert Merrill, and Bruno Prevedi, which premiered on September 24 in the Met's new Lincoln Center home.

M O F F O : Lunt and Fontanne were wonderful because they brought a more theatrical approach to the opera. They were very into the music, but he didn't let it govern Dumas or the action.

M E R R I L L : I'll never forget Alfred Lunt's first rehearsal. He was more frightened than we were. And we had this private rehearsal—just Anna, Richard Tucker, and myself. And we sat around and said, "Well, Mr. Lunt, what do you want us to do?" And he said, "Why don't you do what you've always done, and I'll think about it." And that was very intelligent. Instead of changing things right away, he was learning, too. So we did it in stages.

M O F F O : I remember we didn't have many rehearsals, because *Antony and Cleopatra* was always onstage. The first day we got onstage, all the lights fell down. I remember Lunt was so close, we were talking, and all the upper light fixtures crashed about an inch from the two of us. But that's when the stage was new. Sam Barber wanted to use it to the fullest, so it could hold fifty soldiers or something, and he put a hundred fifty—and everything was broken. We could never get onstage. And because of all this they had to postpone *Gioconda,* and I think *Frau ohne Schatten.* It was an exciting adjustment time, though, and everybody had to have a guide to even get to the stage.

M E R R I L L : Lunt was very worried about the tenor and the soprano singing all those "Addio, addio's." For some reason, composers like to have singers spending five minutes saying good-bye. Finally he took me over to the corner and he said, "Bob, what is all this 'Addio' stuff?" He was cute, you know. But then he took it and said, "We have to do this and this—don't stand in one place, but move around and think about different things as you're saying good-bye."

Lunt and Fontanne had fascinated audiences since the 1920s in works ranging from *The Taming of the Shrew* to Noel Coward's *Design for Living* and Friedrich Dürrenmatt's *The Visit*.

MERRILL: He was very inventive and the performance came off beautifully. The dress rehearsal was wonderful. Lynn Fontanne was in the audience and she came back to my dressing room, and needless to say, I was thrilled. And she said to me, "You know, I always knew you could act—but sing?" And that was a running gag between us for years. When she was celebrating the Kennedy Center awards a few years ago, she was sitting in a chair; she couldn't move very well. And I walked over to her and said, "I always knew you could act, but sing?"

MOFFO: I never believed you got anything from rehearsal by just walking through. I always wanted to rehearse in my hoopskirt. And I remember one day Lynn Fontanne was sitting in the audience and said to me in her low voice, "Miss Moffo, I want to know who taught you to walk." And I said, "Nobody." And she said, "In order to go up and down the steps like you do, we were made to put on sheets"—and she told me this horrible story. I would have broken my neck. Apparently, they always wore sheets that were much too long, and the idea was that as they walked up the steps, they'd kick out and free their feet. I thought this was incredible, and I remember I went home to practice. I had a spiral staircase at that point, and I put on a sheet and kicked out and almost broke my foot.

The third act finds Violetta on the arm of Baron Douphol at Flora's soiree. Adelina Patti got into the spirit of things by adorning her bosom with £200,000 worth of diamonds during a series of farewell performances at Covent Garden in 1895. Costumed detectives onstage ensured the safety of both diva and jewels.

MOFFO: When Alfredo throws the money at you, you can shriek and fall on the floor—really a Dracula kind of thing. . . .

BROOKS: The unspoken thing when he throws the money was always "Yes, go ahead and abuse me. I deserve it; I left you. I went back to the Baron and I can't tell you why, Alfredo, because I have a special understanding with your father that you don't know about, and I can't destroy your sister's life." That's what I was always thinking.

SAYÃO: She's gone back to her life as before, and even though she's sacrificed so much for him, he insults her—and she accepts everything he does—to treat her like a mistress.

MOFFO: Lunt suggested something interesting: that this insult is so great, that her reaction is so internal, she didn't have the strength to fall on the floor. She's always a person who puts up a certain front. That she's got plenty of energy for a good time, that she likes all the exterior, superficial things, but she's really looking for that one great love that I gather—though I've never made a survey—most hookers never have had. The great, consuming, selfless love—not the one you pay for. So Lunt, at this point, had me with this unbearable pain: stunned, but kept standing. And then it took such hold that Flora, the Baron—they came and made me sit down because I started to waver, and they knew I was ill. It was very effective.

A glamorous Violetta and a willing student, Moffo's work with Lunt as rehearsals progressed prompted the watchful Fontanne to remark, "I'm surprised I haven't lost him to all those beautiful prima donnas."

ALBANESE: Alfredo should be very aristocratic. When Violetta sees him there, she says to Flora, "Tell him to come here." And he's not "You called, babe?" Not this kind of man now, in the modern way, where he slaps you in the face, you slap him in the face—no. He comes: "You called me? What do you want?" And I never looked at him: "Because I promised somebody." And you have to see this pain in her face. And he says, "Ha ha, I know, you love him," and I say, "Yes, yes, it's true—I love him."

NOVOTNÁ: It was a promise she didn't want to make. He still loves her, but he doesn't understand why she had left him. He didn't know she was only following the father's desire. So he is ugliest in the third act, when he throws the money, like she was still somebody to be bought. And it's a horrible moment for Violetta.

M O F F O : Also, it makes a big difference whether the director has Alfredo throw you paper money or coins. If he throws coins, it's pretty hard not to wince, because they hurt. I've done performances where the tenor looks like he's pitching for the Yankees. Or, there's another way that is often done in Italy—*disprezzo*—so demeaning: "Here it is." You can't give a big reaction to that; you can't throw a fit and fall into the first row. The relationship is what he gives me.

N O V O T N Á : But we don't see how men really react. And although he was so awful to her, she still loves him—and on and on, into the last act.

M O F F O : The tenor has many ways of doing the scene, and it's his scene. And the Violetta who tries to get all the attention has really missed the point. What he is doing is really what's important on-stage—not how she reacts or how wounded she is. The reaction of an actress is sometimes much more important than always being center stage. That's magnanimous on my part; it's the delivery of the show. You can't always be doing something so the people are all looking at you—or there's no point to having a plot, right?

A brilliantined Rudolph Valentino appeared as Armand in a modernized, 1921 screen version of *Camille.* Armand was resurrected ten years later in the form of Robert Montgomery, playing opposite Greta Garbo in Clarence Brown's *Inspiration,* another updated account. He finally endured as Robert Taylor, starring opposite Garbo in the 1936 *Camille.* Hollywood's number three attraction at the time, Taylor was chosen to give box office assistance to Garbo, who was not far from being branded as box office poison.

K R A U S : I think I approach the role of Alfredo lovingly, because when I started in 1956, I made my debut in Italy as Alfredo, and I wanted to sing it. In general, you know, the tenors do not like this part. They think that Violetta is so important, and over everything in the opera. Also, there is not one very good, popular aria in the opera for the tenor. And the part is very difficult, because even if you sing it in the very best way, almost nothing happens for the tenor, because all the applauses go to Violetta.

M O F F O : Nobody wants to do Alfredo, because it's not a name part, because it's so hard and it's so ungrateful. They'd just as soon do the Duke or Cavaradossi or something that's more rewarding for them.

KRAUS: But when I started to sing it, I said, "This is a beautiful role." I love the character and the music, and I love the singing. I started the role with love and I still love the part today. Also, from the first time I sang it, I had a success with the audience; and somebody said in a review—and this happens often—that "Alfredo, sung by Alfredo Kraus, was a high point in the whole night."

Neil Rosenshein has debuted in houses worldwide as Alfredo. He is one of the few tenors today who sings the role regularly.

NEIL ROSENSHEIN: It's a great opera, and I find a lot of sympathy with Alfredo, but I have to admit I'm really not that crazy about the role. It is just not very satisfying for a tenor. His evolution just isn't there as a character. He's very much at the end what he was at the beginning.

KRAUS: You have to create, of course. I used to sing it without the cabaletta; when I started in Italy, they never used that. But when I discovered it and started to sing it, I found it gives you a little something more about the character—a more complete impression of him. He's more finished, not only vocally but in personality. Your ideas on any character change over the years. As you get more mature, you color the opera more every time you do it, and there are so many wonderful small ideas that give you more of an idea about the man.

ROSENSHEIN: He has beautiful music, but it hasn't touched me enormously. I find her music a lot more interesting. Vocally, Alfredo would seem to be easy, but he's not. The second-act aria is very elusive. It seems lighthearted and it's high. But you have to hold a very high tessitura in a sweet, loving way. And to capture that sort of feeling in that type of vocalism is not easy.

KRAUS: There are two moments for me in the opera that are very delicate: the first duet with Violetta and the last one. They are so different, and the first one has so much passion, but the last one is so much more tender. He has found out she's going to die, and he tries to give her some consolation and more sweet love. They are both very difficult to do, because of the singing, and also exploring all these different emotions.

SCOTTO: Alfredo Kraus is one of my favorite Alfredos. We did many *Traviata*s together.

Audiences, especially nineteenth-century ones, were both fascinated and repelled by wicked women, staples of any opera house. So as one of the looser operatic heroines like Manon, Mimì, Thaïs, or Violetta paraded her wickedness before a titillated public, the composer at least hoped that the audience's disapproval would be mitigated by the poor girl's death in the last act—a moral necessity, and the nineteenth-century equivalent of "I told you so." Unfortunately for both Dumas and Verdi, scandalized society was not much consoled by Camille's suffering and painful death. The public reasoned that good girls also die of consumption.

MOFFO: It's interesting to do Violetta, Manon, and Mimì, and notice how different and yet how similar these three ladies are. They're all courtesans of a sort, but with very different souls. It's interesting to compare—why is Manon what she is? She doesn't have the strength of Violetta. Mimì, Mimì doesn't want strength. She's *comme ci, comme ça*—strong in her own way.

SCOTTO: Violetta has the same disease as Mimì—but she's the opposite. Because Mimì, she's very simple, and a very free woman in the bohemian group of young people. They live day by day, and that's it. She gets in love and would like very much to stay with Rodolfo, but she has to give up Rodolfo because she cannot impose her sickness on him—so that's it. But Violetta, no. She's a much bigger person.

MOFFO: You have to compare someone like Thaïs, who's everything that's the personification of hookersville: flaunting it, looking for it. But she, too . . . There comes a moment when she repents—and it is total. You see, sometimes the most sinful people become the most penitent. I mean, she goes to the convent. It's just interesting to compare the different states of becoming a so-called loose woman. Tosca is a prima donna—and you find me a prima donna who doesn't have a hard time playing Tosca, because she's an open book; she is what she is when you see her. That's what she is. She loves the tenor—that's it.

While *Traviata* is less susceptible to avant-garde stagings than operas like *Rigoletto* or *Salome,* directors have played fast and loose with it on occasion. Corsaro admits his 1960 production caused "something of a controversy": One of the more controversial features was the appearance of George Sand at Violetta's party, carrying a monkey.

M O F F O : I've done a lot of unusual performances of *Traviata.* I did a *Traviata* in Venice, set in 1910—a funny kind of performance, not quite yet a flapper, tootling around with a long cigarette holder. And one in Buenos Aires, designed like an old photograph, everything in tones of brown—quite beautiful to look at, really. My costumes were brown velvet and ivory camellias. Very interesting. I've done *Traviata* in blue jeans. One of the scenes, I remember, I drove up in a convertible, with a cigarette. And instead of a camellia, I stopped smoking and put out the cigarette.

B R O O K S : Frank Corsaro had an enormous amount to do with my Violetta. There was such a unison between all of us backstage, and with the conductor, Maestro Giuseppe Patanè. But there was such outrage at first against Frank, even by the maestro, who would complain to Julius Rudel [then the New York City Opera's managing director], who had to act as pacifier, "You can't do that; it's all wrong!" Finally he turned around and Frank would act as the conductor, while Patanè would make suggestions.

M O F F O : But everyone says, "I want to do something different—I want to do something new." One of the charms of the opera business, perhaps, is tradition. Doing something new, you may draw in people who are not opera fans, but you often lose your main public because they're so offended.

B R O O K S : It was such a blessing having Frank and his wonderful sense of theater, and his almost irreverence for the opera world, which can become a little too much of "Oh, my darlings!" and all that stuff. He was wonderful.

M O F F O : It's like anything else: If you're going to fight with the director all the time, or just give in, it doesn't work. If you both can contribute something . . . When I was first working with Zeffirelli, he said, "If you can convince me your way is right, I'll buy it; otherwise, you have to do it my way." Which is quite true. And if you can't convince yourself, you can't convince anybody.

A L B A N E S E : You have been seeing all these men, luxurious house.

And when she dies, she's dying with her things around her. She dies poor, but they don't take her things away until she dies. At that time, they had a heart. Now, with all the new stagings, they do things without a heart: She dies poor, without a chair, without this or that—she just dies.

SUTHERLAND: They think if she's from a period closer to our own time, it's easier to understand what she's thinking. I don't like seeing something like *Traviata* updated. I don't think that the piece is viable set in a modern world. It's ridiculous to do *Traviata* punk, as the Welsh National Opera did it. It doesn't work at all, because Violetta would tell Germont to go chase himself.

MOFFO: It's a little thing, but if you take away my hoopskirt in *Traviata,* it's nothing. It's like taking my kimono out of *Butterfly.* Because the things that people do are decided by the time they're in. It's the frivolity of that period. Certain periods were just richer. I mean, if somebody came to me and said, "I'm going to do *Traviata* in Ireland during the famine," I'd say, "Good—without me." You can't do anything just for the sake of doing it, to say you did it for the first time. And also the last, is my point.

In between vaudeville seasons, Ethel Barrymore opened at the Empire Theater on Broadway as Marguerite Gauthier in *The Lady of the Camellias.* The play began after the heroine's death and proceeded through flashbacks in a dream by Armand. According to Miss Barrymore's autobiography, her young female fans would come to the theater for every matinee and cry and cry. They would bring men's handkerchiefs and pin them to the seats in front of them, so they could dry. It became a common occurrence that her fans, at some point of the day or night, would cry, "Oh, let's go and see her die." Miss Barrymore was also very fond of the role.

SCOTTO: Dumas's book starts on the grave, and it's a flashback. Sometimes they do the opera as a flashback, but I don't believe it, because Verdi didn't write it.

MOFFO: You know, there's a very big thing about "character development." Well, you can't develop anything unless you know where you're going to end up. Anybody who does Violetta really has to go to Dumas, and realize that's probably why he begins the whole thing with her death, and the flashback. Verdi didn't do that, probably because it takes away from the end. But that way, you see what she was when she dies; and you really have to know who you are and where you're going, and then get there, before you can begin.

R O S E N S H E I N : I did the Ponnelle production in Paris and Houston. When she comes in, there's set on the table a body—her body. She sees the future and sees herself as dead. Everybody else is standing around her, drinking champagne.

M O F F O : I think Verdi was right—a flashback is less effective. I think it is better to see this life in progression. However, I did the movie the other way: It opens when she's beautiful still, and walking through the ruins of her house—it's all boarded up; then it transforms into the way it was. Franco Zeffirelli did it that way at La Scala. But all it really does is fill up the prelude music, and I think it's an orchestral moment. It's such a wonderful piece that I think it should be kept orchestral.

George Cukor, who had directed Garbo in *Camille,* was approached by Risë Stevens in 1965 to direct *La Traviata* for the young Met National Company, which Stevens headed. Though he initially consented with enthusiasm, Cukor was eventually frightened off by the limited rehearsal time.

M O F F O : The third act of *Traviata,* I think, is a terrific setup for the fourth.

S A Y Ã O : She has gotten sicker, and the disease progressed rapidly, because she is so unhappy. In the last act, you see that she loved him so much, she really gives up her life for him. Then she gets the letter and finds out he's all right, and she is joyous.

M O F F O : Lunt was from the school that just accepted, "Opera singers—don't expect them to do anything, like move their left hand and right foot. It just can't be done." He was a detail man. He liked the way I read the letter, "Teneste la promessa . . ." in a whisper that carried. I mean, projection is great, but you don't have to be all over the stage to project, hopefully. The stage business I'd always seen—everybody did too much, I thought. So many big gestures for this frail woman who was so ill—I mean, she didn't have the energy to do all this. But Lunt liked the detail, encouraged it.

NOVOTNÁ : And Alfredo comes to see her, but she's too far gone. She's very sincere in the last act, because she loves him so deeply; she knows she will love him all of her life. It's very sad. You must put everything you have to convey this.

SCOTTO : Through the entire opera, the most difficult thing for me is to give the voice of Violetta this sad shape, through the entire singing, because of this life. Happiness, but not fully—and then completely happy, but ruined. So it has to come through the voice, a sense of continuity.

SAYÃO : The last act is easy, because you have the feeling—it's full of sentiment and full of emotion. And the duet and the aria are not so hard.

BROOKS : Working on the fourth act with Frank was wonderful— really very exciting. It was a coming together with Patton Campbell, the designer, too. We all chose really not beautiful, but warm clothes, because I was sick. So there was this plain nightgown with a woolen coat over it. The reality of the whole situation was there. She was sick; and when you see someone in the hospital or at home, and they're sick, they look sick. That was important to all of us. I would even put on makeup to help this. There were no jewels or satin dresses, like a lot of Violettas have in that act.

MOFFO : I always feel that the music is wonderful because it is driven music. There can't be anything more compelling than "Addio del passato." It's a big piece, but then it's the end. But then, it's not the end, because in comes Alfredo, and it's like Act One.

SCOTTO : "Addio del passato" is one of the most beautiful moments in the opera. She looks back to her life, and says, "My God—what was my life? My youth? I gave everything away, so I wasn't able to do anything with my life." Then she thinks about this young girl who's going to marry, who has everything—only because of society. And at this moment, of course, Alfredo comes back, but it's too late.

MOFFO : I also believe that if the composer wanted something, he gives you an opening. If you take any Puccini opera—he's the greatest director in the world. If you study *Tosca,* you take the score and see everything is in there. He gives you measures to do everything: to kill Scarpia, to fix the candlesticks, to come in, go out, to open the door for Cavaradossi. It's all so wonderfully right there in the score. And so it is a little bit less with Verdi, but his music is very clear. And it's very irritating for me only when a director asks me to do something where the music tells me something else. That's the only thing I rebel against.

SUTHERLAND: I suppose there is a school that feels she should stay in bed for the whole last act, but I think most producers want you to go to the window when the chorus starts singing outside. Usually I play the act lying on a chaise, and I don't dash around all that much. I don't think she should be moving around all that much. But she does have a slight reserve, and there is the despair when she reads the letter and knows that it's all too late. When one's in despair, one does have a certain strength. You do things you normally would not.

BROOKS: There was the moment when Frank wanted me to try to get in the gown when Alfredo's coming, and of course I was too sick to do it. Then, at another point, in rehearsal, Plácido came in and picked me up right off the ground, and Frank yelled, "Keep it in!" He would pick me up and rock me in his arms, and it just felt so wonderful for the moment, so right. It made me feel like a little fragile sparrow. The whole production felt very right and very truthful.

Polish soprano Marcella Sembrich premiered *La Traviata* with the Metropolitan Opera on November 5, 1883, in its first season, and the role was hers for years. Lucrezia Bori was the reigning Violetta of her generation and performed the role forty-six times at the Met alone. Other sopranos who left their mark on Violetta were Lillian Nordica, Nellie Melba, Geraldine Farrar, Luisa Tetrazzini, Frieda Hempel, Amelita Galli-Curci, and Queena Mario. Claudia Muzio, the Bette Davis of opera, chose the unfortunate courtesan for her return to the Met in 1934 after a twelve-year absence. In the fourth act, she languished in a black velvet negligee, her makeup a virtual death mask.

MOFFO: I sing almost the whole "Addio del passato" with my head hanging over the bed. It's effective, but I feel it—she has no strength to go on, and only rises for that last hurrah.

NOVOTNÁ: One can feel her approaching death in that aria. When Alfredo arrives, her hope is rekindled, and they sing the lovely duet "Parigi, o cara," with better promise for the future. Now she really hopes that she will be living—and with him. Unfortunately, it was too late.

BROOKS: In the farewell to Alfredo, Plácido used to give me singing lessons. He'd turn his back to the audience and show me how to place it. He's such a sweetheart—there are very few tenors who would do that. It took a lot of study and I had to work out every measure. That section really needs what the Italians call *coglioni*, which means "balls."

SCOTTO: The singing of *Traviata* is very difficult. You need a very complete tessitura, like Verdi writes. And you need a coloratura—but this is not the point. The point is the right character for every musical phrase.

BROOKS: Having been a dancer and actress, the movement, like going to the prie-dieu in the fourth act, was easier for me. It was so natural—the fever was taking her there. That's why, I think, I had a career.

NOVOTNÁ: We were in some little place on the tour, and in the last act, when Germont comes in, they had forgotten the sofa. The sofa had been sent, but suddenly there was no sofa. So they took an empty crate and put a rug over it. But they had put the rug over the wrong end. So Father Germont comes, and should have sat lightly on the sofa, which he did—and he suddenly disappeared into the crate. And the audience roared. And at the same time, I had to die, and die, and die. It was awful.

SUTHERLAND: Then, of course, there is the last surge of energy before she drops dead. It can't be static. I don't think there's anything wrong with her moving around, and I think most producers like to have you moving just to have you moving.

MOFFO: The energy required, psychologically, that Violette forgets all of this with the father and the sister, and the going away and the disgrace of the money in front of everybody, and she's insulted and chose to sell everything rather than go back . . . So it's a constant calling on the energy of this poor woman—physically, soul-wise, giving everything; and in her mind, not getting anything back. So she gets this surge of energy at the end, when she finally says, "Hey now, you're a little late, but I'm glad you came." But it's too late. I mean, even her last invocation, "Oh gioia!"—she can't even get it out.

NOVOTNÁ : I love to die—also in *Bohème* as Mimì, and as Manon. At these moments, if you can be real, true—well, I think it's the best moment in the opera.

SAYÃO : I studied the role note by note. Then in Naples, I met one of the great Violettas of the time, Gemma Bellincioni. She had studied the role with Toscanini. She was a spinto-lyric, and she was marvelous. I went to many of the great singers of the past for advice, and they were wonderful. They would tell me how to get the feeling, the way to produce those words and feelings that were so important. My voice then was small but sweet, with a good quality to hear— pleasant.

BROOKS : I don't think my voice was that exceptional. It was all right, I guess—I'm probably the worst judge of that. I have no idea how it sounded or what effect it had. I don't think most singers know the effect they have. You do your best, and in this case, with Frank's help and all the wonderful people I worked with, it turned out all right.

SAYÃO : They told me just to go with the voice I had, and caress every word, and I could make it work. They told me, even at the old Met, that they never missed one word when I sang the role. Diction is so important.

MOFFO : I remember my debut in Palermo—God, I was so excited about this role. I got so wound up in it that I was crying real crocodile tears that went maybe not quite as far as the prompter's box. I'd waited all of two years after my debut to do *Traviata,* which is a long time when you're starting. And then I accepted Palermo, and I thought it was terrific, because I had a lot of rehearsal and a great director. And of course, I got bronchitis. But I went on, and it was really pretty good. Well, Miss Tebaldi canceled in *Traviata* at the Rome Opera, and Miss Stella came, and she got sick. You know, distances are so short in Italy—so they called me in Palermo. And after those two performances, Mr. Bing called. He had already invited me to debut as the Queen of the Night and Gilda; he'd heard me sing the Queen of the Night in Venice. Then the following season he'd invited me to do *Otello* and *Faust,* and by advice, I'd turned that down. So he called and said, "Miss Moffo, this is positively the last time I'm calling you. Will you do *Traviata* on—" and before he told me the dates, I said, "Yes!" So I came to the Met for my debut after having done three performances. And everyone was wonderful—people like Charlie Anthony, and my wonderful Baron, George Cehanovsky—they were so terrific.

SCOTTO: I tell you something. I'm not so fond of the libretto, because I don't think the words are always very beautiful. They are always in style with the period, but Verdi goes far beyond the period—there is no period in the music of Verdi. Maybe if Verdi had Boito, as he did later with *Otello* or *Falstaff,* he would have had a better libretto. I think when he found Boito, Verdi could express his music into more profound words; or maybe if Verdi could have written the words himself, like Wagner . . . but this is only my opinion. Anyway, I love the music so much, and I think that everything is in the music.

MERRILL: People ask, "Did you get tired of singing the same music?" No way. Every time I sang the part—a couple of hundred times—I felt something new, every time I walked on that stage. With different Violettas and different tenors, I would find myself doing something different and surprising, found new ways of singing it. I never got tired of singing Germont. It's a masterpiece, and anything that's a masterpiece is always fresh. *Traviata* is very close to me, and if I were to sing it today, I'd find something new in it.

MOFFO: Violetta is a very wonderful part, because every time you do it, you're going to find something more. Something you thought you understood means something else to you now—a deeper conviction. She's an important lady.

CARMEN

~

She is a Gypsy. . . . They believe
in God, in destiny—that it is there, that
you cannot escape it.
And they are right.

—RÉGINE CRESPIN

Music by Georges Bizet
Libretto by Henri Meilhac and Ludovic Halévy
from the novella and play by Prosper Mérimée

CARMEN......................... *Grace Bumbry, Régine Crespin, Rosalind*
Elias, Marilyn Horne, Brenda Lewis,
Anna Moffo, Nell Rankin, Regina Resnik

MICAËLA .... *Lucine Amara, Mirella Freni*

ESCAMILLO................ *Robert Merrill*

When Célestine Galli-Marié stepped onstage for the first time as Carmen, the audience at Paris's Opéra-Comique saw nothing like the "innocent, chaste young girl" librettist Ludovic Halévy had promised the Comique's director, Camille du Locle. When du Locle agreed to the project, he had begged Halévy, "Please try not to have her die! Death at the Opéra-Comique—such a thing has never been seen!" The offensiveness of the subject matter, along with *Carmen*'s radical musical structure, scandalized the first-night audience. By the end, only a few of Bizet's friends remained in the theater—a place where usually half a dozen boxes were engaged every evening for the sole purpose of arranging marriages. *Carmen* played out its scheduled forty-eight-performance run to increasingly empty houses. It never came close to recouping production costs, and Bizet, who died shortly afterward, went to his grave convinced he had given birth to a failure.

Regina Resnik, who began her career as a soprano, moved into the mezzo repertory and became thoroughly identified with the role of Carmen. In addition to staging the work, she produced a documentary on *Carmen,* which was shown on public television.

REGINA RESNIK: I felt the Mérimée character was a better study for Don José than it was for Carmen. And a lot of things that happen in the opera weren't true to the Mérimée plot at all: She was killed by a fifth-rate picador; she was not the mistress of the greatest toreador in Spain; she wasn't free, as she was in the cigarette factory.

Régine Crespin came to Carmen from roles like the Marschallin, Tosca, and Sieglinde. After *Dialogues of the Carmelites'* Mme. de Croissy, Carmen is the role she has performed most often at the Metropolitan Opera.

RÉGINE CRESPIN: I think the main mistake is to play her like a whore—like a street girl, a vulgar one. She is not a whore. She goes to bed with the one she loves. She is herself; she's free. If she wants to show her legs, she does. She's carefree and she does what she pleases.

Rosalind Elias made her operatic debut as Grimgerde in *Die Walküre* at the Metropolitan in 1954 and moved quickly through twenty-six roles before her first Carmen in 1958.

ROSALIND ELIAS: I tried not to act Carmen. I have to be truthful: When I first started Carmen, and I was very young, I thought it was the hands-on-the-hips sort of thing—because this is what I saw. I was brought up to see Carmen do this. And of course, they can do that once in a while, but it's not a pose—it's a natural thing. It's not, "Now I'm going to sing the 'Habanera' and put my hands on my hips." It may not even happen in that scene—it could happen any time, in a dramatic way of saying, "You go to hell."

Grace Bumbry—who, clad in mink, adorned a "What becomes a Legend most?" ad—made her mark on both soprano and mezzo roles. In 1961, she was the first black artist to appear at Bayreuth. In 1967, she sang her first Metropolitan Opera Carmen.

GRACE BUMBRY: I think of her as a young woman, first of all. She is sassy and very sensual. I always see the character as she is in the first two acts of Julia Migenes's film version, also in the ballet version.

When Jack Beeson created the operatic Lizzie Borden, the obvious choice for the ax murderess was Brenda Lewis, the ultimate singing actress of her day. She has performed Carmen all over the world.

BRENDA LEWIS: When I was preparing a role, I always found it's very helpful to go one hundred eighty degrees away from the ordinary perception of what the role is, to find what would be the direct opposite and justify that in the character, in order to play off the expected reaction. I don't feel that Carmen starts off in the opera, you know, out to lay every man she can get her hands on, get into bed with them, and then die. On the contrary, she's a woman with a tremendous lust for life, with a tremendous sense of adventure. And there isn't even a question of caution or courage—she faces life head on. Whatever you choose to use as her background, there's a certain acceptance of what life has to offer.

Alabama-born Nell Rankin brought to the Gypsy a Scarlett O'Hara philosophy—ladylike but a free spirit. Carmen introduced her to Covent Garden audiences in 1953, and she first sang the role at the Met the following year.

NELL RANKIN: I think my Carmen was a little different than most people's. I've lived among the Spanish people, and I've noticed how much dignity the gypsies have. Even in their dance—they come very close, but they don't touch each other. So I never thought of a Carmen being mauled by men as soon as she comes on the stage.

CRESPIN: For me, the two main qualities of that woman are, first of all, the courage: She goes until the end and proves that she is courageous—what she thinks, what she does. Then, you know, very often people who are laughing a lot are quite the contrary. Carmen laughs a lot, is a coquette of course, and very free—but for me, she is one who flirts with the idea of suicide.

RESNIK: The challenge was to be physically what you had to be on the stage, which was visual. But superimposed on that, like some beautiful thing, was the elegance of the score. Every time I went back to doing something major about *Carmen,* I referred to the score, and I always came up with the same conclusion. It's not "thick" music— it's sinuous; it's music which lies over an idea. Of course, that is the sexiest music possible, not the one that forces itself on you.

Carmen is one of the few roles outside the bel canto repertory to which Marilyn Horne returns on a regular basis. In her first public association with the role, she sang for Dorothy Dandridge in the film version of *Carmen Jones.* She premiered the Met's 1972 production with James McCracken and Tom Krause, conducted by Leonard Bernstein, and has gone on to perform the role over forty times with the company.

MARILYN HORNE: Working with Bernstein was a great privilege and a wonderful collaboration. He participated fully in the staging of the opera as well as conducting, and was a tremendous help in that area, as well as musically.

In 1866, nine years before premiering *Carmen,* Galli-Marié had created the title role in Ambroise Thomas's *Mignon.* The adoring public so overwhelmingly identified her with the role that when the producers tried to revive the work, they faced the casting dilemma of a modern producer attempting to fill a Judy Holliday role: "No other artist should sing it," declared the critics.

RANKIN: Carmen was more or less an aloof person, because she was interested in freedom. She lived life to the fullest. She loved life, but she tempted death—and she died. She probably had tempted fate many times before she ever walked on the stage in Bizet's opera—sort of a cat with nine lives, never satisfied, always going a little bit further and further each time. And it got her.

BUMBRY: I don't think about Carmen as a Gypsy. I just think about doing the role and singing the music that Bizet wrote. I'm sure when I started, I thought, "How close can I make her to a Gypsy?" But now I think it's just a given situation. What you do as Carmen has to be attuned to that sort of lifestyle and sensuality—but that's part of the performance.

RANKIN: I played a rather aristocratic Carmen, which got me into trouble with some of the London critics. They said Carmen should be an out-and-out harlot, a real slut. I never thought Bizet wrote this type of personality. She has very lyric music to sing. It's telling—there's a lot of drama in *Carmen,* but there's also a lot of lyricism. And if she had been just a harlot, she wouldn't have been different from other people.

Traditionally, sopranos like Anna Moffo have been drawn to Carmen. She recorded the complete opera with Franco Corelli for RCA, and has starred in two productions on European television.

ANNA MOFFO: I don't like the word *slut.* Let's say Carmen sleeps around—but she's really very selective. She's sexy, I know. I think if she walked down the street or out of the cigarette factory with a bag on her head, she'd be just as sexy. It's something about her—it isn't a strut or a low-cut dress. I get the feeling that when she looks at a man, he can't take his eyes off her.

RANKIN: There were a lot of beautiful Gypsy girls—why would men choose her? She must have had something that wasn't readily available. She was a lithe person, very vibrant, very passionate.

ELIAS: I don't think Carmen has to be beautiful, with a perfect figure. It doesn't matter to me.

HORNE: Carmen can look like anything! What amazes me is that no one asks what it takes to *sing* Carmen! Why has that been forgotten in the world of opera in which we live now?

ELIAS: I saw Régine Crespin do it, and truthfully, she's not the figure of Miss America—but she told me something. And anyway,

I find her a very sensuous woman—very sexy, as far as I'm concerned. And I was sure that a lot of men would find her very appealing; as a woman, I did.

C R E S P I N : In fact, I didn't want to sing the role and I refused it for many, many years, because I thought I was not the type. Usually, you see very thin girls—very bony—and I was not that type. Of course, when I went to do it, I lost something like ten kilos. Also, I felt I didn't have the voice for that. But I had heard *Carmen* many times, so finally, when someone convinced me to do it, I knew the part. It was very easy, because I had it in my ear already—a little bit like when you put on an old coat to wear.

When du Locle offered Galli-Marié the chance to create Carmen, she wrote to her future Don José: "Your little marmoset of a director writes to ask if I wish to create Carmen. What is it?" Then she put it in the wrong envelope, which du Locle duly received. When she eventually brought her own pet marmoset to rehearsal, he commented, "You're really fond of little marmosets, aren't you?"

R E S N I K : As far as I was concerned, in *Carmen* the major portion of the responsibility lay with the stage director and how he fashioned the chorus. Because if you don't make the people onstage crazy— about what she's going to say, what she's going to do—it's like a bubble burst. It lets all the air out. But if there's tremendous tension about the men in the chorus, and the women opposing her, and the men loving her . . . and this doesn't come out right away, because she's tempting everybody; she's starting a new adventure.

Though Geraldine Farrar's signature role was the delicate Cio-Cio-San, her fiery realism as Bizet's Gypsy delighted her legion of "Gerry-flappers" and infuriated her co-star Enrico Caruso, who objected to the physical abuse she heaped upon him. Getting into the spirit of one 1916 performance, Farrar slapped Caruso in the first act, shoved around an irate chorus girl in the second, then bit the tenor in Act Three. Though he finally threw her to the floor, they preserved their battered relationship as Carmen and José and performed together in the opera many times afterward.

R A N K I N : I think an overall good Carmen is very difficult to do. It takes years of study to really build up a great Carmen—I even took castinet lessons from a Spanish Gypsy in Zurich. There are so many facets to this personality. She was a very dangerous person. Like a tigress on the loose, she was looking for adventure. She was a totally selfish person, headstrong—wanted only what she wanted, when she wanted it. And she knew how to get it. She knew how to get men who were really not that interested in her; she saw to it they became interested.

M O F F O : When I was living in Italy, I came into contact with Gypsies all the time—you do, when you're in Europe. They're always carrying babies on their back, and always a little disheveled, and they're always asking for money. And as soon as you put your hand in your purse to get something, they steal out of your pocket. I mean, they're so quick, and they've got the whole thing down to a system.

R A N K I N : Most young Gypsies are lovely to look at. In Spain, they're all beautiful. If you see a bunch sitting around, it's very difficult to tell which is the prettiest—black eyes, black hair, beautiful bodies. But they age quickly and become matronly.

M O F F O : So Carmen, she sizes everybody up very quickly, and that's very Gypsy. Also, she thinks she knows everything. The Gypsies, they're fortune-tellers—they could talk you into anything.

Rosa Ponselle was said to have sung the role "sweetly," but to have lacked a suitable Gypsy temperament. Even Adelina Patti, renowned for her Violetta and Lucia, prompted one critic to note, "Everyone knows that Carmen was a cat; but Patti made her a kitten."

E L I A S : I tell you, these roles like Carmen are the much more interesting protagonists. It's such a strong role, it's got to be controversial. You try to go into the character after studying the role and the music, and knowing it all perfectly. And the text is important. But then you have to come out fresh, come out spontaneous.

R E S N I K : Against tradition and against the tide, the music of *Carmen* in Acts One and Two, until she loses her temper in the second act, is probably the most eloquent, elegant, sinuous type of music. It has the elegance of the French mentality of sexuality and the earthiness of the Spanish.

"Ingenious orchestral details, risky dissonances, instrumental subtlety cannot express musically the uterine frenzies of Mlle. Carmen . . ." observed the critic from *Le Siècle* after *Carmen*'s world premiere.

E L I A S : I tried to learn the role with a capital *T*—truthfulness—which is the person. She was herself-truthful. If she loved you, she loved you. If she didn't want you anymore, that is enough. She is sweat, earth, herself. She doesn't think, "Oh, do I sit this way? Do I walk this way? Do I say the right things?" Nothing is premeditated, everything is spontaneous: "I love you; I don't love you; yes, let's go to the mountains." She is childlike, innocent, free.

M O F F O : Manon is a good person to compare Carmen with. Manon is sexy, she's a flirt, but she really loved. She had sincere traits. Carmen, I decided, was never sincere with anybody. She cons everybody—anyone who'll listen. I mean for me, somebody who loves is Violetta—who, you have the feeling, if Alfredo came in and stabbed her, she'd say, "All right, but I still love you," you know?

R A N K I N : I don't think Carmen was a liar. That would violate Bizet's work, where she says in the last act, "I have never lied." I don't think she ever lied to anyone, just as she says. She tells José, "I'm telling you I don't love you anymore, so you'd better believe it."

C R E S P I N : That's why she's original, in a way: because at that time, or even today, who is going to tell the truth? I don't think she is a liar. She's honest until the death. I think she is speaking real love, real truth, real things. She is truthful.

M O F F O : It's an opera where everybody's kidding everybody else. I'd never had to do a part where everybody was lying, in effect, to themselves. And it's hard for me. Basically, I tell the truth because it's such a bother to remember so I can lie the next time. So my immediate thought about Carmen was "Poor thing, how does she sleep at night when she lies all the time?" Then I decided that she's probably so used to this that maybe she doesn't even know she's lying.

E L I A S : I've sung it everywhere: in South America, Spain, France, Hamburg, at the Met, and all over the United States. Performances always varied. If they didn't, I would be bored—I'm not that kind of performer. The basic feeling of Carmen was always the same, but with duets being different and all that. I'm very happy for it. But the basic inner soul of Carmen is always the same—that's just what she is.

RESNIK: I had a lot of fun with this opera, because I don't think I ever sang it the same way twice. I just did as I pleased at the moment, because Carmen is kind of a spontaneous character. You can't do that with Klytemnestra. For Carmen, there is a prescription, but there's a lot of room in between.

ELIAS: I like to hear directors' different concepts and be open to them. But I've walked out of rehearsals on directors who were not prepared. That's the only thing that bothers me. *Carmen* is a difficult opera to direct, but I won't give them the satisfaction of saying that. It's their concept; then we can agree or disagree—but some directors just don't prepare. In a way, maybe that was better, sometimes; because I got to use my own intelligence, and maybe their ideas would have interfered.

BUMBRY: My first *Carmen* was in Basel, in 1960, at the first opera house I was under contract with. Now mind you, I had done a couple of performances in Paris, where I had my real debut in the spring of 1960. But I was hired in Basel as their dramatic mezzo, and their opening was *Carmen,* so there I was. We had a long rehearsal period—about a month and a half. I do have an acting talent and I'm quick at learning things, so it was one of the best things I did in that period.

RESNIK: I was always aware that when I heard the overture in my room, that it was really the death of Carmen. What Bizet really wrote was a flashback: He starts out with the death of Carmen, and an overture that doesn't end—it ends on a suspended chord—and he said, "Now I'm turning back the page. Here's how it looked in Seville. . . ." The curtain goes up on what *was,* not what is. So I was always imbued with that fatalistic feeling long before I ever made my entrance. I was always conscious that even though I was playing and joking, the fatal Carmen—the Carmen *fatale*—was on the stage the minute she enters.

CRESPIN: You know, Don Giovanni is always looking for women all the time. With men, Carmen is exactly the same in character as Don Giovanni. Maybe underneath that—nobody can be sure—but they might have a sexual problem, like the ones who are running for sex all the time. Maybe Carmen is one of those people.

In his review of *Carmen*'s premiere, the critic from *Le Siècle* went on to say that Carmen "should be gagged, a stop put to the unbridled twisting of her hips; she should be fastened into a strait-jacket after being cooled off by a jug of water poured over her head. . . ."

R A N K I N : Carmen was a tigress. Like a wild animal, she had great dignity. And tigresses, you know, are also soft-pawed. They don't have to strike—they can be very cuddly. But they're also wild and like to be free.

M O F F O : One type of girl I could always imagine as Carmen would be Sophia Loren. The other one I thought would be a great Carmen was Brigitte Bardot—the kitten, not the tiger. I wanted to do it like that, but I didn't have the same presence.

R A N K I N : I think she never liked to be trapped by any man or any situation. This was her undoing. Because most men, like Escamillo, possibly, would have been as delighted to leave her as she was to leave him. But José just happened not to be this kind of a person. I see José's character as something of a mama's boy who is infatuated with this woman, and didn't really intend to give up his life for her, but found himself unable to extricate himself from this person.

C R E S P I N : She absolutely does not change. She is like she is from the beginning. In the third act, for instance, she plays the cards and sings that aria with the cards. And she says, "I know he's going to kill me—I know." So it's very obvious she knows that, but yet she doesn't escape. She could have escaped if she had wanted to, but she doesn't. She goes until the end, to the fate.

R E S N I K : See, it's always been my opinion if the "Habanera" and "Seguidilla" were overinterpreted, then Carmen has nowhere to go for the last act. Because nothing that she says in the "Habanera" or "Seguidilla" really has anything to do with the plot. They really only expose her as she is at that moment, which is not tied to anyone, free. And she treats love like some bird, which lands in one place, then flies away, and all of a sudden it's back again. Except she sees one person, Don José, and picks on him to throw the flower—not knowing that her destiny, with that flower, was that she would die by his hand, because Bizet fashioned the death motif with the throwing of the flower. So she's pronounced her own death with the throwing of the flower—only she doesn't know it yet.

The night after the San Francisco earthquake of 1906, Olive Fremstad reportedly sat in a park across from her hotel and passed out roses she'd received for her previous night's success as Carmen to refugees passing by.

CRESPIN: Her death may be a little bit suicidal, because she could escape if she really wanted to tell him, "OK, I'm going to follow you. Just wait for me—I'm coming back." But she doesn't do that. She goes straight to the truth—she doesn't lie. In fact, though she always seems to laugh, to tease, to dance, she is the courageous one. She doesn't lie to him. And I'm sure she knows he is going to kill her. I think that's an interesting aspect of Carmen. Because she is looking for one man after another man, maybe she is looking for the one who is going to say no to her. Because apparently, all the men are falling in love with her, and she gets everyone she wants—it seems to be very easy. Finally, when she falls in love with Don José, she's a flirt, and it's a very easy thing, like all the others. But finally, in the second act when he suddenly says, "I have to go back to the army," she's absolutely surprised. He is finally the first one who says no to her. For me, that's why she is completely attracted by him—deeply and unconsciously.

RESNIK: The fact that their real affair, whatever it was, happens in the intermission of Acts Two and Three is a revelation, because the side of Carmen that has had it, had enough of his hysteria, happens between Acts Two and Three. At the end of Act Two she goes away with him to the mountains, convinces him to desert. By the opening of Act Three, she's had enough of him. This makes Act Three powerful: powerful enough to read the cards, powerful enough to show her this dignity. She does it in two lines: "Va-t'en, va-t'en"— "Go to your mama." It's all in the music. There really isn't a real, dramatic forte in what she says until the end of Act Two. You see, even though he says he must see his mother before he dies, it's not the mama's boy who goes to see her; it's a very noble person. He wants to see his mother and that's why it's very powerful when he goes.

CRESPIN: He's a truthful one. He goes to his mother in the end, because he's educated this way. He loves his mother all right, but I don't think he is a little boy of mama.

RANKIN: To me, Carmen playing with José is like a cat playing with a ball of twine. It started unraveling and ensnaring her, and she didn't like it. She probably loved these men as much as she could love anybody, and was true to the man she was involved with at the time. But she was young—probably no more than twenty—and vibrant, fun loving. And more than anything, she loved adventure.

RESNIK: She doesn't shock him because he's an innocent bumpkin—she tantalizes him. He does fall in love with her, but it's his temper that gets in her way, his jealousy and his temper. A great many tenors let me build them up. The bigger Don José is, the more daring he is, the more hysterical, the less innocent he is, the better was my interpretation. The more noble, the more cavalier, the taller Don José was, the better it was for my Carmen. Because I don't believe he's an innocent boy from the country. He's not the little country boy, shy, who has this sweetheart, and all of a sudden he's stunned by this Gypsy. To me, that never made much sense. First of all, he's the only one who has the name of a nobleman: *Don* José. He's been demoted to corporal because of his traits—the trait that does him in—not only his jealousy, but his lack of control, his temper. And that lack of control killed a man. So he's seen a lot. I sang it with everybody: del Monaco and Tucker . . . Perhaps the one who taught me more about the opera, only through his interpretation and his presence onstage, was Ramón Vinay. Because he was all the things I thought about José. What a foil he was for Carmen! Because he was all man, all Spanish, all passionate in that Latin sense—never for a moment tough and vulgar.

LEWIS: I did my first Carmen with Ramón Vinay for the Pittsburgh Opera. He was a tall, handsome, and well-built man—very muscular. When we got into the first-act fight that Carmen has with the other cigarette women, I did the usual fighting: the hair pulling, the biting, the smashing, the kicking. I think I was biting when he leaned over and, instead of grabbing me by the waistline and pulling me away, as is usually done, he picked me up and slung me over his shoulder.

It was totally unexpected. It was wonderful, because it was so real and so spontaneous, and it gave an entirely different quality to our relationship throughout the rest of the evening.

Smashing and hair pulling, in fact, were the least indications of the character's ignorance of Emily Post. On first sight, the critic from *La Patrie* called Carmen "a *fille* in the most revolting sense of the word. . . . She is the veritable prostitute of the gutter," and then he went on to accuse Bizet of plagiarizing the score.

C R E S P I N : When I sang Carmen for the first time, it was personally the first time I could laugh on the stage. Before, I was singing all those parts that were *sérieuse,* dying. I mean, Carmen dies, too, but at least for the first two acts she can enjoy, laugh, and run around the stage, and make other people laugh. That was, for me, a big discovery. For the first time in my life, I could enjoy a little bit on the stage. I like to do that, of course; because in life, I like to laugh. But on the stage, it was not always my case, except with Offenbach's Grande Duchesse de Gérolstein, with Carmen—those were the two parts where I could really laugh and enjoy myself. So that was a big attraction for me.

H O R N E : I think personally there is a lot of comedy in the first two acts, but I'm speaking of subtle comedy—repartee with the other characters, like Mercédès and Frasquita, which can be humorous at times.

R E S N I K : Very often, I played Carmen for her humor in Act One. In the fight scene, I always found something funny to do so the audience would have a good time. See, I always believed that she picked the fight in the factory to attract the attention of Don José, because he was the only one in the "Habanera" not to pay any attention to her.

C R E S P I N : She is flirting, she's laughing, she's making fun of people. The first two acts are really funny to play, of course.

H O R N E : When the third act starts, the comic possibilities are over. It is dead serious from that moment on. Tragedy is the underlying theme, isn't it? And certainly, the balance of the opera is very serious.

R E S N I K : The seriousness comes in the second act, where she discovers she's been waiting for Don José for months. She's not become involved with anyone else. And contrary to what people feel about her, in essence, she's very, very honest, completely honest. She says to the toreador in the second act, when he says to her, "You tell me your name; I'll name the bull for you, I'll name the fight for you," and she says, "It doesn't matter what you call me, because I'm not particularly interested."

After Germont *père,* Escamillo was the role Robert Merrill performed most often with the Met, giving eighty performances as the toreador with the company.

ROBERT MERRILL: In the second-act toreador scene, he knows he's attractive, knows everybody loves him. It's not an easy aria, but it lay in my voice very well, so I could have a lot of fun with it. I'd walk by Carmen, you know, and give her the eye—she's going to be my next girl. *Carmen* is the only opera where the baritone gets the girl. It's interesting; you think of all the Verdi operas and the others—the baritone is always the father or the villain, never the lover. So the closest I came was Carmen. I finally get the girl—she's mine. She leaves the tenor. And the tenor winds up killing her, and I wind up with the bull. It's the closest I got, and I blew it.

Bizet, who had already rewritten the "Habanera" thirteen times, remarked while composing the "Toreador Song," "So they want trash? I'll give them trash!"

RESNIK: Carmen says to him, "You wait your turn, I'm involved now." So this flirting with him in the "Toreador Song," and flirting with everybody, for me, was always out. I had to choose my intentions in the first two acts of *Carmen.*

MERRILL: Escamillo was the glamour hero. If the era was today, he could be Sinatra or Joe DiMaggio. He was the bullfighter, the glamour boy. He wooed Carmen, and she was an ordinary gal, a working girl. I guess he fell in love with her, but you never knew. Escamillo was frivolous—that's the way I pictured him—and I tried to play him swashbuckling and carefree.

RANKIN: Even in the third act, she was through with José. It wasn't that she fell in love with Escamillo; she fell out of love with José. He turned out to be a country bumpkin and she just wasn't interested anymore. She left bodies strewn everywhere, mainly because she had the magnetism to attract and played the game of making people love her. She ruined a lot of lives, but I don't think she thought very much about it.

MERRILL: I did several new productions of *Carmen* at the Met. But one outstanding thing happened onstage during the first night of the new production with Risë Stevens. During the "Toreador Song," I was supposed to leap up on the table and sing. But they didn't prop it. You see, those tables had wheels under them, so they could move them out fast when they changed the scene. So some guy forgot to fix my table. I leaped up, and the thing started to roll into the wings as I was singing the "Toreador Song." I rolled right into the wings, past everybody. I'll never forget the look on Risë's face as she followed my movement; everyone onstage was "Where's he going?" But I never missed a beat. I got off in the wings and walked back out and finished the aria.

MOFFO: I loved Risë Stevens's Carmen. I saw it when—I don't want to say I was a child, but I was. She came to Philadelphia, and I was pretty young. I thought it was just terrific. I hadn't thought about it then, but I only remember I loved it. She got a message to me; that's what's important.

At *Carmen*'s premiere, Micaëla was the only character in the entire opera who most critics felt was suited to the Opéra-Comique stage. Charles Gounod was less enthusiastic; he insisted Bizet had stolen Micaëla's aria from him.

Micaëla was the role that introduced Mirella Freni to the operagoing public.

MIRELLA FRENI: I love the name *Micaëla,* so I gave this name to my daughter. But I had made the role first, the year she was born. I made my debut with this role, in Modena in 1955.

Lucine Amara has sung Micaëla eighty-seven times with the Metropolitan alone.

LUCINE AMARA: I find Micaëla not weak, like some people play her. She has to be a strong character, to come through those mountains alone and look for José to give him the message that his mother is dying. Her love for him also carries her along. When she finds him with Carmen as one of the smugglers, she says, "I will not have fear, and I will stand up to her, because my God will help me. He will protect me."

F R E N I : Micaëla came from the country, but she has great character. The way she goes off to find Don José—someone could kill her, you know. There is always the danger around her. When you think about it, it's incredible, the strength she has. In the first act you don't see this so much, because she's safer. But she's afraid, and when she has to go through the mountains, she has the strength inside her to do what she has to do.

A M A R A : She does have this love for God and José, and this makes her strong. My relationship with José is the most important thing in the opera to me. She hopes that he will declare his love for her, but she says she will come back for the answer. Of course she doesn't come back, because he winds up in prison.

M O F F O : I sang Micaëla only once in my life. I always hated all those kids with the blond braids. Oh, I think I was the first one to beg the Met to take the braids away for Gilda. I did a black-haired Gilda, a dark-haired Marguerite—even Lucia. I didn't do any more blondes. On me, instead of making me look pure, I really look very . . . impure, with a blond wig. I mean, look at me! My eyes are dark—I really look like it's not my hair. They always made Juliet blond, and I couldn't figure out why; as a good kid from Verona, nice Italian girl—I don't know. Franco Zeffirelli made her a brunet, so she must have been.

F R E N I : There are roles that are just comfortable for you. Mimì is one of those for me; Micaëla, too. I went back and sang that last year. I am a grandmother now, but I am quiet and relaxed, and it's easy for me to think young. It's strange to go back to a role like that, because I'm not a young girl now and Micaëla is a young girl. When I go onstage, I'm thinking it's hard to convince people I'm young; but you go out there, and the expressions and the music are there, and the audience—not me—they say I'm a young girl. Micaëla is a simple girl, but she's not stupid, like sometimes people say.

Carmens have notoriously been jealous of the beautiful melodies Bizet gave to Micaëla and Don José. Minnie Hauk, America's first

Carmen, rushed onstage during the third act and fiercely embraced tenor Luigi Ravelli, who was about to deliver a crowd-pleasing high note. With the note and his breath gone, he tried to throw Hauk into the orchestra pit, and the battered diva took to the wings.

R E S N I K : I sang Carmen with a great many interesting tenors. Vickers was a very powerful force—and we sang it very often at the beginning of his career and mine—not so much because he was the perfect foil, but because he was so powerful onstage as presence. He was the essence of the man who did not have control over his relationships.

C R E S P I N : Even though Carmen screams, "I don't love you any-more—I hate you," she follows him till the end, really. And appar-ently, she's afraid of nothing. I love the *mise en scène* when, though it is Don José who stabs her, she goes to him, and it's almost like she stabs herself. And to me, the aspect of the almost suicidal side of her is interesting to show off.

B U M B R Y : I enjoy the fourth act of *Carmen* because there is an interaction with two persons only, and if you have a good dramatic tenor, it makes the whole opera worthwhile.

R E S N I K : The Act Four Carmen, that character, does not exist in the play. Therefore, Bizet has built his stance to the very end. It was what he wanted from the librettist. He rewrote the words of the "Habanera," the "Card Song," and several other major things the night before the dress rehearsal. They pleaded with him to take certain things out. But instead, he put the screws on and made it even more poignant, because he wrote in all the things that insinuate what she says in the third act: "Destiny is the master, and my destiny is death."

C R E S P I N : She is a Gypsy; they believe in fate and they don't try to avoid it. They believe in God, in destiny—that it is there, that you cannot escape it. And they are right.

R A N K I N : I liked most of the tenors I did Carmen with. Richard Tucker was a wonderful Don José—very strong. And I liked del Monaco very much—I did it a lot with him.

Displeased with her tenor, Emma Calvé allegedly decided to walk offstage on Jean de Reszke during the last act of *Carmen* one night, but unfortunately waited until after he had stabbed her. The furious tenor chased her into the wings, dragged her back onto the stage, and proceeded to complete the act. The "dying" Calvé retaliated by completing his final lines along with him.

E L I A S : I did a production where the tenor forgot to bring his knife with him so he could stab me. And I'll tell you, he was smart and choked me, and it worked out very well. Because he realized during the duet he didn't have it, and if you give it an instant, it could be laughable; but he gave himself time to kill me, and it was convincing. I guess people thought, "Well, directors do things the way they want."

H O R N E : I remember one night I was singing the "Seguidilla" at the Met, sitting by the edge of the stage with my hands tied behind my back. I got something in my eye, behind my contact lens—hard lenses, mind you—and I couldn't move the lens or pop it out. I cried through the whole aria; I'm not so sure what that did to my interpretation.

R A N K I N : I remember one incident at Covent Garden where we had a tenor who was very good at knife throwing. He was a butcher's son, actually. The director wanted him to throw the knife in the last act, when he's getting very violent because Carmen had already said she didn't love him. Not *at* Carmen, but to hit this wooden box at the back of the stage, while I stood leaning up against the cross at the side of the stage. So it all went very well, until one night the knife was caroming through the air, went into the box, and hit the head of a buried nail; so it left the box, continued to carom, and almost nailed my thumb to the cross. It caught me right at the edge of the thumb, and of course it bled like crazy. But the public didn't mind a little blood, it didn't bother them at all, so I just kept right on. After that, they took out the knife throwing altogether. It did frighten me a little.

E L I A S : I loved singing with Plácido Domingo; Jon Vickers was great; but they were all wonderful.

B U M B R Y : Jon Vickers and Franco Corelli, for me, for my psyche, were the best Josés I worked with. And they complemented what I was doing.

En route to the American premiere at New York's Academy of Music in 1879, Minnie Hauk introduced *Carmen* to London audiences, sung in Italian. One critic concluded, "The story is tragic enough for Italian fancy, and sufficiently improper for the French mind. . . ." Another commended Hauk's acting, singing, and grace, which "lifted the part clear out of the gutter." New York critics found her portrayal "too realistic."

E L I A S : *Carmen* is an opera that wouldn't make any difference in English or French. You see, I'm a big believer that operas, comedies, should be done in English—not things like *Bohème.* But with *Carmen,* English shouldn't make any difference. It wouldn't harm it, because everybody knows the story, and because of the language itself.

R A N K I N : I've sung several translations of *Carmen* in English, one worse than the next, and they were all perfectly dreadful. I like operas in English if they fit. I think *Così Fan Tutte* is very lovely in English, because if you didn't sing it that way, three quarters of the people would miss the fun. But the grand-scale operas like Wagner, or for *Carmen*—it just isn't to be translated into English; it's more beautiful in French.

E L I A S : I don't think Puccini or Verdi lends itself to English. Mozart does; Rossini does. And *Carmen*—well, sometimes it's good to give the audience even more to know.

R A N K I N : If an opera has a long line, it's very difficult to hold a high note on *if, and,* or *but.* And by the time you've finished holding a note, everybody has forgotten what you're saying. And there are no hidden meanings, really, in *Carmen.* You can see it and, like mime, watch what is going on and follow it. *Trovatore* is very difficult in English and *Carmen* becomes almost drab.

M O F F O : I have to say I don't like translations of anything—except for comedy and dialogue, where the jokes are more easily understood in English—for the simple reason that the nuance of the language is never exactly right. It's always lopsided in the accents, where the syllables fall, and you have to make a word to fit the music or add a note. It's never the same.

R A N K I N : My first year in Zurich, I did *Carmen* in German. And I can tell you, a German *Carmen* is not the same as a French one; it's much less subtle. In some ways she's stronger. I always thought of Carmen as being an older woman in German—it seems more mature than the French does. It's certainly not playful, let's put it that way.

It becomes very stark, and in parts like the third act, it becomes much more menacing.

M O F F O : When I was first in Italy, they were still doing *Carmen* in Italian; when I got to Germany, they were doing it in German. I asked my teacher, "Why do they do *Carmen* in Italian?" And he said, "Because it's really much more Spanish than the French." I thought about that for a while. Then we should do *Traviata* in French. I heard Tebaldi do *Lohengrin* in Italian. They all did Wagner in Italian. They said, "You know, he wrote *Lohengrin* and *Tannhäuser* in Bologna." I know—but not in Italian. But translating in the U.S.—English doesn't bend; it doesn't curve.

As a specimen of womanhood, Carmen made the critics shudder. *La Patrie* ranted that the courtesan had taken over the stage, condemning the influence of Manon Lescaut and Marguerite Gauthier.

M O F F O : I was asked to do Carmen for a film with Franco Corelli. Had it not been for the movie, I don't think I'd ever have made the recording. I almost pulled out, because he was an artist who had done so many *Carmen*s before that. I thought I wouldn't measure up.

E L I A S : We're never satisfied with the productions of *Carmen,* are we? Why is that? *Otello* can be a great success, *Bohème* can be a great success, but *Carmen* . . . It's a great opera—but maybe that's why it was so criticized when it was first produced.

M O F F O : I made some mistakes, as we all do. But if I saw something that was totally out of my reach, I was not one of those daredevils. And whenever I did something that other people perhaps thought was daredevil, in my heart, I thought it was good for me. Anyway, it worked out quite well. As it turned out, we did not make the movie—Mr. Corelli decided otherwise. But I'm glad I did the recording.

R A N K I N : It was one of my favorite roles, because it was more of a challenge than any other. The singing part of it is duck soup for anybody. Subtlety, yes—but it isn't very rangy. It isn't really dramatic, it almost sings itself, so it is not what I would term a singing role.

B U M B R Y : Carmen did seem to fit me like a glove, even though I never really liked her character. Still, I've been able to act it very well, and that's what makes the difference. You don't have to have an affinity for a piece of music to do it well. You just have to be musical and have the talent. You can give a believable dramatic performance even if you don't like the character at all.

R E S N I K : I had very few productions of *Carmen* in my life that were done for me, where I sang the first night. I always came into a production. And coming in, you hardly ever meet the original stage director. I always said, "If I come in, I'll do as I want." I always said so—I never went in and did so without stating it. But when I was onstage, I really wanted to play it in the way I wanted to. Otherwise, what's the point? I never had a problem with a single conductor in the entire world. They all appreciated what I felt, because most of the conductors wanted the musical things I felt, and very often couldn't get them.

Conductors and their Carmens haven't always seen eye to eye. When Arturo Toscanini had the audacity to correct Geraldine Farrar during rehearsal, she answered, "You forget, Maestro, that I am the star." Toscanini quietly responded, "I thank God I know no stars except those in heaven, which are perfect."

C R E S P I N : Vocally, *Carmen* is not difficult. The big challenge is that she talks a lot, she sings a lot, she dances; she does a lot of things on the stage. That is why the part is tiring.

H O R N E : The acting challenges of Carmen are the same as in any role, inasmuch as reaching to the other characters and situations. But Carmen has to dance and play the castanets, and she is onstage for a great deal of the opera.

R E S N I K : *Carmen* has the most complicated first act ever written. That's certainly no fun. It's not fun for Carmen; it's not fun for the stage director—it's only fun for the audience. The soldiers and the little boys and the cigarette girls and the smoke and the men and the fight . . . I used to say that the only time you could gargle or have a cup of tea was during Micaëla's aria. From the moment she enters to the death of Carmen, she has no time—'cause if she's not singing or dancing, she's changing her costume. *Carmen* is also very difficult to direct, because in thirty-three of the thirty-five numbers, you've got the whole chorus—masses of people—onstage all the time.

E L I A S : Now that I've made the crossover to stage directing, someday

I want to direct *Carmen.* I have some ideas, but ideas that I never tell anyone. Well, I will—I'll leave them in my will. But with all due respect to the opera, and to Bizet, I feel there is some way *Carmen* should be turned around. I'm sure it's a brutal opera to direct, but I'll get myself a terrific Carmen and do it. I would like to see *Carmen* once again in the real Spanish way: the sense of how they put colors together, you know, with this kind of polka dot and that kind of thing—which is, after all, what it's all about. I'd just like to see a colorful production again.

After witnessing an attempt to turn one singer into a famous Carmen through cigarette ads, film, and radio appearances before she had ever sung the role, Geraldine Farrar remarked, "In my day, artists became Carmen by singing Carmen."

R A N K I N : It's an acting role. Because if you don't act this role with a real knowledge of what you're doing, both José and Micaëla can take the opera right away from you. Each of them has a beautiful aria the public loves.

A M A R A : I always got big applause for my aria in the third act. It's a real showstopper. Risë Stevens's husband used to say, "Whenever Lucine sings Micaëla, she takes the show away from my wife."

B U M B R Y : With Carmen, you work your fingers to the bone for the whole evening; and if you're lucky, you might have a success. Otherwise, José, Micaëla, and Escamillo take over, because they are the bright spots in the opera. Carmen's just not a positive character. It's like Lady Macbeth, who has all this exposed music to sing—and then Malcolm comes in and tears the house down.

C R E S P I N : It's amazing: Everybody gets a lot of success in the first act, in the second act. Escamillo sings one aria, which is fabulous; and the tenor has got a big success; and Micaëla, the big aria—big applause. Carmen, she sings a lot of arias and she gets some applause, OK. But she has to wait until the last act, until the end—and then you get some real big applause. It's a long part, and you have to wait until the last minute to really get rewarded. And it's a tricky part.

R A N K I N : You see, Carmen has the "Habanera," which is over with in a flash. It's interesting, it's known; but the "Seguidilla" is something else—it's just an enticement she holds before Don José. But there's nothing startling—I mean, you're not singing "O don fatale" like Eboli. You've got to get the public through knowhow, through timing, and through really trying to become this person. Now, Don José is a difficult role—you have to be a great singer to make a success of Don José. More than acting, José really has to sing, and so does Micaëla.

M O F F O : It's a wonderful part. In many ways I think it's an ungrateful part. Carmen sings some very difficult and yet simple things. The simpler a phrase, the harder it is, because it's so easily dissected in its simplicity. It's so much more accessible to other people's ears that you have to work that much harder.

E L I A S : I don't care how many people are in the audience; they all have their own idea of what Carmen should be like. It's a role that will never satisfy everybody. Most people will say, "Oh, she's too vulgar, she's this, she's that." It's a strange, strange role. I wish all Carmens all the best, because it's a very difficult part. You can't please everybody—and in some roles you can, believe me. There are some roles where the majority of the people will say, "Oh, she was so wonderful!" But Carmen is not that kind of a role.

M O F F O : The difference between a good Carmen and a great one is, I guess, an involvement that goes a little bit deeper than a kiss or a strut. I always see Carmen fixing her garters or something—that's all part of it, but you shouldn't have to do that.

E L I A S : It's very possible to miss with Carmen, very easy to be criticized, because we can't satisfy the people. They all have their own conception of what Carmen is. Their fantasies of Carmen are so strong, whether it's the man in the audience or the woman or the critic, and it's very difficult to come up with what they expect. Poor Carmen—she puts blood onstage for three hours. Micaëla comes on and sings this one aria and everyone goes wild.

M E R R I L L : My first Carmen was Gladys Swarthout, in New Jersey. I was in awe of her; she was a tremendous artist and a big star. It was a very poor opera company, and since she was the star, she got all the money. We got little, but it was a great honor to sing Escamillo with her. They couldn't afford many rehearsals and she didn't come to any—she only needed one piano rehearsal. I'd rented my costume from Stivanello, in New York, and when I got to the theater, it had arrived without shoes. And I hadn't even met Swarthout yet. I had sport shoes—black and white, I think—and I had to wear them. I looked like a poverty-stricken bullfighter. So I got to her dressing room to meet her for the first time, and she takes one look at me and says, "No! It can't be!" As you might know, I'm very shy, and I was embarrassed. I told her what had happened, and she said, "Well, let's forget it. Let's go out and sing." And we became very good friends. That was my first crack at Escamillo.

Since its premiere, *Carmen* has triumphed in every conceivable form, including ballet, cinema, and Oscar Hammerstein II's all-black version, *Carmen Jones.* After its first unfortunate experience, the Paris Opéra-Comique rallied to present *Carmen* over three thousand times.

R E S N I K : If we use the word *fun,* it's only because it's the world's most popular opera. The audience knows it is, and they look forward to it because they know the tunes. It's fun because they know it—a lot of it's familiar. They also know that at some point they're going to hear the "Toreador Song" four times. The fun, or the attraction, of *Carmen* is the color—not only the subject and the music, but the look of it. It's Spanish, and it has a lot in it for everybody.

C R E S P I N : It's a masterpiece, and also the story is so fascinating. Of course, there are a lot of stories like this, with love and death at the end—that is the whole story of the opera. But this one is really fascinating, because of those characters.

M O F F O : I think Carmen will always be popular because it's just terribly tuneful, and it's had a lot of exposure—violin suites, orchestral selections, movie soundtracks. Every other minute, you hear it someplace. The kids can sing you *Carmen*—although I hope they don't know too much about the story—but they'll never sing you *Hansel and Gretel,* for example, which everybody says "I can take my child to."

C R E S P I N : Again, it's the same picture as Don Giovanni—happy and laughing a lot, but death is there all the time. Maybe the public is fascinated by that.

E L I A S : Any person can come out and hum the toreador aria and the "Habanera," and the story is wonderful—I mean, there's this sexy woman who plays around and gets killed. And it's Spanish.

L E W I S : You can't deny the strength of that music, and the drama.

It has color and it's exotic, and we love exotica. It's a story of passion unleashed. You know, everyone feels inside, "Oh God, I wish I had the guts to dump this shmo and throw myself at the next guy." Nobody in his right mind does these things, but to see someone else do it . . .

AIDA

~

*It's hard to get a good Aida or a good
anything else these days.*
—ZINKA MILANOV

Music by Giuseppi Verdi
Libretto by Antonio Ghislanzoni
from the prose of Camille du Locle and a play by Auguste Mariette

AIDA.................................. *Lucine Amara, Martina Arroyo, Rose
Bampton, Grace Bumbry, Mirella Freni,
Zinka Milanov, Aprile Millo, Leona
Mitchell*

AMNERIS..................... *Rose Bampton, Grace Bumbry, Fiorenza
Cossotto, Mignon Dunn, Nell Rankin,
Blanche Thebom, Sandra Warfield*

RADAMES .... *Plácido Domingo*

AMONASRO............... *Sherrill Milnes*

RAMFIS .... *Paul Plishka*

*T*he first performance of *Aida* was given at the Cairo Opera House on December 24, 1871. Commissioned to write the opera by the Egyptian government, Verdi was paid 100,000 lire upon completion of the score. He retained all but the Egyptian rights to the work. The question of who wrote the libretto is still somewhat up in the air. However, it is generally believed to have been written by Antonio Ghislanzoni after the French prose of Camille du Locle from a play by Auguste Mariette. Providing classic roles for soprano, mezzo, tenor, baritone, and bass, *Aida* has been part of the standard repertory in opera houses all over the world since its premiere.

One prominent Aida, the late Zinka Milanov, is considered by many to have been the ultimate Verdi soprano of recent times.

Z I N K A M I L A N O V : It is not easy these days to get a good singer. They are not growing them on trees, so it's hard to get a good Aida or a good anything else these days. I think there are very good voices around who could sing Aida, but they are not being given the chance. You can't just wait around and cover. You have to be out there. I was very fortunate that I was never a standby. I think it must be a very gratifying job just to step in and sing without rehearsals.

Two of Mme. Milanov's colleagues, Blanche Thebom and Nell Rankin, both included Amneris, Aida's rival, among their many roles.

B L A N C H E T H E B O M : I had the good fortune to be singing at the Met when Milanov was in her full power. And she was justifiably *the* Aida! I can tell you that at any hour of the day or night, I can still hear the incredible sound of her voice. In the Nile scene, I used to come out of my dressing room just to listen to her. I respected her so much and I really loved to sing with her.

N E L L R A N K I N : Milanov was certainly one of my favorite Aidas. She sang the part like a dream and she had a perfect lyric-spinto voice, which for me is the perfect type for Aida, rather than a dramatic soprano or a pure lyric. Her pianissimi were unbeatable.

M I L A N O V : Now in America we have many more singers than we did when I came here. Then all singers were from Europe—Italy or wherever—and now we have good domestic singers, but I feel so sorry they have such trouble getting performances.

T H E B O M : Zinka was very nice to me. She was not a little wisp of a thing, but she was a gorgeous, gorgeous singer.

Along with Grace Bumbry, Rose Bampton was one of the few singers who had the chance to perform as both of Verdi's leading ladies in *Aida*.

ROSE BAMPTON: I had the very good fortune to start singing Amneris with Elisabeth Rethberg as my Aida. When I first came to the Met, the maestro kept saying, "You know, of course, you're not a mezzo-soprano and you will be singing soprano parts." Every time I sang Amneris I'd listen to Rethberg and think, "Rose, you've got to remember how that sounds. You've got to remember those phrases, the way she does it, because if you're ever going to sing Aida, you've got to sing it like that." In my ear and in my mind, she was my idol. Rethberg and of course Ponselle, with whom I made my debut, were my two idols, and I couldn't have had better.

GRACE BUMBRY: My very first operatic experience was as Amneris at the Paris Opera in 1960, and there was very little rehearsal time given to an existing production, so we never rehearsed my last scene and they just assumed I'd know what to do. Well, being in my first operatic appearance, I naturally had little skill in improvising. Well, I made my entrance and I found myself standing out there above the tomb during the entire Aida-Radames duet. What do you do? I was already there and I knew I couldn't leave. So I remained as still as I could—out of fright, I'm sure. The next day it was reported in the newspapers, "How apropos that Amneris dominated the farewell of the lovers." Now I'm asking you! That time I lucked out.

In the operatic world, criticism comes in many different forms. Following an accident onstage by one of the horses in the triumphal scene of *Aida,* the conductor, Sir Thomas Beecham, turned to the audience and remarked, "A distressing spectacle, ladies and gentlemen, but gad, what a critic."

Lucine Amara and Martina Arroyo both debuted at the Met as the Celestial Voice in *Don Carlos* and moved on to sing the Ethiopian Princess.

MARTINA ARROYO: I don't think the ultimate Aida's happened yet and I doubt if I'll be the one to sing it. We're all human beings on the stage and I don't know one of us who's perfect. You've got to realize that "O patria mia" is not just a beautiful song to show how a soprano can rise to the occasion with high Cs. It's really a very, very powerful piece. And when she's in that state of mind, her father comes in and asks her to betray her love. There are a lot of vocal challenges in *Aida,* especially "O patria mia," but when you're young, you don't know that. Later when you find out it's difficult, you begin to tremble. The big vocal challenge for me was going from the powerful, dramatic lady in the confrontation or the triumphal scene and then to have to bring the voice down to nothing as in the death scene.

L U C I N E A M A R A : I feel that too many lighter voices are trying to sing Aida these days. The role is really for a dramatic soprano, and some of them don't have the top, and they push down on the bottom so they lose the bloom at the top. Then there are some who only have a top, and they can't make it either. You have to have a top, middle, and bottom.

A R R O Y O : The other vocal challenge, of course, is just being heard over the chorus and orchestra. For example, she sings all during the triumphal scene. I've seen Aidas simply mouth it. Perhaps they are smart to save it for other things. I'm not making a judgment call. Maybe they could produce more in another scene. But if you stay committed to her as a person, you have to give all night long.

L E O N A M I T C H E L L : Every soprano will say "O patria mia" is difficult because it's so dramatic. Verdi will do that! He likes to project intensity and passion through his music. Sometimes you have the dramatic recitatives and then you have to come back and do the aria, which is very quiet. The way that the high C is written makes it very hard to do, and a lot of people judge whether or not you can do the role on that particular aria. You can sing all night, but it's like Carmen and Micaëla: Carmen is out there singing away all night, and Micaëla has her aria and everyone raves about how wonderful she was. It's like that with Aida. It really gets them if you can sing the high C.

M I L A N O V : There's a lot of repertory that is difficult and big and important. It's not just Aida. But that role is a big selling card and you have to have a lot of strength to do it. *Aida* is more difficult than a lot of other operas. The big aria on the Nile scares every soprano and there are lots of other technical things—the legato and other things. The phrasing is also very difficult.

While conducting the opera at Covent Garden, Sir Thomas Beecham, who was saddled with a cast somewhat below the level he would have liked, remarked to the press that he insisted the orchestra play very loudly to drown out the singers, "in the public interest." A hard man to please, Beecham compared the orchestra at the Met to a Salvation Army band.

At the special request of another maestro, Herbert von Karajan, Mirella Freni sang her first Aida in 1979.

MIRELLA FRENI: The third act is very, very difficult for every soprano—well, maybe not for all, but it is for me. It is not composed easy. That Verdi! It's beautiful, but you really must take care for the high C. Thanks, God was always good for me, but you need a lot of control there because a high C in other places is easier, but not there, not in that act. All sopranos—well, let me say many—take care for that moment and are afraid about it.

APRILE MILLO: *Aida* is written so well. Verdi was such a man of the theater. That's such a glib term, but he really was. For me, the role is all a pianissimo building toward a crescendo.

RANKIN: To get over Amneris, a mezzo needs a strong low and middle voice, but she also needs a strong and ringing high voice to compete with the soprano. It's a hard combination to put together as far as the line goes—to sing that low and then so high. The judgment scene is all over the place. And usually there's a lot of getting around the stage, which I like. But it's not the easiest thing to do with all this singing, and then running up and down steps.

THEBOM: In some of Verdi's earlier works you see the difference in the orchestration. This one has a very rich orchestration, and I love enormously the believable dramatic musical punch he builds for each one of the characters. The differences are so beautifully delineated.

RANKIN: But Verdi should have given Amneris an "O don fatale" aria to sing while she's down on the sofa. But then people would say you wouldn't know whether to call the opera *Aida* or *Amneris.* Something should have been done for Amneris in the second act, and that duet is certainly not the most melodious in the world.

Paul Plishka would seem to agree with this assessment of Verdi's theatrical gifts—at least as far as his treatment of the High Priest, Ramfis.

PAUL PLISHKA: I guess Ramfis gets his chance a little during Amneris's aria in the judgment scene, in the condemnation of

Radames, but I still wish it was more. Vocally, of all the Verdi operas, it's the easiest for the bass. There are no real hurdles, nothing to worry about. All basses do the role during their careers, but it's not one that has any real problems other than *patience.*

B A M P T O N : It's great music and wonderful to sing. And of course, with all of Verdi's operas, you get these marvelous melodies that come and are just so gorgeous at the end. All of his operas have great climaxes.

P L I S H K A : I wish Ramfis were actually a better part, more clearly defined. He's in and out too much, and I also think in the overall picture of what's happening within the opera, he should have more of an influence on what's going on. I'm sure he cares a great deal about Radames, but in the opera we don't get to see that.

M I L L O : I don't approve of the last act being a shouting match. She is hearing this music from another world and you have to capture that feeling.

P L I S H K A : I wish there were a stronger scene somewhere—anything where you could see Ramfis having a stronger influence on Radames and Amneris. Then Aida would be more afraid of him, realizing what a powerful man he really is. But we never get to see that. So you have to try to develop all that in the time you're given.

M I T C H E L L : Musically there are so many things you could take out of this opera and label as a high point. I'm not tired of it yet. You never get tired of a role when you're always finding new things to express all the time. To me, that's a tribute to Verdi, because you find new things every time you sing it. My meaning is to work on the phrasing constantly to make the meaning come out through the music.

M I L A N O V : Verdi said it all. Then you have to come with yourself and bring what's in you to the role.

M I T C H E L L : The very quiet singing is the most difficult. Verdi wants a soprano with a unique personality, and you have to be slightly mezzoish with a brilliant top. It's all combined in there together.

R A N K I N : *Aida* certainly has a grand line and the beauty of the music goes right through to the end.

M I L L O : The style of music in the last act—especially the way I like to sing it—is full of dynamics, which I think we're lacking in today's school of music. Now it's just loud, louder, and loudest.

M I L A N O V : Aida is still not as difficult as Norma because there you have all of the coloratura.

B A M P T O N : Actually Aida was much easier for me to sing than Amneris because I had that "float" in the top, which made it easy for me, and also because I had that memory of what Rethberg did. I know that I absolutely had to try to get that same quality that she had.

M I G N O N D U N N : Well, after all, Amneris is twice the length of any mezzo-soprano part—twice the length of Azucena, the length of Carmen. It requires an enormous amount of stamina, just physical strength, to get through it. It's a grand part. After maybe two hundred performances as Amneris, there may have been maybe six I liked. I always think I can do it better. It's a very difficult role.

A R R O Y O : About a hundred years ago, "O patria mia" was the easiest aria for me to sing. It was in "Ritorna vincitor" where I just didn't have enough of a bottom—I mean a vocal bottom; the other part of me I always had. With the intensity I feel about this character, I just had to back off, just to make any sound come out at all, to stay alive technically. I just couldn't do it then, but with time and age and strength, now I can. Now there are problems today that weren't there thirty years ago, but that's part of it, too.

B A M P T O N : Aida is a very fragile person because she's being what she isn't; she's being a maid to this woman who's very autocratic and overbearing. She has vocally beautiful phrases and wonderful ensembles, and it's a very different type of singing from Amneris, who is more declamatory. Aida always has this big, beautiful legato line.

A R R O Y O : So often the Verdi heroine is just sung and the character is not taken into consideration as much as the acting parts in verismo, like Santuzza or the *Chénier*. But I think we have to give as much to the Verdi heroines.

The legendary diva Adelina Patti was not overly fond of rehearsals and was hardly a Method actress. She was the sort of "singular sensation" they sing about in *A Chorus Line*—a star in every sense of the word. In fact, her contracts frequently included clauses that allowed her to be absent from rehearsals. Her concept of a dramatic demise for Aida was to fluff up the pillows on her chaise lounge, kick off her designer shoes, arrange her costume as decorously as possible, and settle in for whatever might happen—death, sleep, and with any luck an ovation.

A M A R A : You have to be involved in the character of Aida at all times. You have to realize that she's not a slave; she's a king's daughter. Her country is at war with Egypt, but she's alive and in a strange country, and now she's also a woman in love. And Radames loves her, too. There's a lot there to work on.

F R E N I : I do the research first on a character, always. It helps to prepare me psychologically for the role, and then when I prepare the piece musically, I put the research in as long as it still respects the composer's plan. Then I might try to put some of my own personality in and I just hope it works.

M I T C H E L L : She gives up everything for her love and she's torn between Radames and her father.

M I L A N O V : As an actress there are lots of things to do in *Aida*. Lots of love, lots of love duets—with her father and her lover. You have to work on it and never give up. Nowadays, when people have a success, they drop it and never go back.

A M A R A : You do get involved. You can't just stand there and sing. You have to think about what the woman is, what she's doing.

A R R O Y O : I think she changes in the opera. Certainly her love is tested. She has to change when she admits to Amneris that she's in love with Radames. These two ladies have gotten to each other's raw nerves. And she has to do a lot of rethinking. Then, right on top of that, her father comes in, right in the next scene, and she has to deal with all of that. She's got some fast decisions to make. She has a great belief in love and now her father is asking her to betray the man she loves and to ask him to betray his country. She's doing it for her country. So this gets to be a little raw—very heavy and fast decisions.

B U M B R Y : The main reason that I wanted to sing Aida was because of the scene with Amonasro. It's the most beautiful, heartrending music in grand opera. I feel what Verdi's doing with the music, the dynamics, and the text. From day one, I felt if you get a baritone who really feels his oats, it's sheer heaven. Even when I was doing Amneris, I'd always be present for rehearsals for that act because it fascinated me.

F R E N I : These women I sing are not me. I read the score, I study, and then I think of what the composer wants from me. I prefer to discover what I can do with my possibilities, but I would never want to be a copy of anyone else. Everyone is different and I am what I am, and what I can bring to each of my roles will be all mine.

A R R O Y O : When you believe Aida and believe you could be in that situation, she isn't farfetched at all. Her situations are very real if you make them live for you.

A M A R A : I always felt involved and as one with the character when I was singing her, especially, of course, in the scene with the father.

Amonasro has always been a favorite debut role for baritones. After Marian Anderson's historic Met debut as Ulrica in *Un Ballo in Maschera* in 1955 broke the color barrier at that house, she was followed a few weeks later by Robert McFerrin, who debuted as Amonasro. The father of pop singer Bobby McFerrin was the first major black male artist to appear on the Met stage. His repertory there has been passed on to such singers as Sherrill Milnes, who appreciates the intricacies and nuances Verdi allotted to Aida's father.

S H E R R I L L   M I L N E S : The duet in the third act is simply great. It's so powerful and the character has gone through so many emotional changes. He loves his daughter, but perhaps he loves his country more. His kingly priorities are stronger than his father-daughter priorities. He doesn't mind that she betrays her own feelings.

R A N K I N : Amonasro is certainly a big help to the opera. He's an unusual character and he has beautiful music to sing. He's a marvelous asset and it works well with the tenor, who also has beautiful lines all the way through and is very virile and masculine.

M I L N E S : Vocally there is some frustration in singing Amonasro, as Verdi has given him no big aria. This is the only great Verdi part in which the baritone has no set piece. Of course, the soprano and tenor both have great solo moments, but the mezzo also doesn't have a lift aria that starts and stops. This can be a little frustrating.

A R R O Y O : Usually you see Amonasro coming out like a gorilla in a loincloth. But I did an *Aida* in Mannheim that I'll never forget. As the Amonasro walked out in front of the people, he was so dignified. He came out and his attitude was "I won't be a barbarian. I'm the head of my people. I'm a leader."

M I L N E S : It's one of the great baritone roles even though it's shorter than some. He sings an act and a half, but it takes one full act to get all the makeup on and another one to remove it, so it's still a four-act opera for me.

A R R O Y O : The problem might be—as Sherrill Milnes feels—that Amonasro just did not want his daughter with Radames. He wants that stopped. That's the ultimate insult—that he uses his daughter: "Oh, you can be his wife, and you can live happily together if you get him to tell you. Then the two of you escape." Sherrill doesn't believe that he wants her to escape.

M I L N E S : Since he's not really a good father, I guess he is in essence the traditional bad guy. But we baritones are used to that. He really forces Aida to rat on Radames, and in that way he is a total conniver, a villain of sorts.

A R R O Y O : Wouldn't I love to tell some stage director to please teach Amonasro that he is a king. There was a respect set up between him and the Egyptian King—two heads of state. One won, the other lost, and that's the way it is

M I L N E S : The makeup is important in this role, too. He is a king, albeit a captured one, and you need to present him that way, with a look that gives you that enormous pride he has. The love he feels for his country has to show. That's very important in this role.

A R R O Y O : It might be nice one day, if a director were staging a new production, to have some input. And to have input from the other characters and how they might feel. For example, why do you have Radames onstage to be chosen as the general to go off, if there are no other generals there? He's got to be one of several generals; otherwise . . . The only other people in the scene are Amneris, Aida, and Ramfis—and they're not going to go off as leaders. It makes no sense. What's he so happy about? Who else is going to go? It's little things like that.

B A M P T O N : Starting with Amneris, you learn so much about Aida because you're with her so much of the time. You realize the contrast in these two women. Then, by the time I did Aida, I had a much better understanding of what Amneris was going through. It's a marvelous thing. It was a great help to begin with Amneris.

A R R O Y O : The best part of portraying Aida is that she has to be false in front of Amneris. So when you get the confrontation between these two ladies, it's much stronger than if one is originally down-beaten. Though really, what can Aida do? Amneris can have her head if she wants it. So why does the game go on? Aida has to have something. I still hang on to that viewpoint, incorporating it with many different stage directors. For me, that's the one thing that makes Aida very real. She has come from a great deal, and even though she didn't live in her own court, she never really reigned, but she wasn't a babe in arms. She said, "I remember the women being raped and the town being looted."

T H E B O M : Aida has a lock on the audience. Naturally everyone has sympathy for the young lovers. And somebody who's a slave—I mean that's pretty attention-grabbing. You're already interested in these people, emotionally speaking.

A R R O Y O : You know, Aida has great feeling about Verdi's big three: fatherland, love for father, and patriotism. She's really a very big character, never boring.

R A N K I N : I don't think the public admires Amneris or what she's doing or what she's done—not only to herself but to the other people who are victims of her jealousy. She's self-propelled, self-centered, and a jealous individualist who will have her way—at least as far as she can—that will end either in her own doom or in getting what she wants.

T H E B O M : Amneris is not an evil person. As a matter of fact, she's an incredibly wonderful person. Her maneuver to have Radames appointed the leader will elevate him to a status where he would be acceptable to the court, and to her father as her mate. We have this lady who is really stunning; her ladies sing that she is, and she has this great compassion and warmth for her ladies-in-waiting. In the second act, she reminds Aida that she has always treated her not as a slave but as a sister. She always had a close and warm relationship with Aida.

A R R O Y O : Amneris is probably the most truthful person in the whole thing. She's a selfish little girl, but she does love Radames, too, in her way. And she is the princess and she is spoiled. Actually she's very tragic, because in her simplicity and honesty, she loses as well. She doesn't even have the advantage—if that's what you want to call it—of being able to give up her life with the man she loves this much. Now I fear that Martina would not go to a tomb with a man no matter how much she loved him, I don't think. But then, I don't know. I haven't been tested yet. But Aida is strong enough to go.

M I T C H E L L : I have a secret fantasy about Amneris. Is that a great part or what? You know, I find myself secretly singing bits of

Amneris's music at home, just on my own. Sometimes I wish I were a mezzo just so I could sing that part. Amneris and Aida have a really unique relationship and it changes with each director you work with. I've played it where Aida is actually stronger than Amneris, where the Amneris is a little bit afraid and shows it. Mezzos usually hate it when it's done that way. They love to just stomp on Aida, but it gets to be kind of dull if Aida is always cowering.

Radames is often referred to as a killer tenor role. Richard Tucker learned it early in his career and actually recorded the opera in 1949. However, he didn't perform the part onstage until 1965. Like his predecessors, Plácido Domingo approached Radames gradually, starting in 1971, but waiting for full vocal maturity before he made it a standard part of his repertory.

P L Á C I D O   D O M I N G O : It has often been said that Radames is a one-dimensional character. I feel differently about him. Admittedly the character is not as rich as Otello or Don Carlos, to name two other Verdi heroes, but he is a fairly complex man. His political ambitions are in conflict with his emotions.

M I T C H E L L : The relationship between Radames and Aida is very strange. There's also just not enough time in the opera when they're really together, so it's hard to portray. I love their moment in Act Three when he comes in and she's a little bit perturbed, because she thinks that he should just know that he wants to choose her as a woman over Amneris. I really get into that. Actually it's probably the only place in the opera where Aida can be self-revealing; a lot more colors can come out in that scene.

D O M I N G O : Radames is a noble man who prefers to accept the consequences of his feelings and deeds rather than making compromises with his own conscience. Let's face it, he could have saved himself by accepting another woman's love. Instead, he prefers to go to his death for the sake of the woman he really loves.

M I T C H E L L : She taunts him and says, "Do you really love me?" And women have been doing that for years. She's really testing him in that scene, and there's all this beautiful music going on. At that point she's like a temptress to me—not that she's a Salome or anything, but she's a woman, and women have ways to convince men to marry them or go off with them or whatever. That's all in that third-act scene.

D O M I N G O : When I first studied the part, I discovered that the true clue to Radames's character is not something he does or sings, but his silence in the judgment scene.

In *The New York Times,* Donal Henahan described Fiorenza Cossotto's Met debut as Amneris as "not the wall clawing harridan familiar to us all, but a wellborn lady able to command her slaves without throwing hysterical fits."

F I O R E N Z A C O S S O T T O : All the big-name singers that have played the part whom I have seen and learned from always have treated Amneris with more austerity, not as a young girl. It was also the taste at that time to see Amneris like that.

S A N D R A W A R F I E L D : The relationship between the two women is so well written. The way Amneris tries to manipulate Aida is so real. I'm going to get in trouble for this, but it is a very womanly thing.

B A M P T O N : You always have to remember that Amneris is the daughter of the King and very spoiled and very jealous.

T H E B O M : You have this incredible entrance for Amneris. It's a measure and a half of music at a rather rapid tempo. Then she begins to sing. Later when Aida comes on, there's a look between Aida and Radames, and Amneris has the first hint that this man she loves is already emotionally involved—and it's with Aida.

R A N K I N : For me, the opera begins badly for Amneris. The only thing that saves her in the first act is the costume, if it's extremely beautiful. If she can really look like a princess and the costume is a knockout, it's helpful, but she still has nothing to sing.

C O S S O T T O : At the beginning she is a very young princess and a friend to Aida. They are together, though one is the slave and the other the princess. Later she finds that Aida's in love with the man that she is herself. Then she begins to put on her superiority because she is a princess: "You are a slave. He's for me, not you." Everything she does is always to defend her love for Radames. She's not a bad woman, not a mean woman, but she wants to defend her love all the way to the end. Vocally it is a very demanding role. The first note to the last is important. But the duet in the second act and the judgment scene are the most important and demanding. There are many, many feelings: one moment scared, one moment she tried to convince him to defend himself for love. After the scene with the priest, she cries tears. She feels like she's dying, because she has no more hope, no more strength. Everything is gone, drained.

R A N K I N : If I were rewriting this for myself, I certainly wouldn't come in on low-lined phrases. In the first place, half of the orchestra is duplicating what you're saying, which is not good. No voice is a powerhouse down there unless you're a real contralto—and then generally you don't have the top for Amneris. So if you're a mezzo-soprano, it's rather tough going in the first act. All I can say is, she better look good if she wants to make any impression at all in the first act.

C O S S O T T O : For me, the victim in the opera is really Amneris. She doesn't have *amore*—love. Life for Amneris is finished.

B A M P T O N : Amneris is a demanding role because she has a lot to sing— a lot in the low and medium, but in the last act she has to have a good B because she has to be able to sing and still make it very convincing. It's a very strong personality.

R A N K I N : I did another production at the Met in which the stage director had Amneris sitting in what I termed an old gray underslip when the curtain went up. Frankly, I was embarrassed. I felt I should either crawl under the couch or leave the stage. After all, she *is* dressing for Radames's homecoming. But I really don't think she'd have this kind of underwear, let alone have the public viewing it. Then she went behind the screen to dress in full, and came out not looking much better.

T H E B O M : I remember my first costume in Act Two. I had a bare midriff, silver lamé with a bra and big collar, and a skirt that was open in the front, and a very short skirt underneath that. That was quite a smashing sensation, and I thought it highly appropriate. It was an attention grabber. One of the men from the tour committee in Atlanta said they didn't care what operas were being presented or how much extra it would cost, but they wanted Blanche Thebom to put on that Act Two costume and just walk once across the stage and that was all. Fortunately, this never became a problem between Zinka and me. I loved and admired her. She used to laugh about it.

R A N K I N : I'm a strong subscriber to outstanding costumes onstage for anything. It makes an immense difference.

D U N N : If an Amneris speaks the role as an actress and not with any rhythm, it really works. I try to get my students to do this. You have to look at every character and say, "How do I feel about Aida, Radames, Ramfis?"

R A N K I N : In the judgment scene, when she realizes that Radames is not going to leave Aida for her and she allows his death to take place, like any woman would be, she's sorry. But I think she would do it again. I don't think she would learn from the truth. I think if she knew Aida was in that tomb with Radames, she would have destroyed them both with her own hands if she could. There's no solution for people who are like this.

C O S S O T T O : Aida is an incredible character, but I think in the judgment scene, it wasn't Amneris's temper but Verdi's temper in the character, begging not to kill Radames. Verdi dedicated himself to Amneris very much. He felt the torment that she had. Sure, between the two ladies, Amneris has many more sentiments than Aida, who is all the time sweet and feminine—crying, romantic, finished. But Amneris has many black-and-white moments. She has this constant contrast in feeling: hate, revenge, love—she always has all of this. She is always boiling inside for something. That's why the *personaggio* is always very outstanding.

T H E B O M : To understand where I was in the character, I realized very early that ancient Egypt was *the* civilization of the world at that time. Amneris is therefore one of the most powerful women in the world. This is something that I had constantly in my mind. I wasn't just a woman. The things she is called upon to do, and does in connection with her love for Radames, are all the more poignant and tragic because she is who she is.

R A N K I N : In my opinion, without the judgment scene, there is no Amneris. The second act is just sort of ho-hum for her. I know a lot of people don't feel that way. They think the second act is great, but I don't. I think that Verdi either didn't like mezzos at that particular time, or for some reason, he didn't consider that it was important to give her a better singing part.

T H E B O M : I don't know any woman who has the kind of compassion, love, and selflessness she has. She doesn't ask him to marry her.

She just asks, "If you can just promise me that you will never see Aida again . . ." That's the only thing she asks of him. He renounces that, and she realizes that the whole thing is impossible and calls the guards, and he's taken off to trial. She humiliates herself completely before the priests. I don't know anyone who has that kind of depth of love. I personally would not be able to do that. And even that's not enough. When he's incarcerated, she goes to pray to the gods for this man's everlasting peace. Now that's a woman of such nobility and depth of love. I always absolutely adored that scene and found it endlessly challenging.

C O S S O T T O : She has a lot of emotion, very dramatic—crying with the priest, begging him. The High Priest had a lot of authority then—over her, over kings, everybody. But this woman, just to protect her love, doesn't care if she has to approach the priests and talk to them, beg. Then she crosses them. She uses a very offensive word against them. But the strength to do all this comes from love. So she's as good as other people. When she feels she couldn't win the battle, she feels very deep sorrow. She lost all hope.

T H E B O M : Even the second act, where she plays cat and mouse to find out what the true situation is between Aida and Radames, is very believable. She does find out by lying. But why not? I would. Wouldn't you? Any woman would.

C O S S O T T O : She doesn't feel sorry for Aida because Aida was mistreating her in trying to get the same man. She also has this deep sorrow because at the end he dies, and he didn't want to defend himself although she begged him. So she feels very sorry for this love that didn't come the way she wanted.

R A N K I N : I don't think that Amneris would even dream that any young officer would turn down a princess. And I don't think anyone normally would, but Radames does just that. I suppose it could happen, but at that time, for a young person to turn down a position as the husband of the daughter of the King—I mean, what could be better?

W A R F I E L D : I feel there's not one moment where Amneris is truly evil. She just adored Radames and couldn't bear to see him love Aida the way that he did. You can see in the last act that she's a broken woman. She may never recover from that. She's just a very passionate woman in love and it's the end for her, too.

C O S S O T T O : If the opera is set with severe scenery and severe costumes, it gives the character a very different impression. Amneris has to move differently. In the current Met production, she's a young girl, same as Aida. When you have the big, splendid headdresses and the cape and crown, it is a different *personaggio* in the eyes of the public. Then I am not the Princess/girl but just the Princess, and I have the authority and education of the Princess. A lot also has to do with the conductor, if he sees it more soft or more strong. The color, the atmosphere of the orchestra, it changes. If the orchestra is softer, the *personaggio* is younger. Amneris as young is more attractive and more sympathetic to the public than a hard princess.

R A N K I N : I think Amneris is basically an unsympathetic character as far as the public goes. Therefore, she has to try to gain the sympathy of the public, and failing that, she has to get their approval through sheer impact in the judgment scene, in acting and in singing.

D U N N : Everything for the character is right in the libretto. The one thing I want when I am Amneris is Radames, and I can't have him. I think this is the first time in her life that she's ever felt insecure. She's had everything she wanted.

R A N K I N : She isn't a spider lady or a tornado all the time. When she's around Radames, she's trying to use all the wiles of a young woman to get a man. She has all this emotional upheaval because of her love.

W A R F I E L D : It's like *Fatal Attraction:* People do things that are wrong or they shouldn't do in the name of love. You can become obsessive very easily.

T H E B O M : Amneris was the role I sang more frequently than any other. I've always seen her as a woman who was very beautiful and who always exhibited a very elegant compassion with her ladies-in-waiting. I based this on the type of music and the circumstances that Verdi provides. I'm not just making this up.

R A N K I N : If Amneris doesn't square off with the public in the judgment scene, she may as well go into the dressing room, close the door, and not come out again. That's why Verdi gave her that powerful scene to portray.

D U N N : The role is difficult, musically, straight through.

T H E B O M : Interestingly enough, a lot of Verdi's correspondence about it was great concern about what the singer was doing in the part of Amneris. The person not only has to have a large, dramatic, and beautiful voice, but terrific vocal control, because the tessitura is really very demanding.

D U N N : In the last twenty years we've found a lot of—well, sort of psychological reasons for why people act the way they do. Now you can really create a person and not just a strong stock character.

R A N K I N : I don't think you can create a lot of psychological situations. The public doesn't understand this. The artist does because the director has explained it, and you may even like it, but where is the public in this? They're not going to get all those psychological implications, are they? If so, where from? You don't project these things.

C O S S O T T O : Verdi really loved Amneris and he gave her a lot. I don't think he thought she was the most important character in the opera, but he did find her special. I think he felt for the torment that she had.

T H E B O M : I think she's the greatest character in the opera. She's the most real character.

R A N K I N : I think the characters are all very well drawn. Every one of them is strong, including Aida, the protagonist, who has temperament and a lot of it. In a lot of operas, the soprano doesn't have that much. I think this is an asset. You have two leading ladies, both of whom have temperament, possibly because they're both princesses.

M I T C H E L L : The essence of the opera for me comes in the third act, when Aida is with her father. For me, this is why the opera exists. It's the crowning point and very exciting because everything builds up to that point for Aida.

M I L N E S : I must admit that the duet with Aida is really special. There are so many emotions running through it. He has to convince her that if she doesn't betray the man she loves, the country will be in ruins. What could be more powerful than a father talking to his daughter that way and forcing her to do something like this? That one duet is really the reward for singing the role, and believe me, it's reward enough.

R A N K I N : I don't think an Aida and Amneris—a soprano and a mezzo—as personalities on a stage are ever going to clash. They work together to make the opera as good as they can. I've never had too much trouble with colleagues on the stage. I've always felt that most people want an entire opera to be successful.

A R R O Y O : We sometimes forget that we're not just singing notes to make it sound lovely. We're saying words that have meaning. And unless you know and care about the meaning of the words, a lot of the story is missing, and that's what we have to hold on to.

M I L L O : The main thing that I want to get into my Aida is that otherworld feeling, not just gimmicks or pretty sounds.

A R R O Y O : Aida is a real person. The few times I've complained, it was because the director saw her as the pitiful, subservient victim of the opera.

M I L L O : She never admits the confines of her tomb, just as she's never admitted the confines of her country or her love for Radames.

A M A R A : I used to play her as a temptress. When I did the role with Corelli, it was so funny because his wife would be watching from the wings. I would take my arms and move them down his sides and then grab his hands and play with the back of his hair just to entice him. I always enjoyed that.

M I T C H E L L : I listened to absolutely everyone when I was first learning the role. I kind of think that no one can go through the world without soaking up what has been done before you. You take a little bit from here and a little bit from there and try to make it your own.

M I L L O : Anyone who really loves opera has to be familiar with *Aida* because it is the grandest of grand operas. As a student, I listened to Tebaldi, Milanov, Ponselle, Rethberg singing various parts of the opera and I've always been in love with it. Though I've been influenced by other singers, even when you take things, it's always different in your own voice.

M I T C H E L L : I listened to Tebaldi, Callas, and Price and they were very important Aidas for me and they influenced my interpretation. I think they would have said the same about whoever came before them. It's the normal thing to do. When I was nineteen, I won some contest and I said, "I want to sing Aida," because it was the first opera I'd ever heard. So my high school teacher had me sing "Ritorna vincitor"—at nineteen! Now I'm singing Aida all over the world. Even then I felt in my heart it was something I wanted to do and it was right for me, and I knew nothing about the operatic world then. I just knew I wanted to do it.

A R R O Y O : I love her. I really do enjoy singing that part.

D U N N : I remember doing the role for the first time with Jimmy

Levine at the Hollywood Bowl. To do an *Aida* with him is a revelation, and you get rather spoiled with it because you feel that he uncovers things that you've never seen before and never will again.

B U M B R Y : The second *Aida* performance I did was at the Met. It was one of those nights where everyone was inspired by everyone else. Carlo Bergonzi started the evening off in grand style, and I mean grand style! He sang the "Celeste Aida" just as Verdi wrote it. Well, of course, when we heard this, we all knew without even speaking to each other what that meant. There was a glance which said, "I will not be outdone." Well, everyone gave their all that evening and the audience went wild. There's nothing more infectious than a friendly rivalry between artists of the first magnitude. It's too bad audiences don't have that kind of experience more today.

W A R F I E L D : My first Amneris was in Split, Yugoslavia. I was going to do it the following year in Zurich, so this was kind of a tryout for me. I was by myself and it was a wild occasion. We had a Bulgarian tenor who was rather aggressive, but he had the wrong girl. He should have been after Aida. In any case, besides running away from him and being sure I'd hit my B flat, I had to spend my money there because you couldn't bring it back. It was my first time away from my daughter and I wanted to get home. So I thought, "Well, I've done my first Amneris and it went very well. Now I can do it in Zurich and I don't have to worry." So I went to the airport and gave them all my money and said, "Just get me on a plane now. Just get me out of here." I remember thinking it was just like in a movie. I don't do things like that! After that, I did Amneris all over the place.

R A N K I N : I debuted as Amneris when I was about twenty at the Brooklyn Academy of Music. Then I went to Europe and began singing it in German in Switzerland, and then I went to the Vienna State Opera in the early fifties and sang it in German also, and in Italian, depending on whether the cast was more Italian or German.

D U N N : Amneris is one of those parts where you don't get it right the first time. You need ten performances at least before you even begin to cut through. You may sing all the notes, but you need at least those ten before you even begin to understand such a role.

A M A R A : My first Aida was at the baths of Caracalla. It was in 1954 and that is some theater in which to break in a role you've never sung before. We rehearsed onstage, so that was all right, but we never had all the people or the chariot, and I didn't speak that much Italian. We did the first and second acts one day, and the third and fourth the next. We never went through the whole thing at one time. Well, in the performance, I was embracing Amonasro, Tito Gobbi, and the whole back of the stage looked like it was on fire, and I said to him, "The place is on fire!" and he said, "No, that's fireworks. It's part of the production." "Well," I thought, "thanks for telling me." We had none of that during rehearsals. I also wasn't told that a camel was going to walk across the stage during the Nile scene, but one did. And he left his calling card, and then I had to go out there and be on my hands and knees. Let me tell you, I had to be really careful. They also spelled my name as "Lucianna" on the billboard. I guess they wanted to make me Italian.

Animals onstage are often dangerous. The obvious examples are the stories about the horses in *Carmen* followed by the man with the shovel. When Eleanor Steber rode onstage, leading another horse, to rescue Mario del Monaco in *The Girl of the Golden West,* the tenor slipped his neck out of the noose and fled the stage, due to the sudden onset of a severe allergy to horses.

A M A R A : At Caracalla when Radames was supposed to come in, he had always walked in at rehearsals. During the first performance, four white horses came galloping down the stage and came to the very edge of the orchestra before they stopped. If you don't think that was frightening! I thought they were all going to go right into the pit.

Giovanni Martinelli, a legendary Radames, was able to sing the role throughout his career by watching his diet. Before each performance, he would drink beaten raw eggs and eat a "light supper" of so-called Risotto Martinelli. The latter consisted of nineteen mushrooms, one pound of veal kidneys, and six tomatoes simmered for two hours in an onion, oil, and garlic base, and served over hot steamed rice with a thick coating of Parmesan cheese. One can only wonder how the many Aidas he sang with reacted to the aftereffects of this light supper, but it obviously had no adverse effect on Rose Bampton.

B A M P T O N : I sang so many times with Martinelli. I sang so many roles with him. He was wonderful. And Pinza! And Bruna Castagna was a wonderful Amneris. She had such a wonderful, rich voice for it. She was just great.

Remembrances of past performances of *Aida* seem to come easily to artists who have been involved with the work.

D U N N : I must have done hundreds of performances of the role now, both here and in South America, plus Europe of course.

M I L L O : One time in Caracalla, the messenger didn't come on and there was dead silence. So the maestro started singing the role. He said, "I'll sing it for you." He was a wonderful young conductor, Daniel Oren, and fortunately he had a big voice. So he did it and the mezzo just came in later.

W A R F I E L D : The Amneris I did in Vienna for the first time was as a replacement. Jimmy [her husband, James McCracken] was there singing and they asked me at the last minute because I was there to be with him. It was New Year's Eve. I had just done it in Zurich two night before. I didn't know the cast, but at least I recognized Jimmy, so that was a big plus. Forgive me for saying this, but when they had me dressed, they said they didn't know what they had vocally, but they certainly had a beautiful Amneris. The costume and headdress were magnificent. It turned out to be a big success for me and I was asked back right away. It was an important step in my career.

B A M P T O N : When I auditioned at the Met, I was working with Serafin, and he said so many times, "Rose, when you are going to do Aida, no matter where you are, you must come to me to prepare it. I know you can do a fine Aida, but I want to be the one to teach it to you." I was in London singing what I thought was the next-to-last Amneris at Covent Garden, and I got a telegram from New York that I was to do my first Aida in Warsaw. I cabled Serafin, and he cabled back immediately, "Come." So I flew to Rome and stayed there for two weeks working with him every day, which was just great because he was a great master.

M I T C H E L L : My first Aida was in Berlin in 1984 and my son had just been born. He was two months old and it was just pandemonium.

Anyone with a child knows that your baby at that time is not even on a schedule, and then to take him to Germany? It was just crazy. But those performances went so well—I did five—and I remember my manager saying that he thought I'd been doing the role for years. I don't know why, but it all just came together in spite of the minuses. We also had a wonderful cast. That helped.

A R R O Y O : I remember the horror of the first time I did Aida in Salzburg, and the man playing Amonasro had not come to rehearsal and I did not even know who he was. I was running to my father and almost screaming, "Which is Father? Which is Father?" And it's funny. People laugh now. But then it was a nightmare.

W A R F I E L D : I remember another performance in Zurich. I had done *Orfeo* in Geneva the night before, but at that time, I felt I could do things like that. So I got on the train thinking everything was fine and I'd get to the theater by one and have time to prepare. Then I remembered that all my costumes were in Dübendorf, which is about ten kilometers from the center of Zurich. So I got out of the train and raced for a cab and fortunately found a sympathetic driver who got me there, waited while I got the costumes, and delivered me to the theater. Everyone was outside waiting for me on the steps, but the performance did go on.

B U M B R Y : In 1972, I did my first Aida, and it wasn't the Aida that I do today, which I find very, very beautiful and among the best that I know of today.

M I L A N O V : People now don't do the job that they should do because they don't devote their lives to it, and you have to do that. You can't have an easy life if you want to make a career. You can't stay out late at night. You can't eat too much. It's not easy.

B U M B R Y : I'm very happy that I waited to sing Aida. Now I have two points of view, from both Amneris's angle and Aida's. It's been a godsend for me to be doing this role now in such abundance. In the past I sang Aida as a little lift for myself, but now I'm concentrating on it more and more.

M I L L O : This was the opera of my debut in Salt Lake City in 1980 and even then I didn't view her as difficult. It's the type of role you're either born to sing or you never sing well.

M I L A N O V : You have to work on it all of your life. You need the softness, the mezza voce that Verdi would like, and that means soft, sweet sounds, and then the full force. You're never ready, really. With a new partner it always changes and you always need to rehearse. The Metropolitan is a big stage and to sing your first Aida there is a big challenge.

M I L L O : For me, she's now my oldest friend, and she remains fresh every time I sing it.

F R E N I : When I started I was singing Micaëla and Mimì and I never thought I would sing Aida. That was, for me, a big surprise. For me, I never thought to sing those big roles. Perhaps I just grew up slowly, slowly, you know? Karajan asked me to do the Aida and I was very worried about it, naturally. I thought I would try, but I needed time, and it took me four years. I started to look at it, and then I'd leave it and go back, and this was over and over. And then I said, "Maestro, I'll try, but if I feel it's too heavy for me onstage I'll say good-bye and I'll go home." And he said, "OK, OK!" He agreed, but every-thing worked out fine. I had a very nice feeling with Karajan and it's the same with Kleiber and Jimmy Levine. We understand each other without even speaking. We are always together.

B U M B R Y : I think you can sing the role too early. If you're too young, you could do your voice real damage, unless you have one of those flexible, freak voices that are part dramatic and part lyric. I don't think a really young person would have the proper intelli-gence to sing it in a safe fashion. You can sing all the notes, but what happens when you don't have all that youthful power behind you? Then you'd have to learn the proper technique and start all over and learn how to sing the role.

M I L L O : So far the role has presented no real problems for me and I've sung it under every sort of possible condition.

M I T C H E L L : I waited to sing it and I'm glad that I did wait until my mid-thirties. I could have done it, and of course I was asked to, when I was in my twenties, but I choose not to. I feel longevity is the key to singing.

M I L L O : I feel that at every performance I've managed to say some-thing with the role, so of course it's very satisfying for me.

A M A R A : I haven't heard any Aida voices coming along lately. Age isn't as important as vocal stamina and color. The first time I sang Aida, I was twenty-nine. My first Met Aida was five years later, and I was certainly better prepared, but it wasn't just a question of age.

I'm glad, though, that I wasn't allowed to sing it earlier, because I probably wasn't ready for it. A dramatic voice doesn't mature until you're between thirty-five and forty. You have to wait.

B U M B R Y : I don't know why young singers today can't take their time. Aida is like Eboli is for the mezzo or Don Giovanni is for the bass-baritone. You have to give yourself some time. You can't just go out and sing it.

M I L L O : I'm heartened by the way my voice is going, because it's not getting less, it's getting bigger. A role always changes with vocal maturity. I'm getting the richness and sureness you need for a Norma, which is where I'm heading.

M I T C H E L L : I think if you start singing Aida in your twenties, well . . . You know both Madame Tebaldi and Callas did that and for whatever reason—be it psychological or what—their voices were both beginning a decline by the time they were my age. I think it was because they did sing this kind of repertory rather early. Still, they both made fabulous, fabulous music, and the recordings! Still, I'm glad I started Aida and the other Verdi roles much later.

THE TALES OF HOFFMANN

~

I actually did a Hoffmann
with a man named Hoffmann—Horst Hoffmann,
who sang it with me in Australia.
He sings a lot there and has a
damned good voice.

–JOAN SUTHERLAND

Music by Jacques Offenbach
Libretto from a play by Jules Barbier and Michel Carré
based on the stories of E.T.A. Hoffmann

OLYMPIA.. *Judith Blegen, Laurel Hurley, Erie Mills, Patrice Munsel, Roberta Peters*

GIULIETTA .... *Rosalind Elias, Carol Vaness*

ANTONIA.. *Roberta Alexander, Lucine Amara, Judith Blegen, Carol Vaness*

ALL THREE LADIES.................... *Anna Moffo, Jarmila Novotná, Joan Sutherland*

NICKLAUSSE...................................... *Frances Bible*

ANTONIA'S MOTHER................. *Frances Bible, Sandra Warfield*

HOFFMANN.. *Jerry Hadley, Alfredo Kraus, Neil Shicoff*

FOUR VILLAINS .... *Martial Singher*

GUEST APPEARANCE................ *Régine Crespin*

*T*he *Tales of Hoffmann* first saw the light of day in a two-act version at the Paris Opéra-Comique on February 10, 1881. The plot centers on a young poet, Hoffmann, and his search for his true love, the prima donna Stella. He is thwarted in his quest by Councillor Lindorf, who, in three villainous disguises, tries to destroy the poet. This search for true love takes Hoffmann to Paris, where he finds the doll Olympia; to Venice, where he is entrapped by the courtesan Giulietta; and to Munich, where he is smitten by the doomed soprano Antonia. The Epilogue finds Hoffmann alone and drunk in Nuremberg while Lindorf walks away with Stella. The Venetian act was not performed at the opera's premiere.

Now, in its standard form, the opera consists of a prologue, three acts, and an epilogue. Offenbach's only grand opera is a prime example of truly French music, and has provided a challenge for singers for over a hundred years.

ALFREDO KRAUS: I first started singing the French repertory in Italian at the beginning of my career in Italy. We sang every opera there in Italian. My first was *Manon,* and my debut as Werther was still in Italian. Eventually other managers and countries started asking me for different operas and I had to learn them in the original languages. It was difficult for me to go from Italian to French.

What was difficult for the Austrian singer was natural for Régine Crespin, a native of Marseilles.

RÉGINE CRESPIN: French opera is not so difficult. It is a little delicate, but so are the Russian, German, and Italian in their own way. French people have a kind of reserve. We don't show so much what we're thinking, what the feelings are. In French music, there's a little reservation of expression. This doesn't mean that we don't express our feelings, but it's not so outgoing like the Italians.

KRAUS: The change from Italian to French was a real challenge for me, but I found that French, for me, is the most beautiful language for singers. Now I'm happy about the results and everyone seems to like the way I sing French.

Baritone Martial Singher built a career on interpreting French music, a talent he has passed on since his retirement to such students as Judith Blegen, John Reardon, and Donald Gramm.

MARTIAL SINGHER: French music is not necessarily more difficult than any other, but it requires a sense of beauty, a sense of exact color of the vowels. For instance, an American singer, for all his mastery, will find very difficult the diphthonging of the vowels. Each vowel becomes entirely a different color.

LUCINE AMARA: I was always happy singing French music. The art songs have always been important to me and I've always been comfortable with the language and the style.

CRESPIN: For me, what is more difficult than the opera is French songs in recital, because the music is a little delicate. It's difficult to get the spirit.

SINGHER: First there is the sound of the language. For some reason, it is much easier to master the sound of German or Italian than to master the French. I have no explanation for that. In *Hoffmann* there is something in the lightness of the music, even in the orchestration, which is typically French. Also the parts are written in a very melodic way, and they have to be sung with the idea of having the melodic line, and not at all the overpowering quantity of voice. For some of my colleagues, there was a little difficulty there.

KRAUS: I think I have the feeling for the time and the expression of all these beautiful operas I sing. The last opera I sang onstage was *Hoffmann,* and it is certainly a beautiful work, but it is long, very long for the tenor. The extremes, the limits, of the work really test my voice. The tenor has to both sing and act a lot, all evening.

SINGHER: *Hoffmann* is a very beautiful opera. Its simplicity sometimes fails to impress some particularly "sophisticated" persons. It's extremely frank. There is not one moment in the opera when complicated music is written for the sake of writing music. From the beginning, the melodies are flowing freely in such a natural way that people sometimes fail to notice the continuous beauty of the melodic line throughout the opera.

Within the opera, Hoffmann has affairs with three women who represent the different sides of all women, and a pathetic lot they are:

Olympia, a mechanical doll; Giulietta, a courtesan with no feelings; and Antonia, a girl dying of consumption or something else, but definitely dying.

JUDITH BLEGEN: I first started my professional career in Nuremberg in about 1967 and my first role there was Olympia. I see now how poignant that was, because I played her exactly as she should be played. She's a little doll and I was a little doll for so many years. I worked for hours and hours getting every little movement just so. And now looking back at it as both an artist and a woman, I see I was just some little girl, a pretty little thing who didn't really have any brains, just doing what she was told—just like Olympia! It was perfect. Now I'd have to work hard to do that, and there are parts of me that would find it very difficult.

JARMILA NOVOTNÁ: In New York, I sang Antonia and Giulietta. I sang all three of them in Vienna, and I also played Stella.

CAROL VANESS: My first *Hoffmann* was in San Francisco and it was my first job ever. They cast me as Giulietta because I could sing both the high and the low notes. Well, I came out and the bass had this big aria about the diamond ring and blah, blah, blah. So he hands me the ring and it's huge, because we were playing outside and it had to be seen. He put it on my finger, and the stone fell out and I caught it in my other hand. I didn't know what to do. Now I'd say, "What the hell! Who cares about the ring?" But then I spent ten minutes walking around with one hand in front of the other, holding the diamond where it should be and pretending it was still on my finger. Then everyone comes out and you have to do the ensemble and finish the act, and I couldn't do anything because I was still holding the stupid ring. It's funny now. Believe me, it wasn't then.

NEIL SHICOFF: I always say to coaches, "Isn't there another Hoffmann we can find, another role that would be just right for me?" and they sometimes say, *"Pique Dame,"* but that's a little heavy for me. We'll have to wait for that one. All these neurotic, crazy parts!

VANESS: The next time I did the opera was my Antonia at the New York City Opera. It was one of those things where I had no rehearsal, but I did know the role, but that was about it. Well, in that production, Antonia disappears through the mirror. However, they didn't tell me that there was a step when you went through the mirror. So I finished the act and was congratulating myself, thinking I had done pretty well, and I walked through the mirror and proceeded to fall flat on my face. I must be a very clumsy person, I don't know.

In the opera's first full-length version, the composer had the Antonia or Munich act precede the section in Venice with Giulietta. That version went out of style for a long time and the Antonia act was placed after Giulietta. Now both versions are used at the discretion of the director.

SINGHER: A production I recently saw in Los Angeles had, I believe, some twenty-five more minutes of music than the version we used to sing at the Met, and I'm not sure it's an improvement. It seems to me that by the time *Tales of Hoffmann* became part of the usual repertoire, it had to be accepted the way it was. It had found a kind of natural balance by the passing of the years and being performed in a particular way. Now, adding new material creates an imbalance. For instance, in this Los Angeles production, the act in Venice was extremely overlong, creating almost the impression of boredom. I prefer the score the way we had it in the fifties.

ROSALIND ELIAS: Stage directors are going overboard these days. They're taking too many liberties with the score and the libretto. Sometimes they go too far and make too many changes and it just doesn't work.

SINGHER: I think that the modification that has been made recently in the order of the opera is a good one. The first love of Hoffmann's is so obviously not a real person that it requires a great deal of naïveté to believe that he falls for her. The second love is Antonia. Then he is a serious man trying to find a serious love and there is a certain amount of maturity involved. If the Venetian act is played third, then he's fallen into the life of pleasure. The evolution of the character is so much clearer if you have, one, Olympia; two, Antonia; and three, Giulietta. Recently I think it has almost become the rule.

The leading lady in the first act is a mechanical doll. The morbid and macabre stories of German author E.T.A. Hoffmann were the basis for the libretto. This, coupled with Offenbach's affinity for light operetta, could have reduced the scope of the work. It is a testament to the composer's genius that *Hoffmann* is considered a grand opera.

NOVOTNÁ: The doll is, of course, absolutely an automaton. Vocally it is so staccato that it's very demanding. Not like Giulietta, where you have the lovely "Barcarolle," which is beautiful, and Antonia, which is the most appealing role vocally.

PATRICE MUNSEL: I have no idea really of how I approached the role of Olympia. It was so long ago. She's certainly mechanical and maybe I brought too much realism, too much humanism to the role. It was very difficult to play. I wish I had done it later when my voice was more mature and then I could have done all three roles, which would have been marvelous.

ROBERTA PETERS: Olympia was pure fun. Of course, she only appears in the first act, but there's so much to the part. Acting it is very challenging. You'd be surprised how hard it is to make gestures that are so mechanical and do it well while you're moving around the stage. Acting her is a huge challenge.

JOAN SUTHERLAND: She's bounded by her mechanism, but I think one can make a great deal of the way she moves, the way she reacts and so on. Actually I think that it's rather fun that she is mechanical.

MUNSEL: But Olympia must have a human core someplace to have all these people so attracted to her. There must have been something else in her that was not just exemplified by the doll.

PETERS: The other big challenge is the aria, the one big aria that she has. It sits very high and needs a lot of agility and good breath control. That aria isn't done very often because it's much harder than one would suppose.

Her early training as a dancer was helpful to soprano Laurel Hurley when she first enacted Hoffmann's doll.

LAUREL HURLEY: I did the role first at City Opera and it was Tommy Schippers who talked me into doing it. At that time, I was doing mostly lyric roles and not the coloratura. In fact, I did the Countess before I did Susanna. Also, I did thirty or forty performances of Mimì before I ever did Musetta. It was Tommy who brought me back to being a coloratura.

P E T E R S : Olympia actually is very hard because you can't do much. You have to get the words out and adhere to the mechanical things constantly so that people will believe in her. The difficulty is you have to keep yourself rigid to do that, but you can't be rigid and still sing. It's very different from anything I've ever done.

H U R L E Y : When they were doing *Hoffmann* at City Opera, Tommy and I were both there and he said I should do the doll, and I really didn't believe it. I did that production with Robert Rounseville and then went on to do it at the Met, where the production was very different.

M U N S E L : My fondest memory of that role was that Pinza was playing in the production. I had one exit way, way upstage and then I had to make an entrance very quickly downstage. Well, I would run like mad during rehearsals, and one day Pinza said to me, "Darling, I'll pick you up and bring you down to the stage." So every night I'd jump into his arms and he'd carry me down for my entrance so I'd still have breath to sing. Now I think, "Oh, if only I'd been less naïve." I was so mad for that man. He was so adorable. Nobody has ever touched him. He had the most fabulous sensuality that was breathtaking. I still really can't hear anyone else in *South Pacific*. He was so warm and so glorious. A marvelous man!

S U T H E R L A N D : In the majority of performances I've done she has definitely just been a doll, but that's really not up to me, is it? Everything implies that she's a doll. She's only human in Hoffmann's eyes when he's got the spectacles on. But she is a doll. In the majority of the productions I've done, the people at the party have been dolls, too. If they're all automatons, I don't see why Olympia should be different, and anyway, I think it's sort of fun.

H U R L E Y : I remember one time my left shoulder strap fell down while I was sitting on a chair or a settee or whatever. As a doll I couldn't do anything about it because I couldn't feel it. If I were singing a human being, there would have been many ways to fix it easily. This was just hopeless. I tried to get people who who came up to me to adjust it, but they might have been afraid because it wasn't called for, or they didn't hear me or whatever, but I was helpless. I had to wait until I got offstage to adjust it.

In November of 1955, Cyril Ritchard's production of *Hoffmann* opened at the Met. The production, which has now achieved almost historic status, featured Martial Singher, Roberta Peters, Risë Stevens, Lucine Amara, and Richard Tucker, with Pierre Monteux conducting.

P E T E R S : Cyril Ritchard was great. It was very different from working with some of the other stage directors who knew the roles very well but from another perspective. He was very theatrical and wanted all kinds of theatrical things. He wanted very pouty kinds of faces from the doll. He would come up to everybody in the cast and discuss the roles with us. Working on the ending with him, where Olympia goes whirling around before she winds up in a heap, was wonderful.

A M A R A : I remember Cyril Ritchard with great love. I had just gotten back from Glyndebourne when we started rehearsals, and I had an English accent you wouldn't believe. While we were rehearsing, I spoke exactly as he did. The way he directed Richard Tucker and myself was wonderful. I loved it when Richard would sit at the stage piano, which had no keyboard, and really make you feel that he was playing.

E L I A S : When I worked with Cyril on *Hoffmann,* we had already worked together on *Périchole.* He was delightful and a very kind man, a lot of fun, very campy, a wonderful sense of humor. I really liked him.

P E T E R S : Richard Tucker was in that cast and he was a wonderful Hoffmann, and Alessio de Paolis was just marvelous. He was the one who cranked me up when the doll sort of collapses in the middle of the aria. A great character singer and actor!

H U R L E Y : My son, James, was just a little boy when I was doing Olympia, and he was the only child I ever saw who was allowed to sit on the stage during the piano rehearsal at the old Met. You know, they would put chairs along the edge of the stage, so he got to sit there and watch his mother. I remember Mr. Bing—he was still just *Mr.* Bing at that time—came over and shook his hand and very formally introduced himself to James. He asked him, "Do you want to be a singer when you grow up, like your mother?" and James said, "No, sir, I'd like to be a stagehand." At that time, Mr. Bing was going through contract negotiations with the stagehands' union, and he turned around and said to me, "He has a point! He has a point!"

A M A R A : Nicolai Gedda was a wonderful Hoffmann, too. When I
was singing with him, I used to have a problem with nerves attack-
ing my stomach, which caused me to burp. I found out much later
what was causing it. I used to drink a lot of coffee with meals and
that would hit my stomach and I'd be filled with gas, and before
going onstage I was constantly burping. Well, offstage Nicolai
would really outburp me. I would do it and he'd come back even
louder. But we had a wonderful time together—what a great colleague!

B L E G E N : When I think of *Hoffmann,* the place of honor goes to
Martial Singher. He taught me at Curtis and I married his second
son. I was so taken with Martial. Artistically my first allegiance is to
him. He just inspired me, not only with *Hoffmann* but with all my
roles.

S I N G H E R : Returning to the opera, I should stress that it has to be
performed with an idea of elegance. Even the sinister parts should not
be sinister in the way you would deal with, say, *Frankenstein.* There
is a kind of measure which is typical of the French style, and it should
never fall into ugliness or slapstick. Olympia should be a dainty little
doll and not a monster; Giulietta as a courtesan should have class and
not fall into vulgarity; and Antonia should be an aristocratic young
woman, and not an invalid in a wheelchair. We must avoid the
extreme exaggerations.

Offenbach wrote nearly a hundred frothy, extremely popular operettas, only a few of which survive. Like the clown longing to play
Hamlet, he always aspired to serious work. *Hoffmann,* his one grand
opera, was left unfinished at his death. Because of this there has always
been controversy about the order of the three acts and debate over
whether one, two, or three divas should be employed to compete for
Hoffmann's love.

K R A U S : For some singers, doing all three roles in the opera works,
but musically speaking, I think I would always prefer three different
women. After all, they have nothing in common. One is a doll, the
other a courtesan, and the third his real romantic love. I don't think
the voice and the music and the feeling are all different, so why have
just one woman?

SUTHERLAND: I did all three roles very early at Covent Garden, but I never did them all together. We did them in English, actually, and I was never first cast for any of them. There were several other people doing the roles. I was scheduled to do Antonia first, but actually my first was Olympia. I sang it after at least two imported ladies. In fact, I think they were trying to get rid of me by having me sing it. It was a matter of singing Olympia and Aida within one week. Maybe they were trying to kill my desire to sing the coloratura since they wanted me in the Strauss and Wagner field.

ANNA MOFFO: I think it was written for one soprano. That's Hoffmann's dream. He always falls in love with the the same face. By the same token, the bass-baritone should always be the same. It's a flashback. It's not just an excuse for a soprano to have a *tour de force*. She really should have the same face.

SUTHERLAND: I did the doll first and then I think I'm right in saying I did Giulietta and Antonia together. At that time, in that production, it would have been nearly impossible to switch from the doll makeup to the others in time. So there we are.

MOFFO: It had never been done at the Met before, with one soprano singing all three, when I did it, and I was challenged by the whole thing. Actually, each part in its own way felt very good to me.

SUTHERLAND: I did them all together for the first time in Seattle, which was the basis for the production we brought to the Met.

SHICOFF: I suppose ideally, from the director's point of view, all three women should be played by one person. It really doesn't matter that much to me how it's done, because they are all different women but still the same—different aspects of one personality.

SINGHER: It's much more difficult for one soprano than it is for the baritone. It's very difficult to have a person who can sing coloratura and also dramatic. The difference in voices for the women is much stronger than for the four men. It has been very seldom that the impersonation of the three parts, plus Stella, by one woman has been successful.

SHICOFF: Actually, the more I think about it, I suppose it is better if they are the same with one person doing it.

SUTHERLAND: I definitely think it should be one soprano.

Hoffmann was slightly kinky and he saw one woman in all these people. I like to think so, anyway. He had this yearning, longing for something, and as these three women entered his life they did it as separate people, but they were indeed one. I know the original idea was for one woman to sing them all, so that should say it.

H U R L E Y : I think if a soprano can do it very well, it should be done by one person. I really wanted to do it. But I wonder how the audience feels about it. If you're paying a hundred dollars for a ticket, maybe you do want to see three separate artists. From a singer's viewpoint, doing all three is a lovely challenge, but it's very difficult because you have to change the vocal color so much. It's incredible.

M O F F O : The funniest thing about doing *Hoffmann* is that you go back to your dressing room after the first act, and you become Anna again. Then you put on another costume and go out and you're Giulietta. It's fun to be all these characters, but still you're Anna!

Tenor Jerry Hadley is a relative newcomer to *The Tales of Hoffmann,* but received a baptism by fire in the Canadian Opera's lavish new production.

J E R R Y H A D L E Y : I think the three women are metaphors for various stages in his life. It also depends a lot on which version you do. With the Antonia act last, he moves from a youthful affection to the feelings of love we all have when we fall in love in a big way with somebody for the first time. Also, with that trio at the end, you go out with a bigger bang, as it were.

S H I C O F F : The women all represent decades, eras in a man's life. When you're young, you can't see past the surface. You just look at gorgeous blue-green eyes and think you're in love and that's it. We all go through that. Then it depends on the version what happens next. I think it should be Antonia second and Giulietta third. I prefer it that way because I think you have to show that he really falls in love and is hurt in the Antonia scene. She's the one love that he has. Then he goes over the line and goes with Giulietta, the courtesan. That order is the best way for me to deal with who he is.

H A D L E Y : If you assume that these episodes are metaphorical and not real, having one woman helps the metaphor. The symbolism then is consistent, particularly if the villains are all played by the same man. But then it becomes a practicality. Can the same woman sing Olympia and Giulietta? Hoffmann is demanding for us but it's monstrously difficult for the girls.

KRAUS: I feel you need a light soprano for the first act, a mezzo-soprano for the second, and a lyric for the third. It's especially important to have a different sound for Antonia because she is a singer and should sound special. You have to define the characters with different voices. In any case, I love the opera and there are so many beautiful, romantic phrases in it.

SUTHERLAND: I can understand why tenors might like the Venice act last, but for me it certainly lies better singing Antonia last. If you're doing all three, Giulietta lies a bit low to sing at the end. I think the Antonia scene is a much better climax for the opera, too.

SHICOFF: The act with Olympia is fun because it's basically comic. It's light, young, superficial. There's a part of all of us that makes us only look at beautiful people and that's what the scene basically means to me.

MOFFO: If you've ever had Shirley Temple curls, four-inch eyelashes, and a key in your back, it's impossible not to be Olympia as soon as you're onstage. You're wound up to go. She's the easiest to do, actually.

HADLEY: One of the interesting things about the opera is that Hoffmann is learning how to trust his instincts and allow them to take over so he can create. I found when I worried about pacing, I didn't sing as well as when I went from moment to moment.

SHICOFF: Getting back to the three voices, when I'm in the scene with Antonia, I do think, "Yeah, they're all part of the same package." All together they make up the personality of the woman he wants. The three are all part of Stella.

HADLEY: The villains all represent Hoffmann's fears.

SINGHER: I've read essays where they say the characters represent the secret will of Offenbach to destroy himself—a lot of really deep things have been written that we don't necessarily have to believe.

HADLEY: As for the villains, in the first act, Lindorf has to be related to as a flesh-and-blood character and a rival for Stella's affection. Hoffmann sees him as a rival, but I think he's just another of a long line of external forces which Hoffmann sees as obstructing him and preventing him from obtaining happiness. In fact, the happiness was there all along and he just never allowed it to be.

SINGHER: I think it's extremely interesting to have the singer who does the four villains change the character of his voice for each role. It really has to be done. Nothing is more boring for a singer, I believe, than to always have the same sound. It's difficult to do but it's worth trying.

HADLEY: What the villains are about is open to a lot of interpretations. Do they actually represent real people in Hoffmann's life? Or is it just someone there to blame when something goes wrong for us? "It's not my fault. The world is against me."

SINGHER: The first time I sang in *Hoffmann* at the Met, I was surprised to find the parts divided between different singers: I sang Dapertutto, Pinza was Coppelius and Miracle, and Mack Harrell sang Lindorf. But I think it was obvious from the beginning that the composer wanted the same man for all four. They are actually the same character and there must be some kind of common thread.

Unanimous rave reviews can bring a smile to the face of even the most hardhearted of opera managers. Rudolf Bing must have been grinning from ear to ear the day after his triumphant revival of *The Tales of Hoffmann* in 1955. Everyone involved was covered with glory. One critic remarked, "Richard Tucker [with] his beautiful arias easily filled the house. . . . Mr. Singher was his old self—versatile, artistic and reliable. . . . Miss Peters [was] charming as usual. . . . [Lucine Amara's voice] sailed and soared through the house true and pure." Those involved in the opening have fond memories, as do the other singers who followed them in that now-historic production.

AMARA: It sounds immodest, but those reviews were really sensational.

SINGHER: The four parts had never been performed at the Met, before I did it, by one artist—except, I believe, by Lawrence Tibbett once. So my first night I didn't win complete recognition, because the major part of the audience didn't realize it had been the same man. I think my colleagues all did very well in their interpretations, and they were all in very good voice. I remember I took particular pleasure in bringing them to mischief. It was a great pleasure to break

Olympia to pieces and to torment Giulietta and finally killing Antonia—not that I had any particular reason to be happy to kill Lucine Amara.

A M A R A : Martial Singher was an absolute joy. The perfect colleague.

H U R L E Y : I never realized that when I did Olympia I never blinked my eyes, until I got a letter from a lovely lady who said, "We were watching you through opera glasses and noticed you never blinked. How do you do that?" I never knew I did that. I just tried to become a doll and coordinate the movements and not think about it. Well, after that I was so conscious of it, I couldn't keep my eyes open for love or money. My eyes always watered. I just couldn't keep them open. But I loved that production.

Mezzo-soprano Frances Bible graduated from the relatively small role of the voice of Antonia's Mother to Hoffmann's best friend and confidant, Nicklausse.

F R A N C E S   B I B L E : Nicklausse is sort of a strange character because he's always in Hoffmann's shadow and kind of on the fringe of the action. I really didn't think that much about him as a character. I just learned the music and let him develop. I was never one of those people who went in for all that Method stuff. I just let it happen. As a teacher now, I don't recommend this for studying a role. You should do the research and history and everything. I was so into history when I was in school that I absorbed it all and then just used it when I was creating a role. Nicklausse and Hoffmann are kind of like Damon and Pythias. It's hard to explain. Nicklausse is always there to back his friend up. Men have friendships like this, I think. I don't know that women always do.

E L I A S : My first *Hoffmann* was actually on the Met stage. Giulietta's another weird lady. I seem to be drawn to them. Vocally, it's a very difficult role and I worked on that a lot. She's very high and there's a big ensemble and she stays up there through the whole thing.

S U T H E R L A N D : I think the Giulietta section is lovely. I always believed that you have to sing what you have to sing, so her music was no problem for me. You don't muck about with your production or anything. You just sing what you have. But I have to repeat, I like to do Antonia last. It is the perfect climax for the opera.

M O F F O : Giulietta, like most of the girls I do, is a courtesan. So that was just like going home.

E L I A S : She takes a lot of concentration, and if you're at all nervous, that concentration goes. It's a tough role, but it's gratifying because of the acting challenge—the sensuousness of the role, the weirdness, the decadence. Hoffmann's looking at her through rose-colored glasses. It's all his fantasy.

H U R L E Y : When I first came to the Met, Pierre Monteux was still conducting the work, and then Tommy Schippers took over. I loved the Met costume for Olympia. She was like a porcelain type of doll instead of a fun type—a caricature with strange makeup.

A M A R A : Sometimes some of our conductors would get carried away and they took the end trio so fast that it was hard to catch your breath and finish the Antonia act.

H U R L E Y : I made myself up at the Met and I had the blond wig, which was really very pretty. When I did *Show Boat* at City Opera, our director, Bill Hammerstein, took me to a makeup studio where they spent a lot of time to get the look he wanted, and I loved it. The makeup had a kind of shiny, porcelain glow and I used that for Olympia.

With a few exceptions, most sopranos feel an affinity for the tragic singer Antonia.

E R I E M I L L S : I shared a dressing room with Roberta Alexander on the Met's tour of Japan. I sang Olympia and went out and had a good time and then was through for the night. She had to prepare for Antonia all during the performance. I think I'll stick with Olympia!

R O B E R T A A L E X A N D E R : Antonia is really a difficult character to play because she dies singing. I mean, that's the first problem right there. There are a lot of us who wonder about that.

M O F F O : Antonia is like a lot of the other girls I do. They all get sick and die. She's a lovely, fragile figure, though.

A L E X A N D E R : It's a totally incongruous part because she sings a lot and it's very heavy and concentrated. You're standing there and singing your heart out and it's conceivable that after that you would want to die.

SHICOFF: I'd like to say that I wish the music in *Hoffmann* was thought of as stronger so that great conductors would be drawn to it more frequently. Jimmy Levine has conducted it, but I don't know of too many others who have. It isn't Wagner or Verdi for them.

AMARA: There's no way that *Hoffmann*'s insignificant musically. Antonia's first music is not easy. Then the trio! Ending the act on a high E-sharp and singing the C-sharp off in the wings and still being heard—that's not easy.

BIBLE: I enjoyed the music. It was fun. It's not very deep and you don't have that much to do with Nicklausse—just the one aria and then some other little things.

SINGHER: I believe that the version we did at the Met was the unaltered one. In recent years, researchers have found a lot of music which existed in manuscript but hadn't been performed. Now they're integrating that music into performances.

SHICOFF: I don't think it's the greatest music ever written for sure, but it is an all-around great piece—it's total, wonderful theater.

ALEXANDER: Antonia was difficult for me because I'm used to playing real gutsy, forceful characters. My husband said, "For once the people are going to love it because you're not out there beating up on some poor person."

NOVOTNÁ: The three ladies are completely different to play. I especially adored doing Antonia though, because it's such a challenge. She wants Hoffmann and still she loves her singing. Even though she knows that the singing would bring her death, she can't give up. Miracle says, "Go on, sing, sing, sing!" and she dies.

ALEXANDER: Antonia is very high, but there's a lot of middle as well. Usually if you have to sing like that, you've been singing all evening and you're all ready to go, but with her there's no time to warm up out there. That's a big challenge.

SUTHERLAND: I think Antonia is definitely my favorite lady to play. It just builds so well, you know. It's really a *tour de force* as far as acting and the music are concerned. It's really terrific writing.

NOVOTNÁ: Antonia is sensitive and very much in love with Hoffmann. But her desire to sing is so strong she just can't give it up, and Miracle is like the devil wanting to bring her death.

ALEXANDER: I feel she's doomed. From the moment you hear

the first chord, you know this girl isn't going to make it. One of the problems is not to play her as doomed. The same thing with Mimì. It's hard, because you know you're going to die because you've been rehearsing it.

AMARA: Not every soprano can sing Antonia. It sits in an area of the voice where you really need sound! People used to marvel that I would take that last high note offstage and they could still hear me!

BLEGEN: They are so beautiful together, Antonia and Hoffmann. She loves Hoffmann and she wants to marry him, but then she's inherited her mother's talent and she has to sing. She's going to find out she's up against it.

ALEXANDER: She's very young and she hasn't really experienced anything except the dream of seeing her mother, so that's what she wants, too. She has no idea what it's all about. I can identify with that. When I was seven years old, I saw my mother come out onstage in a fabulous black velvet gown and sing arias, and I thought, "I want to do that!" I just saw the glamour of it.

NOVOTNÁ: At one performance, Pinza was singing Miracle and I was sitting on a sofa. He suddenly comes up from the trap behind the sofa, starts to sing, and comes around to the other side. And they forgot to close the door. After we finished, he walked back there and he fell in. My God! At that moment, I thought, "Can I help him? Should I do something?" But somehow—it probably was not too low, and somebody helped him a little bit—and he finally came back up.

ALEXANDER: Antonia is very late in the evening. I first go on at ten to eleven or something at night. That's a long time to be waiting around. You have to keep your energy level down so you don't start bouncing off the walls and you have to start revving up at nine or ten when your energy is at its lowest.

NOVOTNÁ: Stella is the true love for Hoffmann. He was looking for this ideal in every woman. That he saw a real person in an automaton is amazing—but who knows? Maybe he was just after everything in a skirt.

AMARA: I never would have wanted to do all three roles. Never! You do need three different voices and they are three separate women. Stella, at the end, is still another and it's just not believable to have one person playing all four. It just doesn't make it.

P E T E R S : Did I ever want to sing Antonia? Did I ever want to sing Salome or Tosca? Yes, yes, yes. When I come back in the next life, I'm going to do all those juicy roles. I love them, but not in this life.

M I L L S : No, I think I'll stick with Olympia. She's really comfortable for me and I am always the first one to get to the cast parties.

P E T E R S : I could never sing those other roles, even though some sopranos do. The most lyric parts I've ever sung were Mimì and Violetta and I waited to sing them. I don't go any deeper than that, because for my voice I just don't feel it's right.

B I B L E : I enjoyed singing the Mother. It was really something you could sink your teeth into. It was the role I did first. The Mother was in a picture frame and then for some reason, the way it was staged at City Opera, she got out of the frame and walked down onto the stage, and then went and got back into the frame. It was an odd idea, and later I think she just stayed in the frame, but it was interesting.

At the start of her career, Sandra Warfield also found herself a living portrait, at the Met.

S A N D R A   W A R F I E L D : I had never seen the opera before I was in it. That's the way it was for most young American singers back then. There I was, out on that huge stage standing behind this frame. I was just supposed to come to life when I started to sing. But it was great music and I loved that. Tucker was fabulous and Lucine Amara was a wonderful Antonia. We had a great cast—Martial Singher was fabulous.

A L E X A N D E R : That trio when the Mother's portrait comes to life is exhausting. The first time I did it with an orchestra, with the music and action, I was wiped out. I mean, I was so glad to die. I was happy to lie on the floor and say, "Oh, yeah, you really do die from this."

W A R F I E L D : The part of the Mother is, of course, totally static. I just remember standing there and singing the hell out of it because I wanted to make sure that my voice got out when I was stuck upstage in a box. I really gave that little part everything I had. It's a great opera and what an incredible production that was!

B I B L E : Once in Chicago, I did both Nicklausse and the Mother. I had to put the dress on over the boy's costume and get into the picture frame, and then get the dress off and get out of the frame and run onstage. I was very busy.

B L E G E N : Children are helpless against their mothers and that's part of the message in this act. It's an eternal theme. So Antonia sings and she's abandoned. When she collapses everyone runs in, but where have they been? Men abandon women. They do. I find that very poignant. None of them were around at the last minute and she dies that way.

A L E X A N D E R : Even in her most excited moments there is something fragile about Antonia. And she is totally manipulated by men. But that's opera! I was watching *Butterfly* on TV the other night and I just wanted to run up to Pinkerton and smack him. Some characters aren't manipulated—Salome and the sisters in *Così* and Despina. They all actually manipulate the male characters.

A M A R A : The poor thing. She just goes on singing and singing, and if you had a heart condition, of course you could expire. The part was always very believable to me.

A L E X A N D E R : It's so concentrated, too. Everything you're doing is crammed into twenty minutes at the most. You also don't have much time to communicate that this is a real woman. If I were a magician, I'd like to sing all three roles, but I'm definitely not an Olympia.

S I N G H E R : In that production, I was very happy to be the winner over Tucker. It's not often the baritone is the winner at the end of the opera. In this, the tenor is constantly fooled and betrayed and it's a pleasure for the baritone who does that. In *Hoffmann,* the bass-baritone triumphs.

A L E X A N D E R : Singing and death does seem to have a perverse attraction—that what you love to do is going to kill you. In a way, that's what happens when you go out there. You're putting yourself on the line somehow. You want people to like you you, and if they don't, you hurt inside.

S U T H E R L A N D : I actually did a *Hoffmann* with a man named Hoffmann—Horst Hoffmann, who sang it with me in Australia. He sings a lot there and has a damned good voice.

S H I C O F F : I believe—immodest as it sounds—I make a stamp on Hoffmann. I wish that all my roles were like that. Unfortunately, they're not.

H A D L E Y : I think Neil Shicoff is fantastic in the role. I liked Nicolai Gedda, too. He was so stylish and elegant.

S H I C O F F : With Olympia, I play Hoffmann extremely young and naïve and sweet. You can prove that point about his youth if he goes from Olympia to Giulietta. Then he becomes more mature and he's ready for Antonia . . . but you know, I just can't agree with that even as I say it. He should rise up out of the ashes at the end and not be in despair.

S U T H E R L A N D : He's so misled, so misguided. He's duped! I really feel sorry for the poor man. He's such a sympathetic character and it's not his fault. He's put upon by everyone—the villains and the women. He's taken in by Olympia and then used by Giulietta and everyone else.

S H I C O F F : Hoffmann is unable to cope with what he has to offer. He can't live with it. That's at the center of the creativity of that part. You live out what you think great artists and writers are like, and that's what Hoffmann's about. He can't cope with creating and that's the emphasis of the part for me.

H A D L E Y : I like the Giulietta act last because I know it works that way as a steady progression to debauchery. This finally leaves Hoffmann backed into a corner and he has nowhere to go except to give in to the Muse, whether he wants to or not. Obviously it also works with Antonia last, but you have to put yourself in a different set of gears to make the transition.

S H I C O F F : Hoffmann can end the opera either up or down and that depends upon the version you do. He can end it where he's crashed down and nothing's accomplished or where he's found himself at last. There are so many different colors to the piece and you know every director is going to have his say, even to reversing the acts.

H A D L E Y : It also depends on which Prologue or Epilogue you use. I've done the version where Nicklausse and the Muse are one. The Muse has an aria about her poor Hoffmann in the Prologue, then the audience sees her assume the guise of Nicklausse. In that version she has a lot more to sing and almost becomes his alter ego. Then in the Epilogue, she comes on as the Muse again and raises him like a phoenix out of his own ashes.

S H I C O F F : My favorite part of the opera is the Epilogue. I liked myself best there in both the recording and the videotapes I've done. I just wish the opera was more set and the Giulietta act was always at the end. I like to think that he goes from a pure, beautiful love that doesn't work to the courtesan. I just can't see the progression from Olympia to Giulietta. That makes no sense at all to me.

H A D L E Y : The vocal challenges of the role are monstrous. In a sense, you have to have different voices throughout the evening for each section. You constantly have to shift gears, interpretively and stylistically. It's very difficult.

S H I C O F F : When I sing other roles like Don Carlos, I sing more technically than I do in *Hoffmann*. During the evening, there's a complete metamorphosis of a personality. It can be like his turning into a butterfly if it's directed like that.

H A D L E Y : I think Hoffmann's a role that defies a concise definition. It's about searching and trying to find your way as a human being and an artist. It is possible to rise above the normal, workaday stuff we have to do and get in touch with your higher, creative self—in spite of who you are.

S H I C O F F : Hoffmann is a part that I am. I don't do anything. I just am. From the moment I walk onstage, I start digging into my guts and dealing with what I'm feeling in my life and what I think Hoffmann is feeling, and then I become him. It's totally reacting.

H A D L E Y : It's also a bloody long role and I don't think there are many things harder to sing in opera than the aria with Giulietta—it's just abysmally difficult if you're not really on top of your technique. It just climbs up by semitones and just hangs there. And Hoffmann's onstage all night.

S H I C O F F : It's not just the character, but the music also touches me. Once again, I don't think it's great music, but it's so right for the piece and it really gets to me.

H A D L E Y : Hoffmann is, experientially, a lot older than you think, but it's a paradox you run into in opera a lot. Many of the romantic tenor leads are youthful people, but in order to bring substance to them, I'm not sure you can do them as a young singer, as a beginner. A twenty-five-year-old couldn't meet the demands. I know I couldn't at that age. Maybe that's one of the great things about what we do for a living. It forces us to stay young, in a sense, doesn't it? At least in our outlook.

S H I C O F F : I have trouble with my own talent and that's why I've always felt close to Hoffmann emotionally. It's a part that's tailor-made for my psyche. It's one reason that it shines above all the other roles I do. When I do this part, it's a perfect, total experience for me in every way.

HADLEY: When he loses Antonia, I always think, "Is this also about our fears as performers, of not having the 'normal' life and giving up the white picket fence and the two-car garage and all we were brought up to believe in?" In my mind it triggered all sorts of tangential considerations.

SHICOFF: I take the character as I find him in each scene and I never think of him as being horrible. He's just always satisfying.

HADLEY: You know, there's this cliché about the suffering artist—that you can't really be creative unless you've suffered. I'm not sure I buy that completely, but in the case of Hoffmann, he ultimately realizes that those things he initially views as liabilities turn out to be his greatest assets.

SHICOFF: Sometimes I get too nervous or there's something in my personal life that doesn't let me concentrate fully on what I'm doing. I'm an extraordinarily emotional person and that comes totally from my environment, from the moment—absolutely. And that's why this part, which is a very emotional one for me, is so important.

HADLEY: I found when I was exploring it on the stage that I was dragging around a lot of old baggage. I was forced to confront the demons that lurk around my creative self. I think in a sense that's what Hoffmann's dilemma is. The Muse is constantly hovering about Hoffmann. But the question Hoffmann has to ask is "Do I want to take the easy way out and become everyone's friend and the life of the party and tell all these wonderful stories? Or do I follow my higher instincts and really start to create?"

SHICOFF: It's a varied part, and dirty, in the sense that the guy always has his fingernails on the floor. He's out there all night trying to dig up some guts. I don't see it as anything else.

HADLEY: Initially I was frightened of the part because of Hoffmann's struggle. It frightened me that he's trying to come to terms with his creative self. Is he going to choose the high road or the mundane road that everyone else chooses?

SHICOFF: He's a very self-destructive man. I love him. I love the man. He can't find his own sexuality or his grounding. I wish there

were more of these kinds of roles, but I'll take the one that I have
for now. If I had to sing Alfredo in *Traviata* for the rest of my life,
I wouldn't do this. I don't think I could do it. I'd quit. I do it so
I can find something and create, not just for the money.

H A D L E Y : I think at his core, Hoffmann is not happy with who he
is. He doesn't think he's worthy enough to become a great poet even
though, I think, that's what he wants to be. One of the difficulties
and treasures of *Tales of Hoffmann* is that there's so much to think
about.

S H I C O F F : I'm at an interesting time in my career. I think I'm now
one of the leading tenors and it's up to me where I go from here.
It has to do with how comfortable you are with your talent and your
productivity. When people who know me see me in *Hoffmann,* they
know it's me. He is me. It's just like going into therapy for me to
do this part onstage.

P E T E R S : I really think singers jump around too much these days
and don't concentrate on the correct repertory, and that's why they
don't last. They're doing a lot of roles they shouldn't do. They come
up quickly and they go back. When one wants you, everybody wants
you, and you have to be very careful, selective. I was always selective
in choosing roles.

S H I C O F F : I'm a person who works well out of adversity and that's
one reason this role suits me. I work much better when people are
saying, "I don't like you." Then I work much harder to make them
change their minds. I do produce better under those circumstances,
if I have a network of people around to support me. I do what I do.
I'm very together on that one. I'm not going to be anything other
than what I am. I've been criticized right and left by the critics on
this part but. . . .

S U T H E R L A N D : It's a marvelous role for a tenor to sing if he can
sing it, I should think. It's an awfully long role, but then he doesn't
have to change so much and go through so many wigs and makeup
changes.

S H I C O F F : It's more than just the notes that make it hard. It's the
emotions. At the end of the night, I'm completely wrecked, wiped
out. But then I've always had a lot of trouble with my talent and
that's the main reason I've always found Hoffmann such a satisfying
character.

HADLEY: I think if I live with this role for twenty years, it will add to the richness of the way I portray him.

SHICOFF: If it ain't broke, don't fix it. But I do play him much deeper now, much more destructive. I just thought, "I don't want to do a lot of *Hoffmanns* for a while. I'm *Hoffmann*ed out." And having said that, I suddenly thought, "I miss it already. I want to do more and more and more."

DER RING
DES NIBELUNGEN

~

They haven't gotten their
apples for the day, so all the gods
are feeling a little poorly.

—ELLEN SHADE

They'd stick a spear in your hand,
and we seemed to be constantly jumping from
one rock to another.

—SANDRA WARFIELD

Music by Richard Wagner
Libretti by the composer

BRÜNNHILDE .... *Johanna Meier, Birgit Nilsson*

SIEGLINDE .... *Rose Bampton, Johanna Meier, Birgit Nilsson, Ellen Shade*

FREIA .... *Ellen Shade*

FOREST BIRD .... *Betsy Norden*

FRICKA .... *Helga Dernesch, Mignon Dunn, Sandra Warfield*

ERDA .... *Lili Chookasian, Helga Dernesch, Sandra Warfield*

SIEGMUND .... *Richard Cassilly, Gary Lakes*

LOGE / MIME .... *Graham Clark*

WOTAN .... *Jerome Hines, Franz Mazura, James Morris, Thomas Stewart*

ALBERICH .... *Franz Mazura*

FASOLT/ FAFNER/
HUNDING / HAGEN .... *John Macurdy*

ALSO .... *Joyce Castle, Evelyn Lear, Nell*
Rankin, Regina Resnik

Wagner's *Der Ring des Nibelungen* is composed of four separate operas: *Das Rheingold, Die Walküre, Siegfried,* and *Götterdämmerung.* Purists, however, refer to the four collectively as the *Ring* cycle and treat it as one complete work—one very long complete work.

Written between 1848 and 1876, the *Ring* is generally considered to be the masterwork of Richard Wagner. The major themes of the four operas, power and love, were taken from mythology, and there is a universal appeal to the work that has allowed the cycle to thrive as both a unit and as four individual pieces. Despite the fact that the work occupied the composer for almost thirty years, there is a definite continuity and harmonic unity in the cycle, which in part account for its appeal.

But for many, according to Birgit Nilsson, the leading Wagnerian soprano of her day, this appeal has sometimes been elusive at best.

BIRGIT NILSSON: The *Ring* is not something like *Carmen* or *Traviata* where you go to listen and look, and it comes easily to you. You have to work for it. You have to prepare yourself, and that's where the fault lies. Because people mostly want to be entertained. They come after a day of working and they are sitting there looking and listening to Wagner and a loud orchestra. They are tired and they don't know what it's all about—and they fall asleep. You have to be prepared and you have to know. If you get hooked on Wagner, then you will never stop. The more you listen and the more you get involved, the more you can enjoy it and the more you have from it. But if you don't prepare and you are not willing to read, it is hard to get into it.

JOHN MACURDY: When I was a kid growing up in Kansas and I'd turn on the Saturday afternoon broadcasts, and it was going to be Wagner, I'd almost always turn it off because it was going to be too long. Now, with some of those operas, I think it's a shame there's not more. But you know, sometimes the works could be cut. Before Jimmy Levine at the Met, there was discreet cutting.

HELGA DERNESCH: You have Wagner fans and then you have people who just don't like him and that's that. I remember when I was in Bayreuth for the first time, Wieland Wagner told me I was too young for parts and would I mind being in the chorus? Of course, I did it, and I was on a kind of scholarship program where I didn't have to pay. Well, I went to a performance, and I don't remember what I saw, but I could hear all the wonderful music and the wonderful singers. After that performance, I couldn't sleep. I had a high temperature. I was so sick. I was so moved and so impressed. I was just so moved by just the sound of the orchestra. For me, Wagner is like a drug when the public likes it.

NILSSON: At my first *Tristan,* I was rather young, and in the second act when King Marke is singing, I fell asleep.

The first complete *Ring* cycle was performed at Bayreuth, Germany, on August 13, 14, 16, and 17, 1876. A brief summary of the plot is impossible—*brevity* and the *Ring* are a contradiction in terms. So we'll just give you the highlights. It's about this ring. . . .

The work opens deep in the Rhine—actually in the river—where the three Rhinemaidens guard a golden treasure buried in the briny deep. The repulsive dwarf and sometime blacksmith Alberich appears and tries to woo the Rhinemaidens. Although the girls repel his amorous advances, they do tell him all about the gold. The Rhinegold contains ultimate power, and if it's shaped into a ring, the wearer will rule the world. The only condition attached to this is that the owner of the gold must renounce love. Since Alberich isn't doing well in that department anyway, he steals the gold and runs away.

SANDRA WARFIELD: I did one of those Rhinemaidens once very early on, but it was so dark I really don't remember that much about it.

FRANZ MAZURA: With Alberich, you have to be down. You can't be straight up if you feel this music. You can't sing it any other way. It's not like someone says you have to be bent over or on your knees, but the physical part is very important. It affects the way you sing.

Meanwhile, Wotan, the ruler of the gods, and his wife, Fricka, are admiring their new castle, Valhalla, built for them by two giants, Fasolt and Fafner. Wotan, by the way, is missing an eye, and Fricka is consumed with jealousy about her husband's extramarital activities. But they both are very happy with their new home.

J A M E S   M O R R I S : When I first started studying Wotan, I thought, "Oh well, he's a god." He's the head god and all-powerful and all-knowledgable and everything you think of as a god. I was surprised and disappointed to find that he never really has an original idea through the whole *Ring*. All his original ideas occurred in the past before *Rheingold*. Once he made his laws and treaties that bind the universe, he can't violate them without dire consequences. So even though he's a god, he's bound by the laws that he himself has imposed, and when he tries to go beyond them, all the bad things happen.

J E R O M E   H I N E S : You have to go to the background—how Wotan lost his eye, the plucking it out. But I think much of the influence in Wagner is by the music itself. You've got one of the most, if not *the* most, descriptive composers of all.

M O R R I S : There obviously was a genuine love between Wotan and Fricka at one time, and the affairs with Erda and other people do show another human side of him.

M I G N O N   D U N N : If Fricka had been a little more adventurous, they probably would have gotten along, but don't you know couples like that? At one point, she's very hurt and she has the feeling "I wish it wouldn't be this way."

D E R N E S C H : There's no question she loves Wotan, but she knows too much about his unfaithfulness and having children with other women. As I always say, women who are not in a happy marriage seek some other job to do, and Fricka is the minister of justice and the household, and it's her job to keep the house in order and the family together.

D U N N : There is some hurt because he's betrayed her—high, low, everywhere. He's betrayed her. Then she says to Wotan, "At least, guard my honor. Don't wipe my nose in it. Go back to the rules you set and don't let me be an absolute laughingstock."

D E R N E S C H : Fricka is not a spoiled woman like Herodias in *Salome*. In *Das Rheingold,* she is a little bit worried about her husband's faithfulness.

W A R F I E L D : I tried not to think of Fricka as a totally disagreeable figure. I think she suffers and is misunderstood, and she loves Wotan and she's trying to do what she thinks is right. I don't see her as a nag, which is how I think most people see her. I always tried to go down to the human angle of every character. It's a very thankful part to sing.

M A C U R D Y : There's nothing about Fafner and Fasolt that threatening, other than they've made a contract with Wotan to build Valhalla and it's legally binding and now Wotan's trying to back out of it.

D E R N E S C H : Fricka is also upset about giving away her sister and all that, but she's still hoping that her marriage will carry on well.

In return for building Valhalla, the two giants have been promised Freia, who is the goddess of youth and Fricka's sister, and whose golden apples give the gods eternal youth. Wotan has no intention of keeping his promise, but Fasolt and Fafner are insistent, while Fricka and Freia are understandably upset.

E L L E N S H A D E : I don't think Freia understands why Wotan gives her away and I think it hurts her feelings. It's not explained, is it? I, as an actress, just accept what Wotan says in his tired, cavalier way as just another rejection. It's sad, but it all turns out well in the end.

D U N N : Fricka in the *Rheingold* is a much younger, more human, more pliable character than she is later on. She's trying to manipulate Wotan but she's still attracted to him. I feel they've not been married that long. It's more of a human thing. She tries constantly to say, "Remember your responsibilities," which I guess wives have been doing from the start of time. She's really aggravated with him, but she's a much softer character.

Loge, the demigod of fire, who arranged the construction contract for Valhalla, mentions Alberich's theft of the Rhinegold and its potential power as a ring. That gets everyone's attention. Fasolt and Fafner say they'll take the ring in place of Freia. Once the gold is in the hands of Wotan and Fricka, Freia will be saved and order will be restored to the world. So they think.

SHADE: I think the gods are all somewhat depressed because the giants won't let them eat my apples. They haven't gotten their apples for the day, so all the gods are feeling a little poorly.

GRAHAM CLARK: Loge is the most intelligent person in the *Ring* because he knows exactly what's going to happen. He knows what the problem is and he's been out searching. He tells Wotan he knows the problem, but Wotan's not prepared to solve it, to meet the challenge.

MORRIS: He didn't want to give up Freia. He tries to get out of it, but then he got that bad advice from Loge, who had told him to forget about the giants wanting Freia, that they could get out of it once Valhalla was built. He put himself in Loge's hands, and then when it was time to do it, Loge said, "Well, you have a contract and you have to give her up."

SHADE: Freia goes to several of the gods asking for help because she obviously doesn't want to go off with these giants, but nobody can help her. The gods are just tired because of the lack of their juice or fertility or whatever the apples mean.

MORRIS: Wotan is caught between a rock and a hard place. So then the business of the Ring comes up and the giants say, "If we have to give up Freia, give us the gold instead." He gives up his power in order to keep Freia so all the gods can stay young. By this point he's gotten deeper and deeper into it.

CLARK: Wotan isn't prepared and that's why Loge's so interesting, because he knows what's going to happen from start to finish. He actually is like a gas flame that's icy-cold blue and totally under control. Everyone around him is slightly out of control or out of their depth, and searching, and not knowing what they really want. He's totally under control, and every once in a while you turn the gas up and there he goes, and then he's back in control again. He's the only one in *Rheingold* who is in control.

Meanwhile Mime, another dwarf blacksmith, has forged the gold into a ring for his brother, Alberich.

CLARK: There are glorious moments when you play Mime because he's such a bizarre character. He's lived in the forest all his life and he's a mixture of blacksmith and cook. There are a lot of activities in the character, so there are countless ways of playing him.

This is no ordinary ring. It symbolizes power for men, also a husband's fidelity—which Fricka finds very appealing. Wotan and Loge steal the ring from Alberich, who is understandably upset and places a curse on it.

MORRIS: Wotan is scared of Alberich. He treats him with disdain in the beginning: "This dwarf, this nothing, how could he be a danger to the gods?" But he has the power—the gold, the Ring. He sees Alberich as the one danger, the one threat to the gods. He thinks by the end of *Rheingold* he's put an end to the threat, but then in *Walküre,* he voices the fact that Alberich is still a problem for the gods. Erda has prophesied their end and it's coming from Alberich and his offspring.

MAZURA: Alberich is always interesting to me, because I've played both him and Wotan and they are so similar. They are the two sides of the coin. Wotan makes all of these terrible mistakes and then he has to pay for them. He always wants to be the one who has the power, but he's like someone who lies, lies, lies, and then he believes in his own lies.

Erda, the all-knowing goddess of the earth, makes an appearance late in the opera after all the wrangling has disturbed her long sleep.

LILI CHOOKASIAN: For my Erda at Bayreuth, they put me in a body stocking which had markings for breasts. I remember *Time* magazine saying that I was nude from the waist up, which wasn't true!

As the opera ends, Fafner makes off with the Ring and Fricka tries to convince Wotan to stay close to home at Valhalla, while the Rhinemaidens bemoan the evil done by the gods and Loge realizes that the gods are all about to fall.

The beloved Milton Cross, announcer for the Metropolitan Opera radio broadcasts, would always pause for intermission features. Before we go on to the second opera, *Die Walküre* (The Valkyrie), Birgit Nilsson will share an anecdote about her personal history with the *Ring*.

N I L S S O N : There was one time when they had not nailed down the stage during rehearsal, I think it was in 1975 with *Götterdämmerung,* and I fell and I had to go to the hospital. The change of scenery had been so fast that they didn't have time to nail down the steps to the stage. So when I made my entrance in the first act, the staircase just fell on my head, and it was rather high. My right arm was dislocated. I stayed at the hospital for three days and I went home with a terrible headache. The next day I decided to sing the premiere. They had my arm tied to my body. The tailor at the Metropolitan came to my room and made a dress where I could have the arm underneath. So I was a little bit heroic, as I always try to sing and I didn't want to let them down. So when I came onstage with Jess Thomas, they were standing up and screaming—the whole house. I'll never forget it in all my life. I was still under the shock of it and I started to cry when I heard the people. I felt how well they wished me and how happy they were that I was singing that evening. And I couldn't stand it. I leaned over to Jess and said, "I can't go on," and it was in the middle of my singing. He was such a wonderful colleague, and he said, "Birgit, you know that you can." And he held me tight and I completed that. When it was over, people said I had never sung a Brünnhilde like that.

Between the first and second operas, Erda, who warned Wotan to be cautious, doesn't heed her own advice and bears him nine daughters called Valkyries, one of whom provides the name for the second opera. Wotan and Erda's daughters have some of the most popular music connected with the *Ring*. "The Ride of the Valkyries" is almost a musical cliché. In the second opera, the girls have been out gathering heroes to defend Valhalla, since things haven't been going well for the gods. Wotan has also managed to find himself a nice girl and father mortal twins, Siegmund and Sieglinde, who were separated at birth.

M O R R I S : This is the easiest opera to humanize Wotan in and it's my favorite of the four in the *Ring*.

J O Y C E   C A S T L E : When we girls come on, that's the great energy section. It must last twenty-five minutes or so before Wotan comes on and realizes what is going on.

WARFIELD: When I did one of the Valkyries, I was much too busy jumping from one rock to another and trying to come in on time with the music to worry about any kind of characterization. Let me tell you, none of us had ever done much and here we were with armor and shields. They'd stick a spear in your hand, and we seemed to be constantly jumping from one rock to another.

RICHARD CASSILLY: Siegmund is one of the most interesting of Wagner's characters. He's really a three-dimensional animal with all the problems that every animal has. He's also a man, a real man.

ROSE BAMPTON: Sieglinde is very warm, feminine, womanly. I remember seeing Lehmann in the part and that was a wonderful experience.

GARY LAKES: Siegmund has always been very close to me. He's one of opera's most tragic characters. He's a young guy who didn't have any family life at all. He didn't know who his father was for a long time and then he finally finds one thing, Sieglinde, and she's taken from him.

SHADE: Sieglinde speaks of her mother and Siegmund never does, as far as I know. He never mentions her. He's very involved with the father.

MORRIS: In this opera, Wotan is not only a god but a father, too, and he has all these problems and shortcomings and emotions. The love for his daughter is the main thing.

Sieglinde has married Hunding and they live in a house that has been built around a tree with a sword projecting from it. Why the house was built around the tree is never made clear, but the sword is vitally important to the plot. Siegmund shows up at their house and Hunding notices the family resemblance. Something less than the perfect host, Hunding gives his brother-in-law shelter for the night but tells him that the two must fight to the death in the morning. As luck would have it, Siegmund and Sieglinde fall in love.

MACURDY: When I play Hunding, I'm uncomfortable having this man in my house and I realize that he's a Hatfield and I'm a McCoy, but I'll give him food and shelter and then deal with him in the morning. And what does the guy do? He runs off with my wife. That's heroic? When people say that Hunding's a villain, I really don't understand that. One night he's at his dinner table and the next day he runs off with his wife.

LAKES: Siegmund was hard for me at first because of the stamina you need.

BAMPTON: In the first act it's very exciting for her. She's under the control of this stern husband and then this handsome stranger comes in and relates this whole story. I must say that modern performances of it leave me a little bit shocked. We never had an ending like they have now in the first act, where they "go into the woods" right on the stage.

NILSSON: I love Sieglinde because she's a human being, a very loving human being, and it's a very thankful part. The hearts from the public, they go out to her.

Siegmund plucks the sword from the living-room tree and he and Sieglinde run off. Hunding follows and kills Siegmund with the help of Wotan, who is under pressure from Fricka. Wotan turns on his favorite Valkyrie daughter, Brünnhilde, who has crossed him by supporting Siegmund. Brünnhilde informs Sieglinde that she is carrying Siegmund's child. Wotan then puts Brünnhilde to sleep on a rock, stripped of her powers, and surrounds her with a ring of fire.

NILSSON: Brünnhilde is strong. She's a fighting woman. She can take care of herself.

SHADE: Sieglinde has a lot of anger toward Hunding that's just being realized when she meets Siegmund. At the beginning of the first act, she's just a child. Hunding has taken her not only as a wife but as a cook and a housekeeper. It was just incidental to him that she was a woman. I don't think they've had a very happy or strong marriage. Then there is her attraction to Siegmund, which is love at first sight, but that happens in opera. With him, she feels the first stirrings of womanhood—not just sex, but all the aspects of womanhood. In the second act, it's very hard to understand why she's so upset, except that she's run away with a man who's her twin. It's a wonderful combination of impulse and rationality. It's fascinating. I think she's maybe even disgusted with her body for betraying her rational side. On the other hand, she can't stop her body from reacting to Siegmund. It's such a chemical reaction that they have.

Fricka reprimanded Wotan for interfering with the sacred vows of Sieglinde and Hunding, and also pointed out to him that the twins were guilty not only of adultery but also of incest.

D U N N : The unpleasant thing about Fricka in *Die Walküre* is that she's right. No one—especially Wotan—wants to be around anybody who is absolutely right. It's uncomfortable. She insists: "These are the laws you have set down, my husband, and you have broken them."

M O R R I S : At one time he really loved Fricka, but as in any relationship, things crop up. And quite often Fricka is portrayed as one-dimensional—just browbeating her husband. It shouldn't be like that. After all, she is the goddess of marriage and faithfulness and all that.

Wagner has always been controversial. Debussy wrote of his colleague: "Wagner never did anything of real service to music, and he never did much for Germany either."

Before moving on to a discussion of the third opera, *Siegfried,* we'll have a second intermission feature: some thoughts on the composer from one of the world's leading Wagnerian baritones, Thomas Stewart, and his devoted wife, soprano Evelyn Lear—the William Powell and Myrna Loy of opera.

T H O M A S   S T E W A R T : I think the *Ring* should be constantly in the repertory. When you have a new production of it, it's usually because you have the singers and better do it while you can, or you have a conductor who feels the musical world will not survive if it doesn't hear his *Ring.* Either of these elements has inevitably caused the *Ring* to be done, because another production from a theatrical stage viewpoint is no big deal, because nobody's going to come up with something to set the world on fire as far as the *Ring* is concerned. We have some very good singers around today, but I don't agree that there's a whole group available who are responsible for the resurgence

of interest in the *Ring* today. The *Ring* characters are all bigger than
life, but to play them more powerfully, you have to play them as
if they were a part of everyday life, as if they were ordinary people
sitting around talking. Then they become effective. This was not my
discovery but was given to me by Wieland Wagner, and I've seen
nothing to make me doubt this. This went through all my years at
Bayreuth and the work with Karajan. Musically, of course, these
characters are all bigger than life. As far as introducing audiences to
Wagner goes, my darling wife had it right when she said, "You do
it by letting them hear one act of the opera at a time." Never any
more than that, and it has to be done over a long period of time.

EVELYN LEAR: And never start with *Parsifal*!

STEWART: Or *Götterdämmerung*! *Tannhäuser* would be a good
one. There's sex in that. There is a mystique about Wagner—the
Richard Burton movie that was made about him and all that. He was
a character right out of his operas. He was one of those characters
out of whom real-life mystiques are made. He stays alive because of
his music, and it's going to go on and on and never die.

LEAR: There are just layers and layers in all of his work, and all those
melodies—the lush, very intense qualities. I guess he wasn't a nice
man—sort of like Mozart. These were very coarse men, who were
geniuses but still just very basic. The Wagner mystique isn't in the
personality of the composer, but all in the music.

STEWART: There have been thousands of volumes written about
Wagner and his music. Every year hundreds of books come out, and
you delve and dig, and you're constantly coming up with some new
ideas. I don't think there was any other composer who wrote music
quite like Wagner. No one.

LEAR: Did you ever sit on those seats in Bayreuth?

STEWART: She was a dutiful wife.

LEAR: I can't tell you how many hours I spent sitting there. The seats
were devised by the Nazis to make you suffer. Wagner does take a
long time to get to his points.

As *Siegfried* opens, we discover that Sieglinde's son, the title character,
has been raised by Mime, who is trying desperately, but to little avail,
to reconstruct Siegmund's sword. Siegfried is not a very grateful orphan
and mistreats Mime, realizing that he doesn't even remotely resemble

the dwarf who claims to be his father. The boy is not a genius, but not totally stupid either. Wotan, disguised as the Wanderer, shows up and explains to Mime through a series of riddles that the sword can be repaired only by someone who has never known fear.

L A K E S : Young Siegfried is sixteen years old, but you really can't think about singing it until you're in your forties. Maybe someone young will come along who can do it, but I doubt it. It would be nice to see someone out there who was twenty-three years old and looked like Siegfried, but it hasn't happened yet. I get offered Siegfried all the time, but I have to wait. I know one guy who used to bill himself as "the youngest person to sing Tristan." He was thirty and he lasted a year.

C A S S I L L Y : Siegfried is like a sort of operetta hero that the German public has always adored. Give them a blond wig and blue eyes and let him strut, and they're enthralled.

C L A R K : By the time of *Siegfried,* there's a difference in Mime, because he's aged a lot and learned a lot more purely through the passage of time. With all that's happened in the meantime, even watching Siegfried grow up for eighteen or nineteen years, he still doesn't understand. Mime is an interesting character. He's a technician who's very good with with his hands. He's like a foreman in a good workshop, but he doesn't understand the implications of what he's doing. He follows the instructions and he ends up with a very good product. He's not entirely an idiot, but he's a craftsman who doesn't have a depth of knowledge. All that Mime can do is relate to events. He doesn't understand why the events have happened. When he asks Wotan, the Wanderer, questions, they're very simple, very pure.

Be that as it may, Mime plans to kill Siegfried, but first he prods the fearless youth to finish the magic sword and go after Fafner, who has taken the shape of a dragon and is still guarding the Ring.

C L A R K : Another interesting thing about Mime is that he has raised this boy all alone. He's been both father and mother, so he is both slightly female and slightly male.

Siegfried hears the sounds of the Forest Bird in the woods, but can't understand what she's saying. However, he does manage to kill Fafner and claim the Ring. He also tastes the giant's blood, which enables him to understand the bird and read Mime's mind. As Anna Russell once said when talking about the *Ring,* "We're not making this up, you know!"

M A C U R D Y : Poor Fafner! He didn't even want Freia. He knew she controlled the apples the gods needed, and all he wanted was for the contract for Valhalla to be honored. Well, Wotan honored contracts more in the breach than in the observance.

Soprano Betsy Norden was introduced to Wagner when she sang the Forest Bird, who, of course, does not appear onstage.

B E T S Y N O R D E N : The only relationship between the Bird and Siegfried is in the music. Obviously, you can't have eye contact, but it is there in the music. That's the fun part about doing the role.

The Forest Bird tells Siegfried to beware of Mime, and the hero, whose patience by this time has been severely tested, kills his stepfather. His feathered friend then leads him to the mountain where Brünnhilde lies surrounded by fire.

N O R D E N : With the Forest Bird, you have a lot of words and they're important. You have to be understood. I love the music, though, and I think it really is in the patterns of a bird. It does sound like a twittering, chirping little thing. I can picture this pretty little bird flitting around the forest. I love the whole idea of it, of bringing the good news. The role fits in one of the best parts of my voice, too, so I always enjoy doing it.

Siegfried eventually finds Brünnhilde, the first woman he's ever seen, and kisses her on the lips. Well, like a veritable Sleeping Beauty, Brünnhilde comes to life, tells him she's loved him forever—even before he was born—and realizes that she is a goddess no longer, just a mortal. But her love is stronger than any fears or doubts she might have. The soprano singing Brünnhilde in *Siegfried* has to crowd a lot into one scene.

N I L S S O N : The most difficult Brünnhilde is in *Siegfried,* I think, because it's so short. She has to interpret three different faces in that role. She woke up as a goddess by the kiss from Siegfried. Then finally she starts to get human feelings. Then she gets motherly feelings toward Siegfried. She ends up as a loving woman. The part is very short and very stationary. She doesn't move much. To make these three steps in three quarters of an hour, or however long it takes, is hard. There's not much action to it. Through the music and her inner feelings, you have to interpret this change in her. It's very tough. I was always afraid for this Brünnhilde, because I always felt I could not express what I was really feeling. In the other operas, they are longer and there is action, and it comes gradually.

There are many interesting stories that have collected around the *Ring* over the years. One such anecdote concerns the famous battles between Helen Traubel and Lauritz Melchior to see who could hold the climactic notes the longest. Melchior generally won. The soprano remarked that he seemed to enjoy "turning purple." Before we move on to *Götterdämmerung* (The Twilight of the Gods), the last opera in the cycle, a few more remembrances:

BAMPTON: In the beginning of the war, we were still doing Wagner, and then Flagstad went back to Norway to be with her husband. Helen Traubel came in to sing at that time and she was wonderful—beautiful voice, a wonderful colleague, a great sense of humor. They didn't do much German opera then, but there was still a public for it. There's always been a public for it, and nobody accused you of being pro-German because you sang Wagner. There was no thought of that. I remember Helen, in the third act of *Walküre,* when she gives Sieglinde the sword, I always had my back to the audience when she gave it to to me. I remember once I was turning around as she gave it to me, and she stopped singing and said, "Give 'em hell, Rose!" She was a wonderful companion, just great, really.

REGINA RESNIK: Some works require a lot of homework. It's like an acquired taste. I used to hate the taste of scotch, couldn't understand why people were drinking that iodine. Then I got kind of used to it. It became something I could drink. Unless you have a particularly eclectic taste as a youngster, you have to do a *lot* of homework to really appreciate Wagner. Otherwise you could die from all the boring repetition. Let's face it, he does *Rheingold* and then he repeats all of it in *Walküre,* and he repeats those two in *Siegfried,* and then he takes all three and makes you digest them again in *Götterdämmerung.* It doesn't mean that it's not a great work, but it does make the whole damn thing too long. Thankfully, it's shorter for the artist than it is for the audience.

NILSSON: I learned from Wieland Wagner. I was a little bit nervous to move around. When I was just standing, I felt I was not doing enough. He said, "Birgit, listen to the music and believe in your own personality." You have to listen to the music. If you're running your legs off, you can't compete with Wagner's music. The more and the smaller gestures that you do, the smaller the figure gets, and that's not right. When I see the *Ring* and I see how nervously people are acting, I say, "Why do they interpret?" It only makes the figures smaller. There has to be a motive in what they are doing. But then there are those stage directors who brag that they have never seen the *Ring* when they are about to stage it. There are those. But what are you going to do?

NORDEN: The only thing I didn't enjoy about doing the opera was running around backstage trying to find the loft from where I sang. In the production in the seventies I did when Ehrling conducted, I think I sang the role from the third-story walkup backstage at the Met. I remember going up in an elevator on the side of the stage and walking across a catwalk sort of thing, and singing it from up there. It might have been from the lighting grid, but wherever, it was high up and I didn't really enjoy that part. It may have been the best place for the bird to be, but it wasn't very comfortable. I just don't like heights. The next time, I sang it from the sidestage and it was amplified, and a lot more comfortable.

As *Götterdämmerung* opens, we discover that Erda has had three more daughters called the Norns. They sit around singing and weaving all of their mother's wisdom into a long rope. They sing about Alberich and about how Loge, the god of fire, will ignite the giant pyre when the old order of the gods must end.

After they've sung for half an hour and received, at most, polite applause, their rope breaks. This symbolizes the end of the gods, and the Norns go home to their mother.

D E R N E S C H : The Norns really shouldn't be humanized. They are just symbols, that's all.

D U N N : With the Norns, you have to be very careful to keep your energy up. Something very important is happening in that Norn scene when the rope breaks, and it's very scary and it has to be done that way.

Siegfried gives the Ring to Brünnhilde and goes off to find adventure. He meets the Gibichungs: Gunther, Gutrune, and their half brother, Hagen, who was sired by Alberich and has his eye on the Ring. Siegfried falls under the spell of Gutrune.

M A C U R D Y : Most people think that Hagen is much older than Siegfried, but they really were born within nine months of each other if you follow normal human chronology. He's not an old man. He's different from everyone else because he was the son of Alberich, who is so strange. He's described as an ugly character.

N E L L R A N K I N : Gutrune, I think, really got what she deserved, because she gave Siegfried the potion that made him fall in love with her. If she hadn't done that, a lot of the things that happened at the end of the *Ring* wouldn't have come about the way they did. But the part is very short.

Waltraute tries to get her sister Brünnhilde to return the Ring to the Rhinemaidens, but Brünnhilde refuses.

C A S T L E : Waltraute's fun. She's sort of the leader of the Valkyries and very energetic. She has a hell of a long Wagnerian line to get across.

D U N N : Waltraute has a mini–immolation scene. It's incredible. It's probably the best, the most grateful of all the mezzo parts in the *Ring*.

Siegfried tears the Ring from Brünnhilde's finger and turns her over to Gunther. By this point, she realizes that the end of the gods is near. Hoping to get the Ring, Hagen then kills both Siegfried and Gunther. Brünnhilde, realizing that all is lost, builds a funeral pyre for Siegfried, lights it, and rides her horse into the fire, taking the Ring so that it will be destroyed, and with it the rotten old order of the world. The Rhine then overflows, and in the distance Valhalla is seen in flames. Love and not power must now rule the world.

N I L S S O N : In this opera Brünnhilde starts off as the loving woman. Then there is a transformation into the betrayed woman, and then the avenging woman at the end. Then she stands over everything, throws herself into the flames, and she's a goddess again. It comes gradually. Brünnhilde is only half human, you know. I know the public likes to have a very human Brünnhilde with lots of feelings. She's the daughter of a god. So it has to be a character which is not quite human, anyway. Otherwise, in a way, it will be too small.

M O R R I S : One of my favorite moments in the cycle is when Wotan says to Brünnhilde right after the confrontation with Fricka, "If I tell you what's wrong with me, I'll lose my will over you." And she says, "But what am I but your will?" That's a very strong bond there.

N I L S S O N : The most difficult thing is to sing with Wotan in his farewell to Brünnhilde. Some Wotans did this so beautifully, with so much heart, that I closed my eyes so I shouldn't have tears in my eyes. It affects the one who is singing. That was very, very hard. The music there is so beautiful. Very often I was standing there closing my eyes and the tears would brim up under my eyelids. It is so tough. You can harm Wotan, really, because if he's involved and he sees somebody cry . . . That happened to me once. I was singing Elsa in Bayreuth, and the music is so beautiful, and I thought it was my last performance there—it wasn't but I thought it would be—and I started to weep. Lohengrin was Wolfgang Windgassen and he started to weep, too. And he had to sing. Oh, I was so unhappy for him! So there I learned you must never show anybody if you're emotional, because it does have an effect. If I start to cry, I lose my voice immediately.

M O R R I S : Brünnhilde is the favorite daughter because she was the firstborn, or at least that's how I look at it. In any group of children, there is a favorite, and a father tries not to betray this to his other children, but it happens, and who knows why really? Wotan sees himself in Brünnhilde. When he begins his monologue, he says, "When I'm talking to you, I'm talking to myself."

The Rhinemaidens end the *Ring* as they began it, and a twenty-hour musical journey is over.

* * *

In the early part of this century, Olive Fremstad and Johanna Gadski, both of whom were competing for the title of leading Wagnerian female singer at the Met, had to dodge showers of floral tributes at the curtain calls. Gadski, who was a trifle larger, made her way downstage to accept her cheers while Fremstad couldn't make it through the barrage of flowers. At one performance of *Walküre,* Gadski deliberately drew blood from Fremstad near the end of Act Two. During the curtain calls, Olive held Johanna very still while her blood dripped all over Gadski's Brünnhilde costume.

Fortunately, there are other, happier memories of the *Ring:*

C H O O K A S I A N : When I did Bayreuth, I was the shortest and also the leanest of the Valkyries, and I would always go to the back of the stage, because they all had spears and I didn't want to be speared. So I really would hover at the back, and Mr. Wagner would say, "Frau Chookasian, please come to the front. I can't see you." Believe me, I used to make a quick dash when it was time for the Valkyries to get off.

D E R N E S C H : My first dealing with the *Ring* was in *Götterdämmerung* in Bayreuth when I was still a student in 1959. Then I came back in a new production of the cycle as Wellgunde, one of the Rhinemaidens, and then the next year I added Ortlinde, a Valkyrie. Then I think it was Sieglinde and the Third Norn, which I did in Cologne. And then it was the Karajan recording of Brünnhilde in *Siegfried* in '68, and then I was singing it onstage in Salzburg in '69, and then that year there was the recording of Brünnhilde in *Götterdämmerung* and I sang that in Salzburg. In the meantime, I did that and Gutrune in Bayreuth. Well, it went on like that, and then when the change of repertory came, I did Fricka, Erda in *Siegfried,* and Waltraute.

J O H A N N A M E I E R : I'm the first to admit that I'm very conservative about my opera. I believe an opera should be staged in the manner in which it was conceived, because it presents a better blend of music and drama. I never felt a work really benefited from being updated or fiddled with in any way.

R E S N I K : In Bayreuth, you have an aperitif intermission and then a dinner intermission. An opera starts at four in the afternoon and ends at ten or ten-thirty. The dinner break gives your voice and the audience a break, but if your big thing is at the end, it can be a mighty long day.

CHOOKASIAN: My Erda at the Met had grassy things coming out of her face. It was like a mask, and Karajan got so aggravated and said, "That's not what I wanted. Don't wear that." One review said, "Miss Chookasian came up from the back. You had the feeling she was out on Amsterdam Avenue. She was far away." But the voice, apparently, was powerful enough to be heard all over the house.

MACURDY: What a wonderful Erda Lili Chookasian was. The next one came in and complained because she was placed upstage and wasn't downstage singing like it was a concert. No one could hear her anyway. We always heard Lili. She was incredibly effective.

MEIER: One year when we did the *Ring* in Seattle, I was doing Sieglinde, we had a new tenor doing Siegmund, and we got through the German cycle and everything was fine and we got on well. When we began rehearsing the English, we realized that we were going to have a problem because he didn't have the words, and he rehearsed off cards for a week. We did the second version very quickly then. When it came to the performance, I went out on the set and I saw that he had words all over the set at strategic spots—on the table, the tree, anywhere he was going to end up. In the English translation there was one line of dialogue that says, "She moves and smiles in her sleep." So I did just that, and he hissed in my ear, "Roll over! My words are in your hair." I have long hair and I always use it instead of a wig, and he had obviously placed a long strip in my hair and was reading them like from a tickertape. Those days were a little scary but a lot of fun.

WARFIELD: I did the *Götterdämmerung* Erda at the Met, and she comes out of the ground, and they had the elevator already set. First, you've got to remember, I've never seen this opera, and all I knew was I had to come out of the ground and start singing with the low G at the end. Well, they had the elevator set for Jean Madeira, who was at least two inches taller than I was. When it stopped, all you could see was the top of my head. I was trying to see the beat of the conductor, because it was the first time I'd ever sung the role. The prompter must have helped me somewhat, but I was standing on tiptoe and just hoping for the best. I just sang and hoped I was with the orchestra, or at least somewhere in the ballpark.

CHOOKASIAN: The image of Erda never became so poignant to me as when I went to Dallas for a new production there and it all worked wonderfully. Before that I'd always thought of her as a symbol and not a real woman, but that all changed. I became the most beautiful Erda of all. They said, "After all, you've had all these beautiful daughters, of course you must be beautiful." At last I had a gorgeous costume in metallic cloth with a drape, and it was very, very nice.

DERNESCH: Working with Maestro Levine now is a really special experience. For me, this man is a miracle. How he leads and he really listens to singers!

NORDEN: I've always been impressed, to say the least, with the people I was singing with in *Siegfried*. I still remember Jess Thomas doing the role. I thought he had great legs. A great voice—but he really had great legs.

NILSSON: I always missed Sieglinde, and I said this to someone at the Met, and they went to Mr. Bing and told him. And then they had Rita Hunter and Berit Lindholm for Brünnhilde—it was in '72 or '73 or something like that—and he thought that was something new: He could present me as Sieglinde. So I did get to do two or three at the Metropolitan and I loved that.

CLARK: The more I sing the *Ring,* the more I love it. I find it fascinating. Every time you pick up a Wagner score, even one you've sung many times, you discover something new. You have a blinding revelation. There's always something new to look at.

NILSSON: I'll never forget the performance when Jon Vickers pulled the sword out of the tree and it separated and passed by my nose by half an inch and ended up down in the orchestra. It was terrible.

WARFIELD: I loved singing the Frickas in the two operas. That's a beautiful part, beautiful music.

CASTLE: Wagner was very kind to mezzos.

DUNN: He really wrote well for the mezzo voice.

CLARK: I've done over twenty Loges and Mimes, and there's so much in the text about both of them that it's sort of a lifelong quest to fully understand them.

NORDEN: Wagner's music is almost narcotic. I hate to use that word; it's not a good word these days. But that music of his carries you to a different plane. There are so many magical moments in it that can almost take you to a different level. I think that's what gets to people.

H I N E S : I did all the Wagner repertory for almost twenty years at the Met—I did all the bass repertory in everything! But I backed off from doing the *Walküre* Wotan after five years. I just felt it was too high and too long. If it were a matter of singing excerpts that ran ten or fifteen minutes, fine, but to do an hour and twenty minutes of actual singing with that high tessitura—it was too fatiguing vocally.

M A C U R D Y : I'd love to sing Hagen once a week. There are so many nuances and so many things to sing. Fasolt, also, has some of the most beautiful lines ever written, but Hagen is so complete.

R E S N I K : Wagnerian parts are not very physical. You stand a long time and sing. It takes a lot of endurance, but there isn't much acting.

M O R R I S : The thing about Wagner is that there are so many interpretations. I wish Wagner were here so that we could get the definitive interpretation.

L A K E S : The *Ring* is such a mysterious thing to so many people. It draws us into it. I've never been placed in the position where I had to play the allegory, the symbol and not the man. I like the Met's productions. They make sense. The characters are all clear and distinct.

S T E W A R T : Wieland loved to shake people up. And the fact that this young American Texan who had never sung a Wagnerian role in his life was about to sing Amfortas in *Parsifal* really shook them up. The Wagnerians were incensed, but I pulled it off and sang it for fifteen years. Then I sang everything else over the next fifteen years.

L E A R : How many productions of *Parsifal* have you done?

S T E W A R T : I've stopped counting.

L E A R : Oh, you've done it everywhere from South America to Bayreuth and I've sat through them all.

M A C U R D Y : Birgit and I had this wonderful thing that was like a heavyweight fight—anything you can do, I can do bigger and louder. It was fun. There's nothing more exciting than to be out onstage with someone who you're not only singing with but singing against. That was a wonderful experience for me.

N I L S S O N : With Karajan, that production was so dark one could very easily fall asleep. It was all Karajan. He put out all the lights except the one on himself. Backstage it was pitch-dark and we were all breaking our legs. We couldn't see how to walk. I remember before one entrance the stage man who was leading me fell, and his trousers were completely ruined and he hurt his leg. I fell on top of him. For me it wasn't so bad.

MACURDY: That was a fact: The most light in the opera house was shining down on Maestro von Karajan. He's a phenomenal musician, and he could hold a hundred-piece orchestra down to a whisper, but it wasn't the music necessarily we thought it was. In terms of being heroic or epic or gigantic, it wasn't there. It was nice, but . . . well, we did have Birgit with the miner's helmet with the light to show us the way.

NILSSON: Mr. von Karajan is a fantastic conductor, but he hasn't a clue about staging. In the section where Brünnhilde listens to everything Wotan is saying and she has to act or react, but she doesn't sing that much, he put me in the pitch-dark. It was important that the audience could see me. I said, "I could go out and have a coffee. Nobody would ever see me. It's like I'm not part of the opera." But he said, "As soon as you sing, you'll have the light, but not before." But this is the most difficult of all. You have to live. You have to feel the intensity as much when you're not singing as when you are—otherwise the opera is dead. It would be so easy to stage an opera where you only get light when you sing, then when you're listening, you're in the dark. I mean, how far can you go? How stupid can it be? So, I was a little bit—well, not too polite, and I said, "I didn't know it was so easy to be a stage director." But it never changed. Don't speak to me about that! And that scenery, God!

STEWART: Whatever else one says, the *Ring* is a great, monumental work that belongs in the repertory of any and every house that calls itself an opera house.

LA BOHÈME

~

She was so much in love;
she was young and poor; she
makes artificial flowers to live. . . .
He writes poems that have never
been published—what a mess!

–BIDÚ SAYÃO

Music by Giacomo Puccini
Libretto by Giuseppe Giacosa and Luigi Illica,
from the novel *Scènes de la Vie de Bohème* by Henri Murger

MIMÌ... *Licia Albanese, Mirella*
Freni, Anna Moffo,
Jarmila Novotná, Bidú
Sayão, Renata Scotto

MUSETTA .... *Lucine Amara, Barbara*
Daniels, Patrice Munsel,
Carol Neblett

RODOLFO.. *Jerry Hadley, Luciano*
Pavarotti, Neil Rosenshein

MARCELLO .... *Robert Merrill*

COLLINE .... *Jerome Hines, Giorgio*
Tozzi

GUEST APPEARANCE................ *Dorothy Kirsten*

*I*t was Lucile Louvet, a sometime mistress of novelist Henri Murger,
who provided the soul for *La Bohème*'s Mimì. Though the opera finds
her a romantic little seamstress, the real Louvet was described as a
"shameless little hussy, devoid of any moral sense." Though she, too,

contracted tuberculosis, she was denied Mimì's privilege of dying in her lover's arms. Benoit, the landlord, refusing to have a death in his house, sent her to the hospital. Murger received the news of her death too late, and she was taken to the dissecting room, where she gave her body one last time—this time to medical students.

JARMILA NOVOTNÁ: Mimì, Mimì darling. Everything is so true to life—because it could happen to anybody, any way. She is just a seamstress who, by this fate—because the light goes out—meets a man. Until then, he was just an easygoing artist. And he loved her because she was probably quite different from what he saw in the other bohemian loves he might have had.

Among her many experiences with *Bohème,* Renata Scotto has appeared in two opening nights of new *Bohème* productions at the Metropolitan—once as Mimì and the other time as Musetta.

RENATA SCOTTO: Mimì is really a beautiful character. I did *Bohème* at the beginning of my career. I'd say maybe it was my third opera role: Traviata, Butterfly, and Mimì.

Anna Moffo took Mimì to the Lyric Opera of Chicago for her American debut in 1957.

ANNA MOFFO: I don't believe Mimì is as simple as a lot of people make her. I don't believe she's as innocent or as uninteresting.
SCOTTO: Mimì is a beautiful character because she's a woman who knows very well what she wants. I mean, think about it: She's the one who wants to meet Rodolfo, not Rodolfo to meet Mimì. She is against any good rule—that it is the man who looks for the woman first.

In 1946, Licia Albanese was chosen by Toscanini to sing Mimì in *Bohème's* fiftieth-anniversary performance with the NBC Symphony.

LICIA ALBANESE: When you come in and say, "Scusi"—when you knock—I knocked, myself. I didn't want anybody to do it for me. Because the men, they do the knock. And I say, "No. This should be the knock of a woman—and sick," because she's coughing coming upstairs. And the light went out, and she didn't have any matches, and she lives alone. So she says, "Let me ask this guy if he has a match, because I cannot see."

MOFFO: I think she's a very interesting character, because she's smart enough to want to trap this guy with something as old as "Do you have a match?" She knows what she wants and she's decided to get it. I think the whole key to the part is knowing that.

ALBANESE: Then you say, "Scusi"—long and very distant; "Di grazia, mi si è spento il lume"—sick.

MOFFO: When I came in in the beginning, I didn't drop the key or any of that. I've had my eye on Rodolfo for weeks. I've had my eye on all four guys up in that garret. I mean, you live in a place like that—it's a walkup—they're going to run into each other at some point. So anyway, with that pretext, I hate whispering, "Scusi," as if she's really coming into *Suor Angelica* by mistake.

SCOTTO: She wanted to meet Rodolfo. And perhaps they had talked to each other. So maybe she was already in love with him. Can you believe, in five minutes, they go onstage, they talk to each other, they get in love, they go in bed? The same night! I mean, they must have seen each other.

MOFFO: But when they creep in with this little candle, without any feeling in the back of their mind what they really came for; if she comes on and plays it like Micaëla, who has to be a virgin— because nobody goes around in those blond braids unless they're a virgin. . . .

Bidú Sayão sang 225 performances with the Metropolitan, both in the house and on tour. The role assigned to her most often (31 performances) was Puccni's gentle seamstress.

BIDÚ SAYÃO: Mimì, she is a simple girl; she was not extraordinary. She was very easy to—how do you say it?—to conquer, because she lived alone.

ALBANESE: And when she comes in, the heat of the room makes you faint: "È il respir . . . quelle scale . . ."—and then she faints. They did a *Bohème* when she has to faint standing up. Can you imagine things like that? They wanted me to do it; I said, "No—I cannot do that."

SCOTTO: They were bohemians, a group of people who just do what they want to do. And Mimì, if she wasn't that sick, she would be another Musetta.

MOFFO: Because of Musetta, Mimì by way of contrast has become much more—I don't want to say mousy, but she's become a purer character than she was. She's really exactly like Musetta. She just doesn't talk about it or scream about it; she's not as brazen as Musetta, but she knows exactly what she's doing.

After an extensive European career, Jarmila Novotná made her Metropolitan Opera debut as Mimì in 1940. "An accomplished and experienced singing actress," wrote the *New York Post*'s critic, admiring her "superior musical intelligence."

NOVOTNÁ: Mimì is an easy conquest, yes. One must not think she was a saint or something. But it started with the fact that she loved somebody, then one desires a little more. They were bohemians—there is no question about that.

SCOTTO: This is a very nice group of people, free to do whatever they please. I believe Mimì is that kind of woman, very much like Musetta. Of course, she doesn't have health.

MOFFO: Musetta's so flamboyant, she'll do anything to get attention. Mimì, for one thing, is physically unable to get attention. I don't think she's as glamorous as Musetta—I don't think she can afford to be. But she's been around. I don't think that makes her any less adorable—in fact, it makes her more interesting.

SAYÃO: Mimì was not rich. She has occasion to meet this boy, and he was poor, too. Everybody was poor. It's a very simple life, but at the same time it's very touching, very moving—because it's something that can happen. It's not fantasy.

SCOTTO: And the period is so beautiful. To lead her own life, freedom, was the most important thing. And in that period, everyone was too attached to what they had to do: go to church, get married, and many other things. But Mimì was really free to do what she wants. Of course she was sick, and her sickness brought out her weak side.

MOFFO: See, I don't think anyone can fall in love with anybody who's that uninteresting. And I don't think it's possible for a girl to knock on your door and have a mad love affair that lasts for a whole opera if she doesn't have something. She can't come in in this drab plaid dress they always give you with the apron. There must be something more there.

Mimì has become one of Mirella Freni's signature roles, and was the character in which she made her Metropolitan Opera debut in 1965.

MIRELLA FRENI: For me, Mimì is an incredible role. She's so sensitive. When I started to study it, I discovered the character of Mimì in the last act. When she's so sick, and is about to die, she has a nice word for everybody. She never gives problems to anybody—she never wants to. For me, it is so important to discover this in the last act, because it helps to build the whole character of Mimì—and it's not easy.

ALBANESE: Opera should have a *romanticismo*—even the most vulgar opera. Mimì could have sweethearts, but in a nice way. At that time, the men, they want to go with these beautiful girls; and they were beautiful—otherwise they would not. Mimì was sentimental, and that is different than Violetta. Violetta cannot be like that, because she doesn't have time to think about being sick. Violetta was more this splash of beauty, with elegance and jewelry. I don't think Traviata had time to stop and think who she was. But Mimì was different—she knew.

SCOTTO: I have a very nice story about my first Mimì, because it is one of my dreams to become a costume designer. Actually, I did a new production of *Butterfly* recently, and I did the staging, but also designed the costumes. And in my very first Mimì, they gave me a dress that I didn't like. It was in a small town in north Italy—two rehearsals at the piano, then onstage and sing at the performance, take or leave it. And I didn't like the costume, so I designed my own, and I made it. I bought the fabric—I remember it was a little heavy silk, green and brown and yellow, but very dark. I don't know how I did it. But looking at it today, it's exactly in the style of 1835–40: big sleeves and a beautiful petticoat and skirt. And then I made a very beautiful collar in white lace, and a beautiful apron with flowers. And I still have it!

Sopranos of various shapes and dispositions have made a success of the consumptive seamstress. Among them: Marcella Sembrich (pudgy and, like Claudette Colbert, willing to be photographed only from the left side), Geraldine Farrar (glamorous—the Madonna of her day), Alma Gluck (elegant, and also known as the wife of violinist Ephrem Zimbalist and mother of actor Efrem Zimbalist, Jr.), Amelita Galli-Curci (slender, sharp-featured, perhaps better remembered for her rendition of "Home Sweet Home"), Frances Alda (seductive—the Norma Shearer to Met manager Gatti-Casazza's Irving Thalberg, and in some respects the Della Street to his Perry Mason), Grace Moore (a delicate woman who was herself portrayed by a more full-figured Kathryn Grayson in the movie *So This Is Love*), Claudia Muzio (moody and intense, like Joan Bennett in Fritz Lang's *The Woman in the Window*), Lily Pons (diminutive and impeccably dressed by Adrian), and Montserrat Caballé (not a consumptive look, but a glorious voice).

For some reason, Rodolfo's size and personality don't seem to matter. Tenors who have tried their hand at Rodolfo include Enrico Caruso, Alessandro Bonci, Giovanni Martinelli, Beniamino Gigli, Giacomo Lauri-Volpi, John McCormack, Richard Tucker, Jan Peerce, and Jussi Bjoerling.

M O F F O : All the heroines I've ever done have this common element of an inner passion, of wanting to live, of wanting to be very poetic characters—each one manifesting it in a different way. Even Micaëla, who has to be one of the dreariest—*the* dreariest! But not so dreary that she doesn't say in her aria, "Here's José and Carmen—*elle est belle*—and she's so much wiser than I," I mean, even *she* lusts to be a hooker.

S C O T T O : It makes a very weak interpretation if Mimì is just a sweet lady, very childish, very innocent.

M O F F O : What I mean is, sometimes I think every woman dreams of at least one night, having every guy she can find. I think that's part of being a woman. I don't think they do it, but I think it's part of being a vital female, isn't it?

A L B A N E S E : I thought of Mimì as being very quiet on that stage. She was very quiet—happy, in her way. Work and home. She was like a flower: beautiful, and then she went.

S C O T T O : So if you go out and be very weak and very sweet—and very boring! This is what I would say.

M O F F O : I remember that I came in, and I didn't sit on the chair, and I didn't look like I was going to be raped at any minute. I sat on the table and said, "My name is Mimì"—and I swung my legs swathed in black stockings—"but they call me Lucia." The whole thing was in answer to what he said: "Well, I'm this and this, but I'm a poet." She has been turned on by his obvious bohemian love of life, which makes him a creative person.

S C O T T O : Mimì's disease—consumption. Every time she talks, she goes from giving just a little bit—sounding very soft—and then emphasizes every phrase so much. Because I think with that disease, they're so weak; and every time they find a little strength, they overdo it. And then they go again. That's the disease, and you have to understand that to build a character. Because in her first aria, "Mi chiamano Mimì", she says, "Ma quando vien lo sgelo/Il primo sole è mio." It goes up high and emphasizes the phrase. The singer has to understand that. This is in Mimì's character. And Puccini goes from a very soft line to a strong line.

M O F F O : She says, "The first sun is mine." Of course, because she's sick, she feels the warmth of the sun more than anybody. She's always cold in this place.

A L B A N E S E : She's cold all the time—TB people are. And when I sing, "The sun is mine," I do it like I have the sun on me, like a shawl.

S C O T T O : Sun means "hot," means "warm." She's looking to have a warmth by clothing, by heat. In the last act, she asks for something to cover her hands, because she's very cold.

A L B A N E S E : And she sings her aria, her story, in a very quiet way. And she says this like she's in a dream, singing the aria. I used to walk in front of the public—"Il primo sole è mio"—and you come alive; you become healthy.

M O F F O : The words of Mimì's aria are so revealing. She says, "I feel the kiss of the sun." It's a wording that's not for a drab little creepy girl. "It kisses me." That's why he's mesmerized. And she's mesmerized by what he says.

A L B A N E S E : And at the end, she comes down again. She's tired. And "Germoglia in un vaso una rosa"—"One rose is just blooming. And every morning I count the leaves."

M O F F O : He is exciting because what he says is poetic. And what she says is really kind of poetic for someone who's not a poet. They identify.

During Act One of *Bohème*, Frances Alda had problems with her bloomers, so she slipped them off surreptitiously behind the onstage sofa. Not one to let her get away with anything, her Rodolfo, Caruso, picked them up and spread them out over the couch for all to see.

A L B A N E S E : Mimì was a gracious, dreaming girl, living in another world. Even when she was fighting with Rodolfo, she was a very angelic person. She was very religious, peaceful—perhaps that's what makes her soul very calm.

S A Y Ã O : Mimì was a very easy role for me to play, because I feel very deeply about the role. I thought it should be a very simple interpretation. What you need in that role is to be full of heart and soul and emotion and feeling. This was important for me; just being natural. If you give these things to the audience, it makes the interpretation of Mimì. I don't think the drama is very difficult, because it's very real.

M O F F O : Mimì doesn't just embroider flowers—she makes the petals. She talks about it in the aria. That requires a certain amount of creativity—she just doesn't sit there and sew seams. Mimì is intense, with an inner smoldering, of sorts. She lets Rodolfo have a message when she goes in there.

S C O T T O : She must show love for Rodolfo, and give important meaning to the words, and especially emphasize the strong moments in relation to the soft moments. And be a woman in love—and daring, because she's a bohemian.

S A Y Ã O : I never really had a lesson in acting. I had a teacher who said, "I can't teach you your musicality; you must be born with that. I can't teach you your feelings and the emotions inside of you. How can I teach you that? I can say a thousand times, 'Sing with tears in your eyes,' but tears will never come in your eyes if you don't feel it."

A L B A N E S E : The only time Mimì becomes a little coquettish is in the last part of the first act, when the friends call, "Oh, what are you doing? Come now, because it's late." When they call and she says, "Chi sono?" she comes alive again—she forgets she was sick. Then he says, "Amici," and then "Non son solo. Siamo in due"—"There are two of us." Then I used to go behind him and go, "Shhhh!" because it's "Oh, why did you tell him *in due*?" She becomes a little bashful.

MOFFO: By the time the guys are on the back stairs, calling, "Hey, Rodolfo," when she says, "Chi sono?" it's more of a come-on: "You don't mean we're going to be interrupted"; not *"Chi sono*—the troops are coming!"

ALBANESE: See, I think sometimes Mimì feels bashful to have a life which is not—well, she wanted to be a little better.

SAYÃO: It can happen even today. But you must have inside of you this musicality, this feeling. You must think of every word you say, because interpretation is really saying the *words*—not only the notes. This is very, very important. A lot of singers today don't think of what they say. They're just singing the notes. But opera is drama or comedy—and the diction and the words, along with the notes, are very important. This is what I think about.

MOFFO: Mimì is a flirt. She reminds me a little bit of Norina—it's always a put-up virginity, as it were. I mean, it's a play of these bohemian characters who are used to "easy does it." It's part of Paris.

SAYÃO: There's something so intimate about it, and everyone must be in the same frame of mind to make the performance work. I played her very natural, without any artifice. I just gave all my heart and soul—and at that moment, I looked and felt just like I was her. I was not me anymore at all. I felt sick just the way she did.

Because it is one of his favorite roles, Luciano Pavarotti has made Rodolfo the vehicle for his debuts all over the world.

LUCIANO PAVAROTTI: The most remarkable performance of this opera for me is certainly my debut in Milan, at La Scala, with Karajan conducting. When they told me I was going to sing with an orchestra the full opera, with acting and staging—that is the most important thing every young singer wants to hear. I was able to do the whole opera and still be fresh at the end. There is also the record that Mirella and I have done with Karajan. And then the *Bohème* we have done at the Met with Kleiber.

FRENI: On two occasions I have gone to Japan with Kleiber, and last year they wanted *Bohème,* and every night was so special. I think—and you'll excuse me for saying—I was in good form. And Kleiber was so wonderful. He has such a feeling for the music. He asks for so much more, sometimes it makes it more difficult, because I have to expend so much more energy.

BARBARA DANIELS: At the Met with Carlos Kleiber, I couldn't believe I'd ever sung the role before. Musically, dramatically, emotionally, it was just an unbelievable experience. Then we carried it on for six more performances in Japan, with La Scala, at Kleiber's request—and I felt like I died and went to heaven. In one year, eleven *Bohème*s with Kleiber and my favorite Mimì of all time, Mirella Freni—not to take anything away from any of the other Mimìs I've sung with, because I've sung with some of the greatest of our time and they've all been wonderful—but Freni is really special.

Today, audiences are accustomed to operas about the Holocaust, Richard Nixon, cannibalism, Babar the Elephant. Puccini, trendsetter that he was, had begun to outline an opera about Buddha. Fortunately, he was distracted by Henri Murger's novel *Scenes de la Vie de Bohème*.

JERRY HADLEY: It was a revelation to consider that Rodolfo is not a very good poet. Here, he's got this five-act epic in his drawer—a thing that probably makes the *Ring* look like a divertissement—and try as he might to be a profound poet, he just doesn't have the talent. I think Rodolfo is frustrated, because his talent is not equal to his desires. And if we're creative, we all have been in his position.

NEIL ROSENSHEIN: Rodolfo has a really solid evolution. He's definitely not the same person in the fourth act that he was in the first. This for me, is the perfect opera; it's my favorite.

HADLEY: One of the sweetest and most touching things is that everything Mimì says is so heartfelt and uncontrived; in her simplicity, Mimì is more poetic than Rodolfo could ever dream of being. I think he not only falls in love with Mimì the person, I think he falls in love with the idea of Mimì, as the personification of all his poetic aspirations.

While puffing out her chest to christen a new mobile X-ray unit, Lily Pons once boasted she could hold her breath longer than anyone else at the Metropolitan. When she added that she could sing for thirteen seconds without a breath, long-winded company members took umbrage and challenged her to a contest. "I can hold my breath one minute and thirteen seconds," Jan Peerce sniffed, "with my mouth full of pebbles."

M O F F O : Everyone can sing Mimì—I'll say that. It's within anybody who's a soprano to sing all the notes. *How* you sing them is something else. I don't think many people sing it well. It's difficult, because Mimì is not a part which offers any great vocal virtuosity. Traviata, in two of the acts, doesn't either—but she has many things. Mimì is like Liù: They're there for a reason, and they have to sing beautifully.

S C O T T O : Almost every soprano says, "Oh, I sing *Bohème* as a debut, because it's very easy." No, no, no, no!

M O F F O : People are inclined to give the debutante Mimì because it's such a nice showcase, without a lot of nerveracking business. It's not too difficult stagewise.

S C O T T O : It's a mistake, because Puccini's difficult. You go into a style which is very dangerous for your voice. And you have to be prepared for what you're going to do. You need experience first, so you need a bel canto training.

M O F F O : You do not give a young singer Traviata. There's too much going on. I suppose they could sing it, but a young singer doesn't have the poise or experience, unless you have a lot of rehearsal. But who rehearses anymore? A lot of people think Mozart is a good debut. I think Mozart is terribly difficult. So the big debut roles are Mimì, and I don't think Musetta's a debut role but a lot of people do it, and Micaëla, which I think is dreadfully difficult vocally.

S C O T T O : It's like you're going to write a book without knowing the alphabet. So you can't go in to sing *Bohème* before you have at least sung composers in the bel canto style. Then you must slowly get into the verismo area. Not just start with that because you think it's easy. No way.

M O F F O : At Curtis, we weren't even allowed to sing Puccini until we graduated. The word *verismo* was never mentioned. We only did Mozart, and Bellini *maybe,* and Verdi *maybe,* and lots of lieder. But I was a pianist, so I'd play for all my colleagues who wanted to sing Puccini all day long.

S C O T T O : It takes maturity to understand Mimì. You go out as a child, and start simpering, "Sì. Mi chiamano Mimì," and everything is sweet, everything is beautiful, everything is so stupid.

M O F F O : While I was studying, they always told me it was very
risky to go and see an opera, or listen to records, before what I wanted
to do was set in my mind. Because you don't mean to, or don't realize,
but you imitate; you absorb what other people do, whether you think
it's right or not. So finally I saw Tebaldi do Mimì in Italy; then I
saw de los Angeles.

S A Y Ã O : I was not happy to be a coloratura, the soubrette. I wanted
a voice that would let me sing all Puccini, all those verismo operas.
But I never could, because my voice was too small, and I didn't want
to force. You can't force what you don't have. So the only opera I
could touch was *La Bohème*, because the orchestration wasn't so heavy.
I would have given anything to sing *Madame Butterfly*, because I have
the physique. I was short and small and I feel that role so much, but it
was too heavy and too long for me. The orchestrations are so heavy,
you must have a beautiful, big, round voice. Otherwise, you will fail.

Grace Moore made her operatic debut as Mimì at the Metropolitan
in 1928. She was hailed worldwide as the successor to Mary Garden and
Geraldine Farrar. In her dramatic outbursts, Moore preserved the art of
the temper tantrum, and when irritations arose she could be seen stamp-
ing offstage in a cloud of perfume and jewelry, before her good nature
eventually returned. Enormously popular with the fans, her Hollywood
movies, like 1934's *One Night of Love,* and her interpretations of works
like "I Wish I Could Shimmy Like My Sister Kate" enlarged her public
beyond the confines of the opera house.

D O R O T H Y   K I R S T E N : Grace was my mentor; I was her
protégée. She was a wonderful help to me, giving me advice about
the conductors I worked with, the people I worked with. And she
always said, "Don't do what I do, do what I tell you." She was a
wonderful friend, and I owe a great deal to Grace.

F R E N I : My debut here was at the old Metropolitan in September
1965, and I sang with Gianni Raimondi and Maestro Cleva. And it
was a big impression for me, because I was at the Metropolitan and
in America. It was really something. I remember the audience ap-
plauded incredibly for me, and there were standing ovations.

Beginning in 1956, Giorgio Tozzi sang almost forty Collines with
the Metropolitan.

GIORGIO TOZZI: One *Bohème* I'm very proud of is the recording with Thomas Beecham, with Victoria de los Angeles, Jussi Bjoerling, Lucine Amara, Robert Merrill, John Reardon, and Fernando Corena. It's a wonderful recording—I still enjoy it.

Although better known for her Mimì, which she performed extensively, Lucine Amara lent her versatile talents to the role of Musetta for the Beecham recording.

LUCINE AMARA: Having sung many Mimìs, naturally I had an idea of what Musetta should be like, but I had never done it onstage. I prepared the role on my own with an accompanist, and I expected to have a rehearsal with Sir Thomas before we went into the studio for the recording. Not so. We arrived at the studio, he sat at the piano for about five minutes, and we recorded. It was the most nerveracking thing for me, because I had never sung it with orchestra. In my mind, I kept wanting to sing Mimì's lines. It really was traumatic—we just plunged in and did it. The only problem was the waltz: I was so used to the tempo being much faster, when I had sung Mimì with other conductors. But Sir Thomas took things much slower—which is fine, if you're prepared for it.

TOZZI: Beecham was a delight to work with. Sometimes he could drive you absolutely insane, but on the other hand, there were times he was absolutely a delight—which he was on the occasion of *Bohème.*

AMARA: There is such life and excitement to the recording. Beecham's ideas really worked. It was an incredible experience. I think I brought a fullness and the flirtiness, especially in Musetta's waltz. Usually, Musetta's lost in the ensembles, because she's sung by a lighter voice. But I had a thrust and a heavier sound to my voice, and I was happy with that.

TOZZI: Every one of the singers was in their prime. And sometimes recording sessions are fragmented, but every time you got up to do a section, it turned into a performance.

AMARA: Especially the scene in the fourth act, when she helps Mimì. I think that was very effective. I promptly forgot the role as soon as I recorded it, but when I was asked to sing, I always did sing Musetta's waltz.

TOZZI: There was such spirit, such bubbliness about the way Beecham approached the music. But at the same time, he was able to bring the tragedy out very intensely.

Luciano Pavarotti has often indicated that "Questa è Mimì," a short aria in the second act, is one of his favorite moments in the entire opera.

ALBANESE: When Mimì goes to the Café Momus, she becomes young. And Rodolfo says, "Come here, I want to buy a little hat for you." And this hat for her, this *cuffietta,* was all in lace and pink ribbon. And that's the one they give her at the last moment. As she's dying, she kisses it; she says, "Oh, la mia cuffietta," and then she becomes alive again. But in the second act, Mimì goes to talk to Musetta and looks at the beautiful dress she has on. She shows me this and we talk to each other. Then Mimì comes alive—she forgets to be sick.

SCOTTO: Musetta is very strong and she's very beautiful and she enjoys life very much, because she has health.

PATRICE MUNSEL: She is a little more knowing than girls her age, but she is youthful. I did see her as ingenuous, and she cared terribly much about Mimì in the last act, so I don't think she's in the least hard. But she is like one of the first hippies—she was living in that world, which was the French equivalent of the hippie world.

MOFFO: Musetta is interesting. She teaches singing. She's automatically a splash-through, no matter what. She's theatrical. That's where all the plate cracking and making an entrance comes from.

ALBANESE: She is very gay and *allegra,* full of health. That's why Toscanini wanted the voice of Musetta stronger, not coloratura. He said, "I want *healthy!* And Albanese should sing mezza voce, pianissimo." I said, sometimes, "Maestro, can I sing a little forte?" Because to sing piano like this is bad enough with a microphone, and to sing distance—you give more. And he said, "No. The tenor and the baritone will sing a little lower. Just mezza voice."

In the 1950s, Musetta was taken on by tempestuous red-haired soprano Ljuba Welitsch, who created a sensation in the part in London and New York. "I don't know of another woman in opera who is more full of life and gaiety, and yet who, in the crisis, shows that she has real heart too," she reflected at the time. "Also, she is loved by a baritone. Do you realize how exceptional this is? A soprano is in 95 cases always loved by a tenor."

CAROL NEBLETT: Most people play her in a bitchy, conniving way, but I think she's a fun-loving, warmhearted woman with an outrageous sense of humor, and in love with men—Marcello, particularly. She's determined to get him back, and if she has to throw a huge scene to do it, she will.

DANIELS: The role for me is really not work. It's more like getting paid for playing myself. My particular look must be close to most people's idea of what Musetta should look like. I think that's a reason Musetta seems to follow me around.

NEBLETT: She realizes that because of their last fight, Marcello's not going to speak to her. He'll either yell at her or whatever. So she embarrasses him, to get his attention and win him back.

DANIELS: The fourth act continues to grow in my understanding of the depth of her character, which is much deeper than most people think about.

SCOTTO: Of course, she's very much in love with Marcello. Like Mimì, she changes men; because remember, Mimì goes to the Viscontino. See, they are the same, but it is a question of health. Of course, everybody has a different way to show things, to show feelings. But they're bohemian—very free, everything they do.

NOVOTNÁ: Musetta's a little on the lighter side. Part of her likes the man who gives her money and keeps her. But she doesn't love him; she really loves Marcello.

MOFFO: She and Marcello are really exactly like Mimì and Rodolfo, except they manifest it in different ways.

ROBERT MERRILL: I love the role of Marcello very much. He's a marvelous character.

TOZZI: The voice of Robert Merrill as Marcello! I mean, the man who was born with a Stradivarius in his throat.

Giovanni Martinelli once recalled performances in the twenties: "During the café scene, the tables always had bottles of real champagne. It was during Prohibition, of course, but Frances Alda, our Mimì, always provided it. It didn't take too much acting ability to be gay under those circumstances."

M O F F O : The recording I made with Tucker and Bob Merrill was done with Leinsdorf, and it was very exciting to make. I remember that was when they were just starting to work with squares in the recording studio, so people could hear on their stereo speakers when you moved from stage left to stage right—supposedly to enhance the live feeling. It was like a big checkerboard, with all kinds of numbered squares. And it drove the singers crazy, because more important than how you were singing or what the conductor was doing was "Oh, I'm on thirty-four here," or "I'm on twenty-one." So you said, "Mi chiamano Mimì," and went over there. And what happened with the four guys, the four of them would be on one square, and one of them would say, "Hey, this is my place!" It was fun at first, and it all worked out.

A M A R A : I also did another recording with the Metropolitan Opera Record Club, and then another version, with Barry Morell and Brenda Lewis, in English, done for the schools.

M E R R I L L : Marcello's relationship with Musetta is very interesting. She's a little minx, and I try to calm her all the time, and it was fun doing it. I remember once doing it with Ljuba Welitsch. She was running around all over that scene, and she was something. When I picked her up at the end of the scene, her dress went up and she had no underwear on. It was a really historic performance. But she was marvelous.

S C O T T O : The similarity in *Bohème* is a great thing. The only thing is that Mimì and Rodolfo are more romantic than Musetta and Marcello, because Rodolfo is a poet, and everything he says he has to maybe make a big deal about.

N E B L E T T : I was singing in Salzburg and I got a call from Jimmy Levine asking if I could pull my Musetta together. They were supposed to record *Gioconda,* but had to cancel it. They had the singers all set for *Bohème,* but no Musetta. So I flew to London and we did it. Renata Scotto was wonderful. I don't think she'd ever heard me, and I started the aria and had to stop, and she said, "Wella, wella, well, you can sing!" She was so wonderful in the role.

D A N I E L S : Puccini is like a gift. I love those Puccini ladies. There's always something to be pulled out of Musetta's character. There's a lot of woman there, not just this superficial flirt the music sometimes indicates and some sopranos convey. No, this girl is a real survivor.

Murger's Musette was actually Marie-Christine Mariette Roux. More than just a good-time girl, she was an artist's model who sat for Ingres and was described as "remarkably well-made." Good-natured and resourceful, she managed to accumulate a tidy sum of money and set sail for a new life in Algiers. Shipwreck prevented her from reaching her destination, and Mlle. Roux, along with her fortune, lies somewhere beneath the Mediterranean.

MOFFO: I never did Musetta onstage, but I had the good fortune to record it. I think it's easier to do Mimì if you really know Musetta. She's not just a girl who comes out in a red dress. That's why Mimì has to be like her—they're two peas in a pod.

SCOTTO: When I did Musetta, I was looking at Mimì; when I did Mimì, I was looking at Musetta. That's why I wanted to do both parts. I found similarity absolutely in the way they live.

MOFFO: I was *very* insulted that anyone had the idea I should do Musetta. But then, I didn't know the role; and of course, I did Musetta to Callas's Mimì. Her Mimì was very unusual, especially on the recording. That recording took place at La Scala, and it was a magical kind of thing, with di Stefano—the whole thing was perfect. It was so perfect that as a young singer I was very proud to be a part of it. I later recorded Mimì three different times.

NEBLETT: Now I must play Musetta younger than I played her when I was younger—now, I have to consciously think sixteen or eighteen or twenty. Musetta requires a huge energy level.

DANIELS: I think they make a mistake when they cast a lighter voice. All of Puccini is heavily orchestrated. Musetta's sort of on top of the sandwich one minute, in the middle the next, and screaming most of the time. It's certainly not music written for a light, lyric voice, and I don't think it does your voice any favors.

ALBANESE: Pinza sang *Bohème* many times with us. One night he was not singing, and we were sitting at the table in the second act—and there he was, dressed like a chorus member, and came to the table. We used to do that in the second act of *Bohème,* even the first or second act of *Traviata*. We used to go and dress up for fun. To come in, walk and talk and do like the comprimarios, to surprise the colleagues—Pinza, Cehanovsky, de Paolis, Stella Roman . . .

After winning Academy Awards for *All About Eve* and *A Letter to Three Wives,* and prior to his involvement in Elizabeth Taylor's *Cleopatra,* Hollywood director Joseph L. Mankiewicz was invited by Rudolf Bing to stop by the Met and try his hand at *La Bohème.* Working with an English translation by Howard Dietz, who had translated the new *Fledermaus* two years earlier, Mankiewicz staged the new 1952 production, which starred Nadine Conner, Patrice Munsel, Richard Tucker, Robert Merrill, and Giorgio Tozzi. "It's like blowing a perfect smoke ring, to direct an opera at the Met," Mankiewicz said; "if they miss the opening, they never see the smoke ring."

M E R R I L L : I must give him credit, to change the stereotype of acting on the stage of the opera house. And Joe Mankiewicz was a great Hollywood director, and he was wonderful.

M U N S E L : He was so bright and theater-wise. The problem was that it was not a good translation. It just didn't sing—and I love a good translation; nothing could make me happier than a *Fledermaus* or *Périchole* or *Così Fan Tutte* in English.

M E R R I L L : I must say, I'm not for opera in English, except for the comedies. When you break up something like *La Bohème,* it just doesn't fit the music. You would almost have to change the music. We had problems with it and it wasn't very successful.

M U N S E L : Joe was delightful to work with, as anyone is who knows musical theater as opposed to strictly opera. They're so open to any ideas you can come up with, any excitement you can bring. At that time, anyway, opera directors were very rigid about what they would let you do.

M E R R I L L : That very same year, we went back to Italian. I remember my first line as Marcello was "I feel as though I'm painting with an icicle," because his hands were so cold. So one night I decided to say, "I feel as though I'm painting with a Popsicle." I shouldn't have done it, but I did. Maybe that's why we went back to the original. But the staging was marvelous. When Mimì died, she had a little muff, and it suddenly rolled off her body onto the floor, and you knew she was dead.

M U N S E L : It somehow put an emotional button on the opera—more than Rodolfo collapsing and sobbing.

M E R R I L L : Mankiewicz had a problem with the changing casts. If they put in a substitute, Joe was faced with suddenly having to restage it, and he said, "Oh, these tenors are driving me crazy!" I took him aside one day, and said, "Look, Joe, this is the Met; this is what it's all about. You're stuck with it." But the first act with the four guys is very tricky. There's so much going on.

M U N S E L : The singers and chorus people were bothered by these new directors, because they were used to stopping to face the conductor every time they had to sing. This drove Joe crazy, because he gave all the chorus people specific things to do, characters to play. And they would stay in character until they had to sing; then they'd immediately stop and face the orchestra and sing. When they were finished, they'd go back to the character. But conductors always wanted the chorus to face them at all times. Joe would say, "I see no reason, if you know the music—and you've certainly sung it enough—why you can't move while you're singing."

M E R R I L L : There's a lot of action in *Bohème,* a lot going on. Germont in *Traviata* is very static, but Marcello is always moving with his fellow artists. So, believe it or not, it's a difficult acting part—and a lot depends on the relationships.

M U N S E L : Having worked in the musical theater made it much easier for me to work with Joe or a Garson Kanin. My teacher originally taught me that I should be able to sing standing on my head, or throwing medicine balls while I was singing scales or high Fs, or with sixteen books on my stomach while I was lying on the floor, or punching a punching bag. So you're free from just standing there with your hands folded. So with these directors, when they wanted me to do something weird, I just did it—which was good for them, and a lot of fun for me.

At *Bohème*'s world premiere, on February 1, 1896, the Turin public was indifferent. The seeming insignificance of the story and everyday quality of the characters' lives made little impression. But the critics found the whole presentation disgustingly primal: "Just as *La Bohème* fails to leave any very strong impression upon the listener," wrote *La Stampa*'s critic, "so it will fail to leave any strong trace in the history of our opera, and it will be well for the author to regard it as a momentary error. . . ."

NOVOTNÁ: You know, everybody expects—who knows what? Much to-do. But it's a simple story.

SCOTTO: Maybe in that period they considered it as too much sentimentalism. And there is nothing wrong with sentimentalism, but the story of a group of bohemians maybe didn't touch the critics at that time. See, *Manon Lescaut* was such a big success and is such a powerful story. *La Bohème* is not about one person, but about a group of people. One of the critics said, "*Bohème*—in one month we are all going to forget about it." Can you believe?

NOVOTNÁ: The music—my God! It is such a joy. Everybody except Marcello has a magnificent aria.

SCOTTO: The story is very ordinary. It is so human, so real. If I were to say something against *Butterfly*—which I don't want, but if I did—sometimes there are moments in *Butterfly* where it is not real. It goes on a little bit and it's not so important. But with *Bohème,* the characters, everything is so modern.

PAVAROTTI: I was watching the closing ceremony of the Olympics. And when we see an athlete concentrating, we think that he is an old man. But then when you see them afterward, in normal life, that is youth—that is *Bohème.*

FRENI: I thank Puccini for this role every time. Mimì is no problem for me at all. Other roles, like Tatiana or Adriana Lecouvreur, are more difficult; not just the music, but they make more demands on you dramatically.

PAVAROTTI: It is impossible, with time, to change the character of Rodolfo. He is a young boy. He's good in 1835, when he was thought of by the composer, and he's going to be good when man is going to make *Bohème* on the moon. That feeling of youth, of life, happy and terrible . . . He is now, here. If he's not with tuberculosis, he's with drugs or cancer or all these things. And in the meantime, there's the happiness of youth—of the young people, nineteen, twenty.

FRENI: When you're younger, you don't know so many things as a person. But naturally, my mind is fuller now, and I control better everything I do and put more into it.

PAVAROTTI: I think it is an opera that is very good luck for me, one that I love very much, that is still staying with me until the last day of my performances. I hope not like my father, because he's seventy-five and not able to come to New York because he has to sing in the church—solo!

FRENI: I'm really happy because I'm still singing—I'm sorry if I say this—without routine. You know, I detest this, when it becomes routine. I enjoy to sing really every night, especially when you have a conductor like Kleiber, and with Pavarotti and a cast like we had at the Met. You remember the audience, too, was crazy about these.

TOZZI: In my generation, I can think back to certain years at the Met where it was not unusual to have Gedda, Tucker, Peerce, Corelli, Bergonzi, all singing *Bohème* in one season. I always felt I should have bought a ticket, because working with these great voices, I was as much a part of the audience as I was onstage.

Bohème didn't arrive at the Met until December 26, 1900. Mimì was introduced by the Australian Nellie Melba, who, despite her tremendous following throughout her forty-year career, once described herself as "the meanest woman in the world." Though *The New York Times* liked her "neat character acting and delightful singing" in the first act, even the four years since the world premiere hadn't softened critical reaction to the opera. "*La Bohème* is foul in subject, and fulminant but futile in its music," the *Times* review began, and it went on to misspell Puccini's name. "It is better to dismiss it with a smile than to reflect upon it till vexation sets in."

MOFFO: I loved Mimì, and as every soprano, it was one of the first things I ever studied. And by accident, it was my American debut. I had debuted in Italy in *Butterfly,* and after seeing me do Lucia at a theater outside of Milano, Carol Fox engaged me for Lucia in Chicago. But in those days they never had you make the trip for just one role, so the sequence was: debut, Lucia; Susanna—fantastic, with Solti, Steber, and Cossotto as Cherubino, and Gobbi as the Count; and *Mignon* was terrific, with Simionato; and *Bohème* at the end. So, don't you know, Mr. di Stefano canceled sick for *Lucia*. Bjoerling was scheduled for *Bohème* at the end of the season, and Carol Fox said, "He has agreed to do *Bohème* if you will, and we'll move *Lucia* to the end." This was a big decision, because *Lucia* was a much splashier debut and I just felt happier in it. Also, I didn't believe in my own simplicity; I always thought I had to prove something. But I agreed to do it.

T O Z Z I : I did *Bohème* with so many people; each one brought something of their own. Jussi Bjoerling was absolutely wonderful. And Richard Tucker, who had a more spinto kind of voice, wonderful as well—a great, great singer—and Franco Corelli and Nicolai Gedda . . .

M O F F O : I want to tell you, when I was on that stage and I made my entrance and had to sit there while Jussi Bjoerling sang the most incredible "Che gelida manina". . . . And my heart—I can remember it now. I said, "Mi chiamano Mimì"—and I said to myself, "What am I doing here? What have I done?" It was a success, but I don't remember anything except I kept wishing it was *Lucia*.

T O Z Z I : One of the great things about working with great singers— you feel you're participating in something so special; you feel privileged. And great singers always feed one another.

Among the many unorthodox *Bohème* productions was Joseph Papp's 1984 effort at the Public Theater, which tapped the talents of pop singer Linda Ronstadt. The "updating" consisted of reducing the orchestra to a synthesizer and twelve instruments, including a saxophone, and using a "hip" libretto that traded Mimì's traditional "I am so forgetful" for "I know I'm a pain."

S C O T T O : I know very well why they would do a rock *Bohème*. They're modern characters. I wouldn't do it to Puccini, but Ken Russell did a *Bohème* that starts in 1840 with the first act; the second is at the end of the century; the third is in wartime; and the last act, in our own time, Mimì dying not by consumption but by drugs. As an experiment, it was a great idea. I mean, you're not doing a Puccini *Bohème,* but the fact that each act really fits into our own period is very interesting. But it is only an experiment. It should never be in a major theater where you have a regular season, only in a festival that lasts three weeks. The best way is always to do what the composer and the original wanted, but sometimes it's also a good idea to renovate and do something different. Maybe the composer himself would have agreed to it.

M O F F O : I don't think anyone ever worries enough about what happens in intermission. I've always tried to make my scenario— within the realm of what's written—of what happened between the acts. You have to have continuity. In Act Three of *Bohème,* they're obviously separated; they fight all the time. I always say, "Why do they fight?" Well, probably because they're both creative, sensitive people—they're jealous. The worst part about being so in love is that you're incredibly jealous, no?

N O V O T N Á : The strangest thing—he always said she was unfaithful to him, that she is playing with others and on. But she is a natural, simple girl—probably a little coquettish.

S C O T T O : In the third act, she's strong enough that she knows there is no more hope for her. She's going to die; she leaves Rodolfo. And for her to leave Rodolfo is very painful, but she doesn't want to hurt him by having her sick at home, and having Rodolfo take care of her.

F R E N I : Mimì is naturally very upset because she knows she's sick. And she's had this fight with Rodolfo—he's so anxious about her, because he knows she's sick, too, but he has nothing to help her. He lies to her, really in a rude way, and she's upset and goes with this Viscontino, because he has money and can perhaps help her.

A L B A N E S E : She found somebody else who would take care of her and give her a little bit of security. Then she goes to find Marcello.

N O V O T N Á : And Rodolfo is away with his friend Marcello, and he tells him, "I can't stand it anymore. She's so sick, and it will be awful, because she's coughing and dying."

S A Y Ã O : She understands that the tenor is tired. She was a sick woman, and she overhears what he says.

When Grace Moore sang Mimì with Polish tenor Jan Kiepura for the first time in 1937, she was horrified to see him pushing upstage the chair in which she was required to faint. When she finally did faint, she was forced to sing her aria with the tenor positioned directly between her and the conductor. After informing the management that she would never sing with Kiepura again, she swallowed her fury when she found they were contracted for another performance together. Onstage once more, she watched in disbelief as he again bent to move the chair—only to find that this time, sympathetic stage hands had nailed it to the floor.

ROSENSHEIN: In the third act, Rodolfo experiences what we all do. He can't have what he wants. He's confused and he inflicts pain on the person he loves the most; then he suffers for it. This is the beauty of him.

HADLEY: I think Rodolfo possesses the selfishness of youth. He's unwilling to let go of his dreams of being a poet enough to go out and find steady work to provide for her, to keep her alive.

ROSENSHEIN: He's a different person after she dies. I don't know, for example, if Alfredo is a different person after Violetta dies, but you can see that Rodolfo will never be the same.

HADLEY: Even to the very end, Rodolfo continues to deny that she's as sick as she is. Mimì has faced reality—she knows what's going on. I think it's an opera about coming of age. I very seriously doubt that at the end of that opera, any of those people will ever be the same again.

NOVOTNÁ: The poor woman, Mimì, comes to the inn because she hoped that Marcello would help her to resolve this problem, because she sees that Rodolfo has been really ugly to her, yelling at her. And in her greatest need, Rodolfo leaves her.

SAYÃO: The romance was almost over, and she sings this beautiful aria where she says, "I will go away, because I know you don't care for me anymore."

ALBANESE: Then, "We'll separate again in the spring, because the sun keeps me company." She says, "I want to be warm," and "alla stagion dei fior"—"when the flowers bloom again." And she sings really with this sadness, sickness—maybe tired to live.

TOZZI: Although I never sang with Licia Albanese, I heard her sing it. It was wonderful, absolutely stunning, with all the pathos and heart that one would imagine.

Working for the first time with librettists Giuseppe Giacosa and Luigi Illica, Puccini found himself in the midst of an unwieldy, exasperating project he swore would kill him. They faced the impossible task of turning Murger's loosely strung stories of unremarkable incidents into a stage work of dramatic impact. The first draft was fifteen to twenty acts. The usually phlegmatic Giacosa tried to resign. The project was making him "sick to death," he wrote Puccini's publisher. "Curse the libretto! I have already done the whole thing from start to finish three times over, and some of it four or five times."

P A V A R O T T I : First of all, the people are everybody people. I went the first time to see *Traviata,* and I was shocked—beautiful, incredible costumes and richness. And then I went to see *Bohème.* I was three or four—something like that. And when the scene opens, it was "Oh, why so poor?" And then the music came in, and I realized that was the true life and the other was acted. And that is what the people think. Anybody pictures himself there.

M O F F O : *Bohème* was the first opera I ever saw. I saw it in Philadelphia, with di Stefano and Lucia Evangelista, who is Jerry Hines's wife. And I can't tell you how she sang, but I can tell you she had the reddest hair I'd ever seen, and I remember it was all mopped up on top of her head, and it was just beautiful! And in the last act, it all came down. Those are the things that impress kids. I was already about sixteen or so, and I can remember sitting at the Academy of Music, and I was so entranced, when she dies, at di Stefano's "Mimì!" that I think they had to come and tell me to leave the theater after everybody was out.

P A V A R O T T I : Rodolfo is for me the most important role in terms of *significato,* because I made my debut in 1961 with this role, because I choose this role in any important debut in the opera house. I have done this first at Covent Garden, Milan, New York, San Francisco, Chicago, and more and more. So I would say this is what I consider my first love and my good-luck role. And it's one of the roles I've done the most.

F R E N I : It is very difficult, but I adore the character. It makes me famous in all the world—how can I not love her?

P A V A R O T T I : I have three favorite roles: Rodolfo and also *Ballo in Maschera* and *Elixir of Love,* for different reasons. Vocally speaking, *Ballo* is the most complete for a tenor of my voice. *Elixir of Love* is different; made with a full voice, it is a difficult score, even, and very big to conquer.

F R E N I : I am pleased because people write me so many letters, and they wait for me outside the stage, and they tell me how much they love me—and I think it's because I was natural. This makes me happy and very proud.

S A Y Ã O : I originally wanted to be an actress. I never had any ambition to start singing. But my family was terribly against it. There was no show business in my family. Everyone was lawyers and doctors and housewives—you know, a regular family—in Rio de Janeiro. My family would have been really disgraced if I started to go on the stage. But since I was eight or nine, I would want to recite. My mother used to take me to the theater all the time, and I was fascinated. Well, I had an uncle who was a doctor, but he was also musical; and he started to write for me little monologues, and then to compose a little song for me. My voice was very small, very childish, and I decided to sing just to please him. He told me, "If you can start singing, if your voice will be enough for an opera or even a musical, you will be on the stage and you will be able to act." This is the only reason I started to sing. I was thirteen when I started to vocalize, to develop this voice from one note to the other. I was born with hardly any voice at all. I had no volume, no body in the center to sing lyric. It did start to go up as a coloratura, but my teacher said, "You are not developed even as a woman," so it was slow. I was with her for three years—one year only to vocalize. But after that time I could sing opera arias, coloratura.

After Nellie Melba's farewell performance of *Bohème* at Covent Garden, unceasing ovations washed over her as the hour grew later and later. A weary stagehand tried to protect her by closing the curtain, until the diva demanded, "Pull back those bloody curtains at once!"

M O F F O : I always think of Mimì as having this creamy, honey sound—beautiful but expressive. Mirella Freni, who's made a life's work of Mimì, is just incredible—her voice, her persona, herself . . . she is Mimì. Also Tebaldi, Victoria de los Angeles, Licia Albanese . . .

S A Y Ã O : Mimì is very even. The second act is a little heavy—the duet with the baritone.

F R E N I : The difficult parts in the opera—it really depends if you feel good or not. But no, Mimì is in my voice.

M O F F O : If you find you don't have to sing a high C or E flat, that's very nice, for a change. But you have to work in a different way, to make everything she has to sing beautiful. I don't think Mimì has any phrases to sing that aren't per se gorgeous. Every line she has—even the third-act duet with Marcello—it's all beautiful. The difficulty with Mimì is that it has a sameness, where it's up to you to find—in those ten notes, say, arranged differently—a lot of color, expression, which must come from you. "Sì. Mi chiamano Mimì" is certainly not "Sempre libera," "Ah, fors' è lui," or any of the Bellini or Donizetti things. It's so pure, so obvious, that it's difficult.

SCOTTO: Mimì has to be paced. I mean, you can sing through Mimì and find it's very easy, but you have to give an interpretation. It's there where it's difficult to pace, because interpretation is where you get tired, where you don't know what to do. At the middle of the opera, it's "Oh, my God! I have no voice, no breath. I have no strength," because you don't know how to pace.

MOFFO: Puccini obviously loved his heroines, because he always wrote so beautifully for them. In its simplicity, Mimì to me is like a great Schubert song. It is so simple, but it has to be perfectly done—expressive in its limits—because it doesn't have a mad scene, twenty or thirty minutes to hold the whole stage by herself. She doesn't have the solo scene. All her arias are with somebody else, the duets, the quartet; she dies with a lot of people—she's never the center of attention.

FRENI: It is not so hard to [gives a scream of abandon] as to do the quiet and the simple. So every time it is good for me to try to find something different and new. But if you're natural, it's always different, and you find something each time you do it.

SAYÃO: You have to enunciate every word very clearly. I learned this with Tito Schipa. He had a very regular, not a great, voice—not even a very high voice. He transposed sometimes, because he couldn't even reach the high Cs. And the volume wasn't big. He was a really light tenor. But what he had was an artistry that was so great that he had those pianissimos in his diction. You didn't lose one word that he said, and he never forced his voice.

MOFFO: When I was first studying *Bohème,* I was so in love with the music—as I think all young singers are.

TOZZI: The sopranos I sang with were so marvelous: Victoria de los

Angeles, Renata Tebaldi, who was absolutely wonderful in *Bohème*. A very wonderful Mimì was Lucine Amara, who probably had the best singing technique of any soprano who ever came down the pike, consistently. Anna Moffo did a beautiful Mimì.

SAYÃO: I thought my voice was not big enough for opera, and I went to Jean de Reszke to have a master class, because I was prepared to start my career as a recitalist. He said, "You have too much feeling. You must be in opera." I said, "Maestro, I have no voice big enough for opera." And he said, "It's because you're very young"—I was not yet seventeen. He started to teach me a little bit of *Romeo and Juliet*. He said, "In three or four years, you're going to sing this opera," and I did. I learned a lot from him about style and interpretation. After that I learned *Manon,* then *Bohème*.

FRENI: The first time I did Mimì was in Bologna. The first performances were for Victoria de los Angeles there, and it was for me to sing the last three. But after one or two performances, Victoria was sick, and they asked me to do them. I made my debut this way—it was very, very good for me.

Puccini was unhappy with the choice of Turin for *Bohème*'s premiere, at the Teatro Regio. Toscanini, who would later take charge of *The Girl of the Golden West,* was in the pit; Cesira Ferrani, who had created Manon Lescaut, was onstage as Mimì. Nevertheless, Puccini became more uneasy as rehearsals progressed, until he went to the premiere, in his own words, "like a criminal going to execution."

But artists thrive on suffering. "I actually prayed that a car would run me over so that I wouldn't have to die onstage," wrote Rosa Ponselle about her career-long stage fright. Art is never easy.

SAYÃO: My method of learning a score or song was just to read it many times, until I learned all the words. Then I put the notes over this beautiful declamation. I knew all the words that all the people say, even before I read the score, because I had to know how to react.

PAVAROTTI: The very first time, I was lucky, because the stage director was a very famous soprano, Mafalda Favero. She gave us the book to read, and really go inside. She was very, very, good—very simple in detail, but in character. She really makes us see one thing that was written in the score, I think between the first and second acts: "Life, happy and terrible," and the more happy it is, the more terrible it will be at the end. That, I think, you cannot change much. Yes, you can build, you can do one period or another, with different costumes and so on. But the feeling in the music cannot change much for you, if you are lucky to begin good. An opera like *Trovatore* can change for me even now. I have done ten productions of *Trovatore,* but I am sure if a great stage director is coming down, he is certainly helping me to do better. Of that I am one hundred percent sure, because *Trovatore* is an opera made with all the feeling, all the *sentimento. Bohème,* no.

NOVOTNÁ: The sentiment in *Bohème* is so real, so human. When she feels she's really dying, she goes back to him. Still it is, for her, the greatest love.

ALBANESE: She had left Rodolfo to go with the Viscontino. Musetta says, "And then I saw her in the snow—and she was dying. So I told her to come here, and she said, 'Yes, take me to Rodolfo—I want to die with him.'" It's so beautiful: "Voglio morir con lui. . . . Forse m'aspetta"—"I want to die with him. . . . Maybe he's waiting for me." She was looking for Rodolfo.

HADLEY: Women at those tender ages are far more mature than most men are. When Musetta sees she's dying, she says, "What can I do for her? She wants to see Rodolfo? Fine." Then when they have no money for medicine, who takes off her earrings? Musetta says, "Here, go sell them. Get her some medicine." The two women understand what's happening. The men don't.

MOFFO: I like to think she's probably never been in love with anybody as much as Rodolfo—and this takes its toll as she gets sicker and sicker. But her one thought, what she has to admit on her deathbed, is that the only place she wants to be is with him. They fight like cats and dogs, but inevitably, he's her guy.

FRENI: She loves Rodolfo always.

SAYÃO: She was so much in love; she was young and poor; she makes artificial flowers to live; she wanted little things like the muff that Musetta brings her to keep her hands warm.

ALBANESE: She went to sell her earrings, to buy the muff for the beautiful hands of Mimì.

SAYÃO: Rodolfo, he writes poems that have never been published—what a mess!

At the end, when they are giving the muff to Mimì—Musetta tries to take it back! *Why, I wonder? I hope this little incident was not intended . . .*

—GIACOMO PUCCINI,
IN A LETTER TO HIS PUBLISHER AFTER SEEING AN
EARLY DRAFT OF THE LIBRETTO

M O F F O : In the fourth act, Musetta comes out the way she really is, which is more like Mimì—sells her jewelry, helps her friend. They're really like sisters—very, very close.

J E R O M E   H I N E S : When they were going to tear down the old Met, I was part of the opposition and was trying to get the house saved. The last opera produced on the stage was *Bohème,* and I did Colline. So in the coat song, during the performance, I changed the words: from the "old coat" that I'm saying farewell to, to "the old theater"; from "pockets" to "halls" and "rooms"—and made it a very sentimental farewell to the theater. In Italian. Then I blew a big kiss to the theater instead of the coat. I expected to get fired and I had a letter all ready to deliver to Mr. Bing, had he gotten furious. He never even noticed it. He didn't know until I told him about it five years later. And I thought I was going to get such a blast from him. He was trying to fight any opposition of sentimentality to the old house.

A L B A N E S E : Sometimes, as I was dying, I used to get up from the bed and say, "Oh, do you remember—" and come alive again; "here, near the table, and I lost my key—" And then she starts to cough again, and it's "Oh, Mimì," and he puts her back in the bed again. You have to change all these things. They used to let us do things like that.

M O F F O : Then Puccini does something interesting. When Mimì is dying, she sings as the people go out. When she dies, the same theme comes back, when Rodolfo doesn't realize she's dead. And then he realizes—*"Mimì!"*—and it's up a half-step; it's in sharps. And it's like daggers! It's so much more riveting in the key of C sharp than in C minor that it goes through the whole house. That's when everybody starts to cry, this punch of the sharps. I myself have never been able to sit in the opera, or even do Mimì, without tears streaming down my face in that *"Mimì!"*

S C O T T O : To die in Rodolfo's arms is another symbol of love. And it's also Puccini, because look at Puccini: Every opera, every role, every character—love is the main force and the main purpose and the main talk in the entire opera. And in life, because life without love—I mean, look at Turandot. Mimì, the women in Puccini's life, they have one faith—love.

A L B A N E S E : When I went to see the house where Puccini was born, they said, "Licia, you never went to the terrace." And I went up steps and came on this little terrace. And I saw the roses there, and you can see all the red roofs—when Mimì says, "I can look at the roofs, but I can touch the sun." And I said, "Oh, my God, this is really *Bohème*."

OTELLO

~

*Otello may be the greatest opera ever written.
Certainly, I am completely prejudiced in
that direction.*

—JAMES MCCRACKEN

Music by Giuseppi Verdi
Libretto by Arrigo Boito
Based on the play by William Shakespeare
from the translations of Giulio Carcano and Victor Hugo

DESDEMONA.. *Gilda Cruz-Romo,
Evelyn Lear, Zinka
Milanov, Aprile Millo,
Leona Mitchell, Renata
Scotto, Eleanor Steber,
Kiri Te Kanawa*

EMILIA .... *Mignon Dunn*

OTELLO .... *Richard Cassilly, James
McCracken, Ramón
Vinay*

IAGO .... *Cornell MacNeil, Robert
Merrill, Sherrill Milnes,
Thomas Stewart*

GUEST APPEARANCES................ *Mark Baker, John
Macurdy, Sandra
Warfield*

*A*fter being lost in small parts at the Met for four seasons, tenor James
McCracken fled to Europe with his wife, mezzo Sandra Warfield.

He established himself as a leading dramatic tenor and returned to the United States in triumph as Verdi's Otello in Washington, D.C., in 1960. The role took him to all the major opera houses in the world and provided him with an unprecedented two new productions at the Met. At the time of his death in 1988, he had sung the role more often than any other tenor in history.

SANDRA WARFIELD: The saddest thing for me is that we have no visible record of Jimmy's performance that he took all over the world.

The fact that his Otello was never committed to tape or film never dimmed the singer's passion for the role or the opera.

JAMES McCRACKEN: *Otello* may be the greatest opera ever written. Certainly, I am completely prejudiced in that direction.

Following the world premiere of the opera at La Scala in 1887, a critic wrote, "In no other opera has Verdi devoted so much attention to detail as in this *Otello*." The original Otello was Francesco Tamagno, who possessed a voice of astonishing size and agility. The role became his trademark and he introduced it all over the world, even committing excerpts to a recording that is still available. His vocal style and the composition of the role have proven detrimental to the opera's popularity. The scarcity of singers willing to tackle the title role have made productions of the work harder and harder to cast.

The legendary tenor Richard Tucker never attempted the role and he was in excellent company. "Only fools, idiots sing it," Tucker once said. "The best proof is del Monaco. He was a great Otello, but once when I met him in Verona, you know what he said? 'You're the smart one. *Io stupido!*' He couldn't sing legato anymore. Even better proof is that Caruso never sang the role."

McCRACKEN: Advice is easy to come by; sorting it out is a difficult situation. People are well meaning and they say things to you that they mean in their own heart of hearts to be truthful. I don't say you should never take advice—that would be foolish—but there is something about "To thine own self be true." *You* have to be the one to decide. When people come out and say, "I would," or "I wouldn't," or "If I were you," the last part is the key phrase, because they're *not* you. And I really believe this. Pay attention to the critics and to your well-wishers, but in the final analysis, give yourself plenty of time all by yourself in a room somewhere, and you be the one to decide.

W A R F I E L D : He decided to do the role everywhere he could. Oh, there were others and they were wonderful, but they didn't take on the responsibility of taking the role and keeping it alive. One tenor might do three or four performances, but Jimmy did hundreds and passionately believed that the opera must be heard.

M C C R A C K E N : Otello offers the singing actor the entire gamut of emotions to run with. From the heroic "Esultate!" entrance to the final death, "un altro bacio," lie unforgettable moments of tender love, passion, doubt, fear, jealousy, anger, anguish, terror, sorrow, hate, remorse.

All of these emotions were revealed to Gilda Cruz-Romo when she heard him sing the role long before she debuted as Desdemona.

G I L D A C R U Z - R O M O : You know, when you're onstage you don't really see the performances. It's beautiful but you don't see sometimes how really effective it is. At the very start of my career, Jimmy McCracken came to Mexico to sing *Otello*. I will tell you, it was one of the most incredible things in my life. Then I didn't dream to be singing with him some day. He was bigger than life. It was just so special, really inspiring for me, and then he turned out to be such a beautiful colleague, such an artist, and such a gentleman. When I was singing in *Otello* at the Met, he was out. I never got to sing it with him, but in many ways that performance in Mexico City remains very special for me because I got to see it totally, and if I'd been singing with him it would have been a shared experience, but I would never have seen the strength, the full force of his personality, his total performance. Truly, it is one of the highlights of my life to have heard him sing Otello.

M C C R A C K E N : Well, you take one of Shakespeare's greatest plays and add Verdi's music, and you have to have a profound emotional experience. I guess by now I've done the role more than any other tenor and there are a lot of different ways to play him, believe me. It's gotten to the point where I can combine interpretations and mix things up.

Prior to McCracken's triumphant return to the Met, the two leading Otellos had been the Italian Mario del Monaco and the Chilean Ramón Vinay. As performing artists, they were two sides of a coin: del Monaco the Verdian musician, and Vinay the consummate singing actor. *The New York Times* commented on both: "[Del Monaco] because of the stamina and the drive with which he sings . . . showed himself to be one of the few tenors who can carry the heavy part." On Vinay: "The music was brilliantly and dramatically sung. . . . The elemental fury of the part was emphasized—a wild beast aroused and running amok before the end of it."

ELEANOR STEBER: I did *Otello* with Ramón. He was my first Otello and he was unbelievable, unbelievable! He was an *actor*! He was so realistic and gave such fantastic feeling to the role. He tore you apart onstage. It was a tremendous emotional experience every time you were onstage with Ramón.

RAMÓN VINAY: In all the reviews I got for this role as I look back on it, they would say I was as good an actor as I was a singer, and this does not always go together.

RENATA SCOTTO: I remember when I saw del Monaco. He was a great Otello. He had this figure—and when he was onstage, he *was* Otello! Make-believe—del Monaco had that, to make believe that he was the warrior and the conquerer and the big man that Otello was. Vickers and McCracken had that, and I'm sure Domingo does, too. And I've only heard the recording, but it impressed me a lot, with Ramón Vinay. It doesn't matter what approach you use; you have to understand and be able to sing what Verdi wrote.

CRUZ-ROMO: There were some really extraordinary Otellos. I never heard Ramón Vinay, but I did get to meet him and he was an extraordinary artist.

WARFIELD: Jimmy admired Ramón Vinay very much. I remember we went to see him near the end of his career. He was such a great actor.

CRUZ-ROMO: When I was starting, you got to hear great Otellos like del Monaco. He was extraordinary.

V I N A Y : Acting is intuition. If you don't have the basic intuition to move around and give your voice an accent here or there, it's no good. I barely sang Otello in the last scene. It was speaking the words while singing the words.

Verdi would have been pleased with his approach. "After he has confirmed the fact that Desdemona was innocent [when] murdered," the composer wrote, "Otello no longer has any strength: he's worn out, physically and morally exhausted: he is unable to nor should he sing more than in a veiled, half-dead voice. . . ."

Young American tenor Mark Baker may be heading in the direction of Otello. However, he already knows the type of sound he feels the part requires.

M A R K B A K E R : I'm really partial to the stentorian-type Otello, where you get all that energy. I think that's what makes the opera work. It's just like *Peter Grimes:* It was originally written for Peter Pears, who was very lyric, but the minute Jon Vickers made it his thing, the only thing people wanted to hear was the stentorian madman Grimes. It might not be that at all, but it's such an exciting sound because it's always on the edge. The tenor voice, period, is fun to listen to because it has that moment of danger in it, but the big tenor parts always have that line where you think, "Is he going to make it or not?" and that makes it very exciting. Personally, I like the big beefier sound.

V I N A Y : A big advantage that I had also was that I spoke Italian fluently, and it helps enormously when you speak the language the composer wrote in. It makes it much easier.

S T E B E R : I also did the role with Mario del Monaco, and with that glorious voice of his, that was a real experience. His Otello was terribly impressive. He was marvelous.

V I N A Y : The first time I ever met Toscanini was in maybe '43 or '44. I was in New York with my pianist and my manager and all of a sudden this old gentleman with a beard stepped out of his car. I think he was with his son. Then inside he sat down at the piano and without a score he began to play *Otello.* So I sang the role on the radio with the maestro [the NBC Symphony performance in 1947]. I was lucky to meet with him and do this, very lucky. I've been lucky all my life.

Lucky, talented, and willing to share—as tenor Richard Cassilly found out:

RICHARD CASSILLY: In San Francisco, we were doing *Boris* together, which was a mistake for him, but Vinay was determined to go on singing and he had switched back to being a baritone, and he was having troubles. One day I passed him in the hallway and I said that I had gotten to see him in the last two acts of *Otello* when I was a student at the Peabody Institute in Baltimore. We had opera class that night. When it was over, I rushed over to the Lyric Theater and raced up the fire escape, tipped the usher a dollar—which was the way it was done in those days—and stood for the last two acts. It was with him and Warren and Steber, and I think it was John Garris's last performance. He was murdered when the Met moved on to Atlanta.

The tenor's body was found in an alley in Atlanta. Garris had been singing the role of Cassio. The crime has remained unsolved for forty years.

CASSILLY: I told Ramón I had regretted not seeing the whole performance, and he told me to sit down, which I did. There on the steps he went through the whole of *Otello,* explaining his concept of the whole thing. The one big thing I learned from him—besides gratitude and the love he had for his art—was when he said to me, "Remember, when you enter, you have one thing on your mind: You have not yet been to bed with Desdemona. That's the only thing on your mind. You're in a hurry to get to bed with her, and that will make the rest of the opera make sense." I thought that was valuable information. It's a great operatic moment and a great dramatic moment. Then I made the mistake of saying I'd never seen his José and everyone raved about it, so he had me sit down again for another two and a half hours. It was a great lesson for me in the generosity of an artist. He had a message and he had an audience.

VINAY: There have been better voices than mine, but I have the actor in me and the inflection in the words when I was singing. You have to spend hours and hours and hours to learn that.

CASSILLY: Vinay asked me to come to Santiago and be Otello for his Iago. Fortunately, I was busy, because I understand that Ramón ended up in the last act singing Otello. There was no Iago in the last act. He just used it as an excuse to sing Otello's last act one last time.

R O B E R T   M E R R I L L : Sometimes when you'd sing with Ramón, you'd forget that *you* had to sing because you'd get so wrapped up in his performance.

V I N A Y : When I sang my first *Otello,* it was at La Scala in Milano, and I stayed in the hotel around the corner. The morning before my performance, there was a long line under my window going all the way to Scala. I said to myself, "My word, I hope none of them has a pistol."

By the time he completed *Otello,* Verdi was intimately involved in the psychological nature of his characters. When a friend remarked about the glory the work had brought him, Verdi replied, "Oh, glory, glory! I so loved my solitude in the company of Otello and Desdemona. Now the crowd, always greedy for something new, has taken them away from me, leaving me nothing but the memory of our secret conversations, our dear, past intimacy."

A P R I L E   M I L L O : I wouldn't change a thing in *Otello.* I would kiss Verdi's hand.

In the famous production of Shakespeare's play featuring Paul Robeson, Iago and Desdemona were played by José Ferrer and Uta Hagen, who were then husband and wife. Though the subject matter is not conducive to marital bliss, spouses Evelyn Lear and Thomas Stewart have played the same roles in the operatic version.

T H O M A S   S T E W A R T : Iago is obviously one of the greatest acting parts in opera. For a baritone, it's one of the best. My association with the role goes all the way back to when I was a student, almost thirty-five or forty years ago. . . .

E V E L Y N   L E A R : It wasn't that long ago!

S T E W A R T : Yes, it was thirty years ago.

L E A R : All right, thirty, but not forty.

S T E W A R T : I was in college in 1949. What does she want from me? Anyway, I was a graduate of Baylor University, and they had a great theater department. I went there to take theater courses and that's where I first encountered Shakespeare's *Othello.* When I finally came to the part of Iago in Verdi's *Otello,* I couldn't wait to get ahold of it.

LEAR: When we first did the opera together, he was mean, really mean.

STEWART: I guess I was mean, but I looked at Evelyn and I had to see her not as my wife but as Desdemona.

LEAR: That's the difference between us onstage.

STEWART: She found the separation thing difficult to do. I never did. If I see her as my wife, I'm not going to beat her up and slam her around.

LEAR: My first Desdemona was in Budapest with a Wagnerian tenor.

STEWART: A Hungarian Wagnerian tenor?

LEAR: Yes. That was quite an experience. Of course, after that, I did it all over.

STEWART: My first production of the opera was in Germany with Wolfgang Windgassen and Anja Silja, and it was quite an experience—really off the wall.

While Silja was obviously cast for her dramatic talents rather than her vocal suitability, vocally Desdemona fit Zinka Milanov like a glove.

ZINKA MILANOV: Desdemona is not much effort compared to something like Norma.

STEBER: I think *Otello* is Verdi's greatest tragedy, just as his great comedy is *Falstaff.* Mozart also has two. The comedy is *Marriage of Figaro* and the tragedy is, of course, *Don Giovanni.* Wagner has *Tristan and Isolde* and then *Meistersinger.* You could go on and on down the line, but those are, in my opinion, the great operas that have been written.

CASSILLY: My first Otello was in English for the CBC in 1961 or '62. I was very glad it was in English. Later I did the same translation for the BBC. It's wonderful to do something that large in your own language first, because it makes your emotions or your emotional response become automatic, and I'm all for that. I wish I had sung more Otellos.

WARFIELD: Otello was a natural part for Jimmy. It fit him

perfectly. His middle voice was always very strong and could sail through the orchestra. The high notes were always there and the whole *personaggio* was absolutely part of him.

SHERRILL MILNES: Jim found a way to be absolutely convincing, but he never lost control onstage. Strength onstage is certainly a creation of illusion—not without support strength, but the actual force of throwing and twisting has to be done equally or even more by your partner. Then it's safe.

MERRILL: Jon Vickers was a wonderful Otello—very physical, very emotional. Sometimes you can overdo that, but to me he was wonderful onstage. I enjoyed working with Mario del Monaco, too. For some reason, he never got that much credit for his work at the Metropolitan, but he was a wonderful Otello both musically and dramatically.

MILNES: My first *Otello* was in Mexico City in 1965—pre-Met, post–City Opera. I was half virginal, certainly young. I had never even seen the opera, so for the first time in my career I spent three or four sessions with a coach, a fellow at Northwestern. Prior to that I learned all my roles at home and my mother, who was a piano teacher and church choir director, would help me. I was scared to death in Mexico City. Jon Vickers was the Otello, and he's a very powerful personality, and what the Iago does to a certain extent depends upon the Otello. I still have marks from that original staging. Eventually I discarded everything that I wrote. I finally found out it was not sacred.

CASSILLY: The quality of the voice that you need for Otello is incredible. If you go through the score, there are many places where Verdi asks for an ugly voice. He doesn't want it beautiful. I did it at Tanglewood, a staged concert version with Leinsdorf, and I got a review that I treasure. They wrote that I had the courage to do it the way Verdi wrote it and to forgo the beautiful sounds. I remember another critic saying my voice sounded like it was coming from a barrel, and that's just what Verdi was asking for. That's one of the challenges of Otello. You can't just show off your vocal prowess with the role. Along with Siegmund, it's the most rewarding role I've ever had the chance to do.

MILLO: In a way, there's almost something religious about the work.

MILNES: I suppose the first few years around with *Otello,* I was doing a normal human being who was a little twisted. You work with various stage directors over the years and then you grow with something. It becomes part of your blood. The way I feel about Iago now is that he has to be psychotic. No one who is in any way normal could say the things that he does.

Legend has it that Shakespeare wrote the part of Othello to spite his leading actor, Richard Burbage, by giving him a role he couldn't possibly play successfully. Laurence Olivier, possibly the greatest actor of our day, took months off to go into training before he tackled the role because of its vocal and physical demands. Verdi's Otello is no less strenuous.

S T E W A R T : If you're a singing actor, or an acting opera singer, you risk the danger of letting the musical aspect of the role suffer. You have to really sing it. Audiences today don't want to go and hear Verdi sung by lousy voices, no matter how well they can act. If you can't sing the arias correctly and get the high notes, it won't go. You have to be careful to play both sides of the fence—one from an acting and one from a singing standpoint.

M I L A N O V : All you have to do is to sing what Verdi wrote.

S C O T T O : It's very dramatic singing and very tough. Don't forget Verdi wrote the part for Francesco Tamagno, and he had the right voice and the right temperament and Verdi fitted it to him. Otello's a very strong man. He also came from another kind of culture and he dares everything to get where he is. And all this has to come through the music. Verdi gave him the best singing and this has to come through also. The tenor has to be dramatic and sing through the part. You can't have a light tenor. It's a mix: You need good breath control because of the long phrases, and you need a great top register and also a middle register. You almost need three tenors to sing the role.

B A K E R : Sure, I'm aiming for Otello. There are still a lot of things I have to iron out vocally—the Italianate things in the role. In three or four years, I feel I might be ready for it—about the time I'm forty.

S T E W A R T : When the time is right, a new Otello will surface. We don't have many now, but we will. Certain repertory disappears and then it begins again.

M c C R A C K E N : There are certain roles that require so much stamina and energy that I'm wondering if you shouldn't sing them earlier in a career rather than later. I was thirty when I first sang Otello. It was my first successful role as a leading tenor. Probably, had I been offered something else at thirty, I would have sung that—I don't know. But the point is that certain people say they wouldn't sing Otello until they were fifty, and I feel that that's late. Also the Wagner roles. If you're going to do the big roles, you better get started. I don't think you should wait very long.

M I L L O : We have a wonderful lyric Otello now in Domingo. The phraseology is wonderful, and there are all those wonderful lyric sounds along with his understanding of the character.

C A S S I L L Y : There are places where you have to feel the character has nothing left. When a true lyric voice does this, it makes you uncomfortable. When a dramatic tenor does it, it's thrilling. In Europe it's often sung by lyrics, but with the sizes of the houses we have here, the lyric voice can be in trouble. The difference between a career here and in Europe is often about a thousand seats, and that's a lot.

M I L N E S : Plácido is a very vulnerable Otello, so Iago can't be so heavy-handed. It's a different way of doing Otello, but the sound and the timbre in Plácido's case are absolutely right, so it works.

B A K E R : In the Italian repertory, you have a long legato speech, and then you have duets or whatever, and then another long legato line. In the German, there are all those short declamatory sections, which have nice lines but there are sections in between. That's a lot different than *Otello,* where even in the short arias you have to sustain and carry that tone and breath even to the end.

M I L L O : I'm sure the opera is going to have to have a lyric tenor from now on. I shudder to think that the work would never be done again. I guess tenors will just have to keep the voice open.

Cornell MacNeil has sung Iago with all the leading Otellos of his generation.

C O R N E L L M A C N E I L : The reason we don't have more *Otello* productions and more people singing the role is that we don't have people like Jimmy McCracken around. You have to work at that role and totally give yourself over to it. Other things have to go or suffer, and you can't sing everything else. You have to make a commitment to singing the role. That's what Jimmy did, and that just doesn't seem to happen anymore.

WARFIELD: Jimmy's first Otello was in Washington, D.C., and he didn't know what to do. He had no background in it and he studied the role for at least twelve hours a day in Italy. When he came to Washington, everyone was apprehensive. They really didn't know what they had done. They had never heard him and knew practically nothing about him, and when he came in, nobody said a thing. He sang the first act. Nothing. The second act. Nothing. They were stunned. Well, they finally told him that they were in shock at the voice and what he was doing. Then Paul Hume said in *The Washington Post* it was the best thing he'd ever heard, and the next day the Met called him back to "audition."

MILNES: He was a great guy, a great human being. He kind of found a compromise. He had some of the vulnerability of Plácido with the feeling of the oak tree that Vickers had. Jim came into the in-between area and did things with such integrity—that's a vague word but very applicable—but also with such intensity as well. When he's given the papers relieving him of his command and passing it on to Cassio, whom he hates in light of what he thinks has happened, all of a sudden Cassio is the boss and there's nothing Otello can do about it. Well, Jim would give him the scroll and an artificial "Now I salute you." It was a special reading. A lot of Otellos don't do that. Jim thought it gave an irony, and showed his disgust with what was happening to his heretofore organized regime and the hierarchy of command. Orders are orders in a normal military way.

JOHN MACURDY: The first time I heard Jimmy McCracken, in 1972, all I knew about him was that he had left the Met and he was now back. Then I heard him and I thought, "Wow, this is a brighter sound than del Monaco's," and it was really a tenor sound. He carried the role off beautifully. He knew exactly what he was doing. Mr. Bing even said, "We not only have an Otello, we have *the* Otello." Jimmy was something else.

LEONA MITCHELL: I never did *Otello* with him, but we did do *Aida* together and he was really something—an American original. His *Otello* aria in the Met Centennial Gala was so powerful. I wasn't able to watch the tape for a long time after he died, and then the other day I put it on and I can't believe how wonderful he was, the power he had. We were in rehearsal for *Trovatore* the week before he passed away. A gem! A great man and a great singer.

M A C U R D Y : I'm pro-American and I can tell you I've never seen anyone treated as badly as Jimmy was. It wasn't really Mr. Bing. He realized what he had and he had slots that he had to fill. Some of us were able to do more than others, and Bing did take the company from eighteen to thirty weeks plus the tour and the parks.

M C C R A C K E N : When I came back and did my *Otello* at the Met and had a big success, I was so happy. But after a couple of weeks, I realized that I was losing money. I think I was making a thousand dollars a performance then. So I went to Mr. Bing and asked him to double my salary. Well, he gave me all sorts of excuses and talked about all he had done for me and I told him I still had to have the money. So I got the raise, and the next season, I only had one performance. You never beat him; you could just never get the best of that man. Of course, the year after that, I got the money and a lot of performances. God love him—what a man.

W A R F I E L D : In 1978 it was a great hurt to Jimmy when he didn't have even one telecast of *Otello* when they were doing two. By that time he had sung Otello more than anyone else in history. However, he was not an Otello-type man. You could always talk to him and reason with him.

M A C U R D Y : Jimmy had helped out the Met by doing *Tannhäuser* when Jonny Vickers canceled, and then this whole TV thing came up and you just had to say, "What's this all about?" This had been his production and he had helped them out so many times—well, you have to ask why. For Jimmy, the Met was his spiritual home where he felt he belonged and where he did belong, but for whatever reason, they wouldn't do what he wanted and deserved, even though he was totally dedicated and loyal to them.

W A R F I E L D : When it came to the TV thing, it was just something he wouldn't deal with. His leaving the Met at that time was just a matter of principle. He never thought he was being unreasonable, though other people might have thought that. He was just doing the only thing he could do. Jimmy had sung this part all over the world, had toured it for the Met, and had two new productions. He felt at that time if he had stayed at the Met, he really wouldn't have been able to sing, and it might have even been detrimental to his health. He said, "The only thing I can do is leave." Five new productions in five seasons and they wouldn't give him one telecast!

M c C R A C K E N : I turned down the opening night of the Met *Tannhäuser* because I felt they just weren't playing fair with me. What was interesting about that whole situation was what [Met manager] Mr. Bliss said to me. God bless him, I like the man and I think he meant well. But he actually said to me, "Oh, this television, we don't even know if it's going to be successful. It's just an experimental thing and why would you want to make an issue out of this?" And I said to him, "Not only is this television going to work, it's going to revolutionize what's happening in America as far as opera is concerned." And he came back, "Well, that's possible, but we don't really know, do we?" Basically, they tried to tell me television wasn't important and I didn't need it. I was heavier at the time, but Pavarotti and the others I've seen make me feel weight couldn't be an issue. Here I was singing all these roles for years in the opera house and the public paid good money to hear me. Now when they could sit at home and hear me for free, they weren't going to get the opportunity. I wasn't going to reach that whole new audience.

W A R F I E L D : He would take so much until he was fed up, but he never said anything. He was not a divo-type man, not difficult, and everyone who knew him knew it.

M A C U R D Y : I remember one performance on tour when Jimmy had to cancel after Act One and Bob Nagy went on for him. Jimmy asked Bob if they'd given him a nice bonus for going on for him and Bob said no. So Jimmy went to speak to Mr. Bing, who said no way. To him, Bob was just doing his job. So Jimmy went on his own and gave Bob a nice kicker for helping him out and helping the Metropolitan as well. He was not a small man in any way. He was just a good guy.

M E R R I L L : Jimmy McCracken's first Met Otello was with me and it was my first Iago. The last time I'd sung with him, he had like eight words in *Bohème,* and then he went off and studied it with Dr. Herbert Graf, and he came back and was *the* Otello of that period. It was a remarkable performance. He really had learned the role well. It was like a new debut for him, and after debut performances I usually give debut people a silver dollar for luck. I used to work in Vegas in the summers and I'd collect them. So I went into Jimmy's room and gave him the dollar. So the next day he got sensational reviews and mine were mediocre. The next time I saw him, I said, "Give me back that dollar!" That became a running gag every time I saw him. But he really was a wonderful Otello. He knew the role and worked at it very seriously. He didn't have that pure Italian sound that del Monaco had, but with Otello, it really didn't matter. He had that huge voice and all the dramatic touches.

MCCRACKEN: I don't know of anyone I've ever sung with who would have anything derogatory to say about me. I get along very well with my colleagues. Arrogant people, like Mr. Bing, are the only ones I ever had any problem with. You can't imagine how hard it was to deal with him. Oh, he was witty and there were times when I enjoyed him and laughed with him, but overall he was something else! To go into his office as a tenor and see Corelli's picture staring you in the face—"That's my favorite tenor." That kind of stuff wasn't fair. Franco would do the premieres and I'd take over. It never got to the point where it affected my singing or changed my life in any way, but there were a lot of other people who couldn't take that kind of stuff.

MACURDY: One of the funniest things I ever saw was Zinka with Jimmy in *Otello*. He was strangling her and she was desperately trying to pull her peignoir down.

WARFIELD: Milanov was wonderful to him. He did one performance with her, and as he was killing her at the end, he was leaning over her and she said, "Don't sweat on me!" Jimmy got such a kick out of that.

MCCRACKEN: The opportunity to have performed *Otello* all over the world with so many wonderful colleagues is one of my life's greatest blessings.

KIRI TE KANAWA: He was an incredible Otello, probably the most vivid in my mind. A lovely man also. He was very, very committed to the role and loved it, but he also could be unpredictable. His acting was such that each night he became the role. We did a wonderful performance of the final scene at the Maria Callas evening at Covent Garden and it was televised all over. He was just so right in what he did with the role.

W A R F I E L D : I can still picture Kiri and Jimmy sitting around all day in those heavy, heavy costumes waiting to go on. It took all day. So much for the glamour of the opera.

M I L N E S : Jim could fool you in any part into thinking he was totally the character, and if he was going a little berserk, if the epileptic fit was coming on and the eyes were bulging and he was twitching, you could think, "This is it; this guy is gone. He's not there." There are others, whose names I won't mention, who *are* gone. I mean, they grab you by the wrist or something, and you think they've lost it. With Jim, I remember a time when Iago was doing his first little stroking—"Don't worry about this; it's not too serious at all"—and then Otello explodes at him, and Jim was really snorting steam. Then at one point he sort of looked up at me and winked, and I thought, "Thank God, he's there. He's not going to kill me."

W A R F I E L D : He was really thrilled when he opened the season in Rome as Otello, since we had starved there for years. That same night I opened the season in Venice as Eboli, and he heard me sing the part on the radio in the pause between the first and second acts. It was such a wonderful thing, because we both thought Italy would never accept us. Also, after the first time he worked with Zeffirelli, Franco came back and said, "Now I know what Otello is all about." That was fabulous for Jimmy, who thought that Zeffirelli was God himself.

Audiences are still drawn to the opera by the beauty of the music. Again from an opening night review: "The scoring, even on a first hearing, appeared to be of rare beauty and perfectly balanced." Singers are drawn to it, too, in spite of its difficulties.

M E R R I L L : Iago came late in my career purposely. I was offered the role many times, and musically I could have sung it. But I wanted to wait until I had matured, didn't want to jump into it. I think I had been singing at the Met for twenty years before I tackled it.

M I L N E S : Early on, I did feel intimidated by the role, but now I'm really comfortable with it.

C R U Z - R O M O : I love to sing so much and I always love the parts I am allowed to sing, so there was always enjoyment in that. I was always a happy singer and I still am. You must have that love.

M I T C H E L L : As a black singer, I have offered to sing Desdemona at the Met and have not even had a glimmer of a response. They usually just make a list of people who could and have sung the role, and if you're not on it . . . Still, I think it's a little silly.

TE KANAWA: I love the music in the opening scene very much, also the first duet between Otello and Desdemona. In the second act, I love the scene with Otello and Iago. It's so beautifully done for all three of them and it shows the way a worm can be put in the mind of someone like that. The council chamber scene also has incredible music, and the final confrontation scene is always exciting.

MERRILL: I saw Laurence Olivier play Iago in London. He almost played him as a homosexual, very effeminate in his movements. You never do know too much about Iago's relationship with his wife. With Otello, he was always acting—studying him and playing up to him. Then when Iago was alone, he was almost a different person. It was quite interesting and I tried to use that in my first performance. The critics all got on me for it—"How could Iago smile?" But it was sort of a sneering smile, and I told people later, "Well, I saw Olivier do it and it was marvelous." To me, Iago is actually two people.

MCCRACKEN: Otello's pride is what is attacked by Iago. Everything Iago says to him is like a slap in the face. Even though he's losing Desdemona, he feels more upset about losing his integrity as a soldier, and as the opera goes on and he takes action, he also loses his integrity as a person.

MILNES: Iago kind of likes what he's doing, but he doesn't really understand it. He never planned to have both Otello and Desdemona die.

MCCRACKEN: The Moor is at one and the same time self-centered and naïve. The fact that he can take such delight in his career is probably part of the reason why he won Desdemona in the first place, and then she builds his ego and sense of importance. All of these things get mixed up in his mind—his love for her and his power as a warrior.

MERRILL: Musically it's not as difficult as Rigoletto or some of my other roles, but Iago has to be thinking all the time, "How can I get Cassio in trouble? What do I do next?" Vocally, you have to be prepared, because you don't have time to worry about the vocal process. It's difficult that way. You have to keep the audience's attention on the character.

MILNES: I think it's an odd relationship between Iago and Otello.

It's a love-hate thing, but Iago does respect him. It's just that there's another force, a darkness of the mind. When he knows he's caught at the end, he does the only thing he can do, which is to run.

S C O T T O : Desdemona is a symbol of purity, chastity, and the best, purest symbol of love. That's why sometimes people say she's stupid. No, no! We have to understand she is this symbol of fidelity. I solve this by not being childish. We see so often Desdemona come onstage and she is a very young girl. But if you go on in the love duet and play her as childish, it could make the audience think she is stupid. I think she should be very strong and very full of love, emotion. Innocent, yes, but not sweet, because sweetness becomes weak. She's not saccharine. If you do that with Desdemona—no way! You give a statement with her. She likes this man because he's a man—the man she loves.

M I L L O : Desdemona is one of my all-time favorite roles. I have a concept of good and evil in my own life which I think is true, and for me she's the embodiment of all that is good, like Melanie in *Gone With the Wind*. She just can't conceive of badness or ugliness in someone she loves. All of the opera after the love duet is a very rude shock for her, but she keeps persevering. Her love washes everything away. At the end of the opera, she's even able to say an "Ava Maria" for someone who's half crazed.

M I L A N O V : She is human—we all have the good and the bad.

M C C R A C K E N : The last few performances I did were extraordinary for me. When I was younger, *Otello* always exhausted me to the extent that I was worried about myself. But after my last performance, people described my voice as young-sounding, and I have to agree with that. I pushed my voice around a lot over the course of my career. When I went for the high notes, I really went for them. I forced and pushed, but something I was doing while I did that must have been right.

M I T C H E L L : For me, Desdemona was very strong and had her own opinions. This blond lady says she's going to marry a Moor. That shows you right away what strength she had—to approach her father and tell him this. For her father to agree to it shows you her strength.

S T E B E R : She's a victim, but she does have beautiful music. That duet at the end of the first act is sheer heaven!

M I L L O : She's not an idiot. She's just so good and the music is written very simply, very beautifully, and if you flesh it out with radiant sound, the audience goes wild.

M I L A N O V : I did the role many many times. The public always loved me.

L E A R : Desdemona was kind of challenging for me, because it wasn't in my nature to be passive or to play a role that was so full of sweetness and light. But she was persistent and that is one of my qualities. She really is relentless. She also is feisty. I found things in the text that showed me what she really is. Actually, she's not so much passive as a victim of circumstances.

M C C R A C K E N : For me, the opera changed slightly with every performance. Just by accident one night I found Desdemona's night-dress. It just was in a place on the bed where I could reach it, so I grabbed it and used it to strangle her. It was fantastic. But since I did that, it's probably only happened ten more times since. It worked because it was right, but you can't always plan things like that. Also, sometimes I'd embrace Cassio after the "Esultate!"—that is, if he was around, if I could find him. After all, he's the man Otello likes and it's natural to hold on to him and be talking right to him. Then I would make the exit. If Cassio was not placed near me, I'd do the same thing with Montano. In other words, I just didn't try to sing the "Esultate!" and get off. There was always something between the aria and the exit.

C R U Z - R O M O : Musically the opera is extraordinary. From the play, Verdi caught the very special moments so well and Shakespeare did take longer. I'm not trying to diminish any of the merits of Shakespeare, but Verdi took all the meaty parts and it's just magnificent. I feel that Desdemona doesn't really have a weak moment. She's very much in love and the only problem is that they just don't really talk to each other.

M I T C H E L L : The role is perfection for the voice, absolute perfection.

M C C R A C K E N : The role became so much a part of me that spontaneity—or what would seem like it—was actually just recalling something that I did fifteen or twenty years ago. There's always something to learn when you play Otello, which is one reason it's such a great role. A lot of funny things have happened, too, although I must say they didn't seem too funny at the time. One night I was about to sing "Dio, mi potevi scagliar," and I couldn't get the soprano off the stage. She just wouldn't leave. Otello's thrown her out and he's supposed to sing, and she was still making her exit. Well, I turned my back on the audience and shouted the thing. The conductor thought I'd lost my mind. I'll tell you, I was out of breath and out of control, but we did finally get her off.

While Shakespeare's Emilia, Iago's wife, has attracted such actresses as Dames Edith Evans, Peggy Ashcroft, Sybil Thorndike, and Wendy Hiller, Verdi's re-creation has never proven to be a lure for mezzo-sopranos.

MIGNON DUNN: The play has a lot more lines for Emilia. In the opera it's cut to pieces. There's hardly anything for her. It's certainly no Brangäne. Here the soprano just talks and talks and talks, and Emilia listens. It's also difficult to sing. You're really always on top of the ensembles. It's an ungrateful role. It's not one of my favorites.

TE KANAWA: I read the play before I started singing and I loved it, but I've never actually seen it—only the film with Olivier. The mediums are all so different, though. When you see a ballet based on an opera or operatic themes, you always wonder when they're going to sing. Or I do. That's the way I'm geared. Probably ballet dancers and actors feel the same way when they go to the opera. "Get rid of that music!"

MILLO: I never really had a lot of experience in going to the opera, so in my mind, I would create the visuals while I was listening to a recording of Otello. Sometimes that might have been better than what I would have seen.

SCOTTO: Desdemona is so—oh, beautiful, but so different from the Shakespeare, because in Otello we have only part of the woman we have in the play. There is really not enough story on Desdemona. If we would have a little bit at the beginning as we have with Shakespeare, then we would understand a little bit more about her. We don't see it when she goes against her father and family. She dared a lot, because in that period to marry a person like Otello—well, even though he was very important, he was black and he came from another country. She dares a lot.

CRUZ-ROMO: I don't think my Desdemona could be any differ-

Barbara Cook, Leonard Bernstein's original Cunegonde in *Candide*

Andrea Velis as Mardian
in Barber's *Antony and
Cleopatra,* the opening-night
production for the Met at
Lincoln Center

Patricia Brooks in the title
role of the Santa Fe Opera
production of *Lulu*

John Bubbles as Sportin' Life, Todd Duncan as Porgy,
Anne Wiggins Brown as Bess. The opera is *Porgy and
Bess.* The photographer was composer George Gershwin.

The famous portrait of Samuel Barber's Vanessa, featuring Brenda Lewis

Three great singers, three great stars. Regina Resnik, Eleanor Steber, and Rosalind Elias in the original Met production of *Vanessa*

Morley Meredith, Roberta Peters, and Lili Chookasian bringing home a caged George London in the Met production of Menotti's *The Last Savage*

Carlyle Floyd's Susannah brought to life by Phyllis Curtin

Contralto Lili Chookasian's exotic appearance in Menotti's *The Last Savage*

Puccini's Cio-Cio-San as
embodied by Martina
Arroyo

Madame Butterfly in the
person of Licia Albanese

Dorothy Kirsten as Puccini's heroine (the role that
marked her official farewell to the Met)

Brenda Lewis as Salome

Birgit Nilsson performing "The Dance of the Seven Veils"

Roberta Peters and
Theodor Uppman
in the Met's *Don Giovanni*

Eleanor Steber as Donna
Anna in *Don Giovanni*

One of the century's
leading Don Juans, Giorgio
Tozzi

The Met's *Don
Giovanni* with
Theodor Uppman
and Laurel Hurley
as Zerlina

Sherrill Milnes as
Verdi's Iago

Two all-Americans, James
McCracken and Robert
Merrill—in the classic
Shakespearean roles of
Otello and Iago

Kiri Te Kanawa
and James
McCracken
performing in the
Maria Callas gala
as Desdemona and
Otello

Sandra Warfield and James
McCracken after a
performance of Saint-Saëns's
Samson et Dalila

The beloved Licia Albanese in one of her most memorable roles, Mimì in *La Bohème*

In rehearsal for the Met's English-language version of *La Bohème,* director Joe Mankiewicz and his Musetta, Patrice Munsel

Jerome Hines as Wagner's Wotan

Laurel Hurley dressed for Olympia in *Hoffmann* backstage with her daughter, Laurie Kristina, who was wearing a dress that was the gift of another "doll," Roberta Peters

Joan Sutherland as Offenbach's Olympia

Martial Singher as the four villains in *Hoffmann*

Rose Bampton in *Aida*

Lucine Amara as Verdi's
Ethiopian princess

Colleagues and
friends: Martina
Arroyo and Grace
Bumbry as arch
rivals Aida and
Amneris

A Met *Aida* with
Nell Rankin as
Amneris, Robert
Merrill as
Amonasro, and
Lucine Amara
as Aida

Lucine Amara as Micaëla, a role she sang more than eighty times at the Met alone

Regina Resnik: Carmen

James McCracken as Don José restrains the tempestuous Carmen of Marilyn Horne.

Bidú Sayão sharing the
stage in *La Traviata* with a
treasured colleague,
Giuseppe di Stefano

Joan Sutherland flanked by Lynn
Blair and Sándor Kónya in the
Metropolitan Opera's *La Traviata*

A kiss for director Alfred
Lunt from his Violetta,
Anna Moffo

Moffo with Robert Merrill as
Germont in *La Traviata* at the Met

The Met's touring Rosalinda, Brenda Lewis. The soprano later sang the role in the main house with enormous success.

Rudolf Bing's personal choice for his new *Fledermaus* production—Risë Stevens as Orlofsky

As the show-stopping Adele, Patrice Munsel

Regina Resnik, who fortunately remembers "too much" as the glamorous Rosalinda in *Die Fledermaus*

Resnik in the guise of Prince Orlofsky, the role she sang in the gala for Sir Rudolf Bing's farewell

ent or that much different from what any other singer would do. Some people play her a little too passive and that's not for me. I don't think she is passive or she wouldn't have gone out and married him.

MITCHELL: I did Desdemona in Australia and I do think it's one of my greatest roles. They had brought over an Italian tenor for it and it was a big deal in the press, because they said his black would rub off on my white. But the racial angle aside, it was an overwhelming success out there and they were very exciting performances.

TE KANAWA: You also have to remember all the time that it's also Desdemona's tragedy. It's very sad that she and Otello never get the chance to just talk and resolve their problems. That's the heart of the tragedy. I love the role and I love the opera. I think it's some of the best music Verdi ever wrote.

MITCHELL: I love the scene where he throws the handkerchief in her face and calls her an adulteress and she denies it. I play that very strongly, which is not the way a lot of other people do it. When he's abusing her, that's really catastrophic. You just didn't do those things in public. To me they are some of the most beautiful moments in the opera, and the music has all those low notes and you really can put a lot of strength in them. I don't wimp them out. It's a wonderful scene, even though she's degraded down to her toes.

SCOTTO: The rejection scene has to be very dramatic, not crying so much—because if she's childish, she's stupid. And then in the last act also, you must not sing the "Ave Maria" as you sing it right before you go to bed. No, it's a funeral. She understands very well that he is going to kill her. And she doesn't understand why he doesn't tell her what she did.

MILLO: She's not as strong in my mind as Scotto makes her, but I can agree with that interpretation. You have to remember that this was an Italian woman, not a British woman. An Italian woman will accept a lot from her man, especially in the sense that she never knows whether he's going to strike her down or kiss her.

CRUZ-ROMO: Verdi gave all of his women so much tenderness and beauty. His female parts are all so easy for us to sing. They are so right. No, no, no! Desdemona is a fantastic part.

MITCHELL: I felt that here was a young lady who was the daughter of a senator and got to sit in on some of the meetings. Women weren't allowed to do that in those days. She was sort of a forerunner of a feminist today.

CRUZ-ROMO: The jealousy that he has is all out of proportion, but the fact that they don't communicate is the major problem. He never says what's bothering him. This, along with the meanness of Iago, causes the whole tragedy. At the end, when they finally do talk, it's too late.

MILLO: I go back to the play because Verdi did. There are passages that he didn't put into the libretto, but it's still all there. That's how great a genius this man was. It's riveting for me to see how Verdi improved on the original. I think if I went to see the play, I would really miss the music.

SCOTTO: Otello and Desdemona have a wonderful relationship at the beginning. They have love, understanding, a very happy life, but they don't talk to each other. She never thought for one split of a second that he would think she was unfaithful to him. And if for one moment they would talk to each other, he would say to her, "You went with another man." Then there would be an explanation and there would be no killing. But we have a lot of that in the opera.

MILLO: Opera is nothing more than fantasy and what we lose today—and I'm a bigmouth about this—is that we're taking the fantasy away. In opera you listen to the voice and it's there to take you on the flight. It's not about imperfect vocalism and looking great. That's wrong, wrong, wrong!

WARFIELD: Jimmy was different every time he did Otello, and with all those hundreds of performances, he would still get excited about the role.

MCCRACKEN: There were plenty of things I found that nobody told me to do. I had a lot of directors who were watching me do the role, and just by being there, they would say something and it would stimulate me and we'd find new things. Basically, I had to work out my own approach for everything. Take the death scene. It was always different, every night. There were a million ways I died as Otello—some of them good, some not so good,

WARFIELD: He never spared himself. He didn't know what marking was. He gave his all every time he had to perform.

Shortly before his death, McCracken said he didn't want to go out like basketball star Julius Erving, making good-byes in all the arenas he had appeared in.

MCCRACKEN: I can't imagine wanting to sing one last Otello in all the opera houses where I played. Otello's last words are a tragic return to his basic simplicity. He can't cope with all the complicated business that comes with living; he thinks about his past, and he dies.

DON GIOVANNI

~

*My first question on the subject
went to Max Rudolf. And he said,
"Look—Don Giovanni goes to
hell in D major."*
–JEROME HINES

Music by Wolfgang Amadeus Mozart
Libretto by Lorenzo da Ponte

DONNA ANNA .... *Rose Bampton, Zinka
Milanov, Regina Resnik,
Eleanor Steber, Carol
Vaness*

DONNA ELVIRA .... *Roberta Alexander, Lucine
Amara, Jarmila Novotná,
Regina Resnik, Eleanor
Steber*

ZERLINA .... *Licia Albanese, Judith
Blegen, Rosalind Elias,
Patrice Munsel, Roberta
Peters*

DON GIOVANNI............................ *Håkan Hagegård, Thomas
Hampson, Jerome Hines,
Sherrill Milnes, Giorgio
Tozzi*

MASETTO .... *Theodor Uppman*

GUEST APPEARANCE................ *Robert Merrill*

*T*he Don Juan legend dates back to the seventeenth century. It has
been used as the basis for plays, poems, films (both Rudolph Valentino

and Errol Flynn played out the Don's amorous adventures for the cameras), and, of course, opera. Hampered by a structure of two acts and an epilogue, Mozart had to restrict the Don's conquests to a paltry three women: Donna Anna, whose father he kills in a duel; Donna Elvira, whom he has married and abandoned; and Zerlina, a peasant girl he tries desperately to seduce.

G I O R G I O T O Z Z I : Interestingly enough, Don Giovanni is an over-the-hill character. He never really makes it with any of the women. At the very beginning, he's already on the way out.

S H E R R I L L M I L N E S : Certainly, power's part of Don Giovanni—controlling people. In that, there's a touch of Iago in him, Scarpia. The instant his sword hits the Commendatore, and he dies at the end of the trio, an alarm goes off inside the Don's head. And it is dinging away through the rest of the opera. He's violated his own ethics. It increases his manicness and the speed with which he goes through the next twenty-four hours.

T O Z Z I : It's a driven, compulsive freneticism that comes through. And as the story progresses, he becomes more frenetic. It's structured beautifully, from the standpoint of drama.

J E R O M E H I N E S : I did my first Don Giovanni on the Met stage on April Fools' Day. And boy, I lit into the Commendatore with the sword in the opening duel—and I hit his sword so hard I broke it in half. And I got the blade in the face, and had a mouse under my eye and a cut on my forehead that was bleeding all through the first half.

Sherrill Milnes made his operatic debut as Masetto, touring with Boris Goldovsky's opera company. His Metropolitan debut as the Don came in 1974.

M I L N E S : He's elegant, a good swordsman, well educated, wealthy. And he has to appear dangerous. He can't be a good-time Charlie. There has to be something else—some kind of manic, driven feel, a little mercurial stuff about him. And physical elegance must relate to the vocal elegance.

Giorgio Tozzi sang the Commendatore before being reincarnated as his murderer.

T O Z Z I : There is no question about the greatness of the work—it is a fantastic piece. Don Giovanni was a role I enjoyed up to a point. But to tell you the truth, the character with the music that's so awfully wonderful to sing is Leporello. That is a fantastic role, which unfortunately I never did.

Jerome Hines's first experiences with Don Giovanni were also at the business end of the Don's sword before he switched from the Commendatore to the Don.

H I N E S : I did the role of Don Giovanni for a couple of seasons at the Met; then I backed off and didn't do it anymore. I didn't particularly love the role. I didn't feel I had to go around giving the world the impression I was some sort of great Don Juan. I had my fling as a young man and I married happily, and I didn't need the image.

M I L N E S : Giovanni thought it was not only his right but his obligation to go after anybody if he had the yearning. Only his mother and his sister were safe from him. And we don't know he had a sister, and nobody talks about his mom, so everyone else is fair game.

H I N E S : I do think a lot of singers are in love with the image. I know Pinza was a prime example. When he was still at the Met, at the end, he was in his mid-fifties, and he was putting on such an act. If you were in a hotel lobby with him in Cleveland, and a pretty girl came in the door, he'd immediately be fixing his tie and going, "Ahem, *signorina*," and putting on this big act. And he was always putting his hands on the girls, no matter who. He was trying to live up to that image—it meant a lot to him.

M I L N E S : Leporello and Giovanni, although they have a very special relationship, it's still master and servant. It should never be buddy-buddy or frat house.

Z I N K A M I L A N O V : We had a wonderful company. We had Pinza and, of course, Baccaloni.

R E G I N A R E S N I K : Pinza and Baccaloni as Leporello were incredible. They were like two peas in a pod. It was terribly obvious, and more comic. These days, they think that Leporello should look a bit like Don Giovanni, so his disguise is believable. But on the contrary, if I were the director, I would want them to be direct opposites, so Leporello looks idiotic in the disguise.

Don Juan, a sort of James Bond of his day, appealed to both Mozart and da Ponte, each of whom had an eye for the ladies. They based their opera partially on Giovanni Bertati's libretto for Giuseppe Gazzaniga's *The Stone Guest*. *Don Giovanni* premiered in Prague on October 29, 1787, with Luigi Bassi as the world's greatest lover.

T O Z Z I : The element required in Don Giovanni is a great personality, so there aren't that many great interpreters of the role. I just felt that oh, maybe I should have been doing Leporello instead.

H I N E S : I never generated enormous enthusiasm for doing that part. The only time I really felt I could lay into it and really use my voice was in the finale with the three basses. Then you get some really heavy, gutsy singing.

M I L N E S : There is too much Americanization of Giovanni in some stagings. That is, John Wayne, or the fraternity guy with the beer and the joke. That can't be; neither of these guys is elegant. If that goes on long enough, the audience assumes that's the way it is.

T O Z Z I : One should have a beautiful voice, but even without that, with the proper personality and musicianship, one can still do a beautiful job with Don Giovanni.

H Å K A N H A G E G Å R D : Compared to the women, there are not specific places vocally for Giovanni to be successful. And *Don Giovanni* is one of the operas where it's very important to know how they sing the other parts.

M I L N E S : Americans tend to walk with a roll—different than French or Italians. That belies the elegance of the time. Costumes dictated how somebody had to move. If you're wearing a sword at your side, you can't roll when you walk. And there's only one way to sit. Any nobleman—a Rodrigo, a di Luna—must walk straight, tight cheeks, thighs: a Yul Brynner walk. Also, confidence, ego—the way noblemen were brought up. We're getting awfully inelegant in a lot of productions, and that breaks down the whole reason for the piece—the class structure.

H I N E S : I also felt my size was contrary to the part. Being six foot six and a half, I always felt like I should try to come down to the scale of other people, that you shouldn't be *that* heroic looking on the stage. I pictured the ideal Don Juan about six two, and very handsome, of course. But six six was a little much.

Don Giovanni's American premiere took place at New York's Park Theater on May 23, 1826. In a night at the opera that would put the Marx brothers to shame, the performance was sung by Joaquina García, Manuel García, Manuel García, Jr., María García de Malibran, and assorted others—in English, it is said.

TOZZI: During my generation, there were two people who I thought did the role magnificently. One was Cesare Siepi; the other was George London. Siepi gave Giovanni the flavor of a *bon vivant*. Equally as great an artist, with a fantastically electrical voice, was London—absolutely exciting in every respect. He brought a different quality—a kind of compulsive, driven quality. I always felt, if you have them, why bother with anyone else?

ROBERTA PETERS: I did Zerlina a lot with Cesare Siepi, who was a secret love of mine. Well, not so secret—he took me out a few times before I was married. But he was, in my opinion, *the* Don of the day. He was superb. And we were able to act well together—I felt very comfortable with him.

LUCINE AMARA: George London and Cesare Siepi were my Dons, and we had so much fun onstage. Siepi and Fernando Corena always used to change the words and say dirty words onstage to break you up. I think I sang Elvira to Jerome Hines's Don, too—and he was marvelous.

HINES: At one point I redid the part, and a stage-director friend of mine suggested I do a lot of low, sweeping bows and bring myself down. I got a review on that one that said I looked like the Hunchback of Notre Dame, so I gave up trying to do that. I just never really felt it was a part I could identify with.

Donna Annas at the Metropolitan have included Lilli Lehmann, Lillian Nordica, Emma Eames, and Rosa Ponselle. Eleanor Steber sang both of Giovanni's Donnas during her career, arriving at Anna by way of Elvira.

ELEANOR STEBER: Donna Anna, I think, belonged to me even long before I did it, mainly because my maestro in school taught me the "Non mi dir" before I left the New England Conservatory. He said, "This will be your role someday." I did it at a Sunday night concert at the old Met and everybody said, "My God, there's nobody who can sing this like you do." When I was offered Elvira, I took it because I wasn't offered Anna.

R O B E R T A   A L E X A N D E R : Elvira is driven. I think anybody who follows someone all over a country is driven. Women in those times did not travel alone—especially running around after a man. If your husband left you, too bad.

S T E B E R : They said, "Oh, no, you're no Donna Anna." Perhaps I wasn't at that time. Perhaps my voice didn't have the maturity and ripening that came as a result of the years. I did Anna for the first time in Chicago, in '54. I was already at the Met fourteen years before I did it there.

R O S E   B A M P T O N : Donna Anna is very different from the other women in the opera. The Zerlina is enchanting, and I think the sympathy goes out to the Elvira, because she's so maligned. I think Elvira's a very ungrateful part to sing. But I love Donna Anna because she's a noble person, and I found her very expressive. I love vocally what she has to do.

Zinka Milanov sang her first Metropolitan Donna Anna in 1941.

M I L A N O V : Donna Anna is not really more difficult than a part like Aida, but the first aria you have to be careful with. It's difficult to explain, but in *Don Giovanni* the big aria is so difficult that you have to put forth a special effort for it.

C A R O L   V A N E S S : Except for one recitative, her music is very pure and straightforward. She's a woman of great character. She was very much a girl inside a woman's body—someone who had been set up to be married. Her father's death is a great shock to her. But when she calls for vengeance, it's like children do it: "You did this to me, and now I want you to do that to him." Not that she's a big baby or anything, but she's got all the energy of youth.

Rose Bampton, who began operatic life as a mezzo, debuted her Donna Anna at the Metropolitan less than a year after making her soprano debut there in May 1937.

B A M P T O N : Donna Anna is a wonderful part to sing. And such a contrast, because she comes out with such anger and has that first difficult part; then in the end, she has this marvelous, lovely, legato, long-lined aria to sing.

STEBER: Giovanni did rape her, but there's an awful lot of guilt in her singing, and I think it might have been with her consent. I think she was overcome by him. Of course, my first Don was Pinza.

On the occasion of Ezio Pinza's twentieth anniversary at the Met, Virgil Thomson said, "Casts have changed around him. . . . But he always sings Don Giovanni, and the others always outdo themselves to match his workmanship. He is one of the great singing actors of our century, and Don Giovanni is his greatest role." He sang the role forty-six times at the Met, took it to Florence and Paris, and was the first bass to sing the Don in Italian in Salzburg.

Regina Resnik sang Donna Anna at the Met for the first time in 1947. Only three years later, she began appearing as Elvira.

RESNIK: The greatest Don was Pinza; even though he was very Italianate, there was no greater personality on the stage. I'll never forget standing in the wings and watching Pinza come out in front of the curtain and do the "Champagne Aria," with a glass in his hand, dressed in gold and white brocade, and tossing off this aria in one minute flat. And the laughter as he exited—it was the most abandoned, the most elegant, and yet most decadent personality. His physical form was—well, he was not only very handsome, but the voice was remarkable. It was a true bass. I'm not sure he was ideal for Mozart, but he was a super, super man. It wasn't like the baritone voices that sang it later—but it worked.

Voted "Opera's glamour man" by *Harper's Bazaar,* Pinza once entertained the ambition of becoming a professional six-day bicycle racer, and devoted a full year to that pursuit. He claimed his operatic career began in the bathtub after a losing race. While he was crooning and splashing away, he said, his friends emerged from the locker room to inform him that his vocalism was more impressive than his velocity; after that, he enrolled in the Bologna Conservatory.

In addition to singing Donna Anna in international houses, including the Met, Carol Vaness made her Glyndebourne debut in the role in 1982.

V A N E S S : The main thing is the guilt she felt over her father's death. She feels she herself caused it. Any normal woman in her position would, any woman attacked—or in those days, just to have a strange man in your room was like an attack. Directors always talk about whether she's raped or not raped, but it really almost doesn't matter.

S T E B E R : It was his pure masculinity that did it. It's not a knock-down, drag-out kind of rape, if you know what I mean. It really meant something to her. She was never able to relate with Don Ottavio. And of course, I love what George Bernard Shaw does later when he sends her to hell with them, in "Don Juan in Hell," from *Man and Superman.*

B A M P T O N : Pinza as Don Giovanni! When I came out of the stage crying that this handsome stranger had come in my bedroom and tried to rape me, I always said, "I think I was crying because he didn't." He was simply wonderful!

V A N E S S : I don't think it makes Ottavio a wimp just because he doesn't run off and kill Don Giovanni. It makes him a much more modern man, and a better foil for the Don. A lot of people just ignore that: "Oh, he's such a wimp! Who wants to sing him?" God forbid you should sing something that's not macho in the opera.

Jan Peerce said that Don Ottavio was the role that scared him the most, because, he said, he didn't feel equipped to handle Mozart. But he was convinced that Ottavio was a Don, not a "gutless milquetoast." In his opinion, a milquetoast didn't swear vengance. Starting on February 3, 1950, Peerce sang the role twenty-six times with the Met alone, and it was the vehicle for his company farewell in 1967.

S T E B E R : Jan Peerce was my Don Ottavio, and he was so wonderful. He was such a beautiful singer. The sound of Jan's voice is still in my ears.

Lucine Amara sang her first Elvira with the Met in 1954 and performed the role forty-five times with the company.

A M A R A : If you have someone you can play off well, like the Don Ottavio who sings the big aria right before yours, that is ideal. My Annas were Eleanor Steber and Leontyne Price, and there were others. Steber was really remarkable.

S T E B E R : I never really like the way Anna treats Don Ottavio, but she probably will never forget the experience she has shared with Don Giovanni in the bedroom.

B A M P T O N : I think she really cannot make up her mind to marry the tenor. She keeps saying, "Well, just give me another year to make up my mind about this." And he's been so patient. Most men would say, "I'll find somebody else rather than wait around for you another year." I don't think it's completely because of the loss of her father—although that was horrible, of course. Maybe she was a little bit in love with the Don and can't quite make up her mind whether this tenor is going to be the one for her. I always feel she keeps putting him off. And my tenors were always so darling, it seems she'd want to say, "Let's get on with it."

V A N E S S : One of the best productions I did was the famous Peter Hall one at Glyndebourne, with Thomas Allen as the Don. Ottavio was played as an older man, which would explain why he thinks first. But any gentleman in that period would think before saying, "Let's go and lynch somebody who's a fellow nobleman."

S T E B E R : I don't know why more singers won't sing Don Ottavio. But you have to be a very good singer. Also, it's a kind of innocuous role, and it's very hard to make an impression. He seems like an also-ran. You have to have a very strong personality to make it come through. So maybe tenors are protecting themselves if they don't want to do it. It requires very difficult singing—if they can sing it, they should. McCormack used to sing the role—and don't kid yourself about what you hear on old recordings, the voices in those days. They had beautiful placement and beautiful sound that went through a house. Today, you get more bombastic voices without the color. Richard Crooks used to sing Ottavio, too—and that was a voice.

V A N E S S : There was this Alfred Hitchcock on television recently: This woman was raped, and her husband took her home from the hospital. Naturally, she was very freaked out. One day they were driving along, and she sees this man and she screams, "That's him! That's him!" He runs up to this man and kills him. So he gets back in the car and drives, and five minutes later, she sees another man and screams, "There he is! There he is!" Whereupon the man realizes he's killed a man for no reason. Well, especially in that century, noblemen tried to think first.

Whether it appeared in the guise of Ezio Pinza chasing Bidú Sayão around the Met or Errol Flynn pursuing Viveca Lindfors across a movie screen, the legend of Don Juan has endured, fascinating men as well as women. The two most important productions of *Don Giovanni* in the United States during the twentieth century were the Urban-Wymetal Met production of 1929 (revised in 1953) and the company's Berman-Graf production of 1957.

MILANOV: For *Don Giovanni,* we had Novotná and Pinza and Sayão and Baccaloni and everyone—and we all worked so well together.

JARMILA NOVOTNÁ: Oh, that was divine, it was wonderful; really, quite an ensemble. Because, you see, Milanov had a beutiful voice—a wonderful singer. And this charming Zerlina of Sayão—I think it has never been done better.

LICIA ALBANESE: I loved to watch Bidú do that, because she was such a lovely artist.

NOVOTNÁ: And Baccaloni! And then Pinza—God, many try it, but very few succeed. He had the personality. You see, the important thing is if one has personality. You can bring everything so much more to life. And once we had Tito Schipa—he was a wonderful bel canto singer.

MILANOV: You must love all the roles and all the colleagues. Did you ever ask a mother if she likes one child more than another? You must love them all.

Jarmila Novotná sang her first Elvira at the Met in 1941. There, it was her most often performed role in a dress, behind Cherubino, Orlovsky, and Octavian.

NOVOTNÁ: You see, during the war, nobody could get away and nobody could come here from Europe. So we were an ensemble—which, until then, almost didn't exist. Five years together and no changing. That was great, because we improved, almost, on everything. It was a great time. Edward Johnson was a very amiable director—absolutely wonderful. We could discuss things with him. So we had the most wonderful and delightful time those years—unforgettable.

BAMPTON: Of course, the more often you did the performances with the same people, the closer you got, so that you began to know them as people—as friends. So when you were in a situation on the stage, it was like you were with a friend—somebody who was not a stranger, but someone you know. It made it always much easier.

NOVOTNÁ: I think it is wonderful to play together with others, because it inspires you to do just as well or better. Well, not better, but just as good. That's why it was so nice. We understood each other so well off the stage, and it brought these beautiful performances. And now, we are still seeing each other—like Licia and Bidú and Rose Bampton and so on—because we are of the old opera house, because somehow we were really like one family.

BAMPTON: My Elvira was Novotná, and she's such a love. And of course, you are sympathetic with her in the opera, and she's just charming.

Emma Eames, Johanna Gadski, Elisabeth Rethberg, and Gina Cigna were among the tireless Elviras who pursued Giovanni across the Met stage over the years.

NOVOTNÁ: Elvira was a stylish lady whom he conquered long before we see her on the stage. And he was unfaithful to her all the time, yet somehow she could not completely forget him and follows him, as we see. Now she hopes she can get him back, which is not so easy.

STEBER: The role is actually more dramatic than Donna Anna, except for Donna Anna's first aria. Donna Elvira was one one of the great roles of my career. I did five, six, seven years of it, off and on. It was quite a marvelous role. She's the antithesis of Donna Anna, a completely different personality, and I'm certainly glad she proved to be part of my repertory. I think I did thirty-six of them at the Met.

BAMPTON: Once the opera house told me I had to sing an Elvira, and I said, "I can't sing that part—it's just not for me." Johnson said, "Why?" And I said, "It's not my nature. Maybe Donna Anna is my nature. But also the vocal line of the Elvira is very difficult, and it requires another quality of voice."

Roberta Alexander's Met debut was as the peasant girl Zerlina. She has since become a Donna and has taken her Elvira to opera houses around the world.

A L E X A N D E R : Vocally, Elvira's a long role, especially with the ensembles. You have to keep fresh, which is hard, because you come on and have to sing one of the gangbuster arias—it's all over the place. And it's very difficult to portray "If I get him, I will rip his heart out," with that intensity, and not let it show up in your sound. Because the sound then doesn't stay warm—it gets tight.

A M A R A : Elvira was one of my favorite characters. Glyndebourne had asked me to prepare Donna Anna, but I was never happy with it. Anna's character didn't suit me and it sang too high for my voice. But I loved Elvira and was always comfortable with her.

V A N E S S : Elvira is sometimes easier to cast in terms of vocal demands, and I think they look first for a Donna Anna. Anna was never that hard for me; of course, it's hard—it just wasn't a big stretch for me.

R E S N I K : I started off with Donna Elvira. With due respect to all my great colleagues of the past, I've got to say I couldn't have started singing the opera without Fritz Busch and Fritz Reiner. With colleagues from Pinza and Baccaloni to Milanov and Kullman and Peerce, from Ljuba Welitsch to all the great sopranos who were singing the work at the Met, from switching from Elvira to Anna, then back again—I certainly had a great many experiences. And I finally could decide where I fit in the opera.

A M A R A : The Berman production had a slight rake coming down to the stage, and they would carry you in on a sedan chair, then I would walk down this rake. One night, as I started walking, there was no rosin on my shoes and it was slick. And my foot gave out and I almost fell—and I caught myself, but the entire audience went, "Ahhhhh!" Then I had to sing the aria.

A L E X A N D E R : I think Elvira's particularly attractive as a person. When he sees her, he doesn't recognize her but says, "Oh, this is a beautiful woman." Then when she turns around, he says, "Oh, my God, it's her."

A M A R A : Then, the hat I had to wear was enormous, and if you weren't careful putting it on properly, you couldn't see or be seen. It also bothered me because the brim would deflect the sound.

ALEXANDER: Elvira's very compassionate. Even though he betrayed her, she still wants to save him. She can't believe he's a total loss, even though we all know he's a lost cause. She's sexy, obviously very smart, and a product of her time. Unless she's with the Don, she's never outside the code of behavior. She's mortified inside, but she'd never let that show—maybe not even to him. She's very complex.

AMARA: Elvira is a spit-and-fire character, who is taken in by Giovanni's charm. Even to the end, she wants him to repent. She goes in to warn him, "Please give up your ways." I think she must have loved him very much.

The Metropolitan first saw *Don Giovanni* on November 28, 1883, the company's first season, with a cast including Emma Fürsch-Madi as Donna Anna, Christine Nilsson as Elvira, and Marcella Sembrich as Zerlina, pursued by Giuseppe Kaschmann as the Don. The performance was described by Henry Krehbiel of the *New York Tribune* as "a hotchpotch of the good, the bad and the indifferent." He commended the three women for their "excellent work," saying, "If the complete success of the opera had depended on their efforts, it would have been won. All the trouble there was came from . . . notably the instrumental musicians, who made a sad mess of the finale of the first act."

Beginning in 1957, Masetto was the role Theodor Uppman performed most often with the Metropolitan.

THEODOR UPPMAN: I was part of the Berman production, and it seems to me there was hardly ever a bad performance of it. *Don Giovanni* is rather a difficult opera to do, because there are so many scenes. In the old production they used to bring the curtain down, but this time they were able to move things so quickly that there was very little time lost, and the whole impetus of the work could continue. That's one reason I was very happy to be part of that production. Also, the casts were extraordinary: Siepi and Valletti, Eleanor Steber, Lisa della Casa, then Tozzi and Corena, and Roberta, of course, as Zerlina.

Zerlina, in addition to being Roberta Peters's debut role, was, after Gilda, the one she performed most often in her long association with the Metropolitan Opera.

P E T E R S : I stepped in for an ailing colleague—Nadine Conner—as my very first role at the Metropolitan, November 17, 1950. That was Mr. Bing's first year. Truthfully, I had been signed to do the Queen of the Night in *The Magic Flute,* but the *Don Giovanni*s came before. On a Friday at three P.M., I got a call from Mr. Bing: "Urgent—come running down." So I did, and was ushered into his office very quickly, and he asked me whether I would be able to sing Zerlina that night. I think I was numb—but I obviously said yes. And strangely enough, my mother and I were going as standees that night. So Mr. Bing said, "Take a taxicab home and tell the cab driver he has precious cargo— because without you, we can't do the performance. It's four o'clock already." So my mother came home from work, and I said, "Mom, we're going to the opera." And she said, "Yes, I know." And I said, "Sit down, Mom. . . ." Anyway, I had to take a subway to the Met because all the taxis were jammed at rush hour. When we got there, we were ushered into Fritz Reiner's room. I was so fortunate to have him as the conductor. I became a *Reinerkind* after that. He seemed very calm and very nice, and put me at my ease, and said, "Darling, if you need me, I will be there." He was noted for his very tiny beat; so in the performance, there he was with this very small beat—and all of a sudden, when my cue came, he jutted out his hand and found me on the stage, which was really very reassuring.

U P P M A N : Every performance was a great thing for us. Eleanor Steber was in the first three years, and we all enjoyed each other's company.

P E T E R S : Paul Schoeffler was the Don that night, and I think Eleanor Steber was singing. I had fabulous colleagues. And being thrown on like that . . . I had never sung on any stage before; the Met was my first job. But I'd studied in the studio for about six and a half or seven years. My teacher wouldn't let me sing for anyone until Jan Peerce, who was a friend, invited Mr. Hurok up to hear me, and Mr. Hurok brought me to Mr. Bing.

U P P M A N : When we began bringing other people into the new production, it wasn't always for the better, but it always worked. It's a very dangerous opera if you don't have a good, solid cast. We were very fortunate—everyone at the Met who sang it worked out very well.

P E T E R S : Mine sounds like a Cinderella story. But as you know, there's a lot of work that goes before, a lot of studying. I knew the role; I'd studied French, Italian, and German. I'd also watched *Don Giovanni* rehearsals from the audience. But it was all very thrilling.

U P P M A N : The opera has such maturity, especially when you consider how young Mozart was when he wrote it. It's a magnificent gathering of all forces—at times dramatic, but there are moments of great comedy. It just has everything.

Judith Blegen's first Zerlina at the Met was in 1971. Among her other saucy Mozart girls is Susanna, one of her most frequent portrayals with the company.

J U D I T H   B L E G E N : Masetto is really not too smart, but he's adorable. Don Giovanni comes on the scene after getting rid of Elvira and says, *"O, guarda*—look! Look what lovely young people, what lovely women!" Then he says, "Go ahead and stay happy like that." That's profound: The implication is "Because when I come on the scene, I, Giovanni, know what's going to happen."

U P P M A N : Masetto, he's a very simple young fellow who's confused about his whole situation with the Don—he wants to step in and take his girl away from him.

B L E G E N : Giovanni is so wicked; he not only believes in his nobility, but he takes advantage of it all over the place. And Zerlina tells him, "My Masetto's a man of the best heart." The thing they should do is run from this man right away. Masetto should take her hand and say, "Sweetheart, come with me."

M I L N E S : They had the *droit du seigneur*—the right of the master. The feudal lord had the right, if he desired, to the first night with any bride of his people. Because this wasn't feudal time, Giovanni was old-fashioned, in a way. He did have a code of conduct, but it was his own.

U P P M A N : Like everything Mozart wrote, it has its very serious moments; but in the end, you find the forces of evil have been overcome. *Don Giovanni* is probably the strongest of Mozart's statements. The last moment, when the Don goes off to hell, is a great moment. I don't think there's anything in opera that can top it.

BLEGEN: Word by word, we see Zerlina weaken. And a good Giovanni will figure out how to display also with body motions—corporal display of himself. Then she says, "Is it possible that he really means I'm not a peasant? In which case, it would be absolutely wonderful to live in his world instead of this."

PETERS: Zerlina is quite an extrovert as a character, and it's not very difficult to do her. In the end, she really loves Masetto—I really believe that. But she's so taken with this first flush, and Don Giovanni sweeps her off her feet for the moment. But I think, vocally, most soprano voices can do it. There's not so much of a secret as there is for some other roles.

UPPMAN: I did ninety-eight performances of Masetto at the Met.

PETERS: My Masettos were usually Teddy Uppman, and he was such a joy, always easy to work with. So there was a wonderful rapport, and I really feel that helps the performance a lot.

BLEGEN: Don Giovanni is on the make, and he wants it fast, because he wants to go on to the next one. So he says, "In this case, I'll marry you." Mr. da Ponte only gives you, Zerlina, one thing to say: "You? *Voi?*" And there are infinite ways you could choose to do that one word. Innocent or feline. But she's so stunned—he comes on to her so strong.

MILNES: In that time, there was a civil marriage ceremony and a religious ceremony. And until the religious ceremony was held, there was some confusion as to "Were you really making love to someone else's wife?" Goldovsky always said this episode with Zerlina takes place in between. It simply isn't like the twentieth century, with some guy walking into a church wedding and saying, "You—I'm going to seduce you."

BLEGEN: Then comes that famous duet, and Giovanni becomes so slick. Yet this piece is as close to perfection musically as you can get. It's absolutely beautiful, and the beauty there is above everything else. Finally, she says, "OK, what the heck—let's go." The music just goes so naturally and smoothly over into this happiness. Unfortunately, it's not the right kind of happiness.

UPPMAN: The Don has little more than one aria. There are some marvelous moments—showpieces, like the "Champagne Aria." But the real singing is done by the women, both Anna and Elvira. Then, of course, the tenor has lovely music; but I don't think the men overshadow the women.

BLEGEN: I think Zerlina is a little bit stupid, compared to Susanna, but she's smart enough to ally herself with Elvira and Anna. The authors are dealing with eternal truths, as we know them today, in every single line of this piece. It's a great work of art. Operas earn their greatness by all the implications that live within them—if you learn how to listen. And you must live with these pieces; you can't possibly get everything the first time. Every time you find something new—and you're dead before you get to the bottom of it.

UPPMAN: You have every possible human reaction going on throughout the opera—it's remarkable Mozart was able to do this.

BLEGEN: To me, the joy in these notes is greater than anything. It just has to be pure joy. Zerlina should be done with the most charm—charm to make you die. I would not want her to be portrayed like the true peasant that she is, because the music is far, far above the story—or anything at all.

Although Zerlina was not high on Patrice Munsel's list of favorite roles (she much preferred Lucia's mad scene: "All that time out there by yourself to sing and go crazy!"), critics were rapturous about her portrayal. *The New York Times* claimed it was "a delightful surprise . . . sung with a fine sense of phrase, clean diction and vocal control; interpreted with a charm and a coquetry, but with simplicity and tenderness too, for her Masetto."

PATRICE MUNSEL: Zerlina was more or less me playing a character who is like me—which does not stretch you. But I just adored listening to all those other voices. I was always intrigued with the music—Mozart astonishes me.

BLEGEN: When Zerlina comes back to Masetto, she's sincerely sorry for it. She couldn't even help that she went off with Giovanni. Young girls are that way: That's where nasty old men succeed nicely. She's innocent. In the aria "Batti, batti," she says, "Go ahead, beat me, honey—I've earned it." Then she proceeds to wrap him around her little finger: "Listen, Masetto—" And he says, "Don't touch me." It's a typical domestic battle. "Oh, come on, honey, I didn't mean to. I don't warrant this kind of treatment from you." This is feline. It's feminine wiles—and we know it today, as much as they knew it then.

U P P M A N : I try not to analyze too much as I go along, but I certainly think there are psychological things in *Don Giovanni* that are very interesting.

B L E G E N : I was wrong. She *is* intelligent. She's wonderful. Her intelligence is the type that comes naturally. And the first thing Masetto says is "Look at that little witch, how she was able to seduce me. We men are really the ones who are so weak in our heads."

Rosalind Elias put aside her usual mezzo roles to portray the innocent (and almost always soprano) object of the Don's affections, Zerlina. Ironically, of the forty-five roles she sang with the Metropolitan, Zerlina was one of those she most often performed.

R O S A L I N D   E L I A S : I was the first mezzo to do Zerlina at the Met, and I really enjoyed it. You know, it doesn't make sense if you have Donna Anna and Donna Elvira, two sopranos, and then you have another soprano, Zerlina. Three sopranos in one opera? I think it should have the timbre of a mezzo sound, to break it up.

P E T E R S : Personally, I feel it's wrong to give Zerlina to a mezzo. I don't think it's what the color of the voice should be, because the other two women are so heavy and usually dark in quality. So I think you need a lighter sound.

B L E G E N : I think people can get misled by looking at the tessitura of Zerlina and say, "That really should be done by a mezzo."

P E T E R S : It's now become the thing to use them. Many mezzos do it, and I'm sure they do it well. But the quality, the color of the voice, I think, is wrong.

B L E G E N : Also, in an opera house, they want to hire to get that voice heard, and I think they're afraid that if the voice is a little too light and too high, it won't be heard.

P E T E R S : Those *Don Giovanni* performances when I started were some of the happiest performances I've ever done. We also started to have Fernando Corena doing Leporello and Cesare Valletti as Don Ottavio. With Siepi, we became sort of the Four Musketeers. We went out together, and we were even on a television show together.

On December 27, 1899, Antonio Scotti made his Metropolitan debut as the Don, with a cast that included Lillian Nordica, Marcella Sembrich, and Édouard de Reszke. Over the next thirty-four seasons, the Neapolitan baritone went on to sing almost twelve hundred performances with the company, most frequently as Scarpia. Other singers to don Giovanni's costume have been Theodor Reichmann, Jean-Louis Lassalle, and Victor Maurel.

Håkan Hagegård has taken his Giovanni through Europe and the United States. Though he is most famous for his Papageno, which he brought to life in Ingmar Bergman's film *The Magic Flute,* his other Mozart specialties include Almaviva in *Figaro* and Guglielmo in *Così Fan Tutte.*

HAGEGÅRD: A lot of things about the Don are happening while he's offstage. There is no big love story or plot about somebody else. Therefore, the performers onstage must sing in the same conception as he who sings the Don. The one who sings Don Giovanni must almost be a co-director, to make sure the production is united.

MILNES: I try to keep my voice down. I don't vocalize it as high as *Rigoletto, Forza,* the Verdi baritone stuff—they're at least a third higher. And you have long, tonic high notes at the end of scenes. You don't have that in *Don Giovanni.* The highest note he sings is the "No!" when he pulls his hand away from the Commendatore. It's written a middle A, but you usually parlando up and come out somewhere around an A.

HINES: I have a bass voice that has gone particularly fittingly with Verdi and the Russian operas. And until Pinza came, Giovanni was the domain of the baritone. Many times a baritone didn't have a high voice—and Giovanni has a very small range, vocally.

MILNES: Mozart did write fiendishly for women and tenors. Low voices, he didn't write so hard for. *Don Giovanni* is not a hard sing. It's a hard performance: the body energy, control, pizzazz, change.

HINES: When I did my first Don, Fausto Cleva was there, and I asked him, "What did you think of it?" And he said, "Why waste your voice on it?" Now, a statement like that would be shocking to some people. But what he meant was, with a heavy, Verdi-type voice, you have to thin the voice out and lighten it to sing Giovanni, and I couldn't sing with the distinctive sound that was really mine.

M I L N E S : Giovanni is very satisfying to play, although a lot of his stuff is in recitative.

H I N E S : When I think back, I remember when Richard Tucker did his first Tamino in *Magic Flute,* and he was so proud that he could do it. See, Richard had a big, heavy, gutsy tenor voice, and it was a feat for him to try to curb it to sing Tamino. He was proud of it, but he certainly wasn't the world's greatest Tamino—though he was the world's greatest many other things. I felt in a sense that Tucker was wasted in a role like that; he should be singing the *La Forza del Destino*s and things of that sort.

R O B E R T   M E R R I L L : I wanted to sing Don Giovanni. I never got around to it because I was so damn busy. I never really had time and I was a slow study. I could not learn two roles a year. Perhaps I didn't have as large a repertory, but I digested the roles and sang them often.

M I L N E S : All those operas—*Barber of Seville* and *Marriage of Figaro*—were all in twenty-four-hour spans. At the end of that first act, Don Giovanni really doesn't have fun at that party: It's "We're going to have fun if it kills us." Not psychotic, like Iago, but a psychiatrist would have fun with him as well. And another strange thing going on is the way he likes to torment Leporello.

T O Z Z I : I did the role quite a bit. I opted a little more for George London's interpretation. I found it more dramatically penetrating.

B L E G E N : Every single word of da Ponte's is just fabulous. He's talking about every man, when Leporello says, "I would like to be a gentleman, and I don't want to serve anymore." *Don Giovanni* is the struggle of Everyman against the nobility. And how noble is Don Giovanni? In fact, not noble at all. Terrible!

M I L N E S : One of the reasons it premiered in Prague and not Vienna was because the nobleman goes to hell at the end. All of the kingdoms of Europe were feeling their necks at the time.

B L E G E N : Da Ponte is so brilliant—he shows the women being so much more profound than men. And we see right away that Giovanni is absolutely a horrible, horrible person. He's a liar from the word *go.*

N O V O T N Á : Elvira sees the Don not only going after Donna Anna, but after Zerlina. So she is not interfering. But no matter how he behaves, she still loves him, absolutely, all the time.

A L E X A N D E R : One of the larger challenges for Elvira is the trio in the second act. The girl's been singing in a flat key all night—A flat, B flat, nice warm keys—and out of nowhere, here comes A major, which is a bright key. Then, you're hanging out of some balcony with your feet up in the air on one end, and your head hanging down on the other, and you've got to float high As out of nowhere. And you're not even finished: There, all of a sudden, the character becomes different. At that point, it gets a softness.

R E S N I K : Elvira's a trap because she interrupts everything, whereas Donna Anna has a great deal which stems from the plot and the murder of her father. She has growth with everything she does; Elvira has really only one color—her disappointment with the Don. It's hard not to make her appear as a fishwife.

A M A R A : In the second-act scene with Leporello, she is so enamored of him, thinking he's Don Giovanni, that she practically falls into his arms. She's so in love—then later, she's furious when she finds out about the trick, and she's ready to kill them both.

A L E X A N D E R : I had a wonderful production where Elvira was dressed exactly like Don Giovanni—that's how I was able to travel by myself.

R E S N I K : I remember when Ljuba Welitsch was to come to the Met to debut as Donna Anna, with Reiner, me as Elvira, Patrice Munsel as Zerlina, and Jan Peerce. It was an interesting cast. But Ljuba didn't show up. So the management called and asked me, if she didn't come, would I sing Donna Anna? I said I didn't think that was very fair. I had learned Elvira with Reiner and worked very hard on it; now, to make a switch . . . I later found out I was rehearsing both parts because they had put me down as the cover for Donna Anna, so I'd rehearse one part, then switch to the other. Then Welitsch showed up, and I begged them to take me permanently off that cover, which they did.

A L E X A N D E R : For the Don, Elvira is just another conquest. He is totally upset that she is coming back into his life at this moment, when he was all ready to get this little girl from the village and Donna Anna. She's messing up his plan.

N O V O T N Á : And in the moment when the others start to threaten Don Giovanni, she is there. Even in the last act, she is absolutely, completely a woman who doesn't want anybody else but the Don.

R E S N I K : For a few years I switched over to Donna Anna exclusively. San Francisco asked me to switch to make room for Ezio's daughter, Claudia Pinza. And I really learned Donna Anna in six weeks. In retrospect, I never should have done it. I found Anna, while very gratifying, just wasn't for me. It sat very high for me and put a tremendous strain on my voice, so I went back to Elvira. But, of course, a few years later that whole Mozart problem was over for me, because I turned mezzo and never sang Mozart again.

ALEXANDER: "Mi tradì" is, stamina-wise, one of the most difficult pieces in the repertoire, because it never stops. People don't realize how difficult it is until you can't sing it, because it doesn't sound hard. I've always admired people who can make everything look easy, like Carol Vaness.

MILANOV: When I had to sing softly, I did. The public should never think that you have given all that you have to give.

BAMPTON: Elvira's sound doesn't have the warmth that Anna has. She has a lot of fast work, coloratura. Elvira's always crying, complaining that he's not faithful to her. Anna is quite another type of woman.

VANESS: Elvira's music is always fast and it comes in very short phrases, except where she's speaking of her love for him—then there are very long lines. She's passionate and it comes in short bursts. Donna Anna's music comes in very long lines. She's on the top of all the ensembles. I think Mozart did that in terms of her character.

STEBER: I think Donna Anna has the greatest music to sing. Her singing is sublime.

BAMPTON: Vocally, it's a big contrast, because her first aria is such a forceful thing, whereas the last aria is a long, long line—much more legato, long breaths. And there's a beautiful trio for the two women and the tenor.

MILANOV: We had a very good success with *Don Giovanni*. It was a wonderful company with wonderful colleagues.

BAMPTON: And the wonderful, wonderful tenor I had was Richard Crooks. What a love! And what a beautiful voice! And that second aria, he'd have to stand there while you're singing. So he'd look at me with this twinkle in his eye and say, "Now, Rose, comes your stooge aria."

STEBER: *Don Giovanni* is really playing with very heavy emotions compared to a *Figaro*.

MILANOV: I enjoyed singing Donna Anna. Anna was a little perilous for me, but Maestro [Bruno] Walter said, "Don't worry, my child—just use your voice. I'm going to adjust to your voice, don't worry."

VANESS: In all Mozart parts, the music nearly always explains where your character is emotionally and psychologically at any given moment. For Anna, the first trio runs up and down because she is running; she's desperate to get him. The angularity of the recitative that follows, when she finds her father on the ground, shows her complete loss of any control.

RESNIK: You have to remember that in Mozart's time, pitch was a full half-tone lower. The reaches of Donna Anna are enormous, but they aren't if it's a half-tone lower, which is how it was meant to be.

MILANOV: I loved all my parts. I never sang anything I didn't want to sing. This was very fortunate for me. My singing and my career was beautiful, and I wouldn't choose anything else if I had to do it all again.

BAMPTON: My first *Don Giovanni* I had to do without a stage rehearsal, because it had been done already in the season. And I had never seen a performance of it. But I had a concert in Akron which I couldn't go to because I had a bad cold, so I went to the Met instead that night and heard a *Don Giovanni* performance—so at least I could have an idea of what happened on the stage before I went on.

MILANOV: I did my first Donna Anna on tour. Then, everyone went on the tour—you only had the best. That's why it's no more, because today, the best will not go out. I sang how many Aidas—I don't know—but it was always on the tour, too. It was important to bring it to the people all over.

Pinza's 1948 retirement as an operatic idol cast him as a Broadway idol when he opened the following year in *South Pacific*. Many will remember his "Some Enchanted Evening" even more vividly than his "Deh vieni alla finestra." He followed with the Broadway version of *Fanny* along with other projects, including an ill-fated television sitcom, *Bonino*. His Nellie Forbush, Mary Martin, called him the most magnetic performer she had ever known.

ALBANESE: All the great friends of mine used to tell one another to do things on the stage. As Zerlina, I'd tell Pinza, "Why don't you do it this way—take me like this, like that." And he's say, "Some night, Licia, I'm going to kiss you on your mouth." And I'd say, "Eh, dare it—I will step on your foot!" It was so cute, really. What a great man. What a great voice. Nobody had a voice like that.

UPPMAN: I remember in one performance, Siepi was beating me up onstage, and he actually did hit me rather hard on the bottom. He also took this wonderful wooden rifle I had and threw it down on the floor, and split it all over the place. Then Roberta came out to pick me up and take me offstage and sing her little aria to me. Well, she had to pick up pieces of that gun from all over—it was a real mess.

BLEGEN: Zerlina says, "I told you if you were so silly and jealous, you'd only let yourself in for some misfortune." That's "I told you so." Then, "Where did they hurt you?" And he says, "Here, here, and here," and goes on. And she says, "Oh, don't worry, you're going to be all right. That's not so bad if the *rest* of you is healthy."

BAMPTON: The little Zerlina, of course, is just enchanting. And she always steals the show anyway, because she has such a darling way with her. And in love with that stupid boy—no wonder she's tempted by the Don.

BLEGEN: You know, when you're very young, it's sort of cute to watch how embarrassed people in authority get when it touches on these things that are a little embarrassing. This was the first role I studied at Curtis. And when it approached these things that had to do with sex, my instructors didn't know what to say, and they became very embarrassed. But I remember, they did get it out of themselves to try to make that implication to me: "That's not so bad if the *rest* is all right." That's what it means.

PETERS: Vocally, Zerlina is for me quite easy—a breeze. Queen of the Night is another story, but Zerlina is right in the middle range, really. I've always felt that was such an easy range for me, and I believe I was heard in that thirty-eight-hundred-seat house, so I never worried about it. I never felt I had to push in the lower register. One of the reasons I feel I've lasted is because I haven't pushed all these years, and I've done the right roles.

ALBANESE: I'd rather do ten Butterflys than Zerlina or Susanna, because Mozart repeats the same melodies in different ways. But you mustn't be stiff. If a soprano, tenor, or anybody sees the high notes coming, they start to be stiff. Why? Think of the words and, you see, you make this note. I think of the words, I go to the F.

ELIAS: Technically, Mozart wrote so well that it's like a lesson. I always go back to oil up my voice by singing Mozart. It's the best advice I could give to young singers. The way he wrote is not easy, but the musical line is a lesson for the voice, especially when you go to contemporary pieces like *Regina*. I go back to Mozart. And it makes you feel good—it's like meditation, like going to a retreat and finding yourself again.

BLEGEN: Zerlina says, "Come home with me, because if you promise to be less jealous, I'll make it worth your while." That's what this aria is all about. "The remedy I carry around with myself all the time." She's so tender and gentle with him—it's so poetic. She touches her heart, and Mozart writes in the heartbeat. It's absolutely beautiful. She's the beautiful, adoring woman; she's Eve.

ALBANESE: Bidú told me, "Every time I sing Zerlina, I am crossing myself." And I said, "Don't tell me, Bidú. I'm doing the same thing."

The night before *Don Giovanni*'s premiere, as the famous story goes, the opera apparently lacked an overture. Never one to be put off by details, Mozart locked himself up with his wife, Constanze, who read to him about Cinderella and Aladdin and kept him thoroughly amused, while he guzzled punch and penned the magnificent overture—but not before falling asleep several times.

PETERS: Mozart is my favorite composer. Vocally, it's like a bath for the voice. I usually start all my recitals and orchestra dates with Mozart. It just sets me up so nicely. With Mozart, you have to hold in a bit, and everything is more structured than Verdi or Puccini.

UPPMAN: It takes a certain type of placement and agility for Mozart. You can't just fool around with him. I don't want to say Puccini is not a great composer and there aren't beautiful moments in his work, but I think singers can get away with singing a little badly in Puccini, or even in Verdi at times. But Mozart requires perfection.

NOVOTNÁ: Mozart has this clarity, this terrific diversity. People say it is not easy to sing Mozart. That's because there is such a clarity to everything. And people say that once you can sing Mozart, you can sing everything, because there it just the line, the purity of it. You must not exaggerate it, but you must put your heart into it. But then you can't break the line; otherwise it is no longer beautiful. Although Donna Elvira and Donna Anna do have real dramatic moments, in Verdi you have to express yourself much more naturally. Not that Mozart is unnatural, but it has to be somehow kept in a wonderful continuity.

UPPMAN: It's true that Mozart operas are given a lot to young people to sing—*Così* and *Abduction* are young people's operas, and it's very good for them. It's certainly not bad to be weaned on Mozart. But despite that, Mozart is an adult composer. Singing Mozart effectively means that your vocal technique has to be so good that you can put it aside.

HAGEGÅRD: A professional singer should have the skill to sing different composers and different kinds of music. Therefore, we do not put so much difference in performing Wagner from performing Mozart.

MILNES: I was the first American to have sung *Don Giovanni* in the Tyl Theater in Prague, where it was premiered. That was exciting—a special feeling. Tiny little theater; there was a spiral staircase to the dressing rooms—cast iron with wooden treads that had never been changed, worn in the center. Mozart went up and down those stairs while working on the production. It was almost eerie.

The one thing that Donna Anna, Donna Elvira, and Zerlina do have in common is Don Giovanni. The opera is not the only one where an eligible divo is shared by more than one prima donna. In Cilea's *Adriana Lecouvreur,* the Princess de Bouillon beats the competition by sending her rival a bouquet of poisoned violets.

VANESS: *Don Giovanni* is a total ensemble piece—even for the Don. Most Mozart operas are that way, because Mozart was a humanitarian. You can't say, "She's the queen of the opera and he's the king." All the parts have to be cast from great strength. I have no problem sharing the stage with two other sopranos.

RESNIK: I don't even find it extraordinary. When you do *The Marriage of Figaro,* you have three prima donnas—four! You do the *Walküre,* and you have three prima donnas. What about *Elektra*? And what about the male prima donnas? They were the biggest prima donnas of all!

PETERS: It was great. I always stood in the wings when Eleanor Steber did the big aria in the last act, the "Non mi dir," because I always loved to see how she did it. It was wonderful. My part was the soubrette, the ingenue role, so it was never anything like what people think of as temperament. Everybody knew their roles. And of course, everybody was scared stiff of Reiner, because he had a reputation of really being able to zap people if he didn't like them or felt they weren't doing their part well.

AMARA: I'm not really a Mozart singer. I'm more of a Verdi and Puccini singer. When I sang Pamina, I was young enough that I could sing it, but it wasn't really for me.

STEBER: At the time I was doing Donna Elvira, I kind of tossed it off—except when I did the big aria. Bruno Walter told me, "Eleanor, remember the recitative in this is one of the great ones in all musical writing." So of course, I took what Bruno Walter said as God's word.

BAMPTON: The recitatives in Mozart are very difficult. That, for me is the most difficult thing in Mozart, because he has such long recitatives, and they must all be simply conversational. You must stop singing and read it as if you were reading a story; read it with the inflection in the voice, knowing what you're saying, and with the speed that you would be saying it. When there's a rest, it must be just a little break like when you're speaking, but it doesn't mean take a big breath there. Once you've learned that style of recitative in Mozart, none of the others really are difficult.

MILANOV: I was a Verdi specialist, and then I went to Mozart. Naturally, Mozart is different than Verdi. I sang *Don Giovanni* because Maestro Walter wanted me to sing Donna Anna, so I sang it for him. They also wanted me to sing the Queen of the Night, but no. Donna Anna was the only Mozart part I sang.

BLEGEN: Mozart is an excellent vehicle for learning legato, for learning shade of tone.

MILANOV: I loved *Don Giovanni* especially because I got to sing with Maestro Walter. That was always a very, very great pleasure for me. Also, I would do the Verdi Requiem with him, in New York, Chicago, London, South America. It was very beautiful.

B A M P T O N : Bruno Walter was a great specialist. I sang with him, which was a big bit of work, because he was very demanding—to do it just the way he wanted, with all the phrasing and recitatives just so. I had done it with Ettore Panizza, when I first did *Don Giovanni.* He was a wonderful conductor. I must say, I've had a life filled with wonderful conductors—just great conductors, every one of them. And every one of them was kind to me, and good to me, and helpful. In Buenos Aires, in the Wagner, it was Busch, and then Erich Kleiber. Busch also did the Mozart in Buenos Aires.

Fritz Busch came to South America from Germany, where he had defied the Nazi regime. He especially enjoyed working with young, malleable singers. During one South American performance of *Trovatore,* an American contralto lauded for her lush tones took a note and decided to sit on it. It sounded so good, nothing Busch did could pry her off it. He was finally compelled to drown her out by crashing the orchestra in on the next bar. The incident left them both speechless.

M I L A N O V : I gave all my heart and soul to every part I did. I did all the things I wanted to do. I never asked Mr. Bing or Mr. Johnson for any part—they always asked me.

B A M P T O N : The moment before you go onstage—sometimes I couldn't remember the first word. I would be absolutely panicky and say, "Oh, my God, what *is* my first phrase?" But somehow, the minute you're onstage and hear that music, it comes to you.

M I L A N O V : I was never really nervous. That was not really good for the voice. I was anxious to be good—but not nervous. Rosa Ponselle used to get very nervous. She came to me one night in Baltimore and said, "You're so calm. I couldn't do this; I was always so nervous. I envy you."

B L E G E N : Maybe one way I can know in my heart I have really become an artist is that I know that no matter how hard I try, I can't get to the bottom of these works. What it means is that I know how to recognize them; I know how to see all these implications I've never seen before.

MILANOV: I loved the instrument that God gave me, and you have to take care of it. I don't know today that people know how to take care of it. Many people today think if they eat a lot, that will give you more voice—but that is wrong. I don't say you shouldn't eat, but some people eat or drink during a performance. I would just take an apple or something, and not drink anything—not even water.

On December 7, 1896, the Metropolitan revived *Don Giovanni* with Jean-Louis Lassalle, Édouard de Reszke, and David Bispham. If possible, the criticism was worse than at its premiere. The production, which lacked "the slightest regard for coherency and reason in the dramatic department," and "the inability of the majority of the singers to do anything like justice to the music" caused Krehbiel of the *Tribune* to worry that *"Don Giovanni* will soon be a curiosity in our operatic museum."

UPPMAN: I love the opera. I think it's one of the great works of all time.

RESNIK: I wouldn't call it a perfect opera, because it leaves a great deal to be desired, theatrically. It's just one long continuation of arias. Each one's a jewel, and connected by recitative and great ensemble pieces—there's no question about the musical effect. But there are moments when I found the opera lacking, and it was not really the director's fault.

HAGEGÅRD: I would probably agree that it's one of the greatest operas ever written. But we performers always talk about operas that we know very well, that we've done very often.

RESNIK: Certain works play by themselves, because even if you don't have great people, the work will stand alone. But I think *Don Giovanni* will fall apart if you don't have great singers. It's kind of a trap.

BLEGEN: *Don Giovanni* is just so beautiful, and so profound. It is so much more complicated and mature than *The Marriage of Figaro,* for example, musically.

RESNIK: I don't know if I can compare *Don Giovanni* with *The Marriage of Figaro* and say which is the greater. In my opinion, in certain aspects, as a theater piece, I think *Figaro* is a greater work.

H A G E G Å R D : It depends from what angle you talk. Singing-wise, the role of the Don is not the most rewarding part. It doesn't have big, long arias to show off. It doesn't have music like *The Marriage of Figaro*. It's kind of like the difference between Iago and Falstaff: Iago has some really beautiful music to sing, but Falstaff is a more complete character.

B L E G E N : *Don Giovanni*'s overture is so much more profound. It has more colors in it, and he uses more complicated forms.

R E S N I K : I think it's unfair to ask if it's the greatest opera in the world. It's certainly Mozart's most profound work, but I can't certainly say it's a greater work than *Tristan* or *Faust*. You can't really equate Mozart's greatest with Verdi's or Wagner's or Strauss's. There is no question about the musical gifts of the opera. It's certainly Mozart at his best. Musically, it's the most inspired of his works, with the possible exception of his Requiem.

H I N E S : I remember the first major question I asked was, does one take the story to be a morality play, where the Don goes to hell at the end—a deep, serious point of view, that would require psycho-analysis of the Don? Or should one approach it tongue-in-cheek, as a lighter work?

M I L N E S : *Don Giovanni* has to be serious. If he's not tough, danger-ous, mean enough, you don't have a piece. If it's just pranks and misdemeanors, it's not serious enough for him to lose his life and go to hell.

H I N E S : My first question on the subject went to Max Rudolf. And he said, "Look—Don Giovanni goes to hell in D major." Which means, it's a very bright, happy key, and how can one really take it seriously? In that time in history, anything on the stage had to have a moralistic tone and a moral ending to it. So whether the librettist really felt that Don Juan should go to hell or not, he had to send him there. But my feeling was that it should be approached in a lighter fashion—not a psychoanalysis of the character, as many of the Ger-mans are prone to do.

Ludwig van Beethoven, never known as a pixie, was not amused by the Don. "I could never have put such a scandalous subject to music," he commented. "It would be to dishonor the sacredness of art."

ALEXANDER: Well, the Germans are so serious about every-thing. And I'm a serious person, too—but they can take it a little too far for my taste.

HINES: I think it is a rather tongue-in-cheek and clever secular work, in which we are following the world's greatest lover around for twenty-four hours. And in total frustration, he chases every girl in town, and gets nobody.

Baritone Thomas Hampson was chosen by Jean-Pierre Ponnelle to play the Don in his last staging of the opera in Zurich.

THOMAS HAMPSON: That was Ponnelle's last full *Don Giovanni* production. In his last years, he had gotten into this stark, one-color set. Ponnelle thought this Zurich production was closest to his idea of *Giovanni,* and this production was very stark.

TOZZI: You know, there was an old saying back in the thirties and forties: "Just play the tune, Charlie." If we'd only get back to that philosophy of "You've got great work going for you, great music, great lyrics—play the tune." Don't start to use it as an audiovisual Rorschach. All the philosophical discussion—just let it work for itself. Mozart and da Ponte were sufficiently specific. You can psy-choanalyze an opera to pieces, and all the esoteric conjecture really leads nowhere. The work signifies itself. So why belabor it?

MILNES: Mozart wrote the Epilogue later—he didn't write it for Prague, but for Vienna. There are some practical considerations in using it or not.

ALEXANDER: I had one performance when I ran out for the Epilogue and fell into this six-foot hole. And all the men were standing around looking at me in this hole. And the music is going on, and Donna Anna is pulling me out. Typical.

MILNES: Without the Epilogue, the opera is stronger for Giovanni. There's a scream, he goes down to hell, D major chord, D major chord—curtain. Giovanni goes out and takes a bow. It can't be more visceral than that, and the Epilogue does let the audience simmer down after the excitement. However, a morality statement at the end of one of those pieces was normal at that time. Rossini, Donizetti—*Barber* and *Don Pasquale* have it—"Good forces win, bad forces lose, myeh, myeh, myeh!"

ALEXANDER: I do not condone cutting the Epilogue—but I agree with it. It's so much stronger without it. Otherwise, it's anti-climactic. I always feel so stupid running out—and then of course that dreadful finale is so hard to sing. See? There's an ulterior motive here.

TOZZI: I think it's a question of taste. But if Mozart wrote an epilogue to *Don Giovanni,* I certainly am not going to argue with Mozart. The Epilogue is part of the work—leave it in. Is it so bad that people should have to sit a few more moments in the theater before they run for their cars in the parking lot?

HAMPSON: Ponnelle's was a very dark production—in the philosophical sense. Giovanni's very obviously disturbed once he's killed the Commendatore. And he's as much fleeing from his guilt by the end of the first-act finale as he's fleeing Donna Elvira. You could also say that his nonsuccess with Zerlina was because the juices weren't lined up. He's got something pretty big on his mind: "I've killed a man tonight."

BAMPTON: I don't think I was conscious of anything philosophical about it; I was just anxious to sing it well.

VANESS: But the greatness of it allows for all these different views. It is interesting for everyone to talk about Don Juan. What was he? Was he the jokester of Seville? Was he impotent? Was he a great lover? What's the real story? That's why it's such a great opera. Everyone can argue and be right and wrong. It goes beyond what human beings can decide. Mozart was able to leave a great deal of mystery; he made you think.

MILNES: The homosexual talk—was he really a latent homosexual and all that—ludicrous! Ludicrous! Certainly he had his problems, and the apparent necessity to have to make love to all these women.

VANESS: A really avant-garde *Don Giovanni* really wouldn't interest me. The New York City Opera production was pretty weird, but I was younger then. I would never do certain things now that I did then, no matter who asked me to do it.

HAMPSON: Ponnelle's development of Giovanni was that you see him kill, you see him get bothered by it, you see his nervous reaction. Then he disappears. Then you see him trying to deal with life as he knows it. Everything is starting to unravel. When people say, "Why is Giovanni so difficult? Because he never has any success with the women." It's not that—he's just unraveling; he's out of control. He's looking for something else to be victor over to prove that he's in control.

RESNIK: We have to think about the purpose and the aim of the composer. Mozart had the most incredible, spontaneous, inborn, inbred genius for the stage. The Don Juan legend had been touched by many people. This is what came out of it—true genius. But I don't think it can be analyzed as this or that. You have to think about why a play is written in its time.

HAMPSON: By the time he gets to the graveyard and hears the voice, there's almost a cynical laughter in him. He realizes, "Ah. OK. I'm going to meet my maker. All right, I'll meet you." Then, when you see him in the supper scene, it's a very bizarre thing. In every staging, there's nobody else there. He's going to eat. Who does he eat with? Leporello. That's Giovanni's life. Everybody thinks he's a party king, but he's only a party king if he invites people. So you open up with a really bleak scene, and he's doing his little jokes, trying to amuse himself with Leporello. There's a certain tedium and a certain boredom in that, which is fascinating. And then, "Oh, God, here comes Elvira."

ALEXANDER: Elvira even tries to save Don Giovanni. She says, "Look, there's one chance—you can repent and save yourself." And he just laughs at her.

HAMPSON: It's buffo inside of an incredibly demanding, pleading moment. "What is it? What do you want from me? Change my life? Forget it! It's too late for me, sweetheart. I'm not going to change anything." Then he starts to really unravel.

VANESS: The reason people believe it to be the perfect opera is that whatever you do to it, you can't kill it. There's always room to talk about it. You can argue about it forever.

HINES: There are certain philosophical questions in the finale. Pinza used to play it that he was having his final feast with a bunch of ballet girls hanging all around him, and Pinza had that reputation of being a Don Juan in real life also. I do feel, however, that we should make it serious enough—that Don Juan is at his "last supper" totally alone. It's sort of symbolic in his life. One can play it sort of bleak, a little more of a tragedy, more poignant. It's an important consideration.

M I L N E S : I did *Don Giovanni* in Salzburg with Ponnelle, and I was the first American to do Giovanni in Mozartland. In the supper scene, Ponnelle had the Commendatore appear in the back and I reenacted the sword fight. In Berlin, I did a production where Giovanni died of a heart attack, really boozed up at the end. That caused you to start the opera much more dissipated.

H A M P S O N : We had the Commendatore's voice and a distant statue. But what you saw was what was happening to Giovanni. And Leporello says, "L'uomo bianco"—"I'm seeing a very pale man." And Elvira screams and comes over to the table. She sees this man possessed.

M I L N E S : What Ponnelle did was superior, because during the scene with the Commendatore, there are trombone forte accent passages, and then piano again: swirling music. Each of those, Jean-Pierre read as a lightning bolt, force field, whatever—it can certainly have religious overtones—electrical shock to the body. And that makes perfect sense. I liked that demise, because he's really fighting. And if you want to think it's the forces of heaven and hell . . .

H A M P S O N : Some of the critics wrote, "Ponnelle had Giovanni die of a heart attack. That's pretty boring." Usually, it's "How did he die? How much smoke? Gee, you really felt like you were going to hell yourself." But with Ponnelle, no smoke, no nothing. Died of a heart attack, rolled down the steps, and that was that.

M I L N E S : When I went back to the Met after Salzburg, I brought this: cramping, muscle spasms of enormous pain, in those places in the score. Composers wrote for effects, and we should always use those effects onstage. To treat those forte and piano passages exactly the same is foolish.

V A N E S S : Probably the worst production was one I did in Bonn. It was horrible. The producer believed that at the end, the Don is murdered by Masetto, dressed up as the Commendatore, who comes in and scares him to death. The Don would have to be an idiot not to be able to tell that this man is Masetto. I mean, big deal—a man comes in wearing a sheet. It was also negating any influence of God—whether you believe in Him or not. It was the stupidest thing I ever saw!

T O Z Z I : As far as I'm concerned, I listen to the overture, and the first strain of the overture to me is a statement. It says, "This is a tragedy."

But then it goes on to say, "But there are light moments in this," and so forth. What is the combination of tragedy and lightness? It is the same as Caravaggio, with chiaroscuro: You put a little speck of white alongside a speck of black, and the black becomes blacker and the white becomes whiter. So I think if we would just take these great works for their own worth . . . Why put them on the couch? Why try to use a Freudian approach? It's all there. If you play each moment exactly the way it's outlined in the work, it's great—it's self-explanatory.

SALOME

~

This dance . . . was just another accomplishment
for a young princess. In my day, when I was
a young girl, we played the piano.

–PHYLLIS CURTIN

Music by Richard Strauss
Libretto translated into German by Hedwig Lachmann
from the play *Salomé,* by Oscar Wilde

SALOME .... *Phyllis Curtin, Brenda Lewis, Eva Marton, Julia Migenes, Birgit Nilsson*

HERODIAS .... *Frances Bible, Helga Dernesch, Mignon Dunn, Rosalind Elias, Regina Resnik*

HEROD .... *Richard Cassilly, Graham Clark*

NARRABOTH .... *Mark Baker*

*I*n the beginning was the Bible. And if we're to trust it as a historical document, there actually was a Herod and a Herodias, and Herodias had a daughter whom somebody (not the Bible) named Salome, who was the subject of her stepfather's lustful attention. Then Oscar Wilde took over. Wilde's Herodias was very nervous about John the Baptist, whom she and her husband kept locked in the dungeon, to prevent him from inciting the population to riot—and also to shut him up. Never one to turn a deaf ear to the knock of opportunity, Herodias suggested that to please Herod, Salome would do her famous "Dance of the Seven Veils"; Herod in return promised to give her whatever she wanted—as it happened, John the Baptist's head on a silver platter. What else to give the girl who has everything?

B I R G I T   N I L S S O N : This was the only part I ever asked for. I asked Mr. Bing. I never did before, because I'm so inhibited. So I always thought, "Oh my, I can't ask for that—maybe they'll think I cannot do it." But I felt so much for Salome and liked to sing it, and I felt it was good for my voice. So I remember very well, I was talking to Mr. Bing over the telephone one night, and he said, "Is there something else you think you could do?" And after I hesitated for a long time, I said, "Yes, I would please like to do Salome. I would love to." And that planted the idea in his head. I don't think he would ever have been thinking about it, because he would think about a dancer, someone with a slender little body, you know.

Brenda Lewis and Phyllis Curtin were the two most prominent Salomes in the 1947 New York City Opera production, which helped rescue the work from obscurity.

P H Y L L I S   C U R T I N : I had a wonderful time with *Salome*. It was probably pretty controversial when we did it at the New York City Opera. I was new; I think I'd only sung one thing there before. Then I got the *Salome* assignment.

B R E N D A   L E W I S : When I first did it at City Opera, there had just been a big hassle because they had just closed down the burlesque houses on account of the girls coming out dancing nude. And on our board of directors was the commissioner of licensing, and there was a big hoohah. It was the first time we'd done *Salome* at City Opera, and most of the board of directors was sitting out at the dress rehearsal, the commissioner among them. The time came for the dance, and unfortunately they couldn't get the stage lights down as far as they had planned, so it was fairly clear that at the end of the dance, I was nude on top and all I had on was this jeweled G-string. And all hell broke loose. There was this big hassle about "How can

I close all the burlesque houses in New York City and let this go on in the opera?" They finally persuaded him they would fix the lights, and since there was no spotlight on me, it wasn't the same thing as burlesque.

Salome, in any form, has never put audiences at ease. Oscar Wilde's stage play was banned from the London stage and had to be performed in a brothel. Kaiser Wilhelm II banned the operatic version from Berlin. It fared better at its 1907 U.S. premiere, where it ran one night at the Metropolitan before being pulled, following a public outcry. Two years later Mary Garden revived it at the Manhattan Opera House, to protests from Billy Sunday among many others, but she dug in and became the first Salome to do the dance without the aid of a double.

No protests greeted Birgit Nilsson's interpretation. "If there is anyone in the world who can probe more deeply into the many aspects of Strauss's horrendous heroine," wrote the *New York Herald Tribune,* "her name does not come readily to mind."

N I L S S O N : When I first did Salome, I had been doing queens and princesses—very regal women who were walking around being very regal. This one had to move in a younger way, had to move her body. When I did this role with Göran Gentele, who became the manager at the Metropolitan, he was marvelous. And we were lying every evening until twelve or one o'clock on the floor, and he worked on every gesture, everything with me, so I really got it under my skin. And he was so happy, and I was so happy. It was fantastic work. That really helped me to be not such a regal woman.

When the Metropolitan Opera decided in 1989 it was time for a new production of *Salome,* it enlisted two European singers of Wagnerian vocal proportions: Eva Marton as the Princess and Helga Dernesch as her oversexed mother. The production, designed by Jürgen Rose, was set on an inner-city rooftop; but beneath the bizarre and unbiblical costumes, the characters remained unchanged.

E V A M A R T O N : Who is Salome? As a personage, she is a mystery. In the Bible she is referred to in one line, and then not by name, but merely as the daughter of Herodias.

N I L S S O N : There is much more to Salome than just an evil princess. I think she is a spoiled young girl who has gotten everything she wanted.

M A R T O N : Salome is not an evil person, but rather an innocent product of her time, amid the decadence under which she was reared. We see her as sort of a sacrificial lamb amid the terrible surroundings.

N I L S S O N : She's only fifteen years old, and John is probably the first man she is interested in. She wants him; she wants to talk to him and wants to know him. And when he rejects her—well, she has never experienced this before, that anyone has said no to what she is asking for.

New York-born soprano Julia Migenes has made a specialty of flamboyant characterizations.

J U L I A M I G E N E S : She's a child, really; a willful, spoiled child. Yet there is all that incredible sensuality throughout the entire piece. And the dance is so incredible.

N I L S S O N : The first time I did it was in Stockholm—and I was forced to it. I tried to get away from it, but I couldn't. And shortly before, I'd had pleurisy, so I couldn't really dance—I had to dance together with the ballet, and it was very bad. The ballet dancers came in with a big, big tray, and I was sitting on that with crossed legs, like a Buddha, as they carried me in. But the success was so enormous in Stockholm that there was a *Salome* fever. They even named a carpet at a famous store; they called it the Salome Carpet, and I had my picture there.

Wilde was not the only artist to be fascinated with Salome, a subject that has intrigued a long list of writers, composers, and artists for centuries. Flaubert's "Hérodias" inspired Jules Massenet's *Hérodiade,* an opera that enjoyed popularity in its time. Wilde's version was set by French composer Antoine Mariotte, whose opera was assured obscurity by the appearance of Strauss's.

M A R T O N : As an operatic character, she is as elusive as the *real* Carmen or the *real* Tosca, which to my way of thinking means that she can be interpreted in many different ways, and that no one will ever agree on a definitive interpretation.

CURTIN: All you have to do is read the libretto to know she's willful and headstrong. There's no question about that. "The Dance of the Seven Veils" is not even anything that peculiar. It hasn't been too long ago—I daresay up to the twentieth century—when well-bred young women in the Near East learned dances with veils properly. This is something she clearly did lots of times, and she doesn't do it for Herod.

Modern versions of the biblical legend always seems to center on the dance. Hollywood has always found the subject irresistible. Both Rita Hayworth and Yvonne de Carlo shed their veils for the camera, as did a host of nubile young starlets in assorted biblical epics.

MARTON: I often compare her to a starlet whose one big moment on the world stage has arrived. She doesn't care whether she becomes famous or infamous—she hardly knows the difference—as long as she is remembered.

CURTIN: The part is simply extraordinary. I think of the strange ideas that are connected with it: that there is something perverted about Salome. There is nothing perverted about her—not a scrap of perversion! There is in Herod. There certainly is in Herodias. In fact, John the Baptist says so. It's in his speech about her. But when you have a young woman who walks on the stage and says she's like the moon, who's chaste . . . There's one line in the play that's not in the opera, and I wish it was: She says to John, "I was a virgin until I looked on you."

NILSSON: Of course, she has experienced so much—she has seen everything. So she is not a very nice, educated girl. Also, because of that, a life doesn't mean anything very much.

MARTON: Vocally, I cannot compare Salome with any other Straussian role. At best, I would say she might be considered a younger sister of Elektra.

CURTIN: I adore the music. The music for dance is not particularly great music, but if I just hear this music now on the radio, I can't disassociate my life from it. I daresay if she did this dance at other times in the court, which I think she did, it was just another accomplishment for a young princess. In my day, when I was a young girl, we played the piano.

L E W I S : Historically, what Strauss did with the orchestration, in his own way, was the same thing Oscar Wilde did with words. And it's all the same period. It was a kind of artistic breakthrough, with this lush piling of sonority on sonority, dissonance, color—putting things together that nobody's ever heard before. That's why he scared the hell out of everybody, when they heard it for the first time—because it aroused in them feelings that you just don't allow to be aroused in public. If you took this book off the library shelf and sat in your bedroom and slobbered over it, that's one thing. But to sit in an auditorium with a lot of other people and listen to this music, which makes your flesh crawl and creep, and seeing people do things on the stage that you only imagine in your darkest imagination—that's why it was so horrible.

N I L S S O N : It is really a fantastic bel canto opera, but one has to know how. There are a lot of pianos and pianissimos. And those who are screaming it out, I cannot stand it, because it is so beautiful, and they are screaming it out, and you don't know which note they are hitting—forget it. Yes, it is a thick orchestration—it has to express everything. Strauss was very good, to be able to express all the erotic or sexual feelings. And those conductors who want it loud, refer to Richard Strauss—Strauss, who once said, "Loud or louder, I still have to hear the singer."

At the 1907 Metropolitan premiere, after Olive Fremstad slipped offstage and allowed Met prima ballerina Bianca Froelich to perform the dance, a spectator remarked that "women in the audience held their programs before their faces." We assume this implied moral outrage and was not a comment on Miss Froelich's dancing.

L E W I S : The character of Salome appealed to Oscar Wilde. You've got to remember, he made this up. We don't know about this Princess of Judea—there's only a line or two in the Bible. But we do know what Herodias and Herod were historically. We don't know them in the totally decadent way he describes it. He even had in his own mind the design he wanted for the first production of *Salomé*. He wanted an absolutely black, shiny floor and a silvery moon. And he wanted Salomé's skin to be very white and her feet white, so you can see them. So you can understand, just from the germ of an idea, what he saw.

C U R T I N : I think I first read the play when I was a sophomore in high school. I still have the copy on my desk, if you can believe that—a small, black, leather-bound copy of Oscar Wilde's play, which I just love. It was conductor Joseph Rosenstock himself who assigned me to the role. I was so young in my experience then, I didn't know a lot of Strauss.

M A R T O N : It has been said that Strauss's Salome is a dramatic soprano in a sixteen-year-old body. How someone was able to arrive at this definition is a puzzle to me. One must consider the fact that Sarah Bernhardt was rehearsing Wilde's play, before the censors forbade the performance, when she was forty-eight years old. Would Wilde have given his sanction if he wanted the part type-cast by a sixteen-year-old? I don't think so. Is she a dramatic soprano? That depends on the following circumstances: the size of the theater, the choice of the two orchestral versions, and, of course, on the conductor.

M I G E N E S : I love the role. It's a fabulous opera and a fabulous role. If I have a favorite opera, I suppose it would be that one. There's something about the marriage of the words and the music that make it a wonderful acting experience. It's really one of the best acting roles in all of opera.

C U R T I N : The willfulness of this girl who says, "All right, you wanted to see God, but you wouldn't look at me. Well, all right, now you've seen God, and I can do with you anything that I like. I can throw your head to the dogs!" That's a girl who is angry and really mad—but that's just a moment for her.

N I L S S O N : The more he rejects her, the more excited she gets, and she absolutely loses control over herself. And you know, in those Oriental countries, the lives of human beings—slaves or whatever— are not so important. She has probably heard of Herod and Herodias killing a lot of people for not doing what they want. So as an event, she asks for his life. And it went too far, because she probably didn't expect Herod would really do what she wants—but no. And there we are.

C U R T I N : She first looks at the moon, and then says she has left the room because Herod is just so repulsive. Then what she does in demanding John's head is so repellent to people these days, but the whole court would have done that. Come on—Herod has had John the Baptist down in that well, and Salome's daddy was down there for something like twelve years before they did him in. The Princess gets what she wanted, and a beheading is not that unusual.

NILSSON: Herod is also in love with her, but I think nothing has happened between them. She is more or less an untouched girl who starts to become a woman. From the beginning, John is probably more like a toy for her that she's going to have.

CURTIN: Anything she does, Herod will pant over. She knows that. That's why she ran from the table. He looks at her with lust, and she hates him. That's why she finally decides that when she dances, it's for John—not for Herod. She could get him by just standing there.

"The kissing of the bloody head of John the Baptist was too much for nearly everyone who witnessed the performance . . ." observed one critic of Mary Garden's activities. It was only one of many features he found "absolutely revolting." Dismemberment is more commonplace today, thanks to *Friday the 13th* and *Nightmare on Elm Street,* but it's still revolting.

LEWIS: To believe that a present-day audience is incapable of reacting this way is nonsense. Of course we've seen violence and bloodshed—we see it every night on TV. That doesn't mean our senses are totally deadened. We still have the capacity to go and hear that as an artistic experience, and be aroused by it. I'm sorry—I don't think people go away from *Salome* today and are unshaken. And I don't believe people perform it and are unshaken.

NILSSON: Maybe by the end, because she gets going so, and is so upset, she's not thinking anymore. But in the beginning, she tries to seduce John by all the things she does for him: She tells him how beautiful he is, his hair, his body, and everything, and she is sure he will give in. That is a spoiled girl, from my thinking.

LEWIS: I think Salome's a test of endurance, because she's onstage throughout the whole thing. And I was living the part—onstage, I was it. But I was built like a bull and I had a good, strong throat. I survived it—it didn't kill me. But it's the thickness of the orchestration—though at City Opera we did it with the reduced orchestration. And the final scene, which is sixteen or seventeen minutes without a stop, it's a long, long monologue, and it's all pretty much triple forte, except a few places where he wants you to pull out a beautiful head-tone pianissimo on an F, F-sharp, G—right at the point where it's very difficult for a soprano to do after she's been screaming B-flat. If you have temperament, you're going to give it everything you've got. You can't help it. If you don't have temperament, you will sing it gorgeously, but then you shouldn't be singing Salome.

NILSSON: She has to get Herod on her side, because Herod is afraid of John. There is something more to him than to anyone else—he knows that. He's a very strong man, and Herod somehow has a lot of respect. In her thoughts she is also dancing for John. She is seducing the Baptist in her thoughts, and showing that to Herod. She is a smart girl and used to getting her way. In America, when I was starting to do Salome, and everybody was just talking about "the dance, the dance." And I said, "What's the dance? *Salome* is not only the dance—far from it. Don't hang on the dance; it is something on the side. Otherwise, go to the ballet."

LEWIS: You mustn't break the tension in Salome's mind when she finally realizes she has to dance for Herod to get what she wants. She doesn't approach that dance with joy. She doesn't approach it to make him come on to her sexually. She does it against her will, with her teeth gritted, with desperation—and knowing the five Jews are standing there looking at her, too. All of this is hateful to her. She's not an exhibitionist.

NILSSON: I composed my own dance when I was singing it in Vienna. I did it alone. I just did what I felt was expressed in the music. I went from that to the Metropolitan. But of course when I came to the Met, I was hoping to get help, to get it better, but there was no one who understood my difficulties. The choreographers, they looked at it from their point of view, which was difficult for me. Also the stage at the Met was very helpful, because it was not an even plane where you could really do a big dance—it was full of steps up and down, and God knows what. Somehow it helped me. But I remember, I was lying on my knees, and I went back down with my head on the floor, and went up again. And my body was very movable—so it worked out all right.

LEWIS: There's no reason to think Salome has to strip. Really none. We don't know. I mean, stop and think—how many people of the appropriate fifteen- or sixteen-year-old body have the voice to ride out the Strauss score? Nobody. You take it on faith. But I'm sure I was the first to do that. I mean, I don't hang it up with my credits: "opera singer/stripper." I wouldn't want my kids to think that's what their mother had done for a living.

NILSSON: I understand there have been some who just can make fantastic belly dances and undress until they only have one shred on their body, and they have a nice, slender body and everything. But, well, as I say, if you just hang on the dance, don't do the Salome. Because you cannot be sure that you'll get a perfect dance all the time.

"Strauss showed me how he wanted the dance done," explained Göta Ljungberg, who revived the work in 1934 at the Met. "He didn't want the dance to be hoppy and jumpy. It was a thought dance in his conception. And to him, the actual movements of the dance were secondary, symbolical. He intended that it should be symbolical."

LEWIS: This was not a striptease a la Gypsy Rose Lee. Gypsy Rose Lee in burlesque was not only intended to arouse an erotic impulse in the audience, but because Gypsy Rose Lee was also an artist, she understood the underlying humor of it. And the stripping of the gloves, in itself, was such a put-on—the way she took them off. She intended it to be funny, because the whole idea is so absurd. But you can't take Gypsy Rose Lee out of context and have Salome strip herself of a glove, because that whole period won't support that kind of humor. That's terribly sophisticated twentieth-century humor. "The Dance of the Seven Veils" had a separate meaning.

NILSSON: I had one choreographer at the Met; she had a famous name, and she was a small and frail woman. And she did all kinds of gestures in which I would have seemed absolutely out of place, and it did not help me at all. So I started to discuss with her, "When you hear this erotic music, what do you feel about Salome?" And she put up some gestures which were absolutely sexless; they didn't say anything. And if I would have followed that, people would have laughed about me. I got a little bit unhappy. I have a very strong will, and I felt that this is not my way.

LEWIS: I went to Agnes de Mille. I had worked with her when I did *Rape of Lucretia* on Broadway. We were not close friends, but she respected me, and I certainly had great admiration for what she could do. So I discussed it with her, and she said, "Well, honey, I don't know many dances in the repertoire that one person does on the stage for seven and a half minutes, and I think you should look at it as an extension of what the acting scene is about, and not as a 'dance' by itself."

NILSSON: We had this famous stage director, Günther Rennert, so he was standing there, and I said, "May I try, in my simple way, what I feel in the music and what I feel I could do?" "Of course, yes, please do that," he said. So I did the whole dance, just expressing my feelings, my longings for John, and also to try to be a little bit seducing to Herod. So he said, "Let's keep it that way. I have no objection." And the choreographer I was working with, she didn't seem to have anything to say, either. And I had a big success—not because of the dance, I think, but nobody was really saying the dance was bad.

LEWIS: So I began to improvise with a record, and I showed de Mille what I'd done. She said, "Looks great! You don't look awkward; you don't look like you're pretending to be a dancer"—which was the one thing I didn't want to do. Because I ain't a dancer. And if I got up and pretended to be a dancer, I'd look like some idiot.

NILSSON: This is not a real dance, you know. A solo from a prima ballerina takes mostly three or four minutes, maximum. But this dance, as far as I remember it, takes up to twelve minutes. So already, it is impossible for a singer to make a professional dance. I don't think that was meant, either; it was a seducing dance. The dance had a meaning. But I had a big success, and every evening the choreographer from the Metropolitan went out to take her calls, so she wasn't ashamed of me, you see. I was glad for that.

LEWIS: I moved and I was impelled by the music. I knew when I had to remove the veils, and I made a great big deal out of each one of those. And if you flutter them properly, you also use the time to catch your breath in between.

MARTON: The dance is almost a psychological awakening. She may begin it purely for the sake of dancing, but then she feels her growing power over Herod, and uses it through suggestion and mime, more than through actual dance. What I hope to convey in that dance are Salome's thoughts.

"A beautiful, glistening-voiced soprano, Phyllis Curtin, sang the title role with shattering ease," wrote the critic of the *New York Herald Tribune,* "and performed the Dance of the Seven Veils with skill and taste."

C U R T I N : When she dances, all these sexual and romantic and really serious feelings for John come out. I think that's terribly important. It doesn't cross the minds of most people who say, "Salome is a slut." Nothing could be further from the truth. Even if you just read the words to the final scene, the great culminating statement that the mystery of love is greater than the mystery of death, that's not said by a little slut.

L E W I S : I analyzed the score. I'd know when I was approaching Herod, I'd have time in the music to catch my breath a little, and when I have to remove the veils. You're starting with seven veils, and you know damn well the audience is going to count seven. So you know there's a point at which you can remove a veil. And I started to improvise.

N I L S S O N : You have to listen to the music and feel what the music says, and make the gestures, the steps, and everything close to what you hear.

C U R T I N : The music for the dance for such an occasion would not be great music. But what elevated it is all that I feel about why I'm doing this dance at this moment. The music may be something I danced to before, but I never danced to it the way I am now.

M I G E N E S : The first *Salome* I did was for the director Maurice Béjart, who said at last he'd found someone who could sing the role and do the dance, and looked young enough to pull it all off. So that for me was a really exciting experience.

"Miss Garden did her own dancing as she did before," wrote one critic in 1909, "and not very skillfully." Well, nobody's perfect.

N I L S S O N : I had some veils, sort of taped on my breast; I could strip them off. But I didn't make a striptease to the bare skin.

L E W I S : I must admit I had a wonderful costume. When I had about forty seconds when the serving girls come onstage and surround me, I removed the white silk costume I wore as Salome and put the veils on me. When I was finished, beveiled, it was a full costume. My head was covered, my face—my whole body was covered. I had veils attached to my wrists. The two veils crossing my breasts were two different colors. So when I started, I was covered from head to foot. And when I had finished, the G-string was like a bikini panty with a cloth-of-gold thing which hung between my legs, that had jewels on it. On the top, nothing. Not like the ladies today who wear flesh-colored body suits with rhinestones around their wrists and ankles. I went down to nothing—all bare on top.

The opera's other characters endeared themselves to the critics no more than its heroine. Herodias was described as a "human hyena," while her husband fared little better as a "neurasthenic voluptuary."

R O S A L I N D E L I A S : I want to be the Joan Collins of opera—a real bitch. These are the roles I want now. My first Herodias was in Caracas, ten or twelve years ago. Since then, I've done it all over. Musically, it's a very difficult role.

Critics all agree that Strauss provided the most beautiful music for the tenor who sings Narraboth.

M A R K B A K E R : Besides the first part where Narraboth sings that beautiful, haunting line, my favorite part is when she's walking around with the head. There's such an overwhelming sense of horror at that point. You sit out there in the audience, and you know this is pretend—it's a fake head. It's not an enjoyable moment, but it's a tremendously exciting moment as far as what opera and theater is all about.

H E L G A D E R N E S C H : I did my homework long before I first played Herodias. My first performance in this was back in '81 or '82 in Hamburg. For me, this role is fun, absolute fun. The first husband of mine was also called Herod. Herodias is a very ambitious character. I feel she only married Herod because she thought he could be king in Rome. Well, of course that's only a dream, because he's too weak. Later on he was exiled to France and died in Spain.

M I G N O N D U N N : All of her life she's only thought of herself. She's never had anyone take the time to tell her when she's right and wrong. I don't think you can think of her as being immoral—she's amoral. She actually doesn't have any idea of right or wrong, not at all.

E L I A S : Every role in *Salome* is difficult. The music is dissonant in *Elektra,* too. Klytemnestra is very difficult; Herodias and Herod are very difficult roles. He may have made them difficult because they are such horrid people—and it fits.

B A K E R : Narraboth is Oscar Wilde. It doesn't come out of the Bible; Oscar Wilde added Narraboth. He's the victim. His first line is "How beautiful is the Princess Salome," and there's this other guy who says, "Are you crazy? She looks like a ghost!"

M A R T O N : In the Oscar Wilde play, she is described only through the eyes of others.

B A K E R : So there's something going on right away in the text that says Narraboth is not in his right senses.

"There is not a whiff of fresh and healthy air blowing through *Salome,*" an early critic observed, "except that which exhales from the cistern: the prison house of John the Baptist." Not noted for their fresh and healthy characterizations, Charles Laughton and Judith Anderson portrayed Herod and Herodias in the film version.

R E G I N A R E S N I K : Herodias really can't be satisfying to you once you've done Klytemnestra. Then Herodias is just something you do because you have to. There's nothing to look forward to with her. Acting-wise, it's a fine secondary part. It's just vocal hollering. You have to be heard above the orchestra, so you're usually just shouting.

D U N N : I know so many people like Herodias. I don't mean that she's so evil; I think she's past that. Herodias is terribly insensitive. But remember how she has been brought up: Like Amneris, she's had everything she's ever wanted.

E L I A S : When I play Herodias, I like to see where she's coming from, her frustrations. Why is she like this? Her beautiful daughter has something to do with this; is there jealousy? Is she thinking, has her husband ever . . . ? What was she like before? What does she want out of this? I do this with all my characters.

F R A N C E S B I B L E : I did enjoy Herodias, but I didn't do it until I was at the age were I thought it really wouldn't matter vocally. I always felt it was too heavy a role for me. I never sang Ulrica until I turned fifty, because then I thought, "What difference does it make?" You can't do yourself too much harm at that point. I would never have sung these roles when I was younger, because I think you have to keep your voice as light as possible if you want to last awhile.

R E S N I K : Herodias is the same at the beginning as at the end. There's very little interesting to sing except for screaming, and trying to control it. If you're a good actress, it's no problem at all to make an impression. If you have a good Salome and a good Herod, it doesn't make any difference at all who sings Herodias.

D E R N E S C H : Everybody believes that in my repertory now, every role is a bad character, but I don't agree with that. I don't find Klytemnestra a totally bad character, or the Nurse in *Die Frau ohne Schatten*.

R E S N I K : It's vocally the most ungrateful shrew of all time. Talk about a fishwife!

B I B L E : Herodias wasn't very nice, but she was a product of that period in time. If you're brought up in that kind of atmosphere, what are you going to be?

D U N N : There is very little redeeming in Herodias, very little.

B I B L E : I always think there's some redeeming feature to even the worst of us.

Received by the general manager after the first opening and closing night of *Salome* at the Metropolitan:

January 30, 1907
Heinrich Conried, esq.

> *Dear Sir,*
> *The directors of the Metropolitan Opera and Real Estate Company consider that the performance of* Salome *is objectionable and detrimental to the best interests of the Metropolitan Opera House. They therefore protest against any repetition of this opera.*
> *(Signed)*
> *By order,*
> *Frank N. Dodd,*
> *Secretary*

E L I A S : When I first started at the Metropolitan, they gave us, for free, chances to go to the Actors Studio, and I went and observed. I found it interesting, even though I don't believe in the Method that much. But I've studied and learned from every director I've ever worked with. I'm learning from everyone I see: Zoe Caldwell in the theater as Medea, or people on the street. They're my teachers, every one of them.

D E R N E S C H : Herodias is completely bad. When you look at her background, you understand why: She's the granddaughter of another Herod who was called Herod the Great. He killed his wife and his son, who was the father of Herodias; and in the opera, our Herod is the son of my grandfather, so he's a relative of mine. And Herodias has also been previously been married to his half-brother. So it's all in the family.

R E S N I K : She's the ugly stepsister of Klytemnestra. Once you've done Klytemnestra and you've done Strauss, you're obliged to do Herodias.

B I B L E : I think you can find human touches in her; I think I did. The same with Amneris. I always felt there was a person caught up in being just a spoiled child, and when she saw the harm she had done, she was sorry about it. I don't know that Herodias was sorry . . . but she was sort of sick, you know.

E L I A S : I love going into these mature characters. While I was singing Dorabella and Cherubino, there was a woman in me starving to do these roles. But I was too young. I was all wrong for them. I always wanted to get to this time in my life, when I could do these women. These are the characters that are interesting.

"It was disgusting," proclaimed a critic on seeing Mary Garden's "Dance of the Seven Veils." "Miss Garden wallowed around like a cat in a bed of catnip. There was no art in her dance that I could see. If the same show were produced on Halstead Street, the people would call it cheap; but over at the Auditorium, they say it's art."

"I always bow down to the ignorant and try to make them understand," Garden declared, "but I ignore the illiterate."

D U N N : I would like to see a realistic *Salome*. I think someone should go to Israel and look at things, like the color of stones and the country at night, and not have the productions so gimmicky.

D E R N E S C H : I was never able to resolve how Herodias ended her life. I couldn't find out anything about when or where she died. But in the opera, she is the absolute winner of the evening—because Salome's dead and Herod is totally frightened. She's the only one who survives the whole plot.

G R A H A M C L A R K : Maestro Marek Janowski tells me Herod is one of the hardest roles in opera to learn, because there are so many changes within it. It changes from bar to bar, especially at the beginning when he comes on.

E L I A S : I've never done Herodias with a Herod who sang the music correctly. The crazier and more erratic it was, the more it seemed to work. I sang it with someone who was off for a whole page. He wasn't even close to what had been written. He was just running on the stage like a crazy man, and people thought he was the greatest thing they'd ever seen. I think Strauss really meant it to be cuckoo and wrote it crazy.

R I C H A R D C A S S I L L Y : It's very difficult music, but it's certainly not unlearnable, especially by today's standards. I imagine when it was originally done, it must have been very hard because the idiom was very new. But today, it's no harder than Britten or Berg or whatever.

C L A R K : You've got to count from the first beat till the end of the opera. It's tough music and you have to have total concentration.

C A S S I L L Y : There is real melody in *Salome*—at least for the tenor. I was first asked to do it for the production with the director August Everding and Gwyneth Jones, and I said no. I didn't want to do a character part like that so early in my career. It was traditional then to characterize it and really just scream it. But I looked at it and found the music was right for me. We had a tremendous success with it and then recorded it.

B A K E R : I did Narraboth in Spoleto, set at the end of the thirties, before World War II, in Germany—somewhere in a decadent society built only on pleasure, and thinking about the selfish greed of the moment.

D U N N : It was done in a greenhouse—one of the best sets I've ever seen in my whole life. I also liked Lisa Correas as a stage director very much; she worked very, very well.

B A K E R : It worked beautifully. The problem is, people who are dead set on keeping *Salome* biblical, because to them it happened and has a specific place, will see 1930s costumes and be disappointed.

D U N N : You have to realize that in Europe, they have so many performances and so many theaters that a stage director has to do something different in order to be noticed. I enjoyed the new Met production. We wore different costumes, but the relationships were the same. This was a stylized set, which didn't bother me.

"My costume?" Mary Garden answered reporters on the eve of her first New York Salome. "Well, I hardly know what to say, except that I keep it in a safe deposit vault when not using it. It comes under the head of jewels rather than gowns, but it is beautiful and was designed from two pictures in the Luxembourg."

L E W I S : I cannot imagine Salome coming out fully clothed. If an arm was extended, or the tip of a bare foot, that could be sexually exciting to Herod, too. It wasn't necessary for her to strip down to nothing— bare breasts and bottom. But if you start stripping off gloves, it's into a twentieth-century sensibility, which lifts it right out of all the incense and the peacock feathers and all that. When Wilde and Strauss wrote it, they were doing it from a nineteenth-century sensibility. So if you're going to do something out of its time, I say you have to do it with great judgment.

C A S S I L L Y : I think the current production at the Met is so far out that people don't really follow it and just listen to the singers. Ideally, I think the production should just be set in a beautiful moonlit desert night, and then just let this horrible story play itself out.

M I G E N E S : I like the traditional production of the opera, because there's so much there, you don't really need to add any trappings.

D U N N : It never disturbs me if you take this opera out of context and place it somewhere else, if it's for a dramatic reason.

C A S S I L L Y : Ultimately, the opera will work if the one-on-one relationships are clear.

N I L S S O N : There are those who conduct it very well. I did it here with Karl Böhm. He was not a soft conductor, but he did it wonderfully. At the Metropolitan, I always had my biggest success with Karl Böhm.

L E W I S : It's tough on you vocally if you get terribly emotionally involved—which I guess most Salomes do, because how can you do this thing if you haven't got temperament?

N I L S S O N : Of course, there are those conductors who kill the thing.

I was sitting at a *Salome* performance in Vienna, rather close to the orchestra—and that was Karl Böhm! I must have had a bad place, but it was an expensive place, and I did not hear one singer until Herodias sings at the end, because it was a high B. I heard that, but Salome was completely covered. I just couldn't believe it. It was a terrible experience for me, so I hope I wasn't covered—I don't know. But I don't know how it happened. I got so upset, I couldn't sleep all night.

"Miss Fremstad accomplished a miracle," wrote Henry Krehbiel of the *New York Tribune* after *Salome*'s Met premiere. ". . . She sank under the shields of the soldiers while the orchestra shrieked its final horror, and left the listeners staring at each other with smarting eyeballs and wrecked nerves." That Olive Fremstad always was a crowd pleaser!

C U R T I N : It was always one of the easiest things I ever did. I didn't have any places that were stuck or difficult. We had done it in a wonderful way, so that for all the years I sang that opera, it was always, always the greatest joy for me.

N I L S S O N : But of course, it is a tough role. And I wonder whether it was not that role which finished Ljuba Welitsch—a beautiful voice. It was really her role, you know. We were so different. She was all sex, and she was wild. I just wish I would have heard her in person, but I have only heard that final scene on tape. It is just wonderful. But if I may say something, I can understand that the voice took its turn in this big part, because it was more of a lyric voice—but so beautiful, so beautiful. And she was a revelation, you know— Salome with her own red hair! I don't think her planning the dance was something very good, but she was so wild that everybody just bought it.

L E W I S : Listen, if you try to do things which are out of your *Fach*, and you press and squeeze and bang away at it, and if your vocal equipment is not as strong as someone else's might be—and that's a matter of nature—I suppose you can hurt yourself.

N I L S S O N : Sure, it is difficult. I put them in two categories: Either the Salome is a very, very good dancer and a less good singer, or a good singer and not a good dancer. I don't need to tell you which category I belong to.

L E W I S : When I sang it at the Met, and then Los Angeles and San

Francisco, with a full orchestra, it was much easier. The more strings you have, the less exposed the woodwinds are, and the less competition you have from the woodwinds and brass.

MARTON: Salome has been sung, with varying degrees of success, by lyric, *jugendlich*-dramatic, and *hoch*-dramatic sopranos. Even mezzos with a solid extension on the top have portrayed her.

CURTIN: I took it to my voice teacher and he said, "Well, if you are going to do this, we will learn the whole thing as a vocalise on 'ah,' so you will have solved the vocal problems before you turn on all that emotion." It's the only opera role I ever did that to, but I was meticulous with it.

NILSSON: It is a role that can ruin sopranos' voices. And the thing is, you can never leave the stage. But as I hear now, the Salomes are leaving the stage. In the new production at the Met, she has a moment when she's not singing—and now she's leaving the stage, going down into the cistern, and singing "I want the head of Jokanaan" from down there. So she can have a cup of tea or a glass of beer or a champagne or whatever. You get a little bit more rested, instead of just being onstage and sweating, and not being able to refresh yourself. So that does make it easier.

LEWIS: And if you're an actress interested in the text, as I suppose most Salomes are, the attempt is to get those words out. You can't just vocalize it in a nice, lovely line, or swoop up to a B-flat, or swoop away from it. If you bang away, word after word, in German, it takes a greater amount of energy.

NILSSON: There are many who sing Strauss by screaming it out, and I cannot stand it. Before I started to sing Elektra, I was listening to a few singers, and I said, "I am not going to sing that part—it's a scream part." And so was Salome. You could hardly hear any of the beautiful music, because they were screaming it out so much. This has to be sung with a slender voice, and has to be sung beautifully.

CURTIN: It was the greatest transcendental combination of mind and body that I could find. There are certain things that you have to remember in *Salome*. First, she is very young—and to go around sounding like a coarse-voiced singer is all wet. The libretto, which is straight Wilde—except for one or two scenes which Strauss left out—is divine.

LEWIS: I thought if I could make someone feel a pang of sorrow and pity when Salome says at the end, "Why didn't you look at me? If you had looked at me, you would have loved me." . . . I get chills now when I say it. And the way Strauss wrote the music—it's so poignant. It's a fifteen-year-old girl saying, "If only you'd looked at me you would have fallen in love with me, and everything would have been all right. This wouldn't have had to happen."

B A K E R : Except maybe for *Wozzeck* or *Lulu,* this is the *Friday the 13th* of opera. It's so haunting, so agitating in a very beautiful sense, spooky without being total atonality, where you go out with your hair standing on end. But it's got that chromatic and harmonic texture which is so exciting.

L E W I S : I sang this in English somewhere in the Bible Belt. When I got into the scene when I started to sing to John the Baptist's head, I noticed three people in the front row got up and walked out. Later, some people who had brought these three Baptist ministers came back to the dressing room and apologized for them. They had come and had no idea what they were going to see. And this woman from the opera committee said to me, in a southern accent, "You have to understand that the ministers couldn't take *that.* But I have to tell you, I felt so sorry for this girl—I felt so sorry for her!" And it touched me, because it meant what I felt was there: that you have to understand, pity this human being. I think we have to feel that way about all human beings.

N I L S S O N : I just did as well as I could. There may be those who said, "Well, she was impossible—but she sang good."

MADAMA BUTTERFLY

~

Butterfly's fragility is in her soul.
Talk about giving everything up for love!

—ANNA MOFFO

Music by Giacomo Puccini
Libretto by Giuseppe Giacosa and Luigi Illica
from the play *Madame Butterfly*
by David Belasco and John Luther Long,
based on Long's novella

CIO-CIO-SAN .... *Licia Albanese, Lucine Amara, Martina Arroyo, Gilda Cruz-Romo, Dorothy Kirsten, Leona Mitchell, Anna Moffo, Renata Scotto*

SUZUKI .... *Nedda Casei, Rosalind Elias*

SHARPLESS........................ *Theodor Uppman*

DOLORE............................. *Julia Migenes*

"*L*ouder, you beasts! Shriek at me, yell! But you shall see who was right! That is the best opera I have ever written!" Puccini hurled these words at the La Scala audience who had howled and jeered throughout the painful premiere of *Madama Butterfly,* on February 17, 1904. The disastrous reception wounded Puccini deeply. Though he was in love with all his female heroines, Cio-Cio-San was especially close to his heart.

Despondent at his inability to find a suitable libretto after completing *Tosca,* Puccini had waited impatiently for the consent of "that infernal American," David Belasco, to set to music Belasco's Broadway hit, *Madame Butterfly.* When word arrived, Puccini eagerly set to work on the exotic story, only to be forced to abandon it for almost a year after a serious automobile accident.

With librettists Giuseppe Giacosa and Luigi Illica (who had collaborated on *La Bohème* and *Tosca*), Puccini put excruciating care into *Butterfly*'s preparation. Rehearsals were reportedly so inspiring that even the stagehands were daily moved to tears. Puccini, so sure he had created his masterpiece, invited his brothers and sisters to the premiere—a first. "It is superfluous for me to wish you success," he wrote to the first Cio-Cio-San, Rosina Storchio, on the day of the performance. Puccini felt that, musically, he had created the essence of youth, innocence, and beauty.

Dorothy Kirsten embodied all three throughout her career. With forty performances at the Metropolitan alone, her Butterfly was the vehicle of her "official" farewell to the company in 1975. "She went out in a blaze of glory on New Year's Eve," *The New York Times* reported. "Making her farewell appearance after thirty years with the company in nothing but major roles, she sang and acted with the vocal control and dramatic acuity of a prima donna in mid-career."

D O R O T H Y   K I R S T E N : Butterfly is terribly innocent of the world, and life itself. She had such innocence toward what real love was, to be taken advantage of the way she was—because she gave so easily.

R E N A T A   S C O T T O : I always think about when she's getting ready to be married. She sings this entrance, and she's almost afraid to get to the top of the hill, because maybe she'll not find her dream come true. It is a suffering thing. Even though it's supposed to be a happy thing, it's not so, because she's afraid that maybe she will not find this happiness. So she finally gets there, and she's sure she's going to find that happiness. She believes that, and the hope is through the entire opera.

An indisposed Butterfly provided Licia Albanese with her operatic debut at the Lirico, Milan. The role also introduced her to audiences at the Met. "She is that rare songbird, the Italian lyric soprano," wrote

Virgil Thomson. "The voice in all its natural purity and soft brilliance produces a musical effect of such penetrating beauty as has not been my pleasure to hear in many a year."

L I C I A   A L B A N E S E : Every opera has a young girl at the beginning. When you come in, you're a young girl, and you have to act like you're young. You must dress young, look young. It's necessary in *Butterfly* to remember you're fifteen years old—look at the score. And if there are books, read books; there's an atmosphere you have to absorb.

A N N A   M O F F O : I used to worry about being too tall, too American basketball-star type. I'm five eight, and I thought of it as my feminine Rigoletto. I felt I had to always work to make myself look little.

M A R T I N A   A R R O Y O : Butterfly is an incredible woman. I go in ready to be happy and ready for the wedding day, preparing for it honestly and truthfully—sincerely. From the beginning, she has those qualities. She says from the beginning, "My father killed himself at the order of the emperor, and I came from a nice family, but we lost everything."

In a sensational televised performance at La Scala, Anna Moffo made her operatic debut as Cio-Cio-San. She later recorded the role for RCA, with Erich Leinsdorf conducting.

M O F F O : She is a wonderful character because she's so pure—very pure. Butterfly's fragility is in her soul. Talk about giving everything up for love! She's pure in her love for Pinkerton, in her love for this child. And I'm not saying committing suicide is pure; however, in her case it is, and it is in the custom for the culture: "Con onor muore chi non può serbar vita con onore"—"If you can't live your life with honor, enough already."

On Renata Scotto's Metropolitan debut in 1965, the *New York Times* critic wrote, "Her Butterfly was a combination of Japanese grace and Italian volatility, emotions flying through her body and across her face with seeming spontaneity." *Butterfly* was the first opera she chose to stage as a director.

SCOTTO: I never saw Licia Albanese doing Butterfly. When I'm interested in a new character in an opera, I never wanted to listen to anybody else, especially with Butterfly. The character is between me and Puccini—and, of course, the Belasco play. But I didn't want any influence coming from other artists, because I think the interpretation should be very personal. So I really build my characters by studying the score, and before going into the music, of course the play or the book.

Even those who haven't heard Martina Arroyo's Cio-Cio-San have heard her infectious laugh on television's *The Odd Couple* and *The Tonight Show*. Johnny Carson knows a diva when he hears one.

ARROYO: She knows how to give compliments, but they're truthful ones, right from the beginning. She doesn't come in saying, "Well, I know this man has money, and I'm going to have a good time." She comes in saying, "My friends, this is the happiest day of my life. The heavens are smiling."

MOFFO: Butterfly is honest. She's disarming in the first act, when she shows him all the things she has that she's taking to their marriage; and he says, "What's that?" and she takes it he doesn't like the inkwell, so she throws it away. She's so anxious to please: "How old are you?" "Fifteen, but really more." It's an innocence I don't think I've found in any other opera.

KIRSTEN: Butterfly does change. I believe she becomes very strong. Vocally, it is very dramatic singing, and she has to become very strong, because you cannot sing that music without showing great strength. Even though she holds the baby and rocks it in her arms while she knows she has to give it up, I think she becomes very strong there, in that last act. I think her life has made her strong. She grows strong from great, great disillusionment.

MOFFO: It's so solid, because no innocent kid would wait around, have this baby, let it grow up always waving the flag. She doesn't really change except in her decisions. I think that's what's so sad about her—she never gives up. From the moment she walks onstage to the moment she commits suicide, it's the same.

Lucine Amara first sang Cio-Cio-San at the Metropolitan in 1962, eleven years after first appearing as Pinkerton's other wife, Kate.

LUCINE AMARA: My major problem with Butterfly was size. I was not small, and she should be petite. But you can't bend over to make yourself small, which was what I was doing at first. You have to throw your shoulders back, and you can lower your knees, but not your shoulders.

KIRSTEN: I first sang Butterfly in Mexico, in 1946. And I will never forget it, because at that time I wasn't that smart about going to Mexico and being fourteen thousand feet in the air. One has to become acclimated—you can't just go in there and go to work the next day. But fortunately, we were still having rehearsals then; and I remember being on my tummy, thinking about the last act, and being so sick that I could barely get through it. By the performance, of course, things were much better—you became used to the high altitude. And I was a young horse—I was always very, very healthy—and I adjusted quite fast. But at that time there was a wonderful company in Mexico. I remember it so well, and I remember how happy I was to do it. It was the same year I made my Metropolitan debut in the role, so Butterfly has been a part of me for all of those years.

Leona Mitchell did not attempt Puccini's geisha until she was well into her career.

LEONA MITCHELL: I began my move into the heavier roles with Butterfly in 1976, in Sydney. People were horrified, thinking, "She's too young! Why is she doing Butterfly?" Everybody was concerned about whether I would last or not, but that was a role that fit like a glove for me. My coach even said at the time, "Why do it so early? You have plenty of time." But the character appealed to me so much I just wanted to do it, and kept singing it at home. Finally my coach listened to me and said, "I think you can do that part." Since then, I've done it in many places.

Despite his Italian soul, Puccini was determined to give his opera an authentically Japanese flavor. Having never been to Japan, he went instead to Milan to visit the famous Japanese tragic actress Sada Jacco, who he hoped would help him get some genuine color into the music. Next, he called on Mme. Ohyama, wife of the Japanese ambassador. She found the name *Yamadori* unsuitable for a prince, since it was "feminine." Her suggestion apparently had little impact. But she did arrange for shipment to Puccini of hundreds of Japanese Gramophone records, which he undoubtedly enjoyed but never did incorporate into the score.

M O F F O : It's important you know the Orientals—not so much now, but the way they were brought up. They were brought up to be totally servile, to give pleasure, to give love—never to receive it. As an American, I think you really have to go see it. The Japanese women are so graceful. Their whole being is fettered to being a girl. And I think sometime in the world, we're going to lose that, so it was very touching. And that's what I like about Butterfly—she's feminine, she's passionate, she's pure.

A L B A N E S E : Madame Butterfly knew all the languages—she knew how to speak English, French—because she had to entertain all the sailors. They said the geishas were all bad girls; I said no. Because like all the opera singers or dancers—they are bad girls? I said no. Who wants to be bad is bad. Butterfly got money for the first time—and she killed herself.

S C O T T O : I always believed there are symbols in *Butterfly*. In order to understand all the characters, there are symbols for each one. Suzuki, she's the symbol of real friendship. Pinkerton is men—an adventurer. Most of them, in their youth, are adventurers. And Pinkerton, because he's a naval officer, really is. He goes from one harbor to the next, and in every harbor, he finds a new girl. To the audience, he is youth, man, freedom, and adventure.

K I R S T E N : I think in the first place, Pinkerton has to be a warm person. He has to show a lot of compassion, at least in the beginning. Otherwise, he's not going to get this lovely little Japanese girl to fall in love with him.

T H E O D O R U P P M A N : It's difficult for someone to play a role like Pinkerton unless they have complete interest in doing a character where the more "selfish young American" attitude they can get into it, the more successful they'll be. They love to sing the music, but they really don't want to be that type of person. I can understand why a lot of tenors wouldn't want to do it, because except for the music, it can't give them complete satisfaction. But if they sing it well, my God, it's a beautiful role.

K I R S T E N : I can't imagine anyone who wouldn't want to appear in that nice, good-looking uniform. I did it with Jimmy Melton. Jimmy was a very handsome guy, and it was always much more realistic to have someone like that. I liked them to be big and strong enough to pick her up off her feet and carry her into the house. The audience just loved that, when he was really able to sweep her off her feet.

A R R O Y O : Imagine the difference between a man who says, "I'm going to take care of you"—who doesn't know, by the way, he's made you pregnant—loving and sweet and kind, right from the beginning, who makes her believe he will come back; and a man who says, "This is it for the time being. By the way, get me my breakfast, do this and do that." You simply respond. A lot has to do with how you are at that moment. How are you that night? How shy are you? How soon do you fall into his trap, or were you already there at the beginning? How did the chorus set you up? What electricity was in the air?

K I R S T E N : If the Pinkerton is not right, it can't change your interpretation, so you dream, "Wouldn't it be wonderful if I had the right character there?" You have to do the best you can with what's given to you—and believe me, I've been in some very odd situations in opera. Not in *Butterfly,* but I've had some very short ones—and I'm not a big girl.

After Masetto, Papageno, and *Périchole*'s Piqillo, Sharpless was the role Theodor Uppman performed most often at the Met. The sympathetic consul proved a perfect vehicle for the popular baritone.

U P P M A N : Sharpless is considered a minor role by a lot of baritones. After they've done it once, they feel they don't want to do it again. But in my case—and I think I took this attitude with almost every role I did in my career—I feel it's a very important part of the opera as a whole. He's a sort of pivotal person. He has the great job of trying to teach Pinkerton some kind of manners and understanding of humanity. Pinkerton is really destroying Butterfly, and is very remorseful about it eventually. But it's Sharpless who realizes where this is all going to end up, and he tries very, very hard to stop it.

K I R S T E N : Pinkerton is a big, strong American sailor, and she falls in love with his strength. I think this is one of the things that impresses her very much. He can't be a short, fat tenor and make any impression. I just wanted them to be tall and good-looking, to look as a good-looking American guy in uniform would look. And of course the better looking he was, the more it enhanced the whole picture with her.

Puccini first fell in love with his geisha on a trip to London. There, at the Duke of York's Theatre, she came to life in the form of Evelyn Millard, who played the role created on Broadway by Blanche Bates. Puccini was stricken by Belasco's sense of drama, one of his own innate gifts. With John Luther Long, Belasco had adapted the play from Long's 1898 story in *Century* magazine. With his dramatic flair, Belasco had galvanized the meandering story into tragedy. Only one of more than two hundred plays Belasco authored, *Madame Butterfly* opened on Broadway in 1900.

K I R S T E N : She was so warm, so passionate with the man she loved. And that's why her life at the time was almost breathless. She's looking up to him as a god as well as her husband. I don't think she thought of him just as a husband, as much as this very special life on earth.

S C O T T O : The first act, you only see one side of the girl. She's so young, but yet she went through a lot in her life. At fifteen, her life was already a mess, because she had a father who made a suicide. She was alone and had to take that job as a geisha; that was not such a good thing for a young girl, to be in a teahouse. But the most important thing about *Butterfly* is the last act. The drama is really there—when Butterfly is really a human being, finally coming to the audience.

M O F F O : There's drama before the curtain opens. Nobody pays any attention to it, but it's already quite clear that for Pinkerton, all this is just a fling. Goro has gotten this girl for him, and after talking to her, Sharpless says, "You know, you'd better be careful; she believes you"—"Ella ci crede."

S C O T T O : Goro is a fascinating character, because he's a matchmaker. He doesn't care about anything but money, and Butterfly or another girl, it's the same thing.

M O F F O : The drama builds when the Bonze comes in. This all goes over Pinkerton's head—I think that's the drama. He doesn't realize what he's doing, probably because of the culture difference. He doesn't realize how serious it is to take a Japanese girl for a wife—or how serious she thinks it is.

A R R O Y O : Also, remember, by the time she comes in for the wedding day, she has already gone and changed her religion for the day they could pray together to the same God. She is a very sincere, very open flower. Some people may say I'm not an actress at all, but they can't say I'm not sincere.

S C O T T O : Religion is another main point in *Butterfly*. In the Oriental culture, the religion is so different from the Christian, and to give up your own religion means giving up your own culture. So she dared do this, because she is looking to a different life, to a better life. Then she's rejected by her own happiness, her own hope. So she's left alone by everything.

A native of San Francisco, David Belasco was one of the most prominent theatrical producers from the 1880s through the 1920s. Author of plays like *Du Barry* in 1901 and the 1926 *Lulu Belle,* he was criticized for his sensational showmanship, while holding the public's fascination with his lavish productions and scenic effects. In Belasco, with his flair for the theatrical and sense of dramatic realism, Puccini found a kindred spirit. When *Madama Butterfly* came to the Metropolitan in 1907, Belasco worked with the composer to stage it. They would work together again three years later when Puccini adapted Belasco's 1905 horse opera, *The Girl of the Golden West.*

K I R S T E N : Right from the beginning of my career, I had to know every opera I was doing backwards, so I could relax and perform the character. I don't remember when I first saw *Butterfly,* but I do know that I had studied the role so well, I was very, very sure of myself. I knew exactly what I wanted to do. And I had been interested in the role long enough already to know how really to perform that lovely little girl.

A M A R A : When I prepared a role, I would first prepare it musically as well as I could. Then you're so secure musically that the words come naturally. That way, you're free to interpret and you know that you're really prepared.

UPPMAN: Lucine was a wonderful Butterfly. She had the voice, and this is the thing. So many people try to sing the role and they can't do it, because it takes a great deal of strength; and there's so much emotion in it, that sometimes takes over.

SCOTTO: Butterfly is such a human character. That's why the impact on the audience is immediate. And that's why the singer has to be in such control of the character—never let herself be emotional, keeping the emotion for herself. No. The difficulty in *Butterfly* is to keep in control of the character in order to make an audience understand and cry and be emotional—but not the actress. And yet, you can't act fake. But if you act truthfully, to touch the audience—and at the same time you're acting—this is what makes you different, one of a kind, maybe great. I try to say the truth, to be human.

KIRSTEN: The role takes all kinds of vocal strength and technique. It changes so—from the girl being such a lovely young girl, then suddenly learning about life by having a baby by this man, and then by going through the pain that she is going through. This pain has to be shown in the voice.

ALBANESE: The voice should be beautiful. You should choose that best, beautiful quality of voice.

MOFFO: Unfortunately, I do not have that gift of saving myself—in anything. What I do is decide where I'm going, and get there—but not too soon.

KIRSTEN: Before I sang Butterfly, I went up to Connecticut to visit Geraldine Farrar, and discussed the role with her. And we were talking about where the parts were that the voice had to be saved a bit. She was very helpful, because she was also very upset with people who sing the role and should not, people who didn't have the proper vocal technique to sing the role. But it was very interesting talking with Farrar, just taking the score and saying, "Look here, we know we're coming to a grand climax, and we must think about that and save." Of course, you don't save so that anyone in the world can tell but you. It is a saving of strength.

MOFFO: Pacing is the way you color the voice. It doesn't mean singing any less hard—it's just that my expression isn't at its maximum.

After doing roles ranging from Ortlinde in *Die Walkure* to Marguerite and Elena in *Mefistofele,* Gilda Cruz-Romo made her Metropolitan debut as Cio-Cio-San.

GILDA CRUZ-ROMO: You have to learn to pace yourself, in every act. Because even the last part, which is very short, has a lot of problems where you can get caught. So it is very important to learn exactly where to breathe, where to sing.

SCOTTO: The character of Butterfly goes on sometimes very easily; then you have to save for the moment when you really have to get the audience, like "Che tua madre" or "Morta! Morta!" So before those phrases, there are others you can really relax on; let's say, not give one hundred percent. And there are other times where you only give twenty percent. That's how you pace. But you have to know this by experience with the character.

CRUZ-ROMO: Artistically, I guess you could say Butterfly was one of my battlehorses. I did a lot of them, and she is very close to my heart.

MITCHELL: I think it's very difficult to combine that Japanese image, and keep it in the character. Because the singing is so grand at moments that the tininess of the woman, the fragility, is hard to hold on to.

ARROYO: Butterfly has been a growing experience for me as a part, to sing, and to learn about myself. I've always thought there was a lot of me in her—good or bad. And I was very surprised to find out a couple of people who saw repeated performances and said, "You were Butterfly without acting the part." And that was a compliment, in a way.

Rehearsals for the Met premiere of *Butterfly* did not go as smoothly as had preparations in Italy. Puccini, who did not relish extended travel, came to New York for the occasion. In the wake of Belasco's staging, he directed Enrico Caruso's Pinkerton, Louise Homer's Suzuki, Antonio Scotti's Sharpless, and, as Butterfly, the company's new star, Geraldine Farrar, who had debuted at the Met earlier that season in *Romeo and Juliet*. Puccini spent much rehearsal time at odds with the soprano. "Farrar is not too satisfactory," Puccini wrote to his publisher. "She sings out of tune, forces her voice, and it does not carry well. . . ."

"He didn't like me a bit," Farrar recalled later. "I would not sing out full voice in rehearsal. I had always been taught to conserve my voice in the German way."

K I R S T E N : You know, there is an awful lot of running around, too, up and down on the knees—think of all the exercise one gets in that role. She becomes one who's completely distraught. Then she becomes a very strong character in trying to tell the world what has happened to her in the last act. It's such an overemotional role.

A L B A N E S E : It's different than any opera, and you get tired. This opera, my teacher said, is like a little lyric *Tristan and Isolde.*

M O F F O : A lot of sopranos, I think, get so carried away in the second act—carried away in gesture and in singing hard—that they lose the anguish and the final, ultimate desperation of the last act. That is where everything is over. It doesn't mean I don't sing in the second act—oh, yes. But it just means that it's a hopeful singing. In my mind, anyway, it's a bit like *Traviata*—it's never that desperate until, you know, you're in bed and that's it.

A M A R A : In the first act, you can give everything you've got, both emotionally and vocally; then in the second act, you have nothing left.

K I R S T E N : Also, you know, singing sitting on the floor with the baby in your arms is not terribly easy to do. It's a strain, because one fortifies oneself standing and singing with the whole body. Here, you don't have the strength of your legs behind you, which you need when you sing. Your whole body has to be in a very strong position.

A L B A N E S E : My teacher was Giuseppina Baldassare-Tedeschi, a great prima donna. She taught me a lot of staging, and a lot of heart—to recognize I had a heart. I was very young, and my heart got big when I came to this country. I remember the things she told me: Every word has a meaning—you cannot just sing the music; otherwise, just listen to the music. And in that time, I was singing with the great artists who had heart—Gigli and Schipa, Lauri-Volpi and Gina Cigna. . . .

C R U Z - R O M O : The hardest thing about singing this role, in my case, was not to put in too much heart; because it's too close for me, too close to my heart, and I could get emotional very easily. So I had to be always in control, which for me was difficult, because it is very much in my nature to be emotional. After every performance, I was devastated in many ways. It was an emotional drain.

A L B A N E S E : The singing, the voice, and the high notes—you have to be sure of yourself. And then you can even sing with your head down—like Gigli used to sing, so beautiful, or Schipa, singing *Lucia di Lammermoor* on the floor. You have to do that at home one hundred times—then on the stage, you can sing it.

M O F F O : Butterfly is a very special role for me. It was my debut, and of course, it was connected to my falling in love for the first time, getting married. I auditioned for the radio—not for La Scala—with *Otello,* Louise, and the Countess—and I got hired for Butterfly. Don't ask me to explain it. It was not only in Milano, in La Scala, but it was televised—in the days when we really had a captive audience. People had one channel, and everybody would go to restaurants and bars—there was not yet television in every home—so everybody saw this *Butterfly.* It was a press agent's dream. And I'll never forget the next morning: I had a job in Paris, and I got on the train, and everybody said, "Oh, è la Moffo," and I didn't pick it up until people came on the train and asked me for my autograph.

A M A R A : I'll never forget singing the entrance, which is a B-flat, and Alessio de Paolis was onstage and he told me at the next performance, "Don't blast it to get up there. You have it." It almost got away from me. But we had colleagues in those days who would help you. We didn't have any backstabbing or any of the things that seem to go on now.

C R U Z - R O M O : Vocally, for me the role was not difficult unless I let myself go, and then I got in trouble. There were no problems. I always thought Puccini meant her to be sung by someone with a voice like mine—not by a lighter voice.

M I T C H E L L : For me the challenge is to sing quietly, then come back in one or two measures and give the forte note with the orchestra blaring all those horns and trumpets.

S C O T T O : There are moments in *Butterfly.* . . . I remember I sang Butterfly in Brescia, and it was a very emotional evening I will remember forever. Because *Butterfly*'s second chance as an opera was in Brescia. It had failed at La Scala, and then in Brescia it was successful. And that evening, I got too emotional. In the middle of the opera, I had no voice anymore and I couldn't finish, because I started to cry when I sang "Che tua madre," which is a very difficult moment. And I had so much emotion to myself that I cried, and I had no voice to finish the opera. I had to stop. But then I also had my second chance in Brescia, because I had another performance— and I got to the end.

KIRSTEN: It's very dangerous—it may be one of the most danger-ous roles as far as protecting the voice is concerned. Because there is no way I ever sang that role that I didn't really cry—especially in the last act, because it gets to you so definitely. I think that's some-thing you have to be very careful of, because weeping is not very helpful for vocal technique.

SCOTTO: Some singers get very emotional and they say, "Oh, Butterfly makes me cry." That's where you make a mistake. You shouldn't cry—you should make the audience cry.

ALBANESE: If I put on a *Butterfly,* I'd teach those things which I did. Some people wouldn't, because some people are jealous, I'm sure. And I say, "Why are you jealous? You don't want to leave the beauty with it for the young singers?" This is what the public should have, why the public should come to see the opera—not one time, but fifty times, one hundred times. Now they don't come.

AMARA: Today, everyone seems to go their own way. They come in and do their thing and leave. The Met used to be one big, happy family; that was how it was run. When we would go on tour, it was incredible. We had some of our best times on the train and in the tour cities. We used to have parties on the train. Mr. Bing was there, John Gutman was there, Max Rudolf—all of the administration was in the parlor car. When we had these little roomettes, we would all crowd in and tell jokes—George Shirley, eight or nine of us. And we had such a great time—it was wonderful.

CRUZ-ROMO: The biggest mistake is that many people mark when they are rehearsing. If you're rehearsing all day, you'd better—but if you're just doing it once, you'd better sing it in rehearsal. Otherwise, they get caught in the performance, when they give the emotion.

KIRSTEN: The more you feel the role, the more the audience feels the role. You work yourself up to a tremendous feeling of emotion, and this can be done if you know how to sing. If you learn in the first part how to manage your voice, you can show that emotion without any detriment to the voice. You have to learn to get that under control and not do anything to hurt the beauty of your voice. You're singing over great emotion, but I think emotion adds to the voice when it's done properly. But you need the kind of projection of the voice I have had—I never needed to worry about that. My voice was a natural one.

CRUZ-ROMO: I was very blessed that the emotions didn't come hard; they were all there. I didn't have to dig for them.

KIRSTEN: It's probably the most emotional role I've ever done, or that anyone could ever do, because she suffers so terribly.

For months before the premiere, Farrar studied Japanese figurines and mannerisms, working with a Japanese dancing girl to perfect her presence as a geisha. She even shaved off her eyebrows—at which point her mother informed her she looked "perfectly hideous," and they agreed that eyebrows would, after all, be more in keeping with the Puccini style.

MOFFO: After my debut, I got a lot of offers to do *Butterfly*. Thank God I had good advice, and I put it away for eleven years. But see, it's too bad that as a singer of thirty, when you're old enough to cope with the vocal demands of Butterfly, you're really too old. Like Bernard Shaw said about wasting youth on the young: Thirty isn't old, but there's something about nineteen or twenty. It's dangerous— but I was only four years away from Butterfly's age. And it's something about the virginal quality I think Butterfly has to have. Then, you don't have to work at it; later, it's much harder to sing like a fifteen-year-old in this situation: waiting, she really has no family, falling madly in love this way, having this child. I think when I was thirty, I looked at it differently.

KIRSTEN: Most happily, Butterfly seems to be the role people remember me best for. In fact, a lot of people still write to me, "Dear Butterfly." It's the role I did most often—I must have sung it a hundred fifty or two hundred times.

MOFFO: The most glaring thing I hear even now on the recording I did is that I sound like what I was, which was a virgin. I mean, there is something in the voice. . . . I don't think I sound like a boy soprano, but there's something very immature about the sound: pretty, sort of clean, solid—but there's something all goo-goo-eyed about it that perhaps would not have been correct for a worldly lady like Violetta. But people should not be permitted to sing Butterfly at nineteen. I mean, I always wanted to find the person who really engaged me and then commit them.

ARROYO: You've always got to find the truth in what you're

doing. Acting is about truth, which is why a truth for me is not like a truth for someone else, which makes it interesting for the audience, because it will be different. But it doesn't mean other people are going to see that it's good. It might not read for your critics the way you believe it's reading. Because I'm sure if you went to twenty-five different reviews of any of our Butterflys, you would find many different reactions to the same approach. That's the thing that makes it interesting—that's the ball game.

ALBANESE: Conductors, even Toscanini, gave me ideas all the time. And I never said, "Maestro, I know it already"—never. I said, "I just arrived at a moment where I don't know what else to do on that stage, so give me some ideas." And I used to tell the young conductors, "Give me some ideas, please—you must have some ideas." And they gave them to me.

MITCHELL: My first Butterfly was a great success, thank goodness. After doing a role for the first time, you know if it's going to work or if you should save it for five more years or never do it again.

MOFFO: After I had put it away for eleven years, I picked it up again. It was still there; the only difference was I felt I could sustain the part much better. By that time, I approached each Butterfly in a much more disciplined, professional way. I think for everybody, the first one is always—like the first time you make love—it's different. Everything kind of happens—you don't know what you're doing. In my case it was right, but I felt more prepared to do it later.

"I just went out onstage and was Butterfly," Farrar said in an interview years after her retirement in 1922. "It's not really a difficult or complicated part."

MOFFO: I was once asked why I'm not a women's libber. I am, but I don't like the people who are out to kill men. And they said, "But a woman in your position—you have to be." And I said, "Why? I never took a job away from a tenor. I'm just doing my own thing. I'm a soprano and I do what girls are supposed to do if they're sopranos. It's not a question of equality, it's a question of there's a difference—and *vive la différence.*" I'm an old-fashioned girl—I like being feminine and cooking and sewing. It doesn't mean I'm not ambitious and don't want to succeed in my career, but just not losing sight of how much fun it is to be a feminine girl. It also doesn't mean I don't think I can do a lot of things better than a lot of men. But I know it, maybe, and that's enough.

Often a stage performance's biggest complication is dealing with the necessary evil of child actors.

K I R S T E N : They had rules that a child had to be seven years old to appear onstage, or something—but that's much too old. You could hardly pick them up—they weighed a ton.

M I T C H E L L : In Sydney I had a little boy who was four or five—a film actor. And you can imagine what his attention span was like. Once he'd heard the soprano sing, that was it—he didn't care. And he'd get a little bored, night after night. So around the sixth perform-ance, this little one decided to turn around to the audience as I was singing the last aria, pull up his mask, and wave to the audience. Well, I grabbed him and held him so tight. He was about to cry, but was also about to ruin the scene. Later, he said to his mother, "Miss Leona was trying to hurt me." Then the next time I did it there, he was about six, and I met him coming to the theater, and he said to me, "I hear you're having trouble with the new boy." I said to myself, "This is too much—having trouble with all these little Troubles."

K I R S T E N : One time there was a little child, and that child was too young. It should never have been allowed. It was the first time I'd ever used a boy, and I was a little skeptical about it. And he had this little toy that his mother insisted he had to have with him. It had a little sharp edge on it and he kept jabbing that thing into my breast. The mother was so proud her child was on the stage, she didn't think of me at all. All kinds of crazy things like that go on.

J U L I A M I G E N E S : I was torn out of bed to play the little kid in *Butterfly*—I don't even remember where, maybe the old Met or out in Brooklyn. But I was three years old and they threw this blond wig on my head and there I was. I remember there was all this Puccini music, and I was out onstage waving my little flag because they told me to, but not really understanding what was going on. Through it all, I was unbelievably impressed with all this great music. It was all so gorgeous—I was hypnotized by it.

S C O T T O : Dolore is the most important thing, because he's the one who keeps life going on. So life is not finished with Butterfly, because the child eventually goes to the United States and will get married. And he's still Japanese—you can't cancel what you were.

K I R S T E N : I used to have a call and I'd say, "Get all the mothers who want their children on this stage and I will come to the theater and choose the child I want." I looked for a child who, if I quietly whispered an order to her—always her, only once or twice him—she would listen to me. And I really wanted to make a friend of that child before I took her on the stage. I think children are so frightened, with our voices. In *Butterfly,* we're not always singing quietly. So I would always hold the child with one hand over the ear that was open to my sound, and make it look as though I were just cuddling it. It was very helpful.

M I T C H E L L : I love children, so it's not hard for me. I'd hate to be a person who hated children and had to do that part. That would be treacherous.

K I R S T E N : Only once in my career did I actually have to take a child off the stage while singing, then come back and continue. Because the child was yelling and screaming bloody murder, frightened, and crying at the top of his lungs.

Butterfly did not name her child Dolore, translated as "Sorrow" or "Trouble," so that other children would make fun of him. In traditional Japan, it was customary to give a newborn baby a temporary name until a more permanent one could be decided upon. "His name will be Joy when his father returns," she tells Sharpless.

A L B A N E S E : In the second act you must wait for him. This starts the drama.

M O F F O : The drama in the second act is the wonderful way that Butterfly has this patience, this faith, that he's going to come back.

A R R O Y O : I really don't believe she doubts it. If she ever had a real doubt, she would have been devastated long before Puccini wanted her to end her life. What makes it so sad for the audience is that she's the one person who goes through and says, "He *will* come back. I will wait." And no one can destroy it.

S C O T T O : *Hope* is the word she's attached to, even though Suzuki, in the second act, tries to make her understand: "No, he's not going to come back. It's finished—you're stuck with the child."

MOFFO: And constantly, Sharpless comes with the letter and says, "But . . ." Suzuki comes and says, "But . . ."

SCOTTO: The friendship in Suzuki is very strong. Because when Butterfly and she are left completely alone, rejected by everybody, she's the only one who didn't leave her. So it's a true symbol of friendship—she's there from the first moment to the end. Even near death, she's there. This, I think, is a very important character. You know, every time you're alone and you say, "I hope this will come through," you always have inside you another part of you that says, "No, it will not." So in Suzuki, we have a spoken voice of the inside of Butterfly. Every time she says yes, the inside says no.

Rosalind Elias first sang Suzuki at the Met in 1956 and has recorded the role twice.

ROSALIND ELIAS: Suzuki's a strong character. She's not just a prop woman who carries things from here to there, which is usually done—we call her the best prop lady in opera. But she's not that. She's in this household, observing everything. She has her opinions, and I think Butterfly depends on her opinion and respects it to the point that she's always aware Suzuki's there. It's an important character, theatrically.

As Suzuki, Nedda Casei has comforted the leading Butterflys of our time.

NEDDA CASEI: The role of Suzuki is often undervalued. We forget that the legendary Louise Homer created the first Suzuki at the Met. In *Butterfly,* Puccini gave one of the few opportunities in opera for the mezzo to be a kind and compassionate human being. I wanted to show Suzuki's reality as a contrast to Butterfly's dreams. I also wanted to be supportive of the artist singing Butterfly.

MITCHELL: The Japanese relationships are very interconnected. Suzuki will give her life for Butterfly. It just tears her heart out to see this girl pining away. Also, Butterfly was estranged from her family, so she's probably taken Suzuki as a mother figure.

E L I A S : I know Puccini didn't write much music for her, but as a character, you should make her very important. Because she's always there.

M O F F O : Suzuki tries to say to Butterfly, "But he really isn't coming back—let's stop this."

E L I A S : Suzuki's sympathetic but strong. Butterfly has a great dependency on her.

S C O T T O : Once you realize she's the other side of Butterfly, it's better for your own characterization of Butterfly, because it becomes a true character. Suzuki's not the maid—Suzuki is a friend.

C A S E I : Another thing is we have to carry the baby.

K I R S T E N : Sometimes working with the kids was just incredible. When they get nervous, sometimes they become stiff, and you just couldn't bend those legs. It's funny when you think of it, but it wasn't funny on that stage, believe me.

C A S E I : Dorothy Kirsten was the first Butterfly with whom I sang, and what a supreme artist she was! It was at the Metropolitan, and I was thrown on at the last minute for someone who was ill. Darling Patrick Tavernia, the assistant stage director, stood by with instant directions and a helping hand.

C R U Z - R O M O : I was very fortunate, because with every production I got wonderful Suzukis. I sang it with Nedda Casei—oh, she was wonderful. She was always there whenever I needed anything, and I didn't have to tell her. It was just perfect. She was beautiful. She was sympathetic and yet strong when she needed to be strong. She was one of the best.

C A S E I : In the original book, she married the Consul, so Suzuki has a future.

U P P M A N : I have such sympathy for Suzuki. At times, especially in the trio with Sharpless, Suzuki, and Pinkerton, I've had tears in my eyes over the wonderful, plaintive quality of that role.

E L I A S : She mustn't go home and say, "Oh, look, I don't have much to sing." She shouldn't just stay there and be this whimpering little Oriental flower. I don't mean do any crazy shtick, but there's no reason for the public not to say, "Oh, my God, look—isn't she wonderful, taking in everything? She's so strong, though she's not doing anything." As they say, there are no small roles.

A R R O Y O : One time I did Butterfly in San Diego, where the stage director, at the end of "Un bel dì," instead of having Suzuki and Butterfly hug and Suzuki saying somehow, "OK, I'll go into your belief with you," Butterfly sets up with "l'aspetto"—she's waiting for Suzuki to come—and Suzuki bursts into tears and runs out. Do you know what that does to you? It leaves you totally with egg on your face. The one person you expect to come into your world with you and help you, leaves you. And at that moment, Sharpless brings the letter. So it's totally different; we never got applause at the end of "Un bel dì" when that happened. The look on Suzuki's face says, "Don't you see it's all futile?" It left the audience with a gasp— because the audience was ready to go into "Yes, we love you, Butterfly; we know he's going to come back."

Farrar's Cio-Cio-San was complemented perfectly by Homer's faithful Suzuki in the first Metropolitan production. But rehearsals were strenuous, due not only to the concentration of artistic temperament but to Puccini's overbearing perfectionism. At least once, it is told, the composer reduced both women to tears.

C A S E I : Dorothy was worried about communicating with me at first. What a pleasure it was to find we both believed in the sympathetic sharing of life by the two women.

K I R S T E N : I remember Nedda Casei as a warm, compassionate colleague who was eager to support her Cio-Cio-San in showing the love and pity she so deeply felt for her.

E L I A S : These women in these households, what they called the maid, many times ruled the household. Actually, she's the companion.

C A S E I : Every time Dorothy and I did it together, we found new things to add. She had her own gorgeous costumes and had studied in Japan, creating a beautifully touching and authentic Cio-Cio-San. I'll never forget the haunting moment she took the flowers I had placed in her hair, adorning her for Pinkerton's return, crushing the red petals and letting them fall through her fingers to the ground as she accepted the loss of Pinkerton and life. I learned much from her.

E L I A S : I sang Suzuki with all the great Butterflys: Tebaldi, Albanese, Leontyne Price, Dorothy Kirsten—every singer that has had a great success with the part.

C A S E I : Leontyne Price was also a jewel. I did the only two perform-

ances of Butterfly Leontyne ever did at the Met. And what performances they were! At our first rehearsal, she laughed, "I always wanted
a white maid!"

E L I A S : If some Butterflys were more vulnerable, I was vulnerable—
or sometimes would go the other way and help them be stronger. I
never played any role the same way—it's according to what the
feedback is from the other actress.

M O F F O : One of the great moments is when Suzuki comes in, in the
third act, and there is this trio with Pinkerton and it's "But what
am I going to tell Butterfly?" I wish I had one friend like that. We
all do.

The famous story goes that while recording the Act One duet with
Caruso, who had apparently been celebrating on his way to the studio,
Farrar exchanged the words "He had a highball" for "Sì, per la vita."
The technology of the day allowed it to pass unnoticed. There are those
who dismiss the story as myth, but others swear that if one listens
carefully, Caruso's highball is immortalized for all to hear.

E L I A S : I did two recordings. The first one was with Anna Moffo and
Cesare Valletti, in Rome. First of all, that was my first recording with
RCA. That was my debut.

M O F F O : Roz was marvelous! And Pinkerton was not a role that
Valletti did a lot onstage, if ever—and he brought a freshness to it,
a very delicate approach.

E L I A S : To go to Italy, to record *Butterfly*—and that music, in Italy!
I can even now feel the air, and smell the air in the studio and in
Rome and the Borghese and everything. It was a beautiful experi-
ence.

M O F F O : Roz was a perfect Suzuki for me, because our voices
blended so beautifully. Sometimes it's hard, in a duet in thirds—the
"Flower Duet"—but it just came out of both of us without any
trying. Leinsdorf conducted, and we were in Rome and Milano—
back and forth. It was very exciting.

E L I A S : Anna and I were very young. And she was, at that time, in
love with her first husband-to-be. So the air was full of love, but full
of sorrow, too. You know, when you're young, everything's bigger
than life: The tears were bigger; the music was big. And if it was sad,

it was a tormenting sadness, but also a sadness that you wallowed in. You wanted more of this poetic sadness, this beauty of music. It was a very beautiful time and a very, very beautiful experience. You know, it's the music that's in your soul, and you took it out on the street with you; you took it into your hotel room; you took it into the park with you. Thinking about it makes me very nostalgic. It's Puccini—what can I say?

Whenever Geraldine Farrar could be pried away from Cio-Cio-San, Emmy Destinn was the soprano usually chosen to fill her kimono. A favorite of Caruso's, Destinn had premiered the opera in both London and Berlin. Though her vocal and dramatic gifts were generous, so were her proportions. Perhaps because of the public had been spoiled by Farrar's glamour and femininity, Destinn's Butterfly never did capture American audiences the way it had Europe's.

SCOTTO: My debut with Butterfly was in my own town, when I was nineteen. It was not right for me to sing Butterfly at that time, because Butterfly is very long, very dramatic in the matter of heavy voice. You go from the beginning to end without breaking to rest. I wouldn't suggest it for a young singer today, to sing Butterfly as a debut, no. I did it because I wanted to sing, and they offered me that, and I didn't say no. But it took me at least five or six years before I was able to pace the character to get to the end even fresher than the beginning.

Of all his operas, *Butterfly* was Puccini's favorite. "I never listen to my operas with pleasure," he remarked, "with the exception, perhaps, of the last act of *La Bohème*. But *Butterfly*—the whole thing both entertains and interests me."

ALBANESE: So anyway, this is drama, very, very strong drama. This is life for everybody, when he doesn't come and you have a child. At that time it was a disgrace to have a child and not be married. Now they make a joke. I'd be ashamed if I had a child without a husband—I would kill myself.

MOFFO: For me, *desperation* is a big word. I'm desperate, in a way, with Butterfly in the second act. I'm happy as a clam in the first act. But desperate, mainly because I don't understand where Pinkerton is, why doesn't he come home? I have my little baby, and everybody has ousted me. Finally I'm just there with Suzuki.

MITCHELL: The drama really should come through the music. That's the only way for me. It's a combination of the two—the music and the drama. You can't separate them.

MOFFO: There are so many parts to Butterfly. She can change so quickly: She's pretty depressed at the beginning of the second act; then when Sharpless comes in, she's excited—she thinks he's come with the news of Pinkerton, and indeed he has. And she has to go through this "never coming back!" and throw out Sharpless, which is very hard—Japanese people are terribly polite.

KIRSTEN: The Japanese element is most important. She has to learn all the traits and how to behave. And as anyone knows who's ever been to Japan, they're different.

ALBANESE: The Japanese really are young—even when they have many wrinkles. They still have these little youngish moments—which is what I have, me, too. I'll be the oldest little girl in the world.

KIRSTEN: The women seem to be very gentle in their motions. And we had to learn even how to handle the kimono, and it's not the most comfortable attire—especially some of the heavy ones.

SCOTTO: Actually, there is very little Japanese in *Butterfly,* concerning the singing and the matter of words. If you look at the scenery of the first *Butterfly,* it's very little Japanese—there are flowers all over, decoration on the stage. But in Japan, all the houses are very neat, with all the essential things about it. We don't find that in *Butterfly.* The "Flower Duet," where they throw flowers all over the floor, full of things going on—it is very little Japanese, but it is so beautiful, so Puccini. It is a mix of Japan and Puccini.

MOFFO: To make Butterfly a great success, it needs many colors, shadings, and a great study of the Oriental culture. I mean, the music is definitely Italian and definitely verismo. That brings people to want to emote in a perhaps more Italianate than Oriental fashion. But the Japanese, when they cry, their eyes don't even close. You just see rivulets of tears. It's incredible. In many ways, this is more touching.

ELIAS: There's never a time when I've not been wrenched on the stage and crying coming off, or crying onstage, too. In fact, at the beginning of my career when I started doing Suzuki, I was crying so much that Max Rudolf said, "You've got to learn, Rosalind, how not to get so emotional." After the "Flower Duet," when she goes to get the baby—I mean, I can't stand it—my heart—even talking about it makes me sad. I tried every performance to detach, but never succeeded at it. Can you imagine what the Butterfly has to go through?

A M A R A : When I would sing Butterfly, I would get very choked up. I'll never forget. I'd had a miscarriage, and I came to the theater to see Dorothy Kirsten, because I was covering. When it came to the last act, I had to leave the theater, because the tears just welled up. I came out into the old house, and I was sitting in the reception area crying, and Phyllis Curtin came up and said, "What is it?" So I told her, "I just had a miscarriage, and I can't deal with this opera." She tried to comfort me, but it took me a while to really get to the point where I could sing Butterfly. Every time it came to that part, I would choke up and absolutely be in tears. When I was going to do my first Cio-Cio-San, Dorothy said to me, "Be very careful. Don't give everything you have in the first act, because you have the second and third acts to do. Pace yourself well when you sing this opera." I was very grateful to her for telling me that. And I was aware the only way I could get through it was not to think of the words—I had to lock them out.

U P P M A N : I have to tell you a little secret: I would write out Sharpless's letter each night. Then, when Butterfly would kiss it, of course the lipstick marks would be on the paper, and I've saved almost all of them. So I have them, marked "Tebaldi," "Dorothy Kirsten," "Licia Albanese," and I cherish these. Butterfly is one of the most difficult roles in the world to do, vocally, but also getting the right feeling into it. And those I had the privilege of singing with were really great, great performers.

Missing from his collection are the lip prints of Sylvia Sidney, who starred as an unlikely geisha opposite Cary Grant in the 1932 *Madame Butterfly,* a Hollywood treatment of the Long-Belasco story. To ensure more authenticity for its new 1958 production, the Met engaged Japanese designer Motohiro Nagasaka and director Yoshio Aoyama.

C R U Z - R O M O : I was very lucky, because I worked with Aoyama, the very beautiful Kabuki teacher. Also, I was in Japan and had my costumes designed there.

KIRSTEN: I did my own makeup for Butterfly, and I studied that at great length. We couldn't do it the way they really looked, with the very white faces. We tried that at the Met, but it just didn't ring true.

MOFFO: Everything they do is very intense and within. Butterfly is not a character of Tosca or Mimì gestures. She's very much more contained: her walking, talking to the baby or to Pinkerton, or the way she kneels at his feet. I find that very hard to do continuously all night. And those shoes are really murder to walk in!

ALBANESE: When I started, my teacher gave me her shoes. They are very difficult to walk in. And then the kimonos—beautiful. I still have one or two.

SCOTTO: I don't mind having so little that's Japanese onstage. Butterfly, she talks a lot—she expresses all her feelings. This is not Japanese—it's Italian. So what's wrong about that? It's beautiful!

KIRSTEN: I think in certain operas, companies have got to try to create the whole visual picture of the story. That was so terribly important to me—and many times, so disillusioning.

CRUZ-ROMO: It needs that Italianate strength—the Japanese way, but with the Italian flavor.

KIRSTEN: Puccini knew exactly what he was doing. I've worked with his roles more than any other, his whole repertoire, and he gave me so much to work with.

CRUZ-ROMO: The Japanese people still won't go into their house with their outside shoes; they have special shoes for inside—it's just hygiene for them. I was very upset at one production, because they wanted to dress her the way they wanted, with the wrong shoes. But it changes the whole thing. Then they put a little Japanese boy in as Trouble—and I'm sorry, but if he had been Japanese in the story, there wouldn't have been any problem. And that's what I said. I've been in Japan—I know.

ALBANESE: We used to buy our own costumes. And not one, not two, but change every scene. That's the novelty for the public, too.

KIRSTEN: Butterfly I consider the major role I loved so much, and I felt I was so right for, because too many women at the time were coming along who just couldn't look like Butterfly. They were just too tall; they were too fat. And I felt—well, I've always been the same size, I've never changed, not even yet. I'm not a "fat soprano."

And it infuriates me when they use that silly expression, "The fat lady sings." I think being physically suited is terribly important, especially Butterfly, the Japanese being so small. It's not easy for a tall person to try to be Butterfly.

At the Milan premiere, a crowd turned ugly, an overlong second act, or Puccini's detractors—no one knows for certain—caused a near riot. The audience's hostility was unleashed on Butterfly's entrance, which was with a phrase reminiscent of *Bohème*. Rosina Storchio bravely sang out against a mounting roar of catcalls and jeers, as the crowd shouted insults about her private life. Things only worsened when a wayward draft puffed out her kimono. When Suzuki pulled up the window blinds, the audience collapsed into hilarity. On the verge of hysteria as she left the stage, Storchio vowed never again to sing *Butterfly* in an Italian opera house. That summer, she went on to great success in the role in Buenos Aires with Toscanini. Although she sang many other operas in Italy, she kept her vow that Italians wouldn't see her Cio-Cio-San again, until she finally succumbed to an invitation from the Rome Opera in 1920.

M O F F O : They made a movie on the life of Puccini and did a lot of excerpts and premieres. So they asked me to do the premiere of *Butterfly,* and I said, "Oh, goody, that's marvelous." Then I found out it would involve filming and having everyone in the audience boo. And I couldn't do that—I'd maybe never walk onstage again, certainly not for *Butterfly*. So I gave up the film. Then they decided to do the same portion of *Butterfly* when it was done in Brescia and was a big hit. So I did that—and that was very exciting. I never saw the booing part, which Clara Petrella finally did, until just recently, on television. And I thought, "God, I was right!" I wouldn't be here to tell the story today.

"The opera was presented with the strongest forces that the Metropolitan can command," wrote Richard Aldrich of *The New York Times* after *Butterfly*'s Met premiere. "In nothing else has [Puccini] so completely identified the music with the action, the sentiments, the passions, and the surroundings that are shown upon the stage. Puccini has wrought his music into the very substance and spirit of the drama. . . ."

S C O T T O : Sharpless, the consul, is the father—the symbol of protection. For Butterfly, that's very important, because she didn't have a father. So maybe in the consul she finds her father figure.

U P P M A N : I don't know if Sharpless comes off as the hero, but at least he tried. Sharpless is there to provide the balance. He's the father character, who's trying to make things right. He's not perfect. He makes a lot of mistakes, too, but he's a character I can appreciate and sympathize with.

M I T C H E L L : Puccini was so clever at combining the drama and music. With Sharpless, it gets so big and dramatic again. You really have to learn to sing very quietly, and then call on all that power and force and drama again.

U P P M A N : A great thrill I remember is after one of my early performances, Licia Albanese came to me and said, "You are the best Sharpless I've ever had, because you are so understanding and so good." Whether she meant it or not, I don't know.

A L B A N E S E : We always learned the parts of the other singers. Otherwise, if they made a mistake, we made a mistake. When the Consul wants to help her, she is fainting, and she says, "Niente, niente"—she becomes very young again.

U P P M A N : Not that I'm a flag waver or anything, but I felt that being an American, this was a wonderful opportunity to right some wrongs. I feel that often, some ambassadors or whatever, when they go abroad, are a little on the shady side, and I felt I wanted to right that impression. So I made Sharpless as decent and human a person as I could.

Singers who are performing the Japanese characters ideally steep themselves in Japanese culture before going onstage.

A L B A N E S E : When you listen, you have to listen like the Japanese. And when you sit, it's not like we do today; and when you walk, not with an open kimono.

A M A R A : I learned from the Japanese how to get up without touching the floor. You rise with the knees bent.

K I R S T E N : You've got to be in excellent condition physically in order to be able to so gracefully get down on one's knees and get up again without touching the floor. That's very, very important.

M O F F O : Then, she hears *boom!* That's one of the great theatrical things Puccini did: in the middle of all this wailing, the sound of the boat. It's the most wonderful moment. She can't even see—she says, "Please help me to hold the telescope." And then, "Can you read the name? *Abraham Lincoln*—ah!" And then she runs off—she doesn't even want to know anything else. "He's coming back! He loves only me!"

After paying La Scala twenty thousand lire, Puccini withdrew *Butterfly* after the premiere. He immediately set about revising the opera, changing mainly the miscalculated two-act form. On May 28, 1904, the three-act version's Brescia presentation at the Teatro Grande, with Salomea Kruszelnicka and Giovanni Zenatello, was a resounding success. Today the two-act version is occasionally done, though the second act runs over an hour and a half.

A M A R A : I've sung it with no intermission between the second and third act. That is difficult because you're out there and you don't even have the chance to have a glass of water. By the time you get to the end of *Butterfly,* you're really wrung out.

M O F F O : I always think I'm so well prepared. But I did *Butterfly* in Hamburg—and nobody told me the second and third act had no intermission. And I struck my pose at what should have been the end of Act Two and there I was with my hands up, and I thought, "Are they really not going to bring down the curtain?" And I thought my arms were going to fall off, because it was not a stance I took to keep. They were paralyzed, asleep. And I remember I thought, "I will *never* be able to lift this kid now," because after that, I was supposed to pick up the baby and go off.

K I R S T E N : Butterfly's a role in which you have to be so physically fit in every way—more than in any other role I ever did.

In John Luther Long's upbeat ending, "When Mrs. Pinkerton called the next day at the little house on Higashi Hill, it was all empty." So Kate (called Adelaide in the story) doesn't get to abscond with Dolore. Perhaps to compensate for the great injustice he and Belasco had wrought on poor Butterfly, Puccini cut Kate Pinkerton's role to the bone after the Milan premiere.

ALBANESE: The last act is tragedy. Really, Japanese tragedy is worse than the Sicilian. It's very tragic. She wakes up to call, "Suzuki, Suzuki"—not loudly, no, but like you just woke up. And then she doesn't answer. And the third time, she's very mad.

SCOTTO: I always remember, when in the last act you sing a lullaby, the lullaby is a very difficult one, because you have to make a very beautiful lullaby with a top pianissimo. And sometimes a singer tries to do too much with that lullaby, and that is also a mistake. So pace it, by doing that very simply.

ALBANESE: She wants to be seen in a pure kimono, a young kimono, like when she was married. And she says, "I want him to see me like the first night of my wedding." So that's what I put myself in, not those pink or gold things.

SCOTTO: Then you come back onstage, looking for Pinkerton, and he is there. And she hopes that he's coming to stay. I think deep inside, she knows the truth but doesn't want to face it. This is what makes the character of Butterfly—not to face the truth. She sings the phrase very simple, very happy, very nervous, but saves the voice for what comes after.

ALBANESE: And then [gasp] you find this woman. And I used to gasp. They don't do these things anymore. We used to do this, with all the expression. You see something which you don't expect to see—what do you do? You turn around to Kate and say, "Oh, benvenuto"? It must be "Oh! I was not expecting you!"

SCOTTO: And the moment she sees the wife—that is where you have to give one hundred percent.

ALBANESE: Then she goes behind the *shoji* screen. And my teacher said, "When you go there, relax—because otherwise the voice will suffer." They lose the voice in that opera. That's why they say it's like the Isolde part in a lyric way. You never stop from the beginning. You have to rest, go behind the screen, take a deep breath, then slowly come out: "He's not there."

MOFFO: I think it's true of any woman, to know there's another woman—and to know "è sua moglie!" Butterfly thinks, "Oh, so I've really been had—as well as everything else. There's no other escape but suicide."

SCOTTO: When she sees the wife, at that moment, the hope leaves her. There's nothing more left for her, because she's the one who comes to take her child, and Butterfly gives up her life for the child. Because what happiness, what life could the child have with her? So I think this has to come through the character of Butterfly through the entire opera.

ARROYO: I imagine the moment she realizes Kate is his wife must cut her to shreds. With her mentality, she has no choice but to take her own life. It's devastating. I don't think she's the type of woman who would say, "Well, maybe I'll meet another man if I wait long enough." If she had lived, she might have been able to say it. Because you do find that you have more than one love in life that can be a real love. But you have to live and allow the experience to happen.

KIRSTEN: But people have gotten too far away from Puccini's score. All of these crazy companies that try to change operas like *Butterfly* and *Traviata,* and all those marvelous Puccini and Verdi works, are just killing opera, just trying to do something different. Look at the things they've done with *Butterfly*! Hideous! Absolutely hideous!

SCOTTO: When the wife leaves, Butterfly sends them away and says, "Leave, I don't want to see you anymore. Come back and take the child," and Butterfly faints. I think she finally understands, "Everything's finished; I'm going to kill myself." This is a moment where Butterfly really has to pace herself.

ALBANESE: I started to sing with the great conductors—because at that time, we had great conductors. They would accompany me without getting mad, with a smile. Everything they told me to do, I did: "Make this note more mezza voce, more pianissimo."

SCOTTO: "Con onor muore chi non può serbar vita con onore"— in the past, those words were sometimes spoken. I never liked that. Puccini wrote notes there. These words come like you are dead already; that phrase is done very well by Puccini, in order to get ready for the *hara-kiri*. At the end, I always used my body by staying still, not moving, not even my little finger. I try to get myself calm, so people won't take their eyes from me. That moment I say, "Con onor muore chi non può serbar vita con onore"—those are the words that make Butterfly kill herself. Then the child comes in and she sings, "Tu? Tu? Piccolo Iddio!"

ARROYO: The first Butterfly I did was in scenes at the opera workshop at Hunter College, when I really was fifteen years old. I felt a great deal with her, but it was shown externally, not internally. When I started learning about her and how to feel those things, I also learned about myself. Because in the development of character, and supposedly in the development of your life, you learn so many more things about what can force you to do something, and each time you bring something else to it.

ALBANESE: When I hear one of my records, and a long breath, I say, "Did I do that? I thought all the time they were short." I criticize myself all the time and redo it. Now I hear the records and say, "Oh, I would do better. I would give ideas better than that, or do this or that here."

KIRSTEN: Everybody says, "What's your favorite role?" I can't say, because I adored Manon Lescaut, *Bohème*—all of those wonderful roles that I had, every one of them.

ALBANESE: And the public goes home and they cry, they cry. They want to go back and see it again. But crying of happiness, because you go home with such a heart. And that's what they miss now in the opera.

SCOTTO: The "Tu? Tu? Piccolo Iddio!"—that is one hundred percent. You get the audience there. But before that, it's a moment where you have to leave everything to Puccini.

CRUZ-ROMO: The conductor, too, has to know where he must help you. They have to learn about the needs of the singer and what you have to do to get through the role.

ALBANESE: When they say, "The opera house is too big"—no! The orchestra is too big! They don't want to say that. It is not a symphony with voices. The opera was born with a small orchestra. And now they spend a lot of money with the orchestra, and when they have to go overtime, good-bye—that's a thousand dollars. It's too big.

MITCHELL: It's hard to hold on to that little geisha figure and still sing the music Puccini wrote for her. The orchestra gets so big.

SCOTTO: There is so much to the end of *Butterfly*. That's why you have to save yourself so well, to get to the end so fresh that you can really concentrate on the drama.

The sword fell dully to the floor. The stream between her breasts darkened and stopped. Her head dropped slowly

forward. Her arms penitently outstretched toward the shrine.
She wept. The little maid came in and
bound up her wound.

—JOHN LUTHER LONG

A L B A N E S E : So anyway, when I was killing myself, I took my veil—because she is like a bride—and I cover Buddha. Because I didn't want him to see. And sometimes they didn't have Buddha, just a little shrine. And then sometimes I used to take my kimono and put it on the chair where he used to sit, and that was beautiful.

S C O T T O : The last part of the last act—it's where Butterfly finally faces the truth. The drama is there. I was fascinated by the novel, because it was so different. The novel is much lighter—it's not such a big deal, not such a big drama. Belasco put the big drama in it, and Puccini was fascinated by the drama; that was really his field. What Puccini was great at was the theatrical. He wants the drama onstage. And the characters are real. It's always a reflection of life.

M O F F O : It's continuous drama. People are very tired when they come out of *Butterfly.* It's "wring your handkerchief all night." Because there's always something. She always believes in a dream world, and she's always getting hurt. She doesn't win anything. It's too bad.

S C O T T O : Puccini got it so well in his music, much more than in the play. The novel had a happy ending, where Butterfly was making a *hara-kiri,* and Suzuki came out and got the knife—and happy ending. This is not what Puccini or Belasco liked.

M O F F O : The most important thing to me is at the end of the opera, when Pinkerton comes in. The climate should be such that he really is sorry. That's the drama. I don't think he thought this little geisha would wait for him with the baby. He must be sorry. That's what it's all about. He must realize what he's done.

S C O T T O : I always say to every singer, "You are the character, and you are an actress." That is so important, especially for singers, because we are always too much of a singer. We think too much of our own voice and go through the singing. The singing is always difficult—but if you can achieve singing and acting, and really perform, that's something!

K I R S T E N : It was a very exciting role, and I loved every second of it, every time I ever did it.

The first Japanese soprano to sing Cio-Cio-San was Tamaki Miura, who sang the role over two thousand times. A native of Tokyo, she went to Germany hoping to study with Lilli Lehmann in 1914. The onset of war forced her to London, where, shortly after being asked by Lady Randolph Churchill to sing at a charity concert, she debuted as Butterfly at Oscar Hammerstein's London Opera House. The performance coincided with the first air raid in London's history, when a zeppelin began bombarding the city shortly after she had completed "Un bel dì." In 1967, the first "Worldwide Madame Butterfly Competition" was announced in her honor. Held in Tokyo and Nagasaki, the contest's first prize was 1,000,000 yen—then equivalent to $2,778.

A L B A N E S E : I saw the last performance Tamaki Miura did, and I bought all her costumes. I went to see the grave. When I went to Tokyo, I said to my husband, Joe, "I want to go to see Tamaki Miura." I'd seen so many pictures of her with Puccini, so we went.

When it premiered in English, in 1906, *Madame Butterfly* couldn't have come to the United States at a better time. The early 1900s saw the country smitten with all things Japanese. Only a few years later, in 1912, Mrs. William Howard Taft would plant Washington's famous cherry trees, a gift from the mayor of Tokyo.

M O F F O : You know that during the war, after Pearl Harbor, *Butterfly* was not presented in America. I don't believe it was presented again until '49 or '50, long after. I only mention this because I always think politics and music have nothing to do with each other. And I think that's what makes artists, in any field of art, so unique: because they speak the only language that everybody understands, that everybody can communicate in. And as soon as you start mixing up "You can't sing *Butterfly* because of Japan," I think that's too bad, because that's the most incredible part of our business: not ever really having boundaries. And those setups where people from all countries come together in a production, or in an orchestra—it's suddenly like being at the bottom of the Tower of Babel. Even though everybody's saying something else, nobody fails to communicate.

AMERICAN
OPERA

~

We all did eight performances a week,
and it was like the bumblebee: You do it because
you don't know you can't do it.
–BARBARA COOK

Participants (in order of appearance): Phyllis Curtin, Regina Resnik, Giorgio Tozzi, Frances Bible, Thomas Stewart, Evelyn Lear, Theodor Uppman, Joyce Castle, Laurel Hurley, Erie Mills, Brenda Lewis, Rosalind Elias, Lili Chookasian, Morley Meredith, Roberta Peters, Eleanor Steber, Johanna Meier, Anne Wiggins Brown, Todd Duncan, Leona Mitchell, Harolyn Blackwell, Grace Bumbry, Roberta Alexander, Ron Bottcher, Andrea Velis, Jo Sullivan Loesser, Patrice Munsel, Jerry Hadley, Neil Rosenshein, Barbara Daniels, Kiri Te Kanawa, Julia Migenes, Håkan Hagegård, Barbara Cook, Cris Groenendaal

PHYLLIS CURTIN: I started out knowing good composers, and if I had any virtue at all, it was that I could read fast. It's wonderful to be part of the creativity of your time. I have never understood artists who are not interested in it. People would say, "Why are you learning that? You'll never use it again," as if by learning it nothing would happen. When you learn any piece of new

music, you come back to your Mozart and you know how to do it
fresh.

REGINA RESNIK: We don't give the real composers any incen-
tive to write. Everything is just falling by the wayside. I heard the
first *Susannah,* the first *Crucible,* and I think they were important
American works. Now people are so money oriented they don't think
about anything except what will sell.

GIORGIO TOZZI: People don't go to *hear* an opera anymore.
They go to *see* an opera. When production is the almighty god, the
more opulent and gimmicky it can be, the more it's touted as the
supreme. Very often you miss the opera, your eyes are so overwhelmed at what you're seeing. It seems as though the stage director
and designers are the first people signed up anymore, and then as an
afterthought, they say, "Oh, yes, now we need singers."

RESNIK: In the forties the European houses were doing all the
interesting new works and they didn't care if they played at sixty-five
or seventy percent capacity. It wasn't that way here, and now the
avant-garde has taken over, as it were, and people are either buying
Picasso and van Gogh or Jasper Johns. And there's nothing in between: We're either doing the romantic and the baroque or else you
have Philip Glass. Nobody is writing for the voice. They're writing
about subjects to please the public, but within these works there isn't
a composer who seems to care for the human sound.

FRANCES BIBLE: I loved doing Robert Ward's *The Crucible.*
My big aria kept going higher and higher and was really very
rewarding. We all got along so well working on it, too. I wish it
were revived more. I think it's a really great piece.

Evelyn Lear and Thomas Stewart were less fortunate when they
appeared in the premiere of a Ward opera, *Minutes to Midnight.*

THOMAS STEWART: The Ward opera was the only modern
piece that we did together.

EVELYN LEAR: It was about a bomb, and it did. It was the
biggest piece of junk I ever had the misfortune to sing or listen to.
When Miami Opera asked us, they gave us a copy of the *Crucible*
recording, which was fabulous. It's a gorgeous work, but it has a great
story based on the Arthur Miller play. Well, we signed to play a

husband and wife, and what could be better? We were also guaranteed that the music was absolutely great.

BIBLE: When we were doing *Crucible,* Robert was writing it as we went along, and we got a few pages at a time, and we would speak up and say, "Look, that's not a good note for me," or something like that. It was all very amicable.

LEAR: We were told the music for *Midnight* was not finished when we signed the contract, but we didn't get the last ten pages of the score until three days before the dress rehearsal. It was worse than a Broadway musical. Tom's part wasn't so terrible. It wasn't great, but ... The libretto was written by a close friend of Robert Ward's who was a writer on nuclear warfare for *The New Yorker* magazine. He was very famous because he had contracted cancer through his studies.

STEWART: He was one of the first nuclear protesters and he contracted leukemia, probably because of his activities there.

LEAR: But his knowledge of opera and libretti was very limited. There were things in the libretto that you couldn't possibly deal with. My big aria began with the line, "A dictator is on the march again. Have you forgotten what the heck that means?" I've done a lot of contemporary opera and composers usually ask you about changes. So I mentioned to Robert that there were some words in the libretto that would have to be changed to make the work more singable. I had no problem with the music, but just some of the words. And he said, "No, I won't change one word." I told him I wasn't asking him to change the music, but he said that this man was his friend and he wouldn't change one word. Well, I said it was unsingable, and he was just a son of a bitch, really terrible. My opening line was "I'm glad I didn't bake a soufflé." I wouldn't even let my mother come down to see it. Every major paper reported that the text was one of the most ridiculous in the history of opera. The Miami paper reprinted all these lousy reviews and we just stuck them all in the score and sent them back to him. It was a horrible experience and I want the world to know about it.

THEODOR UPPMAN: I just have the feeling that a lot of what's being written nowadays isn't going to last, and that really bothers me. Being an American, it really bothers me that we don't have more American opera.

TOZZI: Ignoring the essentials is causing a breakdown in music today as well as in voices. How many voices are ruined because they sing rock? How many ears are now tuned to raucousness instead of the beauty of line and the bel canto approach to music? A lot of the pop singers today sound like they're trying to pass a peach pit.

C U R T I N : Conservatism now is something I find hard to understand, except in an economic sense. You have to give people *Bohème, Rigoletto,* et cetera, and everyone's upset to see a house that isn't full, but people forget about the early failure of works like *Traviata*. I really don't understand it since people will buy new things in every other area.

T O Z Z I : I was working last year in *Gianni Schicchi,* and a young singer in the company came up to me and said he wished he could work with someone from "the old school." I said to him, "Young man, remember, there's no such thing as an old or a new school. There's just a good and a bad school."

On October 22, 1953, the New York City Opera staged the American premiere of Gottfried von Einem's opera *The Trial*. Although it is not an American opera, the production in English was directed by Otto Preminger and will be remembered mainly for introducing Phyllis Curtin to the operatic world. Curtin went on to become the foremost interpreter of contemporary American works.

C U R T I N : It was very interesting working with Otto Preminger. I was commuting every day from Swarthmore, Pennsylvania, and the schedule was very hectic. In any opera company—especially one with seasons as short as we had at City Opera in those days—you have to plan rehearsals very carefully, and after a two-hour rehearsal for *The Trial,* some of us would have to run off to something else. Preminger had never worked in a situation like this, and he might spend two hours on one little bit of business. Well, he'd be ready to move on and we'd say, "Sorry, we have to move on to something else." And he would be beside himself and he did everything he could with management to hold us.

As an actor, Preminger had specialized in portraying Nazis in films such as *Stalag 17.* As a director, he made actresses out of stars such as Linda Darnell and Gene Tierney. His methods, however, were a bit on the strange side. For example, during the filming of *The Cardinal,* he reportedly calmed an actress having difficulty with a scene by shaking her and screaming, "Relax!"

CURTIN: He was totally exasperated by the musical score. He would get wonderful ideas and they worked, but he didn't plan on the fact that there was music in between our singing, so our movements couldn't be as flowing as he wanted them. Any director who was not musically grounded would have frustrations over that. Lots of them do.

After *The Trial,* Preminger went on to direct the film versions of *Carmen Jones,* starring Dorothy Dandridge and Harry Belafonte, and *Porgy and Bess,* with Dandridge and Sidney Poitier.

CURTIN: He was extremely imaginative as far as the piece was concerned. He was impatient but good to us. I don't remember him making a scene or anything like that. His scenes were all about doing a new opera in a repertory theater. That was his big problem. The production was just marvelous, but unfortunately the music was just not very substantial. It was a wonderful debut piece, though. Who could ask for a better debut than playing three different roles? It never came back to the repertory, though, and to my knowledge hasn't been done in this country since then, although in Europe it continued to turn up. I would have loved to see it as a movie. I think it would have worked beautifully there. But it was my debut in New York and I remember it terribly well.

Douglas Moore's *The Ballad of Baby Doe* had its world premiere in Central City, Colorado, in 1956. A truly American piece, it was set in and around that mountain community and was critically very well received. Among its other virtues, the opera provided star roles for both a soprano and a mezzo. Among those who have benefited from Moore's largess are Frances Bible, Joyce Castle, Laurel Hurley, and Erie Mills.

BIBLE: I was offered *Baby Doe* first at Central City, and I didn't know anything about it but that I would be playing Horace Tabor's first wife, and I thought, "Oh, good, a nice small part and I can have a good vacation at the same time."

JOYCE CASTLE: I love the opera. Augusta Tabor is so sympathetic. She was very strong but very much a New England lady raised for hard work, but in a cold way. She went through all the hardship, a real pioneer woman. It's also a really loud sing.

BIBLE: When I first saw the score for *Baby Doe,* I realized she was in practically every scene and it was a much greater part than I thought it would be.

CASTLE: Augusta is sometimes called the American Amneris. I don't know if I'd go that far, but it needs and shows off the whole mezzo range. It has long, long line and requires lyric singing. It requires a lot.

BIBLE: Augusta's the best-written part in the opera. You can hardly miss. It's written better. She builds into a real character, a real person. The other two parts, Baby Doe and Horace, never really come alive as she does. She's really more of a human being.

CASTLE: Just as she gets her husband through school, this little twerp walks in, and that's one hell of a hurt. I also think she regrets a lot. She sees this free-spirited thing and she sees what she missed. She lashes back, but she still has feelings for the man or she wouldn't come back and fight for him. She's set up fantastically in the opera. The aria in the final scene is just fabulous.

LAUREL HURLEY: When you're doing Baby, you just can't think of Augusta. You just have to throw yourself into it and be totally selfish, because I think that's the way she was. She was thoughtless. If you're playing the part and you start to think about the moral issues involved, you're in trouble.

ERIE MILLS: It's written very weirdly. I don't think people are very sympathetic to Baby Doe, and then you come to the very last scene and people go, "Oh, so what." The only thing is that you've had these brief glimpses of her loving Horace.

HURLEY: I definitely think she was in love with him. Her first marriage was a disaster and this is it.

MILLS: We certainly get the great tunes, but it is a strange part. Augusta shows such strength of character and such torment. Baby Doe is so well written for the soprano, but the character . . .

HURLEY: I loved Baby. I got very involved in the character. I read everything I could about her. When I was in Colorado, we drove up to see the shack at the mine where she died.

M I L L S : I remember reading Beverly Sills's book, and she said that it was hard to make Baby Doe the person that she really was because Moore wrote such glorious music for her, and I agree. I think she has the great tunes, and yet Augusta is the character that most people identify with because she develops, whereas Baby Doe has all this glorious music and yet it doesn't really fit with what the character was.

H U R L E Y : I would get very emotional while singing the part and that was a big danger. I had to control my emotions so I wouldn't go to pieces at the end. I wanted to get involved in it more, but I would have been sobbing on the floor and I wouldn't have been able to sing.

M I L L S : The music is great, great, great, all the way through, but I really think, in spite of all this great music, the composer hasn't allowed for much character development.

The 46th Street Theatre welcomed *Regina,* the musical version of Lillian Hellman's play *The Little Foxes,* on October 31, 1949. Four years later, on April 2, 1953, Marc Blitzstein's musical adaptation was officially sanctioned as an opera when it was revived by the New York City Opera. The one constant in the two productions was Brenda Lewis—an award-winning Birdie on Broadway and the venomous Regina at City Opera. The work has found its way into opera houses all over the world and had a major revival in 1988 at the Long Wharf Theatre in New Haven, Connecticut, directed by Arvin Brown and starring Rosalind Elias.

B R E N D A L E W I S : It was a perfectly natural transition for me, going from Birdie to Regina. With Birdie, Bobby Lewis, our director, left me pretty much alone. There was a section of the set near the staircase which was Birdie's place. I would just sit there and listen so I could respond when I was summoned, but it really separated her from the other characters and allowed her to retire when she couldn't bear to listen to them. It made it easier for me to create my own world and stay separate from the rest.

R O S A L I N D E L I A S : *Regina*'s not a hard piece to think of as theater, because Blitzstein has done the crossover so beautifully from opera to theater.

L E W I S : The charisma of an actor can really be translated into energy which an audience feels. When you're really intent on what you're doing, that's what makes an actor more interesting onstage. I think that was the effect I created with Birdie, because it wasn't a very big role, but Bobbie helped with that and I just did it.

E L I A S : Regina was written for a soprano and that's hard, but she has a low register, too, and I think that would be hard for sopranos except for Brenda, who did have that lower register. I heard her, of course, and she was wonderful.

L E W I S : Compared to Birdie, Regina is a lollipop. It's all there, all written for you, like Carmen.

In her later years, Lillian Hellman admitted that she was upset when friends told her that Birdie's third-act scene was more touching with music than without. She admitted that most authors don't like to hear that they've been improved upon. However, the performance of Brenda Lewis probably had a lot to do with it. On opening night, Lewis literally stopped the show.

L E W I S : When we did it at City Opera, we had Herman Shumlin as director, and he had done the original play with Tallulah Bankhead. From the rehearsals we had, his concerns weren't musical at all. I did what he told me, but it wasn't anything like the work we'd done before with Bobby Lewis

E L I A S : Arvin Brown was a wonderful director. Look at all the actors in his plays who've gone on to win Tonys. He's not at all rigid. He knows how to adjust.

L E W I S : The Long Wharf production was marvelous. It was a heroic effort to bring a classic American opera back to life and Roz Elias was wonderful as Regina. Then *The New York Times* panned it and the work was set back again. I can't believe that a work can be tossed aside when the recording has created such excitement and loyalty from people. I can't believe that such a work can't have a life on the stage. If someone pans the music, I have to question his ears.

Leonard Bernstein described the score as "A kind of apex, a summation of what Blitzstein has been trying to do. The words sing themselves, so to speak. The result is true song—a long, flexible, pragmatic, dramatic song."

E L I A S : Marc's recitative is so special. You're singing and you're talking at the same time, but it's really beautiful.

L E W I S : He was a wonderful orchestrator and he did all his own orchestrations, which is not true for a lot of people on his scale. He knew what he was putting in there and he made everything count. The orchestra underlines a lot of the action in an opera and fills in emotionally when things are not being said or sung.

E L I A S : It's too bad he didn't live longer to write more like this. It's all so singable. As far as contemporary pieces are concerned, he wrote the words theatrically.

George London, Roberta Peters, Lili Chookasian, Morley Meredith, and a cast almost of thousands were gathered together on the stage of the Metropolitan Opera House on January 23, 1963, for the American premiere of Gian Carlo Menotti's *The Last Savage,* a comic look at anthropology, the mores of the day, and life in general.

L I L I   C H O O K A S I A N : *Last Savage* was a lot of fun, but a lot of work, too. We changed things around a lot and added our own little touches.

M O R L E Y   M E R E D I T H : I was excited about the work because I had done a lot of Broadway, and this was by no means a musical comedy but it had a lot of life and movement in it. With *Savage* we had the chance to do comedy, after all the staid, stereotyped operas. Plus, I was pleased that my role was very substantial.

R O B E R T A   P E T E R S : I was so excited about it. To have the composer alive and there! If you wanted a high note, you just asked for it—no, I'm kidding. But there was great excitement at the Met when we did it. It was one of the first new operas done at the Met in a long time. And Gian Carlo being there was wonderful. He wrote it with me in mind. He said he did, anyway, even though it had been performed in Paris before.

M E R E D I T H : Menotti is a wonderful man of the theater, but people unfortunately go to the opera house for the classics. Even something like *Wozzeck*—no matter how well it's done—after the first couple of performances, there's no audience for it. The same is true for *Billy Budd,* which is one of the best productions the Met has ever done, and yet they can never sell the house for it. When you're spending a hundred bucks a seat for a ticket in the orchestra on a Saturday night, it's hard to get a lot of people to try something new.

P E T E R S : There was a lot of rehearsal time given to that opera—learning it, getting the edges on the opera and the roles. Then when we moved to the stage, Gian Carlo was the stage director, too, so it was all very close-knit. My part was a very frivolous, spoiled rich girl. She was an anthropologist and I wore this wonderful pith helmet. It was a lot of fun. Her second-act aria was all over the place: laughing, up and down scales, lots of coloratura—very high, then low. And we had a wonderful cast—Gedda and Stratas, and of course Lili and Morley, and so many others.

C H O O K A S I A N : I think Menotti thought the work out very well and he knew his singers very well. He had chosen us and written for us, so he directed accordingly. The costumes also were great and they spared no expense.

P E T E R S : Gian Carlo really wanted us all to ask him questions. If we didn't like something or feel comfortable, he always wanted to see what he could do to change it. It was just fabulous to have him there.

M E R E D I T H : As a musician you could deal with him and he'd alter things to suit your strengths. Who knows better what he wants than the composer?

C H O O K A S I A N : Everyone was so good. George London in a part like that—such a staid, stately individual to be cast as this savage! And Roberta was delightful.

P E T E R S : We had a great first night. No trepidation and no more nerves than usual.

Then the reviews came out. *The New York Times* was not kind. Audiences did not come and the reputation of the work was damaged.

P E T E R S : I think the *Times* review is what killed it. I really do. Mr. Bing was so incensed at that time. He was really very upset. People mainly read the *Times,* though we had more papers in those days. But I think people are snobs. If the *Times* says it's not good, that's what they're going to think.

C H O O K A S I A N : It obviously wasn't accepted on the level of a bona fide opera by the critics and I really don't know why. The audiences really seemed to love it. The critics take Menotti lightly and I think he's laughing all the way to the bank.

MEREDITH: The average operagoer doesn't care so much about the opera itself as about who's singing. I know what's singable and I know that this score is. However, it was a piece you had to listen to and follow. With something like *Traviata,* you know immediately what's going on, so it's like the lazy man's way out. People don't want to be educated, necessarily. They just want to be entertained.

CHOOKASIAN: As good as Menotti is, he's never been realized as a truly top-notch composer, and I will never understand why. That's just what critics think, not what I think or audiences do.

After the opening *Savage* reviews appeared, Rudolf Bing, never one to back away from a fight, came up with a special ad to refute the *Times* critic who labeled the work "A Broadway musical masquerading as an opera." The ad, which was headlined WHICH PAPER DO YOU READ, quoted other more favorable reviews: "The Metropolitan Opera has a hit on its hands." "It's great fun." "The crowd loved it." ". . . probably the best opera buffa by a living composer."

MEREDITH: My role, Mr. Scattergood, had a wonderful patter song that I could relate to and was very comfortable with. Every performance was fun and slightly different.

PETERS: The music was light and charming. I don't know if it was Verdi or Puccini, but it certainly was singable.

CHOOKASIAN: If you're doing what you want to do and you're enjoying it, what could be better?

PETERS: I'd love to see it revived. I don't know if it would find more acceptance today. Gian Carlo's had a lot of problems with the critics over the years, yet he's gone on to do his thing. People love his work. The audiences were just terrific—warm and responsive and laughing, because the whole thing was a spoof.

MEREDITH: With *The Last Savage* we had a play, a real musical event. With most operas, the story may be great, but the librettos can be ridiculous.

CHOOKASIAN: Strangely enough, it really wasn't successful in New York, but when we took it on tour, it was always the first production and they loved it.

PETERS: Mr. Bing was such a ham and he loved to get in on the act. Well, in this opera in the second act there was a big cocktail party in modern dress; people were milling around. And one night, there he was. At another performance, he came and swept up after the party.

MEREDITH: Leontyne Price appeared in one of the performances in the party scene.

CHOOKASIAN: When we did it on tour in Dallas, they had real lions at the opening night party, but then Dallas has to do things in a big way.

Eleanor Steber created the title role in Samuel Barber's *Vanessa,* which premiered in a production directed by its librettist, Gian Carlo Menotti, at the Metropolitan Opera House on January 15, 1958. The role was later sung by Brenda Lewis and Johanna Meier, among others. Vanessa's niece, Erika, was almost definitively created by Rosalind Elias, the family doctor by Giorgio Tozzi, and the Baroness by Regina Resnik. Steber, Elias, Tozzi, and Resnik are fortunate in that their performances have been immortalized on a recording, still a best seller, that captures the brilliance of that triumphant opening night.

ELEANOR STEBER: This opera was probably one of the truly great experiences of my life. I learned it in six weeks. I had never even looked at the score before someone at the Metropolitan suggested that perhaps I should do it. I was upset because I had not been considered when they were originally casting it. I was, after all, the outstanding American soprano at that time at the Metropolitan. I felt very much left out. I know Callas was approached, but I wouldn't call her—at that time—an American soprano. I saw the work again recently in St. Louis, at the thirtieth-anniversary production, and I was absolutely bowled over. It was such an eye-opener and an ear-opener. The beautiful romantic line and melody and the psychological content and intent in that opera are very deep. For the first time I was able to look at it and see Erika as who she was. As Vanessa I wasn't concerned with Erika's problems, only with my own. Seeing the whole thing just overwhelmed me.

TOZZI: I really do think it is a work that merits being performed fairly frequently. The vocal challenges in the part of Vanessa are really tremendous and Eleanor handled it very, very well. We were fortunate in having her. And, of course, Erika was Rosalind Elias, a very fine artist with a great velvety voice and a marvelous personality.

S T E B E R : It's not an obvious opera for an audience. You have to be psychologically involved, and I think most people want to just enjoy what they can see and hear without a lot of effort. *Vanessa* requires work on the part of the audience.

R E S N I K : I found the opera much more effective than the short life it had would suggest. The greatest thing for me about working on *Vanessa* was the chance to work with Dimitri Mitropoulos, an incredible conductor. He was a master at tempi. I think everything Sam Barber wrote in that score and wanted to say was brought home by Mitropoulos.

S T E B E R : It's a very difficult opera to cast and it's very difficult to sing.

T O Z Z I : It was wonderful to work on in every respect. Menotti was so sensitive to the dramatic and musical values that are wed in opera. I look on it as a very happy time in my career.

R E S N I K : It was all a very harmonious experience. There were very fine performances by everyone. As colleagues we were all very compatible.

J O H A N N A   M E I E R : When we did it, there were some production drawbacks because it was going to be televised, but overall it was pretty effective. What beautiful music it is, too!

L E W I S : The music is lush, but the story just doesn't move you. The characters are all somewhat two-dimensional. I don't think that the music grabs you, except for the quintet at the end, which is as good as the group things that Strauss did.

T O Z Z I : Regina Resnik had the role of the Grandmother, which was not a big singing part. She sat there most of the evening knitting. When she showed us what she had done, if there can be such a thing as abstract knitting, she had achieved it.

R E S N I K : The first thing I think of, when I think of Vanessa, was the day I told Sam Barber that I disagreed with Mr. Bing and didn't want to sing the role, because there was nothing there to sing.

E L I A S : I wonder if the book of *Vanessa* wasn't the problem, and why it's not done more often. That might be a problem for popular acceptance, but not the music. It's great music.

R E S N I K : Sam Barber told me my part required a great actress. But he did level with me about the fact that she didn't sing much, and he was right about that.

T O Z Z I : It's a wonderful thing to rehearse an opera with the composer present. Both Menotti and Barber were present during rehearsals, and of course Menotti directed, and they were both great gentlemen, so it was a very joyful collaboration.

S T E B E R : It was a great experience working with Sam and Gian Carlo. It was hectic, though, to try to learn that role in six weeks. Also, Gian Carlo asked me to do things that were rather difficult. But I managed to do them, and we came up with a wonderful production.

T O Z Z I : Barber actually composed the Doctor's aria in Act Three for me. He put it in to give my character a moment, and it's really a touching, poignant piece.

E L I A S : I auditioned for Sam and Gian Carlo, and I used some of the *Hoffmann* because it showed I could go up as high as they wanted, and they didn't change a note. I had to audition three times and then they took me. I don't know of another time in my career when I enjoyed a role so much. It was a major challenge and everyone needs that in their career.

T O Z Z I : We all had a great sense of camaraderie. There were no prima donnas in the sense of the insecure rantings and ravings that give prima donnas a bad name.

E L I A S : Erika was actually the turning point in my career. And I'll never forget working with Gian Carlo. When the rest of the cast would break for lunch, he would have me stay and work with him. He taught me a great deal about acting; it was really my foundation.

L E W I S : I love Sam Barber's music and I think there are times when he created really wonderful and poignant moments. I don't think this is a work that audiences will ever stand up and cheer for.

S T E B E R : I had just met a man that I was in love with, and it was during the rehearsal period of *Vanessa,* so everything was very rose-colored for me then. And it definitely was my role, and the recording—which I think is beautiful—bears that out.

E L I A S : Erika is *the* role in the opera. It's the best role and I'm grateful I had it. It was written for a soprano, and Max Rudolf, who was then Mr. Bing's assistant, went to Sam Barber and said, "I think I have the right person for this role, but she's a mezzo." And Sam said, "Well, let me hear her."

L E W I S : Erika is a tragic figure, and if Barber had been in a workshop situation like they have today, someone would have told him that she was also the central figure. Maybe then he would have had a masterwork.

S T E B E R : It's not necessarily true that the role of Erika is more developed than Vanessa. She's just more obvious. Vanessa is much more subtle.

T O Z Z I : I think that Erika is really the heroine of the piece, and I don't think Sam Barber intended that, but it doesn't demean his talent in any way.

S T E B E R : I think that theory came from Callas, who said she'd never appear in an opera where she would be second to the real heroine, who was Erika. I don't agree with that.

L E W I S : Something real happened to her. She's a real person who took real chances and paid the consequences. Vanessa is really an airhead, a nothing. Why do you care about her? Call the opera *Erika*.

S T E B E R : You couldn't call the opera *Erika* because she would not come off in the right light. She has to be there as Vanessa's niece. You have to have the contrast.

L E W I S : I sang Vanessa with very little preparation, but no matter how much you think about the role, how much can you think about this woman? How can you get into a person who's so shallow, so wrapped up in herself, and so vain? OK, she's narcissistic, but she really floats on the surface of life and feelings. I just don't care about her.

S T E B E R : There are two protagonists and each is a force in her own way being manipulated by life.

M E I E R : Vanessa was a fascinating character for me. She was ultimately strong enough with young Anatol to take what she could get and settle for it. In a way it's sad, but then again it's not, because this is what ultimately is going to make her happy.

S T E B E R : Vanessa is much more important for the opera to make its statement. So I was not aware that there was any overwhelming personality as far as Erika was concerned, compared to Vanessa.

L E W I S : I couldn't understand how the woman could be so shallow. People who delude themselves the way that woman does, and live with it, and wreak havoc on all around them—the phoniness of it all! I can't relate to that.

STEBER: I love the part and I love Sam and his music. He was a very great part of the latter part of my career. In my concerts, I did many of his songs and, of course, "Knoxville," which he wrote for me and became something of a specialty of mine. Then to do the wonderful Vanessa was just the culmination of a great and wonderful experience.

MEIER: The audience response that we got was warm and that should indicate that the opera should be brought back again and again.

TOZZI: The work itself met with generally good reviews. One of the things that was very interesting to me was the way the musicians reacted to the work. Sometimes they cast a jaundiced eye on new pieces. But when we brought this back, some of them came up to me at rehearsal and said, "You know, we forgot how good this opera really is." That's a pretty good test.

If Alex Trebek asked his *Jeopardy!* contestants to name the greatest American opera of the twentieth century, their answer would probably be George Gershwin's masterpiece, *Porgy and Bess.* The work premiered on September 30, 1935, with Anne Wiggins Brown and Todd Duncan in the title roles and has been performed since then in opera houses all over the world. It premiered at the Met in 1985.

ANNE WIGGINS BROWN: I had no idea of the impact of the work when I first saw the score. I met Gershwin very early on when he was looking for singers and dancers. They wanted technically educated singers as well as jazz singers. Of course, that appealed to me because I was still a student at Juilliard. I wrote Gershwin a letter right away and got an answer in two or three days, went down, and sang a lot of things for them. And this was very early on. From that point, George would phone me and ask me to sing what he had just put down on paper as the opera grew. This was before it was completed.

TODD DUNCAN: I said to Gershwin in a nice way—or at least I hope it was a nice way, a gentlemanly way—that I wasn't sure if I was even interested in doing the piece. Before I first heard *Porgy,* I had been sort of living in a musical cocoon all my own. I was teaching music at Howard University in Washington, D.C. You sort of think you know it all and George Gershwin was sort of, at that time, what I'd consider Tin Pan Alley, and I just couldn't conceive of his writing an opera. So I had to wait and see for myself and I had to be convinced to do it.

LEONA MITCHELL: I've done a lot of Besses onstage in L.A. and Detroit and Atlanta. I don't think a lot of people know that. I'm glad to go back to her now, but I'm sorry about years ago when people had no other choice—or black sopranos had no other choice—than to sing that one part. I didn't want to be put in that slot, so I avoided it for years. I'm sorry about that now, because I absolutely love the part.

HAROLYN BLACKWELL: The first production I did was in Charleston, and it was wonderful to be able to explore Catfish Row, and I had the chance to get the dialect and understand how the people think. It was fascinating. The Met production is so huge, you lose sight of the fact that it's a small community where people are living on top of one another. You need an intimacy. The Glyndebourne production was like that. People were drawn into this community where everyone was living so close to one another.

GRACE BUMBRY: I didn't want to do the role. I went in there kicking and screaming. But I decided if the Metropolitan was going to do it anyway and they had asked me, I was the right person to do it. I thought it should be brought in on a fine note and I thought I could certainly contribute to the production.

DUNCAN: Once I heard the music from "Summertime" on, I knew that here was an idiom that was new; that there was an ethnic honesty, truth, and spiritual awareness in the work that was truly American, and I felt was great—and I could not resist it.

BLACKWELL: As Clara, going out there and starting the opera singing "Summertime," which everyone knows and loves, was terrifying. I realized that I had to go out there and set the tone and I'd better be good.

BROWN: I remember, the first time I heard "Summertime" I fell in love with the melody, and I said to George, "I must sing this in the opera." Well, he laughed at me and explained that Clara was a mother and Bess was as far from that as she can be.

BLACKWELL: Each time Clara sings "Summertime," it's an expression of what's happening in her life. You have the same music, but it's interpreted in three different ways. It has to be.

BROWN: Before the opera was finished, he had written a trio for the first scene in the third act, but one day he said to me, "You're going to sing 'Summertime.'" I was delighted, but I didn't know how he was going to do it. Well, when Clara goes out in the storm, she gives Bess the baby and tells her to hold it until she comes back. Of course, she never returns and Bess sings the lullaby to the baby. I was very proud to have a little finger—even if indirectly—in some of the arrangements.

BLACKWELL: I'm totally convinced it's an opera.

MITCHELL: You have to have very talented people to do it. People love Gershwin's music, but you need good singers and actors, or it's nice but . . .

ROBERTA ALEXANDER: Anyone who's ever sung *Porgy and Bess* would never ask, "Is it an opera?"

MITCHELL: It annoys me when the best people aren't used or they're cast just because they're black.

BLACKWELL: I think Gershwin's intention was to have this piece, which contained jazz and black folk music, accepted as an opera and I think he succeeded. Because of the hit songs, some people assume it's simple, and it's not.

BUMBRY: It's a very difficult piece of music. I thought it would be easy, like an operetta. Having worked on it, I definitely think it's an opera—maybe not a grand opera, but it should be seen at the Metropolitan.

BROWN: I knew Gershwin was a genius even from my high school days, from *American in Paris, Rhapsody in Blue,* and other things. I expected *Porgy and Bess* to be something special, and even though I was a classical singer and really didn't go in for jazz, I loved George's music—all of it. I was happy and very proud to be a part of it.

ALEXANDER: People call this a "folk opera," but whatever you call it, it's a classic—one of the greatest pieces of music ever written. Whatever word you're singing fits right in with that music at that time. It really is a jewel in every sense—one of the most beautiful things ever written.

DUNCAN: I had no idea of the importance of the work when I first became involved in it.

BROWN: I did feel that I was a part of something historic, and I really enjoyed working with all the people, and of course I had a very good relationship—friendship—with Gershwin. I had a lot of criticism, too. It wasn't all peaceful.

ALEXANDER: I don't think Bess is a horrible person. Some people think I make her too sweet, but there has to be some redeeming feature in her or why would all these people be running after her? She does have a drug problem.

BUMBRY: One of the critics wrote that my Bess was too mature or matronly or too old or something like that. I think he said that because he was accustomed to seeing a young Bess, and I don't think that's what the work is about. Anne Brown told me when she did it, they tried to make her look older. In the score, they say that Crown needs a younger woman, so she couldn't have been in her twenties. She had to be a certain age—in her thirties or thirty-five or whatever. Critics should do a little bit more homework.

MITCHELL: I don't think she was a tramp. She was a loose woman, a very free spirit for the thirties. But she was only with two guys, and by today's standards that would be nothing.

BROWN: Bess was in many ways a weak woman, a very weak woman. My Bess was not bad at all. She was just water in the hands of Crown until she met Porgy, who gave her strength. When he disappeared, she was just a ploy. She fell into Sporting Life's hands.

MITCHELL: It's a real challenge playing that part. I really love to kick up my heels. It's a whole different thing for me.

DUNCAN: There really was no special moment for me in the work. That would change from week to week. The entrance always meant a lot to me, and sometimes it was the little crap game where Porgy decides how lucky he is. There were other periods where I really loved "Bess, You Is My Woman Now." I had to learn about breathing and posture, so the fact that Porgy was always on his knees wasn't a problem. Whether I was flat on the floor or crawling up the steps or falling down them, it didn't really make any difference. I always saw to it that I had the right posture so that I could produce the voice. At first I couldn't crawl and sing, couldn't do it. I had to learn to do that. It was difficult because it disturbs the whole breathing apparatus.

BROWN: In the beginning I did all eight performances a week and it was hard, but I was twenty-two then.

DUNCAN: When I hear singers today say they can only sing the role twice a week or once a month or whatever, I laugh to myself and say, "Maybe that's why I had a long career. I learned how to sing. I was doing it right."

BROWN: I listened to a lot of criticism about being a part of this. Even my father said I was just driving another nail into the coffin as far as the image of Negroes was concerned. I just didn't see it that way. I naturally didn't want to do anything that would bring disgrace on the race, but I could think of French or Italian operas that were just as bad—if you can say bad—as *Porgy and Bess* was for my people. Look at *Carmen*! You can go right down the list.

BUMBRY: Once I got past the racial aspects, I was home free, because it really is a part of American history, isn't it? No matter how we look at it, it's still there, and there are a lot of other operas that have librettos that are just as bad. Carmen is certainly not a nun.

DUNCAN: I did the work with an interracial cast in Copenhagen and it worked. It maintains itself beautifully.

MITCHELL: I know Gershwin was against this, but I saw an integrated cast in Zurich with the chorus in blackface, and I didn't even know they weren't black!

BUMBRY: The sound of that chorus at the Met was absolutely unbelievable. Most of them were church singers or had been doing concerts and they were so good. I'm a voice freak and to hear all those beautiful voices in one room was absolutely mind boggling.

DUNCAN: As far as I'm concerned, with American composers, Gershwin was number one. I can't help feeling that way.

BROWN: I remember when we were supposed to play at the National Theatre in Washington and then it was totally segregated. Well, I was from Baltimore and I wanted my family and friends to come those forty miles to see me, so I said, "I'll be damned if I'm going to stand on that stage and play and sing Bess if they can't see me." It created quite an uproar, and people told me I'd be black-balled and "You'll never get another job in the theater." But I didn't care, and one by one other people took it up, and for that week the theater was integrated. We were shy then about making demands and putting things down, but even today if I get mad enough, I don't care what I say. Well, things changed for that one week. Ethel Waters came in next in something called *At Home Abroad* and it was segregated again. It took twenty years before those bans were lifted,

ALEXANDER: I think a generation of black people is going to come along that has not had to deal with any of the things that I've had to deal with, as far as racism is concerned. Then they will be able to look at this piece as strictly a piece of history. For me, it's still too close to the things I've experienced.

UPPMAN: I think you have to have a very clever librettist for an opera in English to work. You need to know where to cut and have an understanding of what's going to go and what's not going to go.

Once thought the shining light of American opera, Leonard Bernstein wrote his one-act opera *Trouble in Tahiti* in 1952. Its sequel, *A Quiet Place,* didn't appear until 1983.

UPPMAN: I think it was especially hard for the Houston cast, as far as *A Quiet Place*'s reception was concerned. There were all these little old ladies sitting there and hearing all these four-letter words and seeing displays of anger and homosexuality. But the work really has its place. It may take a little while for it to be appreciated for what it is, but it's also tremendously American and a very up-to-date work. It grows on you and it's very gripping when you see it.

ALEXANDER: I don't think I want to do any more modern opera. I don't like minimal music. I've done a lot of it—I like to listen to it but not perform it. It doesn't give me any great vocal satisfaction.

From *Susannah* in 1955 to *Willie Stark* in 1981, Carlisle Floyd has been one of America's most prolific operatic composers.

CURTIN: Carlisle Floyd is very much in the mainstream of music. He's not difficult at all. He's not in the twelve-tone position and he's not into minimalism. He's always been mainstream. He showed me *Susannah* in Colorado and I was really taken aback, it was so brilliant. I grew up in the hill country of West Virginia and I just adored this work. I managed to clear time in my schedule and we did the premiere in Tallahassee.

UPPMAN: *Susannah* is a wonderful opera in its folk theme and the feeling for the mountain country. It was an ideal choice to use for an opera.

CURTIN: The other work of Carlisle's that I was mad about and I think should be done over and over was *Wuthering Heights.* That's a nifty piece. It's not easy, but I don't know for the life of me why people don't do it. It's a miracle. The characters are beautifully realized all the way through—every single solitary one of them.

TOZZI: It's wonderful when you find a composer who recognizes the importance of voices. Yes, the orchestra is important, I'd be the last one in the world to deny that, but I think there should be a balance. I'd hate to be starting a career at this point.

CURTIN: Carlisle's *Passion of Jonathan Wade* didn't work. I could say it was not that good, but who am I to judge? I don't really remember the music well enough. It was a wonderful idea and I think it needs to be stronger in the strong things that are are there. When you look at the works of Verdi or anyone, there are strong and weak works.

RON BOTTCHER: It was an interesting piece, but boy, it needed to be cut. I thought there were a few things wrong with the orchestrations, too. It was all too big, an extravaganza. I don't think it would ever be staged again, but who knows?

UPPMAN: Carlisle Floyd is very good and he has done some wonderful work, but in *Jonathan Wade* he just attempted too much. He tried to get the whole Reconstruction period into the opera.

BOTTCHER: His music is great but hard to sing. It goes low and then high, and he brings loud chords in underneath. It was a difficult piece to do.

UPPMAN: We only did two performances, but it actually went very well.

BOTTCHER: One thing I remember was there were three little black boys, and they sat there singing, "I'm free, I'm free, free as a frog and nobody goin' to come after me. I'm free, free, free as a frog. . . ." And this went on and on for a very long time, till everyone screamed, "Get them off the stage!"

When the new Metropolitan Opera House opened in 1966, the inaugural presentation was the world premiere of Samuel Barber's *Antony and Cleopatra,* from Shakespeare's play. It was not a triumph. The physical production and the difficulties the grandeur of the sets produced overshadowed Barber's music. Among the members of the original cast were Rosalind Elias, baritone Ron Bottcher in his Met debut, and the veteran tenor Andrea Velis.

BOTTCHER: There were so many things that didn't work during the rehearsals for *Antony*. The turntable broke down and the orchestra pit kept going up and down. It was chaos.

ANDREA VELIS: I love the opera. I realize I'm one of the few people who did or do love it, but it was just overproduced. We had just come into the Metropolitan Opera. It was the first thing we did there, and Zeffirelli had visions of Cecil B. De Mille, but no one knew how to work the stages at the Met. We were walking around blindly back there with high gaping abysses in front of us, because we didn't really know where we were. If we were doing it today, it would be fine.

BOTTCHER: There was terrific stuff musically in the work. I'd really like to hear the piece again.

ELIAS: Samuel Barber is one of the greatest American composers. Did you ever see the film *Platoon*? It won all the awards and everything and I loved it, but I wonder if it wasn't a *great* film because of Sam's music. All the awards were deserved, but he should have gotten some, too. I even loved *Antony and Cleopatra*. I shouldn't say "even." When we did it, they did a documentary where you didn't see the opera but just heard the music, which was beautiful.

VELIS: It was all too big. It got smaller as it went on—a row of pipes would be taken out or whatever—just so it could be more manageable.

ELIAS: It was too long and should have been cut, but the production did it in. I have great respect for Franco Zeffirelli, but he really missed the boat there. All those pipes—it was like someone was having an affair with a plumber. The whole set was pipes!

VELIS: I sat out in the house with Zeffirelli and saw the piece work. Several times it worked brilliantly. It was like a Hollywood movie, just wonderful, but then other times it just fell apart, because we didn't know how to do things technically, how things worked. So things went wrong even in performance.

BOTTCHER: I enjoyed working with Zeffirelli. He sort of acted it out for you and told you exactly where to go and what to do. I think Barber probably writes better for women than for men. *Vanessa* is certainly a show for the ladies and I think *Antony and Cleopatra* was, too. I only met Barber a couple of times. He was very quiet and withdrawn. He looked absolutely terrified. He didn't know what the hell was going on, either.

VELIS: The part that I did, Mardian, the eunuch, was originally offered to Regina Resnik. It consisted of one page of dialogue with Cleopatra, which was all Shakespeare had in the play. Sam Barber came up to Caramoor, where we were doing the American premiere of Britten's *Curlew River,* and he liked it so much he decided to write an aria for me. So he sent me this gorgeous little aria, and since he had no text, he had Stephen Spender write one for Mardian. Spender did it with the provision that his name would not appear next to Shakespeare's.

ELIAS: I just remember this soulful, dedicated man. He was a different Samuel Barber than I knew with *Vanessa.* He wasn't happy, but he was certainly the right choice to open the new opera house. His music got lost with the camels and everything else. You could barely hear the music, much less know what it was about.

The reviews for the opera and the production were devastating, although the singers were treated very well.

VELIS: I know they've tried to bring the opera back in smaller versions, but *Antony and Cleopatra* is in no way small as a play or an opera. It has to be big or don't bother with it! The play is just scene after scene and Sam didn't change that. I love his music. He was a wonderful composer and a wonderful gentleman. Of course he was; he wrote an aria for me.

Martin David Levy's operatic version of Eugene O'Neill's *Mourning Becomes Electra* was the second American opera to premiere in the Met's first season at Lincoln Center. It received more critical acclaim than *Antony and Cleopatra,* but unfortunately, there was little audience support for the work.

LEAR: Everything about that production was sensational. The cast was unbeatable and the set and lighting—everything.

BOTTCHER: This was not Benjamin Britten, but the music served the drama very well. They cut a lot of my music after the opening, which of course disturbed me, but it was too long. . . . They should have cut somebody else's music.

LEAR: I have to say, in Levy's defense, the vocal writing was beautiful. He wrote beautifully for the voice, but he didn't know how to orchestrate, so all the interludes were messed up. If he had a great orchestrator, I guarantee you that opera would still be done today all over the world.

STEWART: Levy's career as a composer has not been the greatest in the world and that's basically why. He hasn't been able to compete. The musical content was superb and it was exciting and interesting, but no one's going to remember it very much because of the flatness of the orchestrations.

LEAR: He composed at the piano. He wasn't a cerebral composer who knew how to do big orchestral scores. The work suffered for it. It was too sparse.

BOTTCHER: It was one of the best theatrical pieces I've ever seen done on the operatic stage. It was a wonderful ensemble piece and it all just came together. It worked. Why it wasn't recorded and done again, I really can't tell you. I think I learned more as an actor from doing that piece than from anything else I ever did.

TOZZI: Everything today seems to work against melodic writing. There are composers—even Broadway composers—today who are afraid of a musical idea, afraid they'll be thought of as old hat.

PETERS: I wish I knew why there aren't more American operas today. But first of all, commissions are very hard to come by. Opera is very expensive. If an opera is not a success, it's only a few performances and it won't ever be seen again.

CURTIN: Floyd's work is ideal for the typical operatic audience. This points to one of the most serious problems in American music. If you and I sat down and decided to paint a big canvas, we could probably sell it to someone the day after tomorrow. People will buy new art even if they've never heard of the painter. They will go to a new musical on Broadway, but try to get them to a new opera and they're scared to death.

BIBLE: Is it snob appeal? I think that's what holds back American opera. But then I'm a great believer of opera in English and I don't get far with that.

LEWIS: Look at *Regina.* Why the hell take a great play and make an opera out of it, if you're just going to stick Marc's songs in it and direct it like it's a play? That's wrong, too. You're shutting the audience off from the depths of experience you can reveal to them through what the composer has provided for them. You are losing the values.

P E T E R S : I think the problem is with singability. Some of these works are dissonant and they push and stretch the voice. Philip Glass is the one person who seems to be writing the most and is certainly the most successful, so he must have something that people relate to.

U P P M A N : There's so much twelve-tone music being written today that the average audience can't understand, and doesn't want to understand. I don't understand it. I'd hate to sing some of that stuff. It's hard on the voice as well.

P E T E R S : Maybe I shouldn't say this, but I'm not a great admirer of Philip Glass. It's just not my kind of opera. I'm not a minimalist and he likes to do a lot of things on one note. I was not brought up that way.

A L E X A N D E R : You know a composer doesn't know what he's doing when he writes on the weakest part of the voice. You have passages and passages on this part of the voice, which makes you very tired.

U P P M A N : In teaching today, I'm constantly stressing with my students the idea of getting words across. So many of them sing back in their throats and without the head resonance to speak all the words.

L E W I S : Your first responsibility is to make whatever it is understandable to the audience.

T O Z Z I : The problem with new opera today is a lack of singable music. There's also too much of an emphasis on what's not essential. The essential in opera is singing. That's what makes opera what it is. A lot of music and lyrics today sound like gibberish.

L E W I S : People all over the country are hungry for opera, but for most people opera is Pavarotti and *La Bohème,* and in a way that's wonderful. That's the way it starts.

S T E W A R T : You can't hit audiences over the head with new music and make it blatant. The music is there and people just have to accept it.

L E A R : Also, people don't allow themselves to laugh or express their emotions during "serious art." There's something sacrosanct about it and that's a shame.

L E W I S : I have to say that whenever I did *Regina,* there was a standing ovation at the end. Now I think that the theater has the obligation, not to educate, but to give those who want it the opportunity to see and hear works like *Regina*.

T O Z Z I : Essentials have been lost. Even on Broadway today, the star is a falling chandelier. I suppose I sound like a voice crying in the wilderness, but there are a lot of voices crying in the wilderness.

L E W I S : The bottom line is box office, and with the amount of money they charge for tickets now, I guess they have to think of that first. People are very resistant to modern works.

R E S N I K : There are no federations dedicated to the revival of singing saying, "We will give a certain amount of money to a commissioned work provided there are parts in it for four or five wonderful voices."

The recent crop of opera singers tackling the Broadway idiom is not a new phenomenon. But is it good or bad? At the turn of the century, Fritzi Scheff alternated between Marguerite and Nedda at the Met, and Victor Herbert operettas on Broadway. Jarmila Novotná sang the "Barcarole" from *Hoffmann* in Max Reinhardt's *Helen Goes to Troy* at the Alvin Theater on Broadway while still maintaining her status as an operatic diva. Julia Migenes created the role of Hodel in *Fiddler on the Roof* and, while singing eight performances a week, made her City Opera debut on Sunday, her day off from Broadway, in Menotti's *The Saint of Bleecker Street.* Jan Peerce and Robert Merrill both sang Tevye in *Fiddler;* Lawrence Tibbett replaced Ezio Pinza in *Fanny;* Robert Weede was in *The Most Happy Fella.* Examples are endless. But what do those involved think? Should musical comedy invade the opera house? How close are the two forms? What effect does it have on the voice when a singer switches from one area to another?

Jo Sullivan Loesser created the role of Rosabella in *The Most Happy Fella,* with music composed by her husband, Frank Loesser, after she had sung on the operatic stage.

J O   S U L L I V A N   L O E S S E R : Frank was definitely under the influence of opera then. I don't think he wanted to call it that, because he said that if they thought it was an opera, no one would come. But the form is definitely operatic and that says something.

E L I A S : I love the idea of bringing musical comedy into the opera houses.

TOZZI: There should be no problem about putting musical plays into opera houses. When producers and conductors are sensitive to both types of theater, it should be very easy.

PETERS: I rather like it. I don't think it can harm the singer if it's done correctly. There's a lot of crossover today and some singers are doing it very well. In the European houses, opera was done with operetta all the time.

PATRICE MUNSEL: When you start off in opera, people tend to want to keep you there. Whether it's good, bad, or indifferent, you're typed as an opera star. They just don't visualize you as being able to do things like *Mame* or *Dolly*.

JERRY HADLEY: Aside from jazz, American musical comedy is probably the only pure art form we have, and I see nothing wrong with my singing Ravenal in *Show Boat.* I think it's appropriate.

LEWIS: We didn't think of *Regina* as an opera, but as a piece of theater with music in which we believed most intensely. It never occurred to us that it wouldn't be a hit. But the piece was just a little early for people to accept it.

NEIL ROSENSHEIN: In an opera, the music could not be sung by nonoperatic voices, but the reverse might not be true. Operatic voices can sing musical comedy. A work like *Most Happy Fella* is an American opera in some ways, but it also has music of another genre in it and it has more dialogue than you would find in a standard opera.

LOESSER: When we first rehearsed the show, we spoke much less than we did when we arrived in New York. Now when the work is done, the spoken dialogue is very short, no more than ten minutes, and we actually spoke less than that at the beginning.

BARBARA DANIELS: It calls for a whole different type of singing, a style I don't think is being taught anymore. On Broadway, what would they do if their body mikes were disconnected? They wouldn't be heard at all. Where did all the great Broadway voices go? I guess they're all out there trying to be opera singers.

KIRI TE KANAWA: I once heard someone criticize people like me for doing these crossover works, and they said, "How would you get people to come and hear you if you do this?" Well, Jeremy Irons and I did selections from *My Fair Lady* at Albert Hall in London and it was a huge success. The audience loved it. We all change and we all want to do different things, and one does mellow in one's old age, so to speak. It's such fun to do these things and it introduces these works to other people.

H A D L E Y : Up to about twenty-five or thirty years ago, every opera singer who became popular also sang ballads of some kind, so it's not just something that happened in the eighties.

J U L I A   M I G E N E S : I think the crossover things are wonderful. You know what? The life of an opera singer can be really boring, you know.

T E   K A N A W A : The main reason I'm doing these sort of things is that I'm an entertainer. I'm into entertaining rather boring people to death. When I was in Chicago doing *Così,* I watched this lady in the audience who seemed to be looking at the ceiling all night. After a time, I realized she was dead asleep. She had an incredible way of doing it, putting her head back, but she was away. She didn't hear anything. She was the first person out for a drink at the interval. But she had come to the wrong thing. For a lot of people in my game, you have to think we are really entertainers, and there's nothing wrong with that.

M I G E N E S : It finally boils down to seven roles that you sing, and you sing them in every opera house all over the world, and then sometimes there's a new role that comes your way. That's why you often find someone singing a role that's wrong for them, because they're so sick of doing the same roles over and over again. After a while you get to be a Mozart machine or something. The music is always exciting, but how many times and for how many years can you sing the same roles without getting bored? I think any opera singer, after a while, sings that way.

R E S N I K : I had an interesting meeting with Frank Loesser shortly before he died. You know, when he wrote *Most Happy Fella* he was on this road, and he asked me what I would think of Tennessee Williams's *The Rose Tattoo* as an opera—his first opera. I think he would have done something very special with that.

T O Z Z I : You can't answer the question of whether Frank Loesser would have gone on to write operas had he lived. I think that what always caused furrowed brows with *Most Happy Fella* was that people didn't know whether it was a musical or an opera. He made a collage of various styles of music that all worked together. I think the work was a very important one. It still is. If it stands the test of time, it becomes a classic.

RESNIK: If it's a good and interesting work, why not do it in the opera house? People like Gershwin and Loesser, of course.

LOESSER: Yes, Frank was interested in doing *The Rose Tattoo* for Regina, and of course, it was going to be in an operatic form.

MUNSEL: When opera companies do works like *Kismet* and *South Pacific,* I think it would be wise to hire directors who have worked in musical theater before. You have to know where things like the comedy are.

CASTLE: It's all the same package for me and I hate that awful word *crossover.* I think I work in both genres. I did *Brigadoon* and *Sweeney Todd* at City Opera and also standard operas. What's the difference? Is there one? I think it's all really performing.

DANIELS: I had done roles in *West Side Story* and *Man of La Mancha,* and after that I left it alone. That sort of singing is very hard to mix with operatic singing. You can't just drag it around with you on a day-to-day basis. You can't split yourself like that. You can go back to do it from time to time, which I enjoy doing, but it's difficult.

MUNSEL: My work in the musical theater definitely helped me when I did *Fledermaus, Così,* and *Périchole.* They were comic operas and my work away from the opera house allowed me to approach them as comic characters.

TOZZI: When you do a musical, you should get right into the swing of it when you do it every night. It's another thing to expect people to sing a role in *Aida* every night. The demands are much greater. Also, some great opera singers can't do light things, and that's not to denigrate them. It requires a different style of performing. And then when you have a book show, as you do in a musical, you have to be able to do the dialogue and read it convincingly.

LEWIS: Today people go to see *The Phantom of the Opera* and they say, "Oh, what a gorgeous opera." And they love it and really think they're hearing an opera. They fall all over themselves and buy the record and go home and bathe in this wonderful opera. If that makes an audience for Puccini, I say fine! The crossover is inevitable; it's just inevitable.

TE KANAWA: I enjoy these works very much. There's not that much difference between Eliza Doolittle and Desdemona. Why shouldn't opera singers be doing this music? You need ease for it and maybe that comes easier to us. Opera singers sometimes sound strange singing the lighter stuff, but if the music is put in the right key, it really will work.

H Å K A N H A G E G Å R D : I don't have a problem going from *The Sound of Music* to *Tannhäuser,* because for me it's performing. It's all communicating with an audience.

M U N S E L : I adored doing *A Little Night Music* and can't wait to do it again. It is an opera. There's no doubt about that. The opening quartet is so wonderful and all the ensembles are on an operatic scale.

C A S T L E : If a work is of good quality and a company can do it, then that work should be done, whatever you label it.

M I G E N E S : You have to take a lot of head out of the voice. Then you have what's called a more popular sound. That's all.

H A G E G Å R D : Now you can hold this against me, but if a singer is not doing it right and has entered into a field where he doesn't belong, it can backfire. And you know, we have seen examples of this. If you are approaching music with a relaxed mind and know why you want to do it, then it is most likely that you will sing it better.

C A S T L E : I'm very careful in reworking each role. The bottom line is that I cannot push chest voice very high or at all. I'm a fake belter. I just color in the middle or just do a mixed voice and color the language.

T O Z Z I : The reason I was always interested in doing opera and musical theater was because I felt both had great avenues of communication to reach different audiences and to realize different facets of your talent. That's not a unique thing. In the old days, that happened frequently. Fritzi Scheff was Victor Herbert's favorite soprano and she also sang at the Met.

H A D L E Y : I loved doing Ravenal.

H U R L E Y : It's wonderful to bring works like *Show Boat* to the opera house, because they should be heard, and you need real and beautiful voices.

H A D L E Y : It's more akin structurally to an operetta than to an *Evita* or something like that.

H U R L E Y : I have so many wonderful memories of that production. I had such joy doing Magnolia. Robert Rounseville was my leading man and we had a lot of different Cap' Andys. At one time, it was Burl Ives, and I remember he was living on a houseboat then. One day he brought his little boy to the theater. He was so polite and well behaved, the little boy was.

HADLEY: Good words and good music are good words and good music, whether they were written by Verdi or Jerome Kern.

HURLEY: Originally it was Oscar Hammerstein who said he'd allow us to do *Show Boat,* but only if it was introduced during the season as part of the standard repertory.

MILLS: *Candide* is a beautifully written musical comedy piece, but it's not an opera. But why not do it in the opera house with a big orchestra and great singers—well cast, well rehearsed, no microphones. At City Opera, they called it the opera house version of *Candide*—whatever that means. I guess it's just a bigger stage.

BARBARA COOK: I was disappointed in the City Opera production, although I loved the one Hal Prince did on Broadway. The approach was so reverential and the characters didn't engage me, while on Broadway, there was a great sense of fun. I was disappointed by Hal's staging of "Glitter and Be Gay," too. The whole point is that it's a caricature of the very showy aria that's typical of a certain era. It didn't get the applause it deserves and I can't blame that on the performer. When we did it, we even had the most outrageous bows after that number. It's the ultimate diva's greatest moment.

CASTLE: I love doing the Old Lady in *Candide* and I think I have the right voice for it. I sang it for Lenny and he was very pleased, because he wrote it for a real mezzo and not a shouter. You have to know where to go out of chest and show the higher part of the voice.

CRIS GROENENDAAL: When I think of opera, I think of Puccini and Verdi. *Candide* and *Sweeney Todd* started out in standard musical comedy houses and they've been transferred to opera houses only because they bring in money. I approach them as standard musical comedy pieces and from an acting standpoint.

CASTLE: I love the music and I enjoy the humor of the piece, so I have a lot of fun with it.

COOK: From the very start of rehearsals for *Candide,* I knew that it was something I was very proud to be a part of, and nothing's ever happened to change my mind about that.

MILLS: I love Cunegonde in *Candide,* and sometimes I say I hate singing "Glitter and Be Gay" because I think people think it's the only thing I know, but I do love the aria. For a voice like mine, a five-minute show piece like that is wonderful.

COOK: I got stronger vocally while I was doing that show. I thought it was a magnificent show, but we had no idea about the staying power of the show because it wasn't really a hit.

GROENENDAAL: If opera companies are bringing in works like *Follies,* which is a classical musical theater piece which should be revived, and they can't afford to restage it on Broadway, then I think that's great. The show should be seen. Opera companies should be smart enough to realize these works will bring in revenues that will support the standard works in the repertory.

COOK: I'm sure diehard Wagner and Puccini fans think it's dreadful that they're doing works like *The Music Man* in opera houses, but people should be allowed to do whatever they want. The more the merrier.

LEWIS: The one thing that's important to remember is that singers don't have opportunities to do works where they speak in between singing, and that's a technique that has to be learned.

ROSENSHEIN: The difference between musical comedy and opera is not a matter of set arias. It's not a matter of structure. It's not a question of dialogue. There seems to be a never-ending vocal expression in an opera. It never stops during dialogue. If I analyzed *Figaro* and *Annie Get Your Gun,* I think this would hold true—why one is an opera and one a musical. I'm glad when these works come into the opera house because then producers are going to get better voices to sing them.

COOK: I think often singers in crossover albums have just been miscast. Every form of music has its own style and there are very few people who can cross over the lines truly successfully.

GROENENDAAL: I do eight shows a week in *Phantom* because that's the Broadway tradition, but no one would do eight *Figaro*s a week. They wouldn't do it because they respect their instruments a hell of a lot more and the tradition respects their position.

LOESSER: I did eight performances a week in *Most Happy Fella.* It's not that difficult. I think people have become very spoiled, and there's no sense in not doing what you have to do. Theater people of my era did it, that's all!

C O O K : We all did eight performances a week, and it was like the bumblebee: You do it because you don't know you can't do it.

B L A C K W E L L : I used to do eight shows a week on Broadway, but there was no way I could have done Clara in the Glyndebourne *Porgy and Bess* eight times in the same week.

H A G E G Å R D : We all listen to many different types of music. Very often a performer, if he has made the right choice and is doing the the music well, can add to his performance in a *Tannhäuser* by doing something like *The Sound of Music.*

H A D L E Y : If you're going to do crossover works, you have to make sure that the demands they make on you are consistent with what you do. In retrospect, knowing what I know now, I wonder if I would have done Freddy in *My Fair Lady.*

L E W I S : The Broadway production of *Regina* wasn't something we thought of as an opera. It was a musical work that we sang and talked.

H A D L E Y : Remember, in the forties, they had Ezio Pinza with Mary Martin, and no matter what you thought of her, Ethel Merman had one great set of pipes.

C O O K : Opera was such a huge part of my growing up. I don't quite know how it happened, because nobody cared about opera in particular. When I was a little girl, I would always ask my mother or my grandmother to call me when the Saturday afternoon broadcast was beginning. It was a beautiful, beautiful part of my life.

Most American singers seem passionate in their devotion to American opera.

L E A R : I think *Porgy and Bess* is a great, great opera! Americans don't trust their own emotions. We're simple. We're not complicated. That's why our musicals are so successful. I think Stephen Sondheim is coming close to writing a great American opera. Had Robert Ward listened to us, his opera might have been more successful. It's not that I'm patting myself on the back and saying, "I know better than anyone else." I'm the first person to want to learn, but there are certain areas where I do know. He was pigheaded and stubborn. . . . I guess I'm unconventional. I'm an antidiva.

EPILOGUE:
JUST LET ME
SAY THIS!

~

*My life was renunciation on
top of renunciation!*

–BIDÚ SAYÃO

Participants (in order of appearance): Bidú Sayão, Renata Scotto,
Anna Moffo, Patrice Munsel, Roberta Alexander, Evelyn Lear,
Thomas Stewart, Franz Mazura, Catherine Malfitano, Patricia
Brooks, Julia Migenes, Nedda Casei, Martina Arroyo, Robert
Merrill, Sandra Warfield, Zinka Milanov, Rosalind Elias, Giorgio
Tozzi, Regina Resnik, Nell Rankin, Licia Albanese, Jarmila
Novotná, Rose Bampton, Roberta Peters, Theodor Uppman,
Blanche Thebom, Eleanor Steber, Mignon Dunn, Sherrill Milnes,
Marilyn Horne, Brenda Lewis, Jerome Hines, Frances Bible

When Mme. Sayão admits to her renunciations, the promise of
intimate revelations rears its ugly head. So many people with so much
to say! The more than eighty articulate artists we interviewed for this
book were at times hard to confine to our choice of operas. How do
you stop a singer like Evelyn Lear from talking about her first great
triumph as Berg's Lulu, and who would want to? Would it be fair for

us to conceal how these great artists feel about their favorite roles, the special colleagues they worked with, their choice of repertory, the nature of their art, and even such modern innovations as "surtitles"? An exceptional group of people opened up to us, and it is only fair that we let them have their say on a variety of subjects.

Our first interview was with Bidú Sayão. It seems fitting that she should be the first to make some parting remarks.

BIDÚ SAYÃO: My life was renunciation on top of renunciation! I gave up Butterfly, but what I wanted to sing was the lyrical roles with beautiful stories. With the coloratura, what do you have? Mad girls on the stage, very peculiar women. For many years I stayed a coloratura, because I didn't want to force my voice. So I lasted longer—a thirty-year career is long for a voice like mine. I knew my limitations, but I was always so unhappy to sing *Lucia,* then *Puritani,* then *Sonnambula. Rigoletto* I liked because there was a little bit of drama.

RENATA SCOTTO: It is very different when you do a romantic character and when you do a verismo character. In the romantic period, you have to pace absolutely differently—the way you say things, the phrases in music and in acting—much more slowly and intense. But there is not so much in the verismo. If I sing Traviata, then I sing Mimì, the similarity is only in the disease, let's say. Different story, different style—a romantic and a verismo one. So every time you talk about your sickness, it's different. Violetta takes three pages to cough and feel very sick. Mimì only takes one bar. This is the difference.

ANNA MOFFO: I don't think people would want to see these pieces over and over if they didn't really suffer with these characters, whether it's Butterfly, Canio, or whoever. And you always feel guilty, at least I do, when you do an opera like *Daughter of the Regiment*—who has her problems—but I always felt people wanted to see me die, or get killed, or go mad. I think people always preferred to see me die as Violetta, die as Butterfly, die as Mimì, die as Lucia—and actually, I love to make people laugh. I love to clown and I've not had too much occasion to do it. When I do things like the lesson scene in *Daughter of the Regiment* or *Barber,* they're not my most favorite roles, but I love to do Marie and break up all the furniture—things I probably could never do on my own.

PATRICE MUNSEL: I think of all my roles I loved *Rigoletto* and Lucia most. I loved being onstage for that twenty minutes or whatever of the mad scene—and I loved to die. That mad scene in *Lucia* is unique. It is really just you and that flute out there. I loved the Italian repertoire. I loved doing *Romeo and Juliet* because I love dying so much, and that death scene is just glorious!

ROBERTA ALEXANDER: I'm not real thrilled with dying onstage, but I get to do it often. Mimì's death is good, I do enjoy it—but it takes a long time. *Traviata* is also another interesting death. I once had to die as Elettra in *Idomeneo*—it was Ponnelle's idea that she dies from pure ire and choler. That was probably the strangest death of all.

Perhaps the most bizarre death in opera occurs at the end of Alban Berg's twelve-tone masterpiece *Lulu*. After having destroyed everyone who loves her, the protagonist and one of her current lovers, the lesbian Countess Geschwitz, are murdered by Jack the Ripper. The controversial and taxing title role made a star of Evelyn Lear in 1960.

EVELYN LEAR: When I first saw the score of *Lulu,* I nearly fainted. I'd never seen this kind of music before.

THOMAS STEWART: In those days, the brash audacity of Americans offended a lot of Europeans. In America, you succeed if you're not afraid, and you don't let obstacles stop you. Certainly, if you're an American opera singer, you have to scrounge just to stay alive—which we did. You take any job. You say, "Yes, I'll take it. What is it? What do you want me to do?" In the fifties in Europe, they didn't understand this.

LEAR: So I said, "Sure I'll do it. Lulu sounds wonderful. The Vienna Festival, my big opportunity. I can do it." Have you ever seen the score for *Lulu*? It's frightening! So I sat down at the piano and I made little sections where I would play something harmonically which was not harmonic, just to get it in my ear. I was just so determined to learn it that I did.

STEWART: Just to learn the thing, you memorized it virtually, didn't you?

L E A R : The first time was a concert version, but by that time I knew it so well, of course, I didn't need a score.

S T E W A R T : The hardest music ever written, and she learned it in three weeks. They'd never encountered anything like that.

L E A R : Well, there wasn't a third act.

S T E W A R T : Well, there's still enough there. In those days it was completely unheard of, and a lot of Europeans were offended by it.

L E A R : Then we got such sensational reviews that they decided to put it in the festival with Otto Schenk staging it. None of the people who sang with me in that production were well known, because in those days, you know, modern music was done primarily by the lesser-known singers. The known people would not bother with it. But I was an American and I was determined I was going to get ahead—and if I could do it that way, so be it. Anyway, it was an unbelievable experience. My mama was there, and Mr. Bing. . . :

F R A N Z M A Z U R A : The score of *Lulu* is very hard. It's difficult to learn, a lot different from other modern pieces. With these twelve tones, everything does not fit in. I'm a very rhythmic person, and I suppose it was easier for me. After all these different productions, it is now one of my favorite pieces.

C A T H E R I N E M A L F I T A N O : The score is so diverse and multilayered, it takes a while to decipher the different lines.

L E A R : The role is such a challenge vocally: high, low, all over the place. It's beautiful music to sing—not all of it, some of it is awful—but most of it was very exciting to sing and very challenging. It was a type of role I'd never done before. Well, actually, it was one of the early roles in my career.

M A Z U R A : The thing about both *Salome* and *Lulu* is that while they're both difficult, they're not really killers, like some people say. You just have to learn them correctly. It's just like anything else.

P A T R I C I A B R O O K S : For me, there was really nothing very hard about the music of *Lulu*. It's beautiful, and beautiful to sing, and it never affected my singing other roles that I had done before.

M A L F I T A N O : At first I was attracted only to the character of Lulu, the drama. Now, the music sounds tonal and romantic to me.

L E A R : It was all Greek to me, because even though I was a musician, it was all serial music. I was horrified—I didn't know these notes. I had nothing to hold on to. They had hired a woman who had done it before, and she was three hundred and fifty pounds. It was a concert version of *Lulu,* and they decided they needed someone who looked more like Lulu.

M A L F I T A N O : I approached it like Rossini, Mozart, Puccini—not like a fringe, freak part.

B R O O K S : It's strange sounding to the audience, but when you study it, after a while it's not far from Wagner—as strange as that sounds—actually lightly written for a voice. But it was vocally very rewarding.

L E A R : To be a successful Lulu, you have to be a good musician. That's even more important than the voice. A good voice, of course, is helpful. You have to have the high and the low, and in the middle you have to be able to sing and speak over a big orchestra. Also, you have to have the right kind of figure to wear those clothes. You don't necessarily have to be thin, but you have to have a voluptuous figure. Alwa talks about her thighs, and they have to be OK.

B R O O K S : I got to enjoy it very much and even got to the point where I could whistle the tunes—which is strange, since it's Berg and everything. At first the music was very hard for me, but then I found that as bizarre as the music was, it did get easier; and I really found myself identifying with the part.

L E A R : Musically, you just pull yourself together and say, "I've got to learn it." You force yourself to learn it—even though while you're learning it, you may hate it and feel uncomfortable with it and don't understand it. You might find it difficult to absorb, but then it just becomes part of you. You really have to just drum it into yourself.

S T E W A R T : The repetition is the big thing, the key.

L E A R : And histrionically.

S T E W A R T : That was no problem.

L E A R : What?

S T E W A R T : That was no problem for you.

L E A R : No, I guess it wasn't, because I saw her not as a little slut but as a victim of circumstances. She really was a Marilyn Monroe type who was pulled in because she was the incarnation of sex without being sexy—not the Jane Russell type of sex, or whoever. She was just "woman"—and that was why everyone couldn't resist her.

S T E W A R T : Male or female.

L E A R : Yes. She was never knowingly evil. She's certainly not a sympathetic character; she's someone who causes so much grief for other people. But I never saw her as an evil person.

J U L I A M I G E N E S : You take a girl like Christine Keeler, the girl who was a prostitute in London—that's what this is. Lulu is a Christine Keeler in a way. I'm sure she also went to bed with women, men, anything. She's that type of person. Except Lulu has a tremendous evil streak, and a tremendously destructive one. And in the face of anyone's emotions, she's totally cold and unmoving; there's no way to reach her.

L E A R : I loved doing that type of woman, because by nature I like to shock. It's part of my personality. I'm a shocking person.

S T E W A R T : Definitely. She is, and it's much more fun.

L E A R : Often times I say things that get me into a lot of trouble.

M I G E N E S : My training and background as an actress were a big help to me with Lulu, because the role is demanding dramatically as well as vocally.

M A L F I T A N O : It's a full evening for an actress. When I get to the third act, I feel as though I've done two operas already.

B R O O K S : The amorality of the woman is fascinating. It's not that she was sexually depraved, it's just that she was what she was—and people came and touched her life, and she just went with it.

M I G E N E S : Her character is one of total sensuality. Of course, there are a lot of different choices you can make. But she gives up any thought of anything else in favor of her sensuality. I don't see her as a victim. In no way is she a victim. In a way, I think, there is an evil streak in her that causes her destiny.

M A L F I T A N O : Her responses to life are based on difficult beginnings. I have enormous compassion and love for her, and I feel angry that she's treated the way she is—especially by the men in her life.

B R O O K S : I began to feel very natural within the role. That had something to do with power, I'm sure. It's as if she became the predator after her beginnings, and she would set things up so that they would fall into her lap. It didn't matter who she was dealing with, whether it was a woman or a man. It was a very subtle kind of predatory behavior.

M A L F I T A N O : I tend to live the character moment by moment and not overanalyze things. Lulu just lives. For most of the evening, you see no calculation in her at all. She's savage and charming at the same time.

Though Lulu begins the story as the wife of old Dr. Goll, she is no Loretta Young. She provokes his death by a heart attack; is the cause of her next husband's suicide; torments her third husband by keeping company with, among others, his son and the lesbian Countess, before shooting him; allows the Countess to take her place in the cholera ward during her jail break; and ends up supporting her fans by prostitution. The most illustrious of her clients turns out to be Jack the Ripper.

M A Z U R A : Geschwitz is absolutely the only one in the whole piece who feels a true love for Lulu, but Lulu feels nothing for her—only when she needs her in the third act. When she leaves, it is like she can't take herself away, because Lulu is her whole life.

L E A R : Whenever I sang Lulu, I always had such an affinity for the role of Geschwitz. It was very difficult for me as Lulu to be harsh to her. The Countess is the only really sympathetic character in the whole opera. She's generous. She gives not only her wealth and her money but her life for the woman, the person, she loves. Geschwitz is also very much appreciated by the audience because she is such a relief. When I was doing Lulu, I would be up there singing my guts out all night and then she comes along with these two pages of the most beautiful music in the whole opera—and she walks away with the show.

M A Z U R A : She is a lesbian—and when you have a very feminine woman, it becomes very hard to make it believable. With Yvonne Minton in Paris, she was too ladylike, and it took a long time to bring her to the point where she would be believable. It was very difficult, but she was eventually wonderful. But it is so difficult when you have these ladies and you have to make them into this creature who is not feminine and not a lady—but a good person who loves, who is the good person in the opera.

M I G E N E S : It's the same thing as with all the men. You know, you see these girls again and again who play on the emotions of lesbians. Excuse me, but it's as simple as that. Lulu uses her, that's all there is to that. I'm sure that maybe they had something together—it wouldn't be beyond her.

L E A R : John Dexter can be a very difficult director. He also has a totally phony concept of homosexuality among women. He sees them almost as female Oscar Wildes. If it had been up to him, he would have put a leather jacket and pants and studs on me. Obviously, these people don't read what's in the libretto. They have a caricature in their minds that's totally false. All the lesbians I've known in my life are more feminine than I am. I'm a toughie—I'm masculine—I'm a heterosexual. But the homosexual women I've known have been feminine almost to the point of embarrassment, some of them.

NEDDA CASEI: *Lulu* is a wonderful theatrical piece. It's wonderful musical theater. I wouldn't say it has a beautiful vocal line, but it brings out the best in a lot of great singing actors and actresses, and there's wonderful dramatic music. The combination of the two can be very exciting. It's just a high level of dramatic theater, with great music.

MAZURA: If you compare *Wozzeck* and *Lulu,* well, *Wozzeck* is maybe better musically, but it doesn't have the appeal of *Lulu*. *Wozzeck* is a great piece musically, but *Lulu* has a lot of action. I think *Lulu* sells for the audience much better than a lot of modern pieces.

MALFITANO: Lulu is fascinating to audiences, so there's no question about whether they will sit up and watch. I always want them to sit up and listen.

LEAR: I think there are more people around who can sing Lulu now. That's why it's grown in popularity. And it's not unlike some of the depravity you see on miniseries on TV. I think people are more into that sort of depravity now.

Under the stress of a messy divorce, Geraldine Farrar began to develop vocal troubles. She made her Metropolitan Opera farewell in Leoncavallo's *Zazà* before a legion of hysterical fans. In her curtain speech she decreed, "I don't want any tears in this house! I'm leaving because I want to." Gerryflappers adorned her with a crown, robe, scepter, and garlands of flowers, and when Farrar finally did leave the Met, she was carried out through the stage entrance onto a fan-packed Thirty-ninth Street. Fortunately, her vocal troubles weren't severe enough to prevent her from singing 123 *Carmen*s in 125 days on a cross-country tour.

MARTINA ARROYO: One of my favorite sopranos when I was very young was Renata Tebaldi. I used to stand there and just close my eyes and listen to that sound. She could read the telephone book—I couldn't care less. But as I grew older, I found out I was as much interested in the characters, that I wanted more than just a beautiful sound. I wanted the character to do something, to be different, the way she said this or that. Sometimes we have singers who emphasize the beauty of sound, and sometimes those that emphasize the importance of the words. And I'm hoping we are thinking in terms of one that can do both—to say something interestingly and beautifully.

MOFFO: I think singers have to become more involved than actors—and I'm probably going to get killed by the actors for this—because the vocal instrument is so much a part of us, what we eat, what we do. It's the most personal, sensitive instrument there is. Air conditioning, rain, sun—whatever the case, we're always open to something happening to it. And we're not responsible. But if people really thought of themselves exposed to a plane ride or whatever, and what can happen, and then expect us to always be out there perfect, you know. . . . The public has no idea—they think you just open your mouth. Now, you can't spend your career worrying about what could happen, but it's good that you know, so you can guard against it.

BROOKS: When I first did Violetta, I went to Italy and worked with Luigi Ricci, who had coached Bjoerling and worked with Puccini. I got to see more of what that world was like. It certainly helped to make the role richer for me. I think the fact that I was overtrained, having been a dancer and actress and finally a singer, made me kind of a freak for a while in the opera world—because they didn't know what to do with me. It did help, though, when it comes to a really special part like Camille.

SCOTTO: When you sing a phrase in *Traviata* or Desdemona, and then you sing Francesca da Rimini or Manon Lescaut perhaps, you must sing differently. And some singers don't—they sing exactly the same, with the same amount of voice, amount of phrasing. No, you can't do that. You have first to understand the different styles. And I learned that from conductors, from studying, from reading all the different letters of the composers—and from the music. It's beautiful to study and to prepare, to get ready to do this onstage.

SAYÃO: When I first arrived in this country, I didn't know one word of English. At that time in South America, we didn't learn English. Today, everybody learns it. But I knew French and Spanish. I had everyone translating for me—my manager and everyone. I had an accompanist who was British and spoke beautiful English, but not one word of anything else. He taught me American songs, but it was all phonetic—I didn't know anything that I was singing. I knew I didn't give it any feeling, and after I learned a little bit and could think in English, those same songs were so different—because I took my feelings and could think the words. And that's how it should be for American singers. They should learn other languages, and not just phonetically. They sing beautifully, but they really can't communicate the feelings.

When Feodor Chaliapin was asked what he would do if he lost his voice, he replied, "I'd be the greatest actor in the world."

A R R O Y O : So often the case is that you learn the arias, but it's not emphasized that you learn the entire role from beginning to end. And it's one of the things I try really hard to make students aware of. First of all, it's not only a matter of learning the whole role; it's that very often the aria has nothing to do with the part. I mean, I can sing "Vissi d'arte" till the cows come home, but singing "Vissi d'arte" after running around that room—you've been chased by Scarpia, you have seen your lover tortured and bloodied, you are in such a state when you say, "God—why me? Will you please help me?"

R O B E R T M E R R I L L : Italian was always easier for me. I didn't sing many French operas—*Faust* and *Carmen,* I think that was it. Italian was easier because of the vowels, but I had no trouble singing in French, because I didn't change my production. I found some of my colleagues did that, to get that guttural sound in French, but I never understood why. It's the same thing—you sing with an open throat, so it doesn't make any difference. But I did prefer Italian.

M U N S E L : I think we're in the era of the conductor now, and that might be doing a lot of damage to singers. Conductors have become such prima donnas that they force each singer to do the role musically the way they imagine it. I find, for instance, when I listen to a *Rigoletto* these days, and I remember the nuance someone like Leonard Warren gave to the character, so much is missing now that I'm just flabbergasted they don't hear what is there. I can only think the conductor is imposing things and doesn't allow the artist to do it differently. That really amazes me. I hear the same thing in *Hoffmann*. I just had been so used to the wonderful things and dramatic nuances that Pinza did—and they're just lost now. It's very upsetting.

MERRILL: Longevity is in the mind and the body and the technique that you have. I was fortunate to have studied well and to have a good technique. I was given a voice that I did not abuse. I didn't sing too many heavy roles early in my career. The *Traviata* is a lyric role, *The Barber of Seville, Faust*—they're all lyric. I waited several years before I sang Rigoletto and the heavier roles. So I paced myself and I never thought of longevity. I just went on singing one role after another. The dramatic roles—the Rigolettos, the *Toscas*, and *Otellos*—came in time, when I was ready not only vocally but maturity-wise, as an artist.

ARROYO: Poor choice of repertoire with the wrong type of voice is always very dangerous. A young voice doing a part where they say, "Yes, I'm going to do it really well in five years, but I'm trying it now," can be the most dangerous thing in the world, because you can hurt yourself in that little trying period. The hardest thing, of course, is to say no to something that might mean an opportunity for your career to go on. All of us have gone through that.

SANDRA WARFIELD: I never really longed to sing any of the parts outside my repertory. I was satisfied with Carmen and Amneris and Azucena—who wouldn't be? I never felt I should be a diva. I got to do *Favorita* a lot, and a lot of performances of Fidès in *Prophète*. I did around forty performances of that—with me eating *Traubenzucker,* which is a sort of compressed sugar, which I had hidden in various parts of my costume. With the way that opera's written, I needed the energy. I didn't realize you could transpose the score.

MOFFO: I hate when people transpose, because it's a whole different piece. Transposing any aria, to me, is worse than cutting or any other modification of what the composer wrote. Because he heard it in that key, it should be in that key—if you can't do it in that key, you shouldn't be doing it. And a half-step one way or the other does not make that much difference to you, really—except it makes you happier or maybe more relaxed.

ZINKA MILANOV : I was never too ambitious to do too many
parts, but what I was doing, I wanted to do close to perfection. For
years I didn't do Tosca here, because I thought maybe I wasn't ready.
And then Madame Tebaldi canceled, and Mr. Bing said, "Will you
do it, so we don't have to cancel the performance and give back the
money?" So he was hoping when I sang my first Tosca, it would be
a success—and he was right. He was a good businessman. The people
came and instead of returning the tickets, they wanted to buy more.

ROSALIND ELIAS : My favorite role is unfortunately not box
office. It's Charlotte in *Werther.* I love Massenet, but unfortunately,
he's not box office. And of course, I love *Rosenkavalier,* and who
wouldn't say Carmen is a great role?

GIORGIO TOZZI : My favorite of all time was Hans Sachs in
Die Meistersinger, and I was very pleased and happy to be able to do
it extensively in Germany and in the States as well.

REGINA RESNIK : I can't say that out of eighty, I've had one
favorite role, but usually the last part I sang was always my favorite.
I can give you four accomplishments, and each one I would say was
my favorite, because they all allowed me to do something different.
And I was able to be myself, and still be an interpreter. Klytemnestra
certainly, and I found things in Carmen that were very special, and
I found the kind of actress I wanted to be in *Pique Dame,* and the
kind of comedienne I wanted to be in Dame Quickly.

NELL RANKIN : I think everybody likes to play the bad characters. They seem to have more to them than the sweeter-natured
people. Their strength is their greatest weakness. Their incredible
strength, it's a tremendous weakness. And they succumb to it eventually. But while they're going, they're really veritable tornadoes of
destruction in every direction. It is fun playing bad characters.

In her Connecticut retirement, the advent of television prompted
Geraldine Farrar to remark, "It is better for a singer to sing for an
audience of 500 in person, than an unseen audience of 5,000,000."

SAYÃO : What I see today doesn't please me and ruins my fondness
for going to the opera. It's so different now. The singers of the past
dedicated themselves completely to this profession, and it was not
easy at all. We didn't want to sing just for money or publicity. We

wanted to please the audience and to please the critics—and, of course, the management. These were our goals. Now people go because of the publicity. The publicity says it's good, so people go and think it is. It should be the audience who judges you and tells you you're great. You should be judged on the stage, and not in the papers. We have three great tenors now—but when they finish, who will take their place?

LICIA ALBANESE: They gave great artists every performance. Now I read in *The New York Times* they don't do this because the artist is too expensive. My God! Nine thousand dollars or thirty thousand dollars a performance! What are they doing? And they don't sing well—I tell you the truth. You can put this on the radio; I don't care. Because really, if they have a conscience—my God, to be paid like that! I didn't even ask how much I wanted to be paid. What they want to give me, it's right. For me, singing is a beauty. For me, singing is something that I loved so much. And I never went behind and said, "No, I want this or I cannot. . . ." Now they say, "If you give me only this, I cannot make it." They make the contract, they don't come. Is bad, very bad. They don't have conscience, and then they don't treat the art beautifully. Because if you don't think so much of the money, you sing better for the public. You have to give to them more than what they give to you. And you know, they love you, they applaud you—it's better than to have money. I used to sing with Gigli free, to send the little kids, the poor people, to the country for the summer. I was young, and Gigli was singing free, so I sang free.

MERRILL: I occasionally do seminars when I have time, and I can see in the students' eyes when they ask questions that they're not really interested in the past. Sure, they're interested in my career and when I started to sing. But when I talk to them honestly, and say they have to be prepared vocally and they have to work hard for years before you learn how to play your instrument, to be careful, and you might have to wait for years to sing certain roles—I can see in their eyes they don't really care. Their minds are already made up. It's a different era.

MOFFO: The Golden Age was the Golden Age, as everyone's said before me, because they weren't running around on planes. They took forty days and forty nights on a ship to get from place to place. It's a lean year if we only sing a hundred five times; they had a big year with thirty performances. Bruno Zirato, who was not only manager of the Philharmonic but had been Caruso's secretary for many years, would tell stories that would set your hair on end: that Caruso would sing once every two weeks. Well, that's not exactly true; he would sing maybe twice in a week. But he would only do that for three weeks, then he'd take three months off and go to the Baths of Montecatini and make the rounds of all the thermal cures. It's very different today.

SAYÃO: I started to learn languages in my country, from the first teacher. Afterward, I went to France and I learned lots of interpretations with Jean de Reszke. He was Polish, but he loved singing in French, and always he preached that the diction and the words were so important; that without that, you can't be an artist. I tried to make my diction as perfect as possible.

MERRILL: I listened to Titta Ruffo records and all those great baritones—not to copy their style, not to sing like them, but to get a feeling of theater and interpretation. I mean, if you get onstage, you're on your own—Titta Ruffo's not singing. I read all the books on all the great artists. The young people today are just too impatient, and there are too many quick opportunities. You have to be patient and you have to be honest with yourself. I didn't rush—and when I finally did sing, my instrument was prepared. There's very little longevity today. Not with all young singers, I'm generalizing—but generally, I find this to be true.

SAYÃO: The Massenet *Manon* is a glass of champagne, and the Puccini is a glass of Burgundy. I learned Massenet's *Manon* from Maria Massenet. I was always very lucky in learning roles from great people who had the experience with them. I don't know why, but she took me in her wings and taught me every little thing. She also told me in private how unhappy she was—how he liked beautiful girls and beautiful sopranos; and this was bad, but she knew every moment of *Manon* just like he did. And she transmitted to me all the interpretation. She took me to the house where they made all the costumes, so I had all these costumes. And when I left her, she gave me the death mask of Massenet in plaster. This is in the museum in Brazil now. She taught me the way to walk and the way to bow and everything. This is the way I like to sing—to learn from the best I can.

L E A R : When I was doing the staged version of *Lulu* for the first time, we went to see Mrs. Berg, in the home she had shared with him. And she had kept every pencil shaving—everything was on his desk exactly as it was the day he died. She never changed a thing in the room. She was a lovely, warm, beautiful woman. She always wore these turn-of-the-century long skirts and jackets, and sometimes she wore hats. She came to rehearsals all the time, and I'm not saying this to pat myself on the back, but she always said, "You are exactly the type, physically, dramatically, and vocally, that Alban had in mind for the role of Lulu." That made me feel great.

S A Y Ã O : My husband was my teacher Giuseppe Danise, who was one of the great baritones of the Metropolitan. He said, "No, you can't touch certain roles, because you want to have all your voice." I wanted to have my agility, my pianissimos, all of the things that were good, and I didn't want to lose them just to sing a performance where the music wasn't right for me. This was my life.

During a Chicago performance of *Romeo and Juliet,* Jean de Reszke was awaiting Nellie Melba's appearance on her balcony when a man came onstage and threatened him with a gun. While stagehands dragged off the interloper, de Reszke sang on. Melba however, stood behind the balcony screaming, "Bring down the curtain, my voice is gone!" "For God's sake, keep quiet, Melba," de Reszke barked. "Just open the windows and come out!"

A L B A N E S E : We used to tell one another things. I did many *Manon*s with Bjoerling, Tucker, di Stefano, and other artists, and we used to tell each other, "Say, tonight, let's do it this way. This is what I thought—let's change this scene." These were great artists. And then we loved each other—we were singing the same performances so many times.

J A R M I L A N O V O T N Á : Lawrence Tibbett was an excellent father in *Traviata.* He was such an excellent actor. I remember especially his Iago in *Otello*—extraordinary, really.

M E R R I L L : When I first saw *Barber,* I was a student, and I took the subway to the Met and stood on line. The Barber was the great baritone Giuseppe de Luca, and I'll never forget—he was always moving, always thinking. His eyes were always alive. As luck would have it, when I first did the role he came to New York and I studied it with him. I had twelve hours to work on my interpretation of Figaro with my idol, and I got so much from him. I did exactly what he told me, and after my first performance, which was outdoors in Montreal, one of the critics said I reminded him of the great Figaro, Giuseppe de Luca. I was fortunate to have him to work with.

ROSE BAMPTON: Giovanni Martinelli was wonderful. With Martinelli you'd be up there, and he'd give you a very big hug. And I must say that sometimes, that was just so comforting, knowing that he was just there, singing with you, and knowing everything was going to be all right. Melchior was the same way.

WARFIELD: It was incredible to stand next to Milanov onstage— "Don't touch me." I stood next to her in *Gioconda* at the end of the first act. She took a high B or something—and nobody breathed. I know I didn't. It was unbelievable to hear how this woman could sing. And she was so nice to me. She would make me come into her dressing room and she'd test out my voice, because she said the first notes you sing are the most important, and you must be right on. I wasn't singing leads, so my mind was just to learn and wait until I got to sing Amneris and Carmen. I had no idea of the importance of what I was doing, but she did, and every performance, she'd bring me in there and go over my roles.

NOVOTNÁ: Of the women colleagues, Sayão I liked very much, and we liked each other—also outside of the theater. And Licia was always a very sweet, lovely woman. That's why we keep on seeing each other, even now. Swarthout was an excellent singer. And Lily Pons—my God! And we were very good friends. Later on, I sang a lot with Kostelanetz in his light programs. And once I was at Lily's apartment, and she had a parakeet, and she must have taught him— and the parakeet was singing just like Lily! She was wonderful.

ALBANESE: Sometimes they can tell so many funny stories about what happened on the stage. Never happened to me. In the opera, if you had a flower in your hair and you go on the stage and it fell down, you paid a fine. It was a theater rule. And if you had underwear or a hoop that you could see . . . Now it is a joke. And that's why, never—I lost nothing. I wore pins.

WARFIELD: In Europe, they used to refuse to let you wear nail polish on the stage. It was part of the contract, like you couldn't go skiing. I don't know if they still do that.

BAMPTON: I was brought up with an English father, and my mother was of German descent and very straitlaced, and to show any emotion just wasn't ladylike. Melchior used to say, "Rose, do you know—this is our big moment! Would you try and forget that it's me here, that I'm Melchior—just think it's Pelly," my husband [conductor Wilfred Pelletier]. And Lehmann had such a time with me. She would say, "Rose, do you really love Pelly?" And I'd say, "Of course I do." And she'd say, "I don't think you know the least thing about love." And I'd say, "Well, I certainly do, but I don't have to go around advertising that." She'd say, "That's where you make a big mistake. Every experience that you have in life, you've got to use when you sing." She broke down that barrier for me.

Cyril Ritchard, sometimes referred to as an Australian Noel Coward, made his Metropolitan directing debut with *The Barber of Seville* in 1954, and after staging a *Hoffman* for the company went on to direct Offenbach's *La Périchole* (in which he also played the Viceroy), *The Marriage of Figaro,* and *The Gypsy Baron.* However, he will probably be best remembered as Captain Hook in the musical *Peter Pan* on Broadway, with Mary Martin.

MOFFO: When I did *Périchole* with Cyril Ritchard and I had a chance to rest, I would always stand in the wings and watch him— every single night, if he was on the stage. I'd go watch, and I would laugh and just enjoy what he did. And it was never the same; every night was different. I thought he was one of the most incredible people I ever saw on the stage in my life.

MUNSEL: I was very angry with Cyril for a very long time. I had known him before *Périchole* and adored him. . . . So of course I was delighted when I knew he was going to direct the production and be in it. We got to the dress rehearsal and he said, "Pat, darling, I have the most wonderful ending for you. Ted Uppman is going to bring on a donkey and put you on it and lead you offstage as the curtain comes down." But what he neglected to say was that while I was going off on my ass, he was coming on, on this huge white horse that stood center stage facing forward, as the curtain came down. I thought my father was going to kill him. I should have said, "This is not *Le Vice-roi.* This is called *La Périchole!*" For years I wouldn't have anything to do with him; but then we did a show together on a cruise, and then later on Broadway, and I forgave him. But I thought it was all terribly irresponsible—especially the horse!

TOZZI: Fortunately, I never intend to write a book on opera, because what the world does not need is another autobiography by an opera singer, just as we don't need another book on singing. Writing a book on singing is like writing a book about how to ride a bicycle. But if I had to write a book, I would write it in two volumes: one very large volume of people I have known and loved as singers, and one very thin one called *People I Abhorred.*

In the 1930s, Lawrence Tibbett argued, "Grand opera, to be a stimulating art, should be understood. It's asinine to think that foreign tongues are the only cultivated means of producing opera. Most of them could be translated into English without losing any of their art. Sung in English, people would know whether they like it or not. It's ridiculous to say English isn't a singable language."

ELIAS: Most Mozart in English I like. Puccini, Verdi, and Wagner, no. English is not easy to sing in. French is the next most difficult. Italian and Russian are great. I don't mind German; that's fine. But English is the most difficult because you have to bite into every word. You can't sing it with tricks, like you can in Italian, and I always do try as hard as I can to be understood. But when you have to bite into the words, you are right there and it has strength, and people will understand.

MOFFO: I couldn't stand seeing *Fledermaus* at the Met with German singing and English dialogue—what does that mean? It doesn't make any sense. Also, anything above an F-sharp or a G, certainly in the female voice: You can sing *bacio,* you can sing *kiss,* you can sing *Kuss,* whatever—and it's going to sound like "What was that?" So why are we so busy saying, "It should be in English?"

ROBERTA PETERS: I like some of the comic operas in English. I really do. We did a wonderful Mozart *Così* years ago, with a great translation. It's the translation that counts.

THEODOR UPPMAN: Doing Mozart in English is wonderful in certain cases, but I don't think *Don Giovanni* is one of the pieces that would work. When I came to the Met, I did *Così Fan Tutte* over and over again in English, and *Marriage of Figaro* has a wonderful translation. The Mozart comedies, the real comedies, go awfully well in English, because the audience responds so well. They hear all the funny lines—if they hear all the words—and they respond.

BLANCHE THE BOM: Bing was extremely wise to choose the Martins to do the translation of *Così*. Tom and his wife, Ruth, had this delicious sense of humor, and they enjoyed English as a language. When I was with them, they tossed words back and forth, and twisted and turned them. It was sort of a game with them. I think the Ruth and Thomas Martin translation of *Così* was superb and still is. I can't listen to another translation; it's terribly inferior. But ours played so extraordinarily well. And they were so clever in putting words that fit where the vowels were, so you could sing the word. That was a talent they had.

ELEANOR STEBER: Opera in English is absolutely right for an English-speaking audience. Certainly, translations have to be good for it to be right, and certain operas lend themselves to translation. Other works are just not right. They get a little heavy. The original language, in some cases, gives it much more color.

MIGNON DUNN: I wish we would be as finicky about our language as the Germans are about theirs. They would opt for a lesser voice if their language was sung well. Here we let people get away with murder when it comes to our language. *Jenůfa* is a lot harder to sing in English than it is in Czech. It's hard to memorize Czech. It's like memorizing an eye chart. But when you memorize it finally, it sings much, much easier. But if you're going to sing in English, then you'd better sing in English and you'd better learn it like you would a foreign language. If you don't close the ends of words with English, then you're not understood.

RANKIN: I usually made my own translation, when I could get by with it; sometimes I couldn't. I usually got the best word group I could get—the most singable words, especially in the high voice, that I could think up that still made sense. I'd just take the English translation, and in parts that seemed particularly difficult to understand, I would change it, if there was not too much objection. I think every opera singer does this. Sometimes the person who writes the translation will object, but not often, when they realize what you're doing and why you're doing it.

SHERRILL MILNES: Before surtitles, I said there was a place for opera in English—not only for audiences, but as first-time experiences for singers. It can put sharp edges on all your emotions. When you sing in a language that you only vaguely know, it tends to make everything round—it's not precise. Now, with surtitles, it's only a learning experience for the performer.

In recent years, the use of surtitles (or supertitles) in opera has created a major controversy. Projected translations above the proscenium do promote "instant understanding," as the New York City Opera insists, but they can also be distracting, promote faulty diction among singers, and, when malfunctioning, cause confusion and unintentional laughs. Their growing use has both defenders and a strong opposition.

RESNIK: My first opera was *Macbeth* and the first opera I saw with supertitles was *Macbeth.* I was sure I was going to hate it, and suddenly I found myself not paying attention to them because I didn't need them. Then I looked up and looked at the meaning of the words for the public, and I really quite understood what a great idea it was. I don't think it's necessary everywhere, but I do think it's necessary with new works, and certainly necessary for Slavic works. I must say I was not put off at all—well, that's a miracle, and also a first. I truly enjoyed watching the audience being wrapped up and understanding what was going on.

MOFFO: I hate them! I hate them! Because they have nothing to do with what's going on. What does this tell us? That the people who are on the stage, or the composer, that we're unable to give you our message? That we are either so uninteresting or indistinct that you feel compelled to read? And you do not ever look or listen, if you're reading. I don't care what anybody tells me, you do not come away knowing the opera. If you want to know the opera, you should read the libretto. And on top of the stage—your eyes never go down. Not to mention losing any effects of night or dark or suddenly a sunlit stage, with this thing in neon.

MILNES: As a performer, I don't think there are problems in the principle of it, only in the realization—like you get laughs when you're not supposed to. It's not a total panacea. Nevertheless, lots of people come without any fear of appearing stupid because they don't know what's going on. It's absolutely good for the art form. Music reaches out. Opera movies, *Live from the Met,* Luciano's or Plácido's whatever—all of it reaches out, breaking down this cultural inferiority complex we've had as a nation. I hate to use the word *education,* because it sounds stuffy and boring, and music is anything but boring. You can like the Beatles *and* Mozart. But there's a whole group that doesn't see that. Television and surtitles are breaking that down, getting rid of that foreign-language stigma.

P E T E R S : I don't like supertitles, because I think it takes away from the stage, and from concentration. That's the one side of the coin. The other side I know very well—that it's important for people who don't know opera. I've heard it over and over again from friends of mine, who say, "Oh, it's wonderful; now we know what's going on." But somehow it hurts me that they can't get it, they can't really receive it and enjoy it without that. As I say, I understand the reason for it; people say, "I've never been able to drag my husband to the opera—now he understands it and likes it." I just did *Lucia* in Salt Lake City and they had it. I wasn't even aware of it. If it's done well, I guess—if they don't laugh in the wrong places. But then *Lucia*'s an opera where there are no laughs—intentionally.

M A R I L Y N H O R N E : I think surtitles are a mixed blessing. An artist hates to think that some subtle moment or expression may go for nothing because people are glued to the screen above just at that moment. And of course, I have had those experiences where everyone onstage has had to slow down to accommodate a laugh coming from the surtitle and not the actual language being sung.

U P P M A N : If they're handled correctly they can be very helpful. I'm upset when I go in and I hear an audience laughing before the phrase where the joke has been sung. I've been to some performances where I thought it was marvelous. The first time I saw supertitles was in Toronto when they were doing *Elektra.* The whole audience was on the edge of their seats and they loved it. Everyone was saying, "Wasn't that the most marvelous thing you've ever seen?" I think they must go on and just find a way of doing them better.

E L I A S : I'm all for the supertitles. I know Italian, but when I went to see *La Rondine* at City Opera, I was happy that everyone else in the theater knew what was going on. They were enjoying it because they knew every word.

BRENDA LEWIS: I've only seen one production with supertitles and I found myself so busy trying to read that I wasn't following what was going on onstage. You can't become involved on the stage if you're busy reading. Think of yourself when you go to a French movie and you're busy reading the subtitles: You know you're going to miss an expression. If you miss that lift of the eyebrow on that twitch of the nostril, you have missed something of what's going on in that character—and that's what movies are so great at. If opera was just about understanding the story, they could hand that to you and you could read it and that would be that. But opera is about experiencing what a character, a person, is going through as it happens—and then it happens to you.

JEROME HINES: Yes, I do like them. It's a very practical thing. It's a little distraction, but doggone it, it's worth it.

STEBER: I think the business of putting the translations above the proscenium is horrendous! That's a statement! If people want to go and hear an opera in its own language, even if they don't understand every word, they certainly understand what's going on. To be distracted by having to look up and down all the time takes away from the opera itself.

RANKIN: I think it is good, because I don't think people look at it that much, but just enough to understand it much better. And I think it will open up a new public that we've not had before in opera. I don't like it because it's annoying to look at it, even on television, and it's especially annoying to look at it on the stage. I've seen it in *Butterfly,* at City Opera, for instance. But with all the competition opera has today, with hard rock, soft rock, whatever you want to call it, I think it is necessary in order to build up opera for the future generations, and a wonderful addition. As a performer, I would accept it with grace. Yes, I think it takes away, but still I think it is something one must suffer—although people will say, "Well, you've had your career, and you didn't have to go through this." But I believe if it had come during my time, I would have felt the same way. Also, it gives you another challenge. The stronger you are, the less they'll look at that.

FRANCES BIBLE: I don't care for them too much, but I guess they serve a purpose. I think people could read the libretto before going to the theater. You have to do a little homework before you go.

D U N N : I fought it for a very long time. I think it's wrong for operas that are very well known. If people can't take a little time to find out what's going on in *Bohème,* then I think that's stupid. If you're going to do Czech opera like *Jenůfa,* then I think the surtitles are fine. There's not anything wrong with it. It helps a great deal. But I object to it being done for all operas.

H O R N E : They certainly help unravel involved plots for the public and I would say that ninety-nine percent of the people I talk to are in favor of them. By the way, I hear that there is much less sleeping during performances since the advent of surtitles.

M O F F O : You don't understand it. If you want to understand by reading, then you shouldn't come to the opera. You should get a recording and read it while you're listening. I don't see any surtitles for the ballet. So, because they're not talking, you don't want to know what their feet are doing, what it is they're trying to express? I don't know—you might as well put surtitles on the circus—any art form. You want to put surtitles over monkeys or gorillas? You have to know the art form with which you're dealing.

R E S N I K : If the audience gets distracted by the reading, well, half the audience might be riveted to me—and if the other half is riveted to understanding me, so be it.

L E W I S : To enter into opera, you really have to let yourself go. And if you're reading supertitles, you can't concentrate on what's happening to the people on the stage.

M O F F O : The magic of an evening of so-called creativity, even if you've heard it a million times, is—well, why do people keep going back to see *La Bohème*? Because no two people do it the same way. It touches everybody—*everybody.* Would it touch them any more if they read, "Mimì just died and dropped her muff"?

L E W I S : You go to the theater for a catharsis. You go not just to spend the evening, but to be taken through an experience that you can live through safely and get you out of your ordinary, mundane life. Only opera singers have all these things: divorces and murders and abortions and miscarriages and poisons—we have our bellies full. This is why we are as we are. But ordinary human beings sit on the side and say, "Oh, how glamorous, how marvelous." Their lives aren't full of these things and they know that that's really living, so they go and watch somebody else do it. That's what theater has always been, and that's why theater will always survive. That's why people go to theater, to music; why opera is the ultimate theatrical performance. Because you not only have this beautiful thing, theater, but it's aided and abetted by music that lifts you so. That's one reason opera isn't a one-time experience. People want to go back and have that feeling, that experience, again. That's why people go to *Bohème* over and over again. When people stand up and roar at the end, they roar for a reason.

BIOGRAPHIES

LICIA ALBANESE, SOPRANO
Bari, Italy

After studying with Giuseppina Baldassare-Tedeschi, she replaced a sick
Butterfly to debut at the Teatro Lirico
in Milan. The role also brought her to
the Met, and American audiences had
the chance to enjoy her Micaëla,
Susanna, Mimì, Violetta, and Puccini's
Manon at the house, on tour, and on
recordings and radio. The founder of
the Puccini Foundation, she came out
of semiretirement for appearances in
Sondheim's *Follies* both at Avery
Fisher Hall and at the opening of the
new opera house in Houston.

**ROBERTA
ALEXANDER**, SOPRANO
Yellow Springs, Ohio

Graduated from the University of
Michigan and studied with Herman
Woltman at the Royal Conservatory
in The Hague. Her roles at international opera houses include Pamina,
Antonia, and Donna Elvira. She made
her Met debut as Zerlina and went on
to sing Jenůfa, Mimì, and Gershwin's
Bess with the company. Although she
resides in the Netherlands, she keeps
abreast of American affairs via satel-
lite, as an armchair *Jeopardy* fanatic.

LUCINE AMARA, SOPRANO
Hartford, Connecticut

Studied with Stella Eisner-Eyn before
making her Met debut as the Celestial
Voice in the opening night *Don Carlos*
of Rudolf Bing's regime. She repeated
the role as a special favor to Sir Rudolf in his final year with the company. Her repertory spanned over
forty roles and took her from Wellgunde and the Third Norn to Mimì,
Aida, Liù, and Ellen in *Peter Grimes*.
A regular on television, she went Hollywood for an appearance alongside
Mario Lanza in *The Great Caruso*.

MARTINA ARROYO,
SOPRANO
New York, New York

Studied with Joseph Turnau, won the Metropolitan Opera Auditions, and made her professional debut as the First Chorister in Pizzetti's *L'Assassinio nella Cattedrale* at Carnegie Hall. Following her debut at the Met as the Celestial Voice in *Don Carlos,* she went on to sing over 170 performances with the company in roles including Aida, Santuzza, the *Ballo* Amelia, and Cio-Cio-San. When she appeared in an episode of *The Odd Couple,* her good nature prompted the most enthusiastic outpouring of charm Howard Cosell ever exhibited on television.

MARK BAKER, TENOR
Tulsa, Oklahoma

After studying in his home state, he made his Met debut as Paris in *Romeo and Juliet.* His other credits at the Met include Ruiz in *Il Trovatore,* Narraboth in a new production of *Salome,* and Loge in the complete *Ring* cycle. He has a doctorate in music and has performed with regional companies in the United States and Europe.

ROSE BAMPTON, SOPRANO
Lakewood, Ohio

Made her operatic debut as Siebel at Chautauqua, New York, and sang mezzo roles with the Philadelphia Opera before making her Met debut as Laura in *La Gioconda.* Her Metropolitan debut as a soprano was as the *Trovatore* Leonora. Her roles included Sieglinde, Kundry, Amneris, and Aida. Married to conductor Wilfred Pelletier, she also had an outstanding career at the Teatro Colón in Buenos Aires, where she expanded her repertory with such roles as the Countess and Agathe in *Der Freischütz.* She is on the teaching staff of the Juilliard School.

FRANCES BIBLE,
MEZZO-SOPRANO
Sackets Harbor, New York

HAROLYN BLACKWELL, SOPRANO
Washington, D.C.

Studied with Queena Mario at the Juilliard School and made her operatic debut as the Shepherd in *Tosca* with the New York City Opera, where she remained a principal artist for over thirty years. Her roles included Cherubino, Herodias, Hansel, Amneris, Adalgisa, and the Nurse in *Medea.* She created the roles of Elizabeth in *The Crucible* and Augusta in *The Ballad of Baby Doe.*

After graduating from the Catholic University of America, she made her Met debut as Poussette in *Manon* and went on to sing Adele in *Fledermaus* and Sophie in *Werther* with the company. Other appearances range from the *West Side Story* revival on Broadway to the Glyndebourne production of *Porgy and Bess* to Sister Constance in *Dialogues of the Carmelites* for the Canadian Opera.

JUDITH BLEGEN, SOPRANO
Missoula, Montana

An accomplished violinist and a graduate of the Curtis Institute, she made her operatic debut as Olympia in Nuremberg. Her Emily in Menotti's *Globolinks* in Sante Fe required her both to sing and to play the violin. She arrived at the Met as Papagena and has been heard there as Gretel, Susanna, both Sophies, Adele, Oscar, Adina, Gilda, and Juliet.

RON BOTTCHER,
BARITONE
Sandpoint, Idaho

PATRICIA BROOKS,
SOPRANO
New York, New York

Played Escamillo and Sharpless with the Metropolitan Opera National Company before debuting with the main unit as Scarus in *Antony and Cleopatra* on opening night of the new Met at Lincoln Center. He created the role of Peter in *Mourning Becomes Electra* later in the same season. His New York City Opera debut was in Ellstein's *The Golem.* He had the honor of sharing the stage with Giovanni Martinelli when he sang Ping to the tenor's Emperor in a Seattle production of *Turandot.*

Appeared in the Off Broadway production of *The Iceman Cometh* at the Circle in the Square, studied dance with Martha Graham, and was one of the nuns in the original Broadway production of *The Sound of Music.* Her New York City Opera debut was as Marianne in *Der Rosenkavalier,* and she later moved on to sing Sophie in the same work. Her Covent Garden debut was as the Queen in Rimsky-Korsakov's *The Golden Cockerel,* and she created the role of Abigail in *The Crucible.*

ANNE WIGGINS
BROWN, SOPRANO
Baltimore, Maryland

Studied at the Juilliard School and was described by *Musical America* as "an artist of unlimited means." She created the role of Bess in *Porgy and Bess,* and appeared on Broadway in a straight dramatic role in *Mamba's Daughters* with Ethel Waters. She turned down the lead in Hammerstein's *Carmen Jones* to pursue a concert and recital career, and moved to Oslo with her husband in 1948. She has directed productions of *Porgy and Bess* in France, Sweden, and Norway.

GRACE BUMBRY,
SOPRANO
St. Louis, Missouri

Studied with Lotte Lehmann and debuted at the Paris Opera as Amneris. Her Venus at Bayreuth in 1961 was the first appearance by a black singer at the festival. She later debuted as Eboli at both the Met and Covent Garden. She moved from the mezzo into the soprano repertory and her roles now range from Carmen to Salome, and Amneris to Aida. She was Bess in the Met premiere of *Porgy and Bess.*

NEDDA CASEI,
MEZZO-SOPRANO
Baltimore, Maryland

After making her Met debut as Maddalena in *Rigoletto,* she went on to sing such leading roles as Rosina, Adalgisa, and Carmen with the company. She served as president of the American Guild of Musical Artists and, in addition to singing extensively in South America and Europe, she has made frequent appearances in both opera and concert in the Far East.

RICHARD CASSILLY,
TENOR
Washington, D.C.

Made both his operatic and Broadway debuts as Michele in *The Saint of Bleecker Street.* After singing extensively with the New York City Opera and in Chicago, Berlin, and Hamburg and at Covent Garden, he made his Met debut as Radames. His repertory includes Otello, the Drum Major in *Wozzeck,* Vere in *Billy Budd,* Tristan, Tannhäuser, Samson, Canio, and Jimmy in *Mahagonny.*

JOYCE CASTLE,
MEZZO–SOPRANO
Beaumont, Texas

Debuted at the Met as Waltraute in *Die Walküre* after performing such roles as Mrs. Lovett in *Sweeney Todd,* Baba the Turk in Stravinsky's *The Rake's Progress,* and Meg in *Brigadoon* with the New York City Opera. Among her recordings are her City Opera performance as the Old Lady in *Candide* and a special collection of the music of Stephen Sondheim.

LILI CHOOKASIAN,
MEZZO–SOPRANO
Chicago, Illinois

A protégé of Rosa Ponselle's, she made her operatic debut as Adalgisa in Little Rock, Arkansas. Her Met debut was as La Cieca, and she went on to sing over three hundred performances at the house in roles ranging from both Erdas to Auntie in *Peter Grimes,* from Mistress Quickly to Geneviève in *Pelléas et Mélisande.* She debuted at the New York City Opera as the Medium and at Bayreuth as Erda.

GRAHAM CLARK, TENOR
Littleborough, England

Made his professional operatic debut as Roderigo in *Otello* with the Scottish Opera. An audition with Richard Bonynge led to an international career, which brought him to Canada as Camille opposite Joan Sutherland in *The Merry Widow,* and his Met debut as Števa in *Jenůfa.* His performance as Mephistopheles in Busoni's *Doktor Faust* with the English National Opera won him the Laurence Olivier Award for outstanding achievement in opera.

BARBARA COOK,
SOPRANO
Atlanta, Georgia

Made her Broadway debut in *Flahooley* and followed this with—among others—*Plain and Fancy, Candide, She Loves Me,* and *The Music Man,* for which she won a Tony. As a concert artist, she has appeared on Broadway, in London's West End, and at Carnegie Hall. She was Sally in the Lincoln Center concert version of *Follies.*

RÉGINE CRESPIN,
MEZZO–SOPRANO
Marseilles, France

Studied at the Paris Conservatory, but made her first big impact on the operatic world in the German repertory. The Marschallin served as her debut role at both Covent Garden and Glyndebourne, and Sieglinde brought her to Vienna. Midway through her career, she switched from dramatic soprano to mezzo roles, and since her Met debut as the Marschallin she has appeared there in such diverse roles as Carmen, Brünnhilde, Kundry, Charlotte in *Werther,* and Mme. de Croissy in *Dialogues of the Carmelites.*

FIORENZA COSSOTTO,
MEZZO–SOPRANO
Crescentino, Italy

Studied at the La Scala School with Ettore Campogalliani and made her operatic debut as Sister Mathilde in the premiere performance of *Dialogues of the Carmelites.* Her Covent Garden debut was as Neris in *Medea,* and her debut role at the Met was Amneris. Her repertory includes Laura, Eboli, Santuzza, Adalgisa, Azucena, Mistress Quickly, and Carmen. She is married to bass Ivo Vinco.

GILDA CRUZ-ROMO,
SOPRANO
Guadalajara, Mexico

Studied at the Mexico City Conservatory and debuted there as Ortlinde in *Die Walküre.* Her New York City Opera debut was in *Mefistofele,* and her seasoned Cio-Cio-San brought her to the Met. Her repertory includes Nedda, Puccini's Manon, Suor Angelica, and all of the major Verdi heroines. A truly international artist, she has sung in Moscow, Vienna, London, Milan, and Paris.

PHYLLIS CURTIN,
SOPRANO
Clarksburg, West Virginia

Made her operatic debut with the New England Opera Theater and went on to become one of the leading champions of modern American opera. She created the title role in *Susannah,* was Cathy in *Wuthering Heights,* and appeared with the New York City Opera in premieres of *The Passion of Jonathan Wade* and *The Trial.* She sang in Vienna and at Glyndebourne and debuted at the Met as Fiordiligi. Her other Met roles included Donna Anna, Violetta, Rosalinda, and Ellen in *Peter Grimes.*

BARBARA DANIELS,
SOPRANO
Cincinnati, Ohio

Studied at the University of Cincinnati and made her operatic debut, on short notice, as Susanna in a touring production of *The Marriage of Figaro.* She sang extensively in Europe, with contracts in Innsbruck, Kassel, and Cologne, along with appearances at Covent Garden, before making her Met debut as Musetta. With that company she has also sung Violetta, Rosalinda, and Marguerite.

HELGA DERNESCH,
MEZZO–SOPRANO
Vienna, Austria

Studied at the Vienna Conservatory and made her debut as Marina in Bonn. Early in her career, she switched from the mezzo to the soprano repertory, and made her Covent Garden debut as Sieglinde. She has sung all of the major female roles in the *Ring* cycle, along with Isolde, and created the role of Goneril in Reimann's *Lear*. Returning to mezzo roles, she made her Met debut as Marfa in *Khovanshchina*.

PLÁCIDO DOMINGO,
TENOR
Madrid, Spain

Made his debut as Borsa in *Rigoletto* in Mexico City, and also appeared there as one of Alfred Doolittle's cronies in *My Fair Lady*. His New York City Opera debut was as Pinkerton, and he appeared as Ginastera's Don Rodrigo in the company's opening performance at the New York State Theater at Lincoln Center. His official debut at the Met was as Maurizio in *Adriana Lecouvreur*. His conducting debut was with *La Traviata* at City Opera. He created the leading roles in both Torroba's *El Poeta* and Menotti's *Goya*.

TODD DUNCAN, BARITONE
Danville, Kentucky

Made his operatic debut as Alfio with New York's Aeolian Opera. His New York City Opera debut was as Tonio, and he also sang Escamillo with that company. He was the original Porgy in *Porgy and Bess* and created the role of Stephen Kumalo in the Broadway production of Weill's *Lost in the Stars*.

ROSALIND ELIAS,
MEZZO–SOPRANO
Lowell, Massachusetts

MIGNON DUNN,
MEZZO–SOPRANO
Memphis, Tennessee

Studied with Karin Branzell and made her debut as Carmen in New Orleans. Her Met debut was as the Nurse in *Boris Godunov,* and after a period away from the United States, she returned to the Met as Azucena, Marina, Fricka, Brangäne, and Herodias, as well as other roles including both Mother Marie and Mme. de Croissy in *Dialogues of the Carmelites.*

Studied with Luigi Ricci and Nazzareno de Angelis and made her Met debut as Grimgerde in *Die Walküre.* She sang over 450 performances there, in roles including Cherubino, Carmen, Octavian, Hansel, and the Witch. She created roles in both *Vanessa* and *Antony and Cleopatra.* Her New York City Opera debut was as Mrs. Lovett in *Sweeney Todd,* and at Glyndebourne she was Baba the Turk in Stravinsky's *The Rake's Progress.*

MIRELLA FRENI, SOPRANO
Modena, Italy

Debuted in her hometown as Micaëla after studying with Ettore Campogalliani at the Bologna Conservatory. The role of Nanetta introduced her to audiences at La Scala and Covent Garden. At the Met, she debuted as Mimì, and returned as Adina, Liù, Micaëla, Juliet, Susanna, and Puccini's Manon. At the urging of Herbert von Karajan, she moved into a more dramatic repertory, which now includes Desdemona, Aida, and Elisabeth in *Don Carlos.*

CRIS GROENENDAAL,
TENOR
Erie, Pennsylvania

Studied at the University of Exeter in England and made his Broadway debut as Anthony in *Sweeney Todd,* the role that took him to the New York City Opera, where he also sang the title role in *Candide.* His other Broadway credits include *Sunday in the Park with George, Into the Woods,* and the title role in *The Phantom of the Opera.* He has also sung in the operetta series at City Opera and in its production of *Kismet.*

JERRY HADLEY, TENOR
Princeton, Illinois

Debuted as Lionel in *Martha* in Sarasota, Florida, and bowed at the New York City Opera in *Lucia di Lammermoor.* His other roles there included Tom Rakewell in Stravinsky's *The Rake's Progress* and Werther. His Fenton brought him to Covent Garden, and des Grieux in *Manon* to the Met. He sang the role of Gaylord in the first complete recording of *Show Boat.*

HÅKAN HAGEGÅRD,
BARITONE
Karlstad, Sweden

Studied at the Royal Academy in Sweden and also with Tito Gobbi, Erik Werba, and Gerald Moore. His operatic debut was as Papageno in Stockholm, and he re-created the role in Ingmar Bergman's film version of *The Magic Flute.* His Met debut was as Malatesta in *Don Pasquale* and his other roles there include Figaro, Wolfram, and Eisenstein.

THOMAS HAMPSON,
BARITONE
Spokane, Washington

Abandoning his dreams of law school, he pursued vocalism at the urging of his teacher, Dr. Sister Marietta Coyle. He went on to study with Martial Singher at Music Academy of the West, Horst Gunter, Jack Metz, and Elisabeth Schwarzkopf. While in college he was a singing waiter in a German restaurant. Since then, he has sung Don Giovanni, Figaro, Almaviva, and Guglielmo worldwide.

JEROME HINES, BASS
Hollywood, California

Made his operatic debut as Monterone in San Francisco, and his Met debut as the Sergeant in *Boris Godunov*. He later graduated to the title role in that opera and sang it all over the world, including performances at the Bolshoi. His repertory includes Sparafucile, Sarastro, the Grand Inquisitor, and Ramfis. He composed the opera *I Am the Way*, based on the life of Christ. Married to soprano Lucia Evangelista, he is the author of *Great Singers on Great Singing*.

MARILYN HORNE,
MEZZO–SOPRANO
Bradford, Pennsylvania

Studied with William Vennard and Lotte Lehmann before making her operatic debut as Háta in *The Bartered Bride* in Los Angeles. She provided the singing voice for Dorothy Dandridge in the film version of *Carmen Jones*. Her historic Adalgisa, opposite Joan Sutherland's Norma, brought her to the Met, where she also has performed Rosina, Carmen, Isabella, Amneris, Eboli, and Dalila.

LAUREL HURLEY,
SOPRANO
Allentown, Pennsylvania

Sang and danced on Broadway in *The Student Prince* before making her New York City Opera debut as Zerlina. With that company, she also sang Magnolia in *Show Boat,* Baby Doe, and Rosalinda. Her Met debut was as Oscar in *Un Ballo in Maschera* and her subsequent roles there included the Queen of the Night, Gilda, Olympia, Musetta, and Susanna. She and her husband are senior ice dancers.

GARSON KANIN, DIRECTOR
Rochester, New York

Made his Broadway debut as an actor in *Little Ol' Boy.* As an assistant director, he worked with George Abbott on *Room Service.* He wrote and directed *Born Yesterday,* which was rescued out of town by the appearance of Judy Holliday, who replaced Jean Arthur and went on to capture the hearts of the public and an Academy Award. With his wife, Ruth Gordon, he wrote two screenplays for Tracy and Hepburn, plus two for Holliday.

DOROTHY KIRSTEN,
SOPRANO
Montclair, New Jersey

A protégé of Grace Moore's, she made her operatic debut as Poussette in *Manon* and arrived at the Met as Mimì. She played a leading role in the film *The Great Caruso* with Mario Lanza, and was a regular on television singing both classical and pop music. Among her favored roles were Cio-Cio-San, both Manons, Marguerite, Violetta, Tosca, and Louise, which she learned from the composer, Charpentier.

GARY LAKES, TENOR
Dallas, Texas

ALFREDO KRAUS, TENOR
Las Palmas, Canary Islands

Cairo was the site of his operatic debut as the Duke in *Rigoletto,* the role that also brought him to the Met. A master of the French school of music, the tenor has limited his repertory to such roles as Werther, Faust, Hoffmann, Alfredo, and Romeo, and is noted in the profession for the total dramatic conviction and elegant musical style he brings to each of his roles.

Made his operatic debut as Froh with the Seattle Opera and his Met debut as the High Priest in *Idomeneo.* His other roles at the Met include Don José, Samson, and Siegmund. His many concert appearances have included stops in Chicago, Houston, Paris, and Milan. With the Prague Symphony, he made his debut in Japan at the Osaka Festival.

EVELYN LEAR, SOPRANO
Brooklyn, New York

Studied with Maria Ivogün, among others, before making her operatic debut as the Composer in *Ariadne auf Naxos.* Her Met debut was as Lavinia in the world premiere of *Mourning Becomes Electra.* Her vocal versatility has allowed her to excel as the Countess and Cherubino, as Octavian and the Marschallin. A specialist in modern opera, she created roles in works by Klebe and Egk, made her film debut with Paul Newman in *Buffalo Bill and the Indians,* and frequently sings with her husband, baritone Thomas Stewart.

BRENDA LEWIS, SOPRANO
Sunbury, Pennsylvania

Sang with New York New Opera Company and City Opera, where she debuted as Santuzza. She created the role of Birdie in the Broadway production of *Regina* and later sang the title role in that work with City Opera, where she also created the title role in the premiere of Beeson's *Lizzie Borden*. Musetta brought her to the Met, where she also sang Venus, Salome, Marie in *Wozzeck*, Vanessa, and a record number of Rosalindas in *Fledermaus*. She also starred on Broadway in Romberg's last musical, *The Girl in Pink Tights*.

JO SULLIVAN LOESSER, SOPRANO
Mound City, Illinois

A Columbia University graduate, she appeared on Broadway in Mike Todd's *As the Girls Go* and in *Let's Make an Opera*. Off Broadway, she created the role of Polly in Lucille Lortel's production of *The Threepenny Opera*, costarring with Lotte Lenya. She has toured in *Guys and Dolls, A Little Night Music,* and *The King and I,* and created the role of Rosabella in the Broadway production of *The Most Happy Fella*. Since the death of her husband Frank Loesser, she has appeared in *Perfectly Frank,* a revue based on his work, and performs his music in concerts and cabaret.

JAMES MCCRACKEN,
TENOR
Gary, Indiana

CORNELL MACNEIL,
BARITONE
Minneapolis, Minnesota

Made his operatic debut as Rodolfo in Central City, Colorado, and his Met debut as Parpignol in the same opera. With his wife, mezzo Sandra Warfield, he pursued a career in Europe, where he attained stardom before returning to this country, where he sang over four hundred performances at the Met alone. His repertory included Radames, Samson, Canio, Manrico, and, of course, Otello. His last operatic performances were as Florestan in Washington, D.C.

Studied with the great bass-baritone Friedrich Schorr and created the role of John Sorel in *The Consul*. He debuted with the New York City Opera as Germont, at Covent Garden as Macbeth, and at the Met as Rigoletto. His other Met roles included Amonasro, Alfio, Tonio, and Scarpia. He also served as president of the American Guild of Musical Artists.

JOHN MACURDY, BASS
Detroit, Michigan

After singing with regional opera companies all over the country, he made his New York City Opera debut in Weill's *Street Scene*. He went on to the Met, where he has sung in over seven hundred performances so far. He created roles in two new operas, and has sung in Paris and Milan and in Joseph Losey's film version of *Don Giovanni*.

CATHERINE MALFITANO, SOPRANO
New York, New York

Debuted as Nanetta in Central City, Colorado, as Mimì with the New York City Opera, and as Gretel at the Met, where her father, Joseph, is a member of the orchestra. She sang her first Lulu at the Munich Festival before taking the role to Chicago and the Met.

EVA MARTON, SOPRANO
Budapest, Hungary

Started small, debuting as Kate Pinkerton at the Margarteten Island Festival, before moving on to such substantial roles as Tosca, the Empress in *Die Frau ohne Schatten,* Gioconda, and Brünnhilde. Her Met debut was as Eva in *Die Meistersinger,* and she sang the title role in the premiere of the Met's Zeffirelli production of *Turandot.*

FRANZ MAZURA, BARITONE
Salzburg, Austria

Debuted in Kassel and eventually went on to become a member of the Deutsche Oper Berlin. His roles at Bayreuth include Gunther, Alberich, and Klingsor. He created the role of Dr. Schön in the first production of the three-act version of *Lulu* in Paris. That role also served as his Met debut. In addition to opera, he appears frequently in straight dramatic plays.

JOHANNA MEIER,
SOPRANO
Chicago, Illinois

Studied with John Brownlee at the Manhattan School of Music, and made her New York City Opera debut as the Countess in *Capriccio*. Her roles with that company ranged from Tosca to Rosalinda and from Ariadne to Marguerite, the role that brought her to the Met. She has appeared in the *Ring* cycle with both the Seattle Opera and the Met, as both Brünnhilde and Sieglinde. She also has the distinction of being the first American artist to sing Isolde at Bayreuth.

MORLEY MEREDITH,
BARITONE
Winnipeg, Canada

After an extensive career in musical comedy and operetta, he made his operatic debut with the New York City Opera as Escamillo, and went on to the Met in all four baritone roles in *The Tales of Hoffmann*. Along with appearances all over the world, he has managed to sing well over four hundred performances at the Met alone.

ROBERT MERRILL,
BARITONE
Brooklyn, New York

Made his debut as Amonasro in Trenton, New Jersey, and his Met debut as Germont, a role that introduced him to opera houses all over the world. He appears on television and in musicals, and his recordings range from countless operas to such popular works as *Man of La Mancha* and *Kismet*. As an honorary New York Yankee, he can be heard singing "The Star Spangled Banner" before each home game, and "Take Me Out to the Ball Game" at the seventh-inning stretch.

ZINKA MILANOV,
SOPRANO
Zagreb, Yugoslavia

JULIA MIGENES, SOPRANO
New York, New York

Made her official operatic debut as An-
nina in *The Saint of Bleecker Street*
with the New York City Opera,
while appearing on Broadway in *Fiddler on the Roof* as Hodel, a part she
created. Her Met debut was as Jenny in
Mahagonny, and her appearances in
Europe have included film, recordings, and her own television series. She
also starred in Francesco Rosi's film
version of *Carmen.*

After studying with her compatriot
Milka Ternina, she made her debut in
Ljubljana as Leonora in *Il Trovatore.*
After singing the Verdi Requiem with
Toscanini in Salzburg, she made her
Met debut, also as Leonora. Tosca
brought her to both La Scala and Covent Garden. Her final Met performance as Maddalena took place in the
last season at the old house, and is re-
garded as one of the highlight eve-
nings in the Met's history.

APRILE MILLO, SOPRANO
New York, New York

The daughter of two opera singers, she
also studied with Rita Patanè before
making her operatic debut as Aida in
Salt Lake City. Her La Scala debut was
as Elvira in *Ernani,* and her Met debut
as Amelia in *Simon Boccanegra.* She has
appeared frequently with Eve Queler
and her Opera Orchestra of New
York.

ERIE MILLS, SOPRANO
Granite City, Illinois

Made her operatic debut as Ninetta in *The Love for Three Oranges* in Chicago. Her La Scala debut was as Giunia in Mozart's *Lucio Silla,* and her Met debut as Blonde in *The Abduction from the Seraglio.* For the New York City Opera, she was Cunegonde in *Candide,* a role she also recorded. In the historic concert version of *Follies* at Avery Fisher Hall, she sang Young Heidi and shared the song "One Last Kiss" with Licia Albanese.

SHERRILL MILNES,
BARITONE
Downers Grove, Illinois

After studying with Hermanus Baer and Rosa Ponselle, he made his operatic debut as Masetto with the Boris Goldovsky company, and both his New York City Opera and Met debuts as Valentin. A Verdi specialist, he has appeared in every major opera house all over the globe and has made over thirty complete operatic recordings. He is married to soprano Nancy Stokes.

LEONA MITCHELL,
SOPRANO
Enid, Oklahoma

Made her operatic debut as Micaëla in San Francisco, and that role also brought her to the Met. For Lorin Maazel, she was Bess in the first complete recording of *Porgy and Bess.* Her career has steadily moved from such roles as Pamina and Liù on to Aida and Desdemona.

ANNA MOFFO, SOPRANO
Wayne, Pennsylvania

Studied at the Curtis Institute and debuted at Spoleto as Norina. Her Cio-Cio-San on Italian television turned her into a star overnight in Europe, before coming back to the United States for a Mimì in Chicago. She debuted at the Met as Violetta and at Covent Garden as Gilda. She has recorded extensively and has appeared in numerous feature films, both operatic and strictly dramatic. While studying, she worked as an X-ray technician, and she can type ninety-seven words a minute.

JAMES MORRIS, BASS
Baltimore, Maryland

Trained with Rosa Ponselle and Nicola Moscona before his debut in Baltimore as Crespel in *The Tales of Hoffmann.* The King in *Aida* brought him to the Met, where he quickly moved on to such roles as Figaro, Claggart in *Billy Budd,* and the Grand Inquisitor. Before moving into the Wagnerian roles that have become his specialty, he coached with the great Hans Hotter.

PATRICE MUNSEL,
SOPRANO
Spokane, Washington

Her Met debut at seventeen as Philine in *Mignon* made her the youngest singer ever to bow there in a major role. She went on to sing all the leading coloratura parts, played Nellie Melba in the film version of her life, had her own television series, and appeared in musicals both on Broadway and all over the country. Her Adele, Despina, and Périchole proved especially delightful to both critics and audiences.

CAROL NEBLETT,
SOPRANO
Modesto, California

Studied with Lotte Lehmann, among others, before bringing her Musetta to the New York City Opera. Her Met debut was as Senta. Her recordings range from Marietta in *Die Tote Stadt* to Minnie in *La Fanciulla del West,* the role that served as her introduction to audiences in Vienna and at Covent Garden.

BIRGIT NILSSON,
SOPRANO
West Karup, Sweden

A legend in her own time, she debuted as Agathe in *Der Freischütz,* moved on to Lady Macbeth, and then conquered all the major dramatic-soprano roles. Her Met debut as Isolde, and the attention and excitement surrounding it, made the front page of *The New York Times.* Her recording career was extensive, and she became the reigning Brünnhilde and Isolde of her day. Among other accomplishments, she recorded two complete *Ring* cycles.

BETSY NORDEN, SOPRANO
Cincinnati, Ohio

Studied at Boston University and joined the Met chorus in 1969 before moving on to solo roles in 1972, starting as a peasant girl in *The Marriage of Figaro.* Her repertory includes Oscar, Marzelline, Sister Constance in *Dialogues of the Carmelites,* the title role in *The Cunning Little Vixen,* Gretel, and Adele.

JARMILA NOVOTNÁ,
SOPRANO
Prague, Czechoslovakia

After singing Rosina and Violetta in the Czechoslovakian provinces, she became a member of the Prague National Theater, and was also a member of the Berlin State Opera. She made her Met debut as Mimì. Her repertory included such roles as both Manons, Octavian, Pamina, and Cherubino. She starred in numerous films in both Europe and America, including the classic *The Search,* with Montgomery Clift.

ROBERTA PETERS,
SOPRANO
Bronx, New York

Equally beloved as an opera singer and a recitalist, she made her debut on the Met stage itself as Zerlina. She then went on to conquer all the leading coloratura roles, including Lucia, Zerbinetta, and Gilda. Her frequent television appearances, including her American Express commercial, have made her a household name. She consolidated her prominence with her numerous recordings, and appearances in such musicals as *The King and I* and Noel Coward's *Bitter Sweet.*

LUCIANO PAVAROTTI,
TENOR
Modena, Italy

Debuted as Rodolfo in Reggio Emilia. This role also served as his entry to opera houses in Vienna, Naples, Chicago, and Philadelphia, as well as the Met, Covent Garden, and La Scala. His roles range from Cavaradossi to Idomeneo, from the Italian Singer to Radames. His recordings and television celebrity status make his concert appearances sellouts all over the world. He established a competition for young singers at the Philadelphia Lyric Opera, and he appears each year in performance with the winners.

PAUL PLISHKA, BASS
Old Forge, Pennsylvania

Studied with Armen Boyajian and debuted with the Paterson Lyric Opera in New Jersey. After touring for a year with the Metropolitan Opera National Company, he joined the main unit as the Monk in *La Gioconda*. His big break into major roles came as an emergency replacement for the scheduled Oroveso in a Texaco radio broadcast of *Norma* with Joan Sutherland and Marilyn Horne. Since then, he has sung all the major bass roles in leading houses all over the world.

NELL RANKIN,
MEZZO–SOPRANO
Montgomery, Alabama

Studied with Jeanne Lorraine and Karin Branzell, and debuted in Zurich as Ortrud, at Covent Garden as Carmen, and at the Met as Amneris. At the Metropolitan, she sang more than 140 performances in more than 15 different roles, including Gutrune, Ulrica, and Azucena. In addition to opera, she had a successful career in concerts and recitals, appearing with most of the major orchestras in the United States and abroad.

REGINA RESNIK,
MEZZO–SOPRANO
New York, New York

After graduating from Hunter College, she debuted with the New Opera Company in New York as Lady Macbeth, and at the Met as the *Trovatore* Leonora. She sang all the major soprano roles before switching to the mezzo repertory, where Carmen, Klytemnestra, and Mistress Quickly became her specialties. She played Clare in the U.S. premiere of the operatic version of *The Visit* in San Francisco. She was also nominated for a Tony for her performance in the Broadway revival of *Cabaret*.

NEIL ROSENSHEIN,
TENOR
New York, New York

Debuted at the Met as Alfredo, the role that has introduced him to opera companies all over the world. He has performed with such conductors as Mackerras, Bernstein, Muti, Ozawa, Davis, and Mehta, and appeared in the title role in Argento's *The Aspern Papers* at the Dallas Opera, a performance televised by PBS.

RENATA SCOTTO,
SOPRANO
Savona, Italy

Her hometown witnessed her debut as a teenage Violetta, and the same role served as her formal debut at Teatro Nuovo, Milan, a few years later. Her La Scala debut was as Walter in *La Wally*. She replaced Maria Callas as Amina in *La Sonnambula* when La Scala played Edinburgh, and her Cio-Cio-San took her to the Met, where she sang most of the leading soprano roles, participated in such little-revived works as *Francesca da Rimini* and *La Clemenza di Tito,* and staged a revival of *Madama Butterfly.* Her autobiography, *More Than a Diva,* appeared in 1984.

BIDÚ SAYÃO, SOPRANO
Rio de Janeiro, Brazil

Studied with Jean de Reszke and debuted in Rome as Rosina, the role that also took her to La Scala. Her Paris debut was as Juliet. Her New York recital debut brought her to the attention of Toscanini, who hired her for a concert that led to her Met debut as Massenet's Manon. She sang over two hundred performances with that company, and also appeared frequently in both Chicago and San Francisco. Among her most beloved roles were Mélisande, Gilda, Violetta, Susanna, and Mimì.

ELLEN SHADE, SOPRANO
New York, New York

Studied at the Juilliard School and debuted as Liù in Frankfurt, as Eva at the Met, and as Donna Elvira at the New York City Opera. She has worked her way through all the major female roles in the *Ring* cycle, and has developed a reputation as a specialist in offbeat repertory, making her Chicago debut as Emma in *Khovanshchina*. She created the role of Eve in Penderecki's *Paradise Lost*.

NEIL SHICOFF, TENOR
New York, New York

After studying at the Juilliard School, and with his father, who was a cantor, he made his professional debut at the Met as Rinuccio in *Gianni Schicchi*. Subsequent roles included the des Grieux of both Puccini and Massenet, Rodolfo, Lensky, Don Carlos, and his two favorites, Werther and Hoffmann. As the Offenbach hero, he can be seen in two different videotaped versions.

MARTIAL SINGHER,
BASS–BARITONE
Oloron-Ste.-Marie, France

A master of the French repertory, he debuted as Oreste in Gluck's *Iphigénie en Tauride* in Amsterdam, as Athanaël in *Thaïs* at the Paris Opera, and as Dapertutto in *The Tales of Hoffmann* at the Met. In addition to his French roles, he also sang Verdi and lighter Wagner parts. He taught, among others, Judith Blegen, Donald Gramm, and John Reardon.

RISË STEVENS,
MEZZO-SOPRANO
Queens, New York

ELEANOR STEBER,
SOPRANO
Wheeling, West Virginia

Studied at the New England Conservatory and with Paul Althouse, and
debuted as Senta with the Common-
wealth Opera of Boston. As a winner
of the Met auditions, she made her
debut there as Sophie in *Der Rosenkavalier,* and went on to sing more
than three hundred performances in
thirty-three roles there. Her career also
took her to Edinburgh, Florence, and
Salzburg. Recognized as a Mozart specialist, she created the title role in
Vanessa and was the Met's first Ara-
bella and first Marie in *Wozzeck.*

Her debut in *The Bartered Bride* with
the Little Theater Opera of New York
followed studies with Anna Schoen-
René at the Juilliard School. Her Met
debut was as Mignon, and she went on
to sing over three hundred performances with the company. She starred
in several films, including *Going My
Way* with Bing Crosby and *The Chocolate Soldier* with Nelson Eddy. She
also played Anna in the Lincoln Center production of *The King and I,* and
served as a director of the Metropolitan Opera National Company.

THOMAS STEWART,
BARITONE
San Saba, Texas

Debuted as La Roche in the U.S. pre-
miere of *Capriccio* at the Juilliard
School, and subsequently debuted at
the New York City Opera as the
Commendatore. A member of the
Städtische Oper in Berlin, he made his
Covent Garden debut as Escamillo and
his Met bow as Ford in *Falstaff.* In San
Francisco, he sang the title role in the
American premiere of Reimann's
Lear. He frequently sings with his
wife, soprano Evelyn Lear.

JOAN SUTHERLAND,
SOPRANO
Sydney, Australia

Made her operatic debut in her native
city as Goossens's Judith, her Covent
Garden debut as the First Lady in *The
Magic Flute*. Her husband, pianist/
conductor Richard Bonynge, steered
her into the more florid coloratura
repertory, and her big breakthrough
came with a Covent Garden Lucia.
This role also served as her debut vehicle at Chicago, La Scala, and the Met.
While singing in such varied works as
Bellini's *Beatrice di Tenda* and Massenet's *Esclarmonde* all over the world,
she always finds time to return to her
homeland for regular appearances.

KIRI TE KANAWA,
SOPRANO
Gisborne, New Zealand

Studied at the London Opera Centre
and made her professional debut as
Carmen with the English Northern
Opera. Her Covent Garden debut was
as a Flower Maiden. After she debuted
the role in Sante Fe, the Countess
brought her back to Covent Garden in
triumph. Her Met debut was on three
hours' notice as a broadcast Desdemona. Her superstar status was rein-
forced by her first pop album with
Nelson Riddle, and a series of "crossover" albums including *West Side
Story* and *South Pacific*.

BLANCHE THEBOM,
MEZZO-SOPRANO
Monessen, Pennsylvania

Studied with Margarete Matzenauer
and Edyth Walker, and made her Met
debut as Brangäne. She appeared with
the Met for twenty-two seasons and
sang close to sixty roles there. She also
sang in San Francisco and Chicago,
and at Glyndebourne and Covent Garden. She created the role of Baba the
Turk in *The Rake's Progress* and recorded the work with Stravinsky.

GIORGIO TOZZI, BASS
Chicago, Illinois

Debuted as Tarquinius in Britten's *The Rape of Lucretia* on Broadway, and went on to appear in musicals in London before changing his vocal category from baritone to bass. He made his Met debut as Alvise in *La Gioconda,* and went on to sing over three hundred performances with the company while also establishing an international career. He returned to Broadway as Tony in the revival of *The Most Happy Fella,* and is remembered for a brief but striking appearance as a gangster on TV's *The Odd Couple.*

THEODOR UPPMAN,
BARITONE
San Jose, California

Studied at the Curtis Institute and made his concert debut in San Francisco as Pelléas, the role that first brought him to the New York City Opera and the Met, where he was especially known for his Papageno, Piquillo in *La Périchole,* and Masetto. His place in operatic history was secured when he created the title role in *Billy Budd.* He teaches at the Manhattan School of Music, and with his wife, Jean, is an active part of New York's musical life.

CAROL VANESS, SOPRANO
Los Angeles, California

After studying in her native state, she seemed to make a career of singing Vitellia in the little-heard *La Clemenza di Tito,* using it for her debut at the New York City Opera and also singing it at the Met, where she debuted as Armida in Handel's *Rinaldo.* One of her Met Vitellias was sung from a wheelchair when she had a broken leg and had to watch another singer walk through the role.

ANDREA VELIS, TENOR
New Kensington, Pennsylvania

Studied in both Pittsburgh and Rome before making his Met debut as Joe in *La Fanciulla del West.* He went on to sing more than fifty roles with the company, including Spoletta, Bardolfo, and the Witch in *Hansel and Gretel.* He has also specialized in modern music, particularly the works of Benjamin Britten.

SANDRA WARFIELD,
MEZZO–SOPRANO
St. Louis, Missouri

After playing minor roles at the Met, she and her husband, James McCracken, went to Europe, where they starved for a few years before both their careers took off. She returned to the Met as Dalila, and sang leading mezzo roles with all the leading opera companies in the world. Her repertory included Azucena, Amneris, and Fidès in *Le Prophète,* along with *La Favorita.* Her daughter, soprano Ahna McCracken, is carrying on the family tradition.

RAMÓN VINAY, TENOR
Chillán, Chile

Studied in Mexico City, where he first debuted as a baritone, as Alphonse in *La Favorita,* and ten years later as a tenor, as Don José. The latter role also brought him to both the New York City Opera and the Met. He sang Otello first with Toscanini and the NBC Symphony Orchestra, and then at the Met, Covent Garden, Salzburg, Mexico City, La Scala, and on and on. Later in his career, he returned to baritone roles with a Telramund at Bayreuth, and also sang Iago and Rossini's Bartolo.

INDEX

About the Authors

Dennis McGovern has worked in the Metropolitan Opera Archives. Deborah Grace Winer is a playwright. They both contribute articles to *Opera News* and live in New York City.